JOURNAL FOR THE STUDY OF THE OLD TESTAMENT
SUPPLEMENT SERIES
192

Editors
David J.A. Clines
Philip R. Davies

Executive Editor
John Jarick

Editorial Board
Richard J. Coggins, Alan Cooper, Tamara C. Eskenazi,
J. Cheryl Exum, John Goldingay, Robert P. Gordon,
Norman K. Gottwald, Andrew D.H. Mayes, Carol Meyers,
Patrick D. Miller

Sheffield Academic Press

Biblical Studies and the Shifting of Paradigms, 1850–1914

edited by
Henning Graf Reventlow
and William Farmer

Journal for the Study of the Old Testament
Supplement Series 192

Copyright © 1995 Sheffield Academic Press

Published by Sheffield Academic Press Ltd
Mansion House
19 Kingfield Road
Sheffield, S11 9AS
England

Typeset by Sheffield Academic Press
and
Printed on acid-free paper in Great Britain
by Bookcraft
Midsomer Norton, Somerset

British Library Cataloguing in Publication Data

A catalogue record for this book is available
from the British Library

ISBN 1-85075-532-9

CONTENTS

APPENDIX
Henning Graf Reventlow:

ABBREVIATIONS

AEK	*Allgemeine Evangelisch-Lutherische Kirchenzeitung*
AHR	*The American Historical Review*
Bib	*Biblica*
CUB	*The Catholic University Bulletin*
CW	*Christliche Welt*
DR	*The Downside Review*
DubR	*The Dublin Review*
EdR	*The Edinburgh Review*
EH	*Europäische Hochschulschriften*
EncBr	*Encyclopedia Brittanica*
HMPEC	*Historical Magazine of the Protestant Episcopal Church*
HZ	*Historische Zeitschrift*
JAAR	*Journal of the American Academy of Religion*
JMH	*Journal of Modern History*
JSNT	*Journal for the Study of the New Testament*
JSOT	*Journal for the Study of the Old Testament*
MM	*Macmillan's Magazine*
NovT	*Novum Testamentum*
NRT	*La nouvelle revue théologique*
PJ	*Preussische Jahrbücher*
PKZ	*Protestantische Kirchenzeitung*
PM	*Protestantische Monatshefte*
PSTJ	*Perkins (School of Theology) Journal*
RB	*Revue biblique*
RE	*Realenzyklopädie für protestantische Theologie und Kirche*
RG	*Revue germanique*
RGF	*Revue germanique et francaise*
RGFE	*Revue germanique et francaise et etrangère*
RGG	*Religion in Geschichte und Gegenwart*
RM	*Revue moderne*
RT	*Revue de théologie*
RTP	*Revue de théologie et de philosophie*
SAUL	St Andrews University Library
TJ	*Theologische Jahrbücher*
TLS	*Time Literary Supplement*
TRE	*Theologische Realenzyklopädie*

TRu	*Theologische Rundschau*
TT	*Theologisk Tidsschrift*
VSWG	*Vierteljahresschrift für Sozial- und Wirtschaftsgeschichte*
ZG	*Zeitschrift für Geschichtswissenschaft*
ZRGG	*Zeitschrift für Religions- und Geistesgeschichte*
ZTK	*Zeitschrift für katholische Theologie*
ZWT	*Zeitschrift für wissenschaftliche Theologie*

LIST OF CONTRIBUTORS

William R. Farmer is Emeritus Professor of New Testament at the University of Dallas, Dallas, Texas.

David P. Peabody is Professor for the New Testament at the Nebraska Wesleyan University, Lincoln, Nebraska.

Henning Graf Reventlow is Emeritus Professor of Theology and Exegesis of the Old Testament at the University of the Ruhr, Bochum.

Gunther Scholz is Professor of History and Theory of the Humanities within the the Institute of Philosophy of the Univeristy of the Ruhr, Bochum.

Christian Simon is Associate Professor for Modern History and Swiss History at the University of Basel.

Ronald E. Clements is Emeritus Professor of Old Testament at King's College, University of London.

Friedrich Wilhelm Graf is Professor of Protestant Theology and Social Ethics in the Universität der Bundeswehr, Hamburg.

Hans Rollman is Professor of Religious Studies at Memorial University of Newfoundland, St John's, Newfoundland, Canada.

INTRODUCTION

The following pages contain the contributions to a symposium in which specialists in different fields worked together in an attempt to throw more light on the conditions—the theological convictions and worldview, the political climate, the state officials, educational institutions and churches—which were influential in the development of biblical studies in the second half of the nineteenth century.

The discussion originated with a special problem: how to understand the role of Heinrich Julius Holtzmann, the protagonist of the so called Two Source Hypothesis,[1] in the development of biblical studies in the second half of the nineteenth century. The co-editors of this volume have differing views as to how far it is possible for the historian to speak of state *Interesse* in the appointment of Holtzmann to the prestigious chair of New Testament in Strasbourg in 1874. Was it the result of a direct intervention by the imperial chancellor Bismarck, who may have wished to procure a place for this well-known liberal scholar because of Holtzmann's undermining of Papal supremacy?[2] Both of us agreed, after the problem had been discussed at a first meeting in Latrobe in 1990, that the existing material concerning Holtzmann's appointment to his Strasbourg professorship in the Strasbourg archives does not contain express statements which could contribute to a solution to the problem. Charles McClelland, an expert in the history of German universities, pointed out in the same conference that the way of teaching German history in German universities differed remarkably before and after 1870. After 1870 a situation developed where there was only one way to teach German history, namely, from the perspective of Germany as a nation state. Was this development the result of a changed intellectual climate? Or shall we presume that the state intervened in the appointment of professors? The statistical evidence, according to McClelland,

1. Holtzmann declared Mark the oldest of the Synoptic Gospels.
2. We are in the period of the *Kulturkampf* (1870–78) between Bismarck and the Curia (cf. below, pp. 16ff.).

suggests that there were ideological concerns which affected the process of appointing professors of German history in German universities after 1870. Yet, the official correspondence preserved in the university archives contains no explicit statements to clarify how such ideological concerns may have affected the appointment process.

Both of us agree that the whole matter of how state *Interesse* may have affected the appointment process for theology professors in Prussian universities in the period 1830–1914, merits further investigation, and that the case of Holtzmann could be an interesting test case. At issue is how to develop a revised methodology combining the merits of a history of ideas approach with the merits of approaching the problem from the perspective of social history. Is statistical evidence admissible? If so, how is it to be used?

The discussion of the Holtzmann case led to the conviction of all who were interested in the field, that it would be essential for coming to deeper insights into the conditions in which biblical exegesis was enacted in the nineteenth century to broaden the scenery and to include other aspects that might throw more light on a period widely unknown to many current scholars. This recognition motivated the convening of a second symposium in which specialists from different fields should cooperate from their respective view points and interests in elucidating basic themes and methods of biblical exegesis, scientific theology and the relations between state and universities in the nineteenth century, especially during the period of the Second Reich. However, the themes were not restricted to that area. They included also a broader picture of the first half of the century and across the borders of Germany into other European countries. In this way, a specialized research interest led to an interdisciplinary and international discussion by which all the participants have profited very much. Most of the papers read at the Bochum symposium are included in this volume. Since H. Graf Reventlow's contribution made to the meeting in Latrobe is important to understanding the whole discussion, the editors are in agreement that it should be included.

The meeting in Bochum would have been impossible if the Stiftung Volkswagenwerk, Hannover, had not supported this symposium with a grant covering most of the expenses. The Evangelical Church of Westfalia generously added what was needed to guarantee the conditions for a successful symposium. We thank both for their help.

We also thank the editors of Sheffield Academic Press for their readiness to publish the Congress Volume. May it stimulate a discussion which has only just begun. We are thinking about a third conference in which the problems debated could be reopened and perhaps further results might be reached.

Bochum/Irvin, TX, July 1994
Henning Graf Reventlow
William Farmer

STATE *INTERESSE* AND MARKAN PRIMACY:
1870–1914*

William R. Farmer

Introduction

Social philosopher Rosenstock-Huessy visualized the Gospels serving the Church as the lips of Jesus. Using this image we can see that in order for these fundamental documents of Christian faith to function as they should in the church, it is necessary for them to be properly disposed one to the other. Rosenstock-Huessy was well enough acquainted with German academic history to know that something happened during the nineteenth century that had served to distort the twentieth century voice of Jesus. He recognized that an influential 'assured result' of nineteenth-century German Protestant Gospel criticism, namely the primacy of the Gospel of Mark, had in fact never been established, and that this revolutionary reversal of the relationships between the Gospels had far reaching canonical consequences. This placed Rosenstock-Huessy fundamentally at odds with the established world of theological scholarship, since it was inconceivable to most of his colleagues that German New Testament scholarship could be mistaken on such a fundamental point as the assumption of Markan primacy.

The theory of Markan primacy has led to the academic practice of interpreting the text of the Gospel of Matthew, the foundational Gospel

* Originally prepared for presentation at Dartmouth College, August 17, 1988 at a Conference marking the 100th birthday of Eugen Rosenstock-Huessy, and revised for presentation at Saint Vincent Seminary, September 9, 1990, at a Conference on 'Kulturpolitik and the Entrenchment of Marcan Primacy in the German Universities 1860–1914'. All references to Rosenstock-Huessy in this paper are based upon lengthy interviews with him held during the summer of 1965 in Heidelberg and Göttingen. An important literary locus for his thinking on these matters may be found in M. Davis Battles (ed.), *The Fruit of Lips or Why Four Gospels* (Pittsburgh: The Pickwick Press, 1978), especially ch. 2, 'The Heart and the Lips', pp. 9-18.

of the Church, in the light of Matthew's presumed changes to the text of Mark. The twist of Jesus' lips that followed from this paradigm shift diminished the Jewish content and character of his message. In this way Markan primacy ironically helped pave the way for anti-semitic German Christianity in the Third Reich. Moreover, Christian interest in the book of Isaiah (in which book Rosenstock-Huessy could see the whole of Christian faith prefigured), was discounted as due to a subsequent preoccupation of the Apostles, rather than as due to Isaiah's place as a decisive beginning point for understanding Jesus' own reading of the Law and the Prophets.

Part I

In 1977 Rosenstock-Huessy's recognition that Markan primacy was never established in the nineteenth century received dramatic confirmation in a book published by Vandenhoeck and Ruprecht: *Geschichte und Kritik der Markus-Hypothese* by Hans-Herbert Stoldt.[1]

In 1987 the late Professor Bo Reicke of Basel University published his study of 'Synoptic Theories Advanced during the Consolidation of Germany, 1830–1870', in which he traced the history of the idea of Markan primacy from Strauss to Holtzmann. In passing, Reicke noted that the appointment in 1874 of Holtzmann to the prestigious chair of New Testament at the reconstituted University of Strasbourg gave this young scholar's career (and thus the Markan Hypothesis) an important boost.[2] Stoldt had analyzed Holtzmann's influential work published in 1863 in his 1977 work, and had demonstrated its critical untenability. This had been done independently as early as 1866 by Hajo Meijboom, eight full years before Holtzmann's appointment to the chair at Strasbourg.[3] Thus it is an unsolved question in the social history of biblical studies how and why this important appointment was made.[4]

---

1.   English translation by Donald L. Niewyk, *History and Criticism of the Marcan Hypothesis* (Macon GA: Mercer University Press; Edinburgh: T. & T. Clark, 1980).
2.   'From Strauss to Holtzmann and Meijboom: Synoptic Theories Advanced during the Consolidation of Germany, 1830–1870', *NovT* 19.1 (1987), pp. 1-21, p. 18.
3.   Hajo Uden Meijboom, *Geschiedenis en critiek der Marcushypothese* (Amsterdam: Gebroeders Kragg, 1866).
4.   The correspondence between Bismarck and Ledderhose, who represented the University in the appointment process, focuses on Holtzmann's church politics.

This leads me to focus on the decade in which this happened—1870–1880, the era of the *Kulturkampf*—in order to see whether it is possible to discover how and why what was still only a very popular 'scientific' hypothesis in 1870 was eventually transformed into what Bo Reicke designates as a *theologumenon*. It should be said in advance that this bit of social history cannot settle the vexing question of whether Mark was or was not the earliest Gospel. That question can only be settled on the basis of historical and literary evidence. This bit of social history can, however, help explain what might be called the sociology of Markan primacy.

By *Kulturkampf* is meant that conflict which dominated relations between Germany and the Vatican during the decade of the eighteen seventies. This conflict arose soon after the close of the first Vatican Council and pitted the Iron Chancellor Prince Otto von Bismarck against Pius IX. This issue was an age old question of the power relations between Church and state. Constantine had simply announced to bishops of the Church that he had received a revelation from God that he was to exercise the office of Bishop on all matters outside the Church, just as they were to exercise jurisdiction on all matters internal to the life of the Church. Therefore, it has always been tempting for the head of any government in Christendom to presuppose the right of a Christian ruler to exercise sovereignty over Christian subjects. Kaiser Wilhelm was no exception, and Bismarck was his appointed minister. Pius IX, on the other hand, was the inheritor of a tradition according to which, as the head of the Roman Catholic Church, he was responsible for every Roman Catholic, including those who were German citizens. At issue was whether Catholics in Germany, in a showdown, were to obey the Pope or the Iron Chancellor. From the Pope's point of view it was a matter of whether these Catholics were going to obey human rule or God's, he being God's appointed representative by way of Christ who had been sent by God. Christ in turn had sent Peter whose infallible successor he (Pius IX) was. From Bismarck's point of view it was more a matter of whether these German citizens were to be subject to the laws promulgated by elected representatives of the German nation, with him guiding the legislative process by means of influence over a

There is no reference to the work of Meyboom (nor, for that matter, to anything Holtzmann had ever published) in any of the documents preserved in the file on Holtzmann in the University archives in Strasbourg. The whole correspondence deserves publication and literary and social analysis.

Protestant majority within the dominant Prussian parliament.

The conflict broke out when Dr Wollmann, a Catholic instructor of religion in the gymnasium at Braunsberg in East Prussia, having refused to signify his assent to the Vatican decrees of 1870 on the supremacy and infallibility of the Pope, was excommunicated and deprived of his right of giving instruction in the Catholic faith.[5] It helps to know that although Dr Wollman was giving instruction to Catholics, he, in fact, in accordance with a long-standing arrangement, had been appointed by government officials, and his salary was paid by the state. Ordinarily this arrangement worked well, since such appointments were made in consultation with Church authorities. The state in turn took for granted that no local bishop would dismiss a government appointee without due cause.

Here is the crux of the matter. What, in this situation, caused a breakdown in a system that for so long had worked well in maintaining a viable relationship between Prussia and its Catholic minority? At issue was the way the Vatican Council decrees of the preceding year were to be implemented, not only in Germany where Bismarck could control the situation through his influence within its dominant state, Prussia, but in France and Austria too, whose governments were vulnerable to pressure from ultramontane forces within their Catholic majorities.

It was among the ultramontane elements in French and Austrian society, with their reaction against liberalizing tendencies arising out of the Enlightenment embodied in some of the forces behind Bismarck, that the Jesuits had found support for their plans to persuade the Pope to convene the Vatican Council. The aim had been to strengthen the Papacy by issuing decrees on universal Papal jurisdiction and Papal infallibility. A strengthened Papacy was perceived by these Europeans as offering the best hope for maintaining an effective defence against a rising and ruinous tide of rationalism and social unrest.

Meanwhile, in response to Wollmann's excommunication, the Prussian minister sent a rescript to Bishop Kremenz, who had excommunicated Wollman demanding that Catholic students should continue to receive religious instruction from Wollmann. The bishop protested. The state responded by issuing an ordinance stating that 'in the eyes of the state, the excommunicated teacher remained a member of the Catholic

---

5. Sir Adolphus William Ward, *Germany 1815–1890*. III. *1871–1890* (Cambridge Historical Series; Cambridge: Cambridge University Press, 1918), pp. 56-57.

church'.[6] The Prussian bishops, rallying around their fellow bishop, collectively sent an immediate remonstrance to the Emperor against 'the interference of the state in the Church's internal sphere of faith and right'.[7] In response to this incipient episcopal rebellion, the German sovereign communicated to Pius IX that 'the Prussian government had acted in strict accordance with the existing law' as hitherto approved by the Pope.[8] A high ranking official issued a declaration that 'the state was under no obligation to treat the adherents of the unchanged Catholic Church as seceders from it'. This paved the way for state recognition of property rights and legal status for that portion of the Catholic clergy which refused to assent to the Vatican decrees and organized itself accordingly (that is Old Catholics). In August, the *Provinzial-Correspondenz*, the organ through which the government was in the habit of elucidating its views for the benefit of the public, explained that no bishop could be allowed to force teachers subject to state control to give their assent to a dogma imperilling the relations between the state and the Church of Rome.[9]

If it is asked: how could the dogma of papal infallibility imperil the relations between Germany and the Church of Rome?, the answer is clear. Germany was a nation in which Protestant principles were dominant. This dogma seemed to Protestants to be anti-Protestant to the core!

The decrees had been promulgated by the Pope in St. Peter's on July 18, 1870. One month later, the *Allgemeine Augsburger Zeitung* delivered this judgment:

> The monstrosity has taken place. The paramount party in the Church, [that is the Roman Catholic Church] has committed the crime of declaring to be a heresy the oldest principle of the Catholic faith that revealed truth is made known only by the continuous consent of all Churches, and, on the other hand, has declared as a dogma by the mouth of the unhappy Pius IX the crazy opinion of mere human origin that the Pope by himself is infallible. It has ventured to threaten with excommunication from the Church all those who may decline to agree with this overbearing outrage. It was not a formally valid resolution of the Council which delivered this verdict. It was merely a remnant of the Vatican gathering which [1] on account of the scornful contempt dealt out by the court and that faction to the independent members, [2] on account of its departure from all rules of

6. Ward, *Germany 1815–1890*, p. 57.
7. Ward, *Germany 1815–1890*, p. 57.
8. Ward, *Germany 1815–1890*, p. 57.
9. Ward, *Germany 1815–1890*, p. 57.

ecumenical Councils in order to thwart free deliberation, [and] [3] on account of official calumniation of the minority, had long forfeited the reputation of an ecumenical Council, or in truth had never won it. This remnant of a sickly corporate body has attempted to turn the Church upside down by the overthrow of its constitution, and Pius IX has lent himself to confirm this criminal undertaking.[10]

From 1830 onwards, the unification of Germany had required a *modus vivendi* between Protestants and Catholics. In response to this ideological need of German society for change and accommodation, German liberalism had carefully worked its will within both communions.

Lillian Wallace, in her work entitled *The Papacy and European Diplomacy, 1869–1878*,[11] writes that in the period before the Vatican decrees were issued:

> The leading German churchmen had been building up a powerful Catholic party which (1) aimed at harmony with the world of science, (2) resented Jesuit influence over the Pope, and (3) strongly opposed further centralization of power in Papal hands.[12]

Wallace goes on to note that 'the ambitions of this group were clearly grasped and set forth' by the Papal nuncio in Munich, who wrote to Cardinal Caterini as follows:

> Almost all of these people pride themselves on forming what they call the great party of German savants. Their aspirations consist in general of encouraging and pursuing to their furtherest limits scientific progress, and that with liberty, complete independence, maintaining dogma intact but sacrificing certain doctrines which are associated with it and have not been defined by the Church; their aspirations also consist of laying aside old-fashioned methods of scholasticism, these antiquities of the Middle Ages, as they call them, which are incompatible with modern progress; most important, their aspirations consist of rendering the scientific research of Catholicism as similar as possible to the scientific research of Protestantism, in order to demonstrate the superiority of Catholic theology over Protestant theology; finally, their aspirations include giving to Biblical, philological and historical studies a very large place, leaving only a very small place for true and positive theology. This party is dominated by pride. It resents the rein of authority which, according to its views, hinders

---

10. Karl von Hase, *Handbook to the Controversy with Rome*, 7th edn of the *Handbuch der protestantischen Polemik gegen die römisch-katholische Kirche*, I (ed. with notes by A.W. Streane; London; 1906), pp. 311-12 (bracketing and italicizing mine).

11. (Chapel Hill: The University of North Carolina Press, 1948).

12. Wallace, *The Papacy*, p. 154 (enumeration mine).

progress. It takes little account of the decisions of the Roman
congregations; it esteems highly the university system of 'learned'
Germany and prefers it to the seminaries of foreign lands; it regards with
an eye of pity, if not scorn, the decree of scientific culture possessed by
other countries, and considers theological science in the seminaries of
Italy, France, and other nations as in a state of infancy; thus it is explained,
also why this party never seems favourable to the founding of scientific
institutions depending on the authority of the bishops, and prefers sub-
ordination to the civil government, in order to preserve a greater liberality
in institution.[13]

It should be noted that this liberal Catholic party aspired to render the
scientific research of Catholicism as similar as possible to the scientific
research of Protestantism. This clearly included biblical and historical
studies, as these studies were carried out within the German universities.
The fact that Germany's state controlled universities were financially
dependent upon the civil government and subject to its influence
appeared to these Catholics to pose no threat.

In taking this ecclesiastical letter and subjecting it to sociological
analysis it is found that it affords striking confirmation of the view that
these liberal Catholics were profoundly implicated in facilitating the
subsequent assimilation of the German Catholic intelligensia within a
predominantly Protestant regime. To be sure, in order for this assimilation to take place there needed to be a compatible Protestant majority
equally willing to abide by the *modus vivendi* which would emerge out
of this kind of cultural and intellectual accommodation.

Before I explain the sociological function of German liberalism in
greater detail, let this one point be underscored: it is the German
university system and more precisely German science or *Deutsche
Wissenschaft* that was to provide the *magisterium* (that is the final court
of appeal) in the ideological struggle for the salvation of the German
nation. How shortsighted and problematic this unguarded reliance on the
German universities was only began to become clear during the Nazi
period.

---

13. George Goyau, *L'Allemagne Religieuse, le Catholicismse 1800–1870*, IV
(Paris, 1872), pp. 299-300, as translated and commented upon by Wallace, *The
Papacy*, pp. 154-55 (all italicizing mine). There was at this time no Papal representative to Germany. 'The Nuncio was to the kingdom of Bavaria, a post that Eugenio
Pacelli held during the First World War, and he subsequently became the first Nuncio
to Germany after it became a Republic', so Winthrop Brainerd in a letter to me dated
4 May 1987.

Part II

It should be self evident to any student of literature that the ideological needs of a society inevitably affect the way literature of that society is interpreted. However, in the established world of Biblical scholarship this influence of the ideological needs of society upon literary interpretation is not always recognized. To be quite specific, there is today a reluctance to recognize the way in which the ideological needs of nineteenth-century German society influenced the way in which the Bible was and continues to be interpreted in our theological schools and our universities. The reasons for this reluctance require exploration.

I begin by asking: what were some of the ideological needs of nineteenth-century German society that have affected literary interpretation of the Bible? There was, for example, the need to be up-to-date in relation to science. In order for Biblical faith to be credible, it was necessary for it to be defended on scientific grounds. In the nineteenth century, one science that provided some ruling models was biology. Since life appeared to develop from simpler forms into ever more complicated forms, it became credible to think of literary forms as developing from the simple to the complex. Thus, for the Old Testament, relatively early J and E were united in various combinations with the more developed D and P to make up the even more complex texts of the books of the Pentateuch. For the New Testament, the more simple Mark and 'Q' were combined to make up the more developed Gospels, Matthew and Luke. Parables of Jesus like that of the leaven in the loaf and that of the mustard seed were cited as evidence that Jesus was ahead of his time in thinking in scientific terms, that is, in the terms of growth. In fact these parables became known as the 'parables of growth'.

This approach to the Bible resulted in the attempt to distinguish earlier from later levels of the tradition. This made possible chronological rearrangements of the fragmented parts of the Bible which could then be reworked into 'scientific' histories of Israel on the one hand and 'scientific' histories of the Early Church on the other. In this way the grand, richly diverse, yet unified story of the Bible, from creation in the Book of Genesis to the eminent coming of a new heaven and new earth in the Book of Revelation, was fragmented. This is true not only of the Bible as a whole, but also of individual books. We can test how this has affected the interpretation of a particular book by considering the Gospel of Matthew. We find a story in this Gospel which, following the canonical model of the Servant in Isaiah 53, begins with the birth of Jesus in Bethlehem of Judea and runs continuously to his death in Jerusalem and his resurrection appearances in Judea and Galilee. It is all narratively connected in the form of a well developed story. But by the end of the nineteenth century this Gospel had been hopelessly broken up and dissected into an incomprehensible set of separate sources. Some parts came from a source called Q; other parts came from Mark or a source overlapping with Q called *Ur Markus*; still other parts came from other putative sources. As a consequence, the canonical character of this book was destroyed.

Every commentary or book about Matthew written out of a commitment to this nineteenth-century model (which by now has assumed an anti-canonical function) borders on being unintelligible. Try as they will, scholars are unable to discover any convincing authorial purpose out of a study of these separate parts, when they are arranged according to what, on this model, is believed to be earlier and what is believed to be later. This is no less true for redaction critics than it was for the earlier form and source critics. The Gospel which remains foundational for the Christian church has become, at the hands of all who rely on this German critical tradition, largely incomprehensible. As a consequence, Matthew, for many Christians, and for most Eurocentric theologians, has lost a great deal of its authority and much of its literary value.

For my purposes, however, it is the political side of the ideological question that is of paramount importance. For example, Bismarck managed to exclude Roman Catholic Austria from the ever expanding Prussian state. This means that the Second Reich in reality became a Protestant dominated Empire led by a Protestant Kaiser. However, while nineteenth-century Germany was predominantly Protestant, it should not be forgotten that it contained a very significant Catholic minority. At the same time, while it was predominantly Christian, it contained also a relatively small but very influential Jewish minority.

Among the important ideological needs of nineteenth-century Germany were a *modus vivendi* between a Protestant majority and a Catholic minority, between a Christian majority and a Jewish minority. Protestants, Catholics, and Jews, following the Enlightenment, were, by 1870, all recognized as citizens of the Second Reich. These culturally diverse German citizens had to accommodate their inherited differences and work together if the German Empire was to fulfill its ascending role in world politics.

Nineteenth-century Biblical criticism served German society well in enabling it to meet these pressing ideological needs. The state supported universities facilitated the inevitable process of intellectual accommodation and/or assimilation. From a post-Holocaust vantage point it is shocking to see how far Jews were willing to go in facilitating the possibilities for a German Jew to become a 'better' German. Not only were the dietary laws given up, some Synagogues were willing to move their main worship services to Sunday. Enlightenment Biblical criticism which became state supported Biblical scholarship smoothed the way for this accommodation.

On the majority side, sacrifices made by Christians were less radical. However, all passages in scripture which had fed Christian anti-semitism throughout the middle ages needed to be discounted. This meant that not only the terrible words in Matthew 'let his blood be upon our heads', needed to be relativized; but also the stinging condemnations of the Pharisees in Matthew 23. This was effectively achieved by denying the foundational role of Matthew in the constitution of the Church, and by turning this foundational role over to earlier hypothetical sources which were sanitized as much as possible from anti-Jewish polemic. The two chief results of this nineteenth-century deconstructive process were Proto-Mark and the *logia* source later called Q.

The breaking up of the text of Matthew into many parts with the earliest and most reliable coming from Mark and Q, and the later and less certain (which tended to include material that was troublesome) coming from the Church or from the hand of the Evangelist, made it possible for liberal theologians to pick and choose what made the most sense to them as they composed historical reconstructions of Jesus serviceable for the time. Ideally Jesus was a Jewish rabbi of the liberal school of Hillel. He could also be a Jewish prophet. Both liberal Jews and liberal Christians could experience relief and joy over this socially and nationally unifying achievement made possible by German *Wissenschaft*.

However, it was just this gentle liberal Jewish teacher or eschatological prophet that proved inadequate as a basis for theology for disillusioned, post-World War I, liberal Christians in Germany, when they were expected to make sense out of the devastating defeat of their imperial armies. The defeated German people needed a theology with a redemptive doctrine of sin. In Germany, this led to a rejection of the 'historical' Jesus and a turning to a Pauline dominated dialectical theology, and, in the United States, eventually to Pauline dominated neoorthodoxy. An appropriate canonical role for the Gospels, however, still eludes liberals, some of whom today toy with the idea of canonizing Q and the Gospel of Thomas.

State initiated pressure on German Catholics to accommodate and/or assimilate to the Protestant majority was at first successfully resisted by the Vatican. But eventually, through the state supported universities of Germany, aided by British and American universities which followed the lead of German scholarship, German *Wissenschaft* triumphed over Church tradition, over revelation, over the oracular. Sociologically speaking, within Germany, the critical tradition that developed in and was fostered by these state universities was one that went a long way toward serving the ideological need for Catholics, Protestants, and Jews to accommodate their differences, in the interests of a unified and purposeful Germany.

The societies of every country which faced essentially the same ideological needs readily embraced this liberal Protestant German criticism. These included England, Scotland, Holland, Scandinavia, the United States, Australia, and New Zealand. The most talented and aspiring young Biblical scholars from these countries flocked to the German universities. But societies in which these particular ideological needs did not exist turned a deaf ear to this critical tradition. These included those of Ireland, Austria, Hungary, Greece, France, Italy, Ethiopia, Spain, Portugal and all Latin American countries. The presence of students from these societies in the lecture halls of the theological faculties of the universities of Berlin, Göttingen, Marburg, Tübingen, and Strasbourg, was negligible.

Part III

With this survey of the sociological aspects of the topic in view, I return to the struggles between Bismarck and Pius IX. Each of these titans lived out of and represented his own world of discourse. That of Pius IX was Catholic; that of Bismarck was Protestant. At issue was the figure of the Apostle Peter, and how the Pope was to be understood in relationship to Peter.

It should be borne in mind that the protagonists of these two worlds of discourse were playing out their roles on a stage of history where both sides had committed themselves to a certain measure of religious toleration. Blood should not be shed over this issue. There should not even be torture, and certainly no capital punishment—there could only be arrests, trials, banishments or imprisonments. It is against this background of religious tolerance that measures taken by Bismarck to break down Catholic resistance appear so shocking. By 1876 every Prussian bishop was in prison or had left the country.[14] It is estimated that at the height of the controversy, as many as 989 Prussian parishes were without priests.

But how and when were these persecutory measures first initiated? As early as May of 1871, Bismarck had told the Prussian legislators that

> the Prussian Cabinet is determined to take measures which shall henceforth render it impossible for Prussians who are priests of the Roman Catholic Church to assert with impunity that they will be guided by canon rather than by Prussian law [Bishop Kremenz of Ermeland had so expressed himself]... We shall maintain the legislative power of the State against all comers.[15]

The next month Bismarck told a government official that he 'proposed to move vigorously against the clericals...' Wallace conjectures that this decision, which contemporaries said came so quickly it seemed like an inspiration and could be fixed almost to the day and hour, was possibly the result of a report from Rome that: 'the Papacy was assuming an anti-German attitude.'[16]

Three days later an article appeared in the *Neue Preussische Zeitung* which declared that the Jesuits, who had exhausted every resource to prevent the unification of Germany, were responsible for the formation of the Centre Party [that is the Catholic Party]. Although the Papal See, it went on, had at first greeted the establishment of the German Empire with approbation, Rome's action had belied its word. The government of Germany would never consent 'to strengthen a party whose sole aim was to resurrect the powers of the Papacy...' This article, in Wallace's view, was the clarion call to arms in the *Kulturkampf*.[17] This was June 22, 1871.

Two days later the periodical *Germania* carried an article in which science and religion were juxtaposed as hopelessly at odds and concluded that an 'ultramontane, that is a Catholic, cannot love his German

---

14. Ellen Lovell Evans, *The German Center Party 1870–1933: A Study in Political Catholicism* (Carbondale: Southern Illinois University Press, 1981), p. 76.

15. Wallace, *The Papacy*, p. 193.

16. Wallace, *The Papacy*, p. 194.

17. Wallace, *The Papacy*, pp. 194-95.

fatherland; he is a stranger in his own house'.[18] Clearly such a person's influence in society, in the press, and in politics was to be curtailed. The conflict escalated and according to one count made early in 1875, 136 editors had been arrested, 20 confiscations of newspapers had been executed, 210 centre Catholic party members had been arrested, 74 house searches had been executed, with 55 dissolutions of meetings and organizations, and 103 expulsions and internments.[19]

The question of what to do about the Jesuits was brought up in the German Reichstag. On May 14, 1872, a bill was introduced calling for their expulsion from Germany. Speeches were heated and the supporters of the bill proved in the end to be unstoppable. One evening in the theatre, following a day of debate, songs were performed about the Jesuits, the Pope, and infallibility.[20] This theatrical reference to infallibility makes it clear that the decrees of 1870 were certainly at issue in the minds of those who wanted to expel the Jesuits.

One month later, after word about the results of the debates in the German Reichstag had reached the Pope, he had the opportunity to address the German reading club in Rome. While he could agree that God wanted citizens to obey and respect magistrates, God also wanted them to speak the truth and fight error.

> We find ourselves under [a] persecution [that has been] prepared for a long time, but [is] now making itself felt. It is the minister of a powerful government who after great success on the battlefield [victories over Austria and France] has placed himself at the head of this persecution. I have let him know (it is not a secret, the whole world may know) that triumph without moderation cannot last, that a triumph which combats truth and the Church is the greatest madness. Who knows if soon a little stone may be detached from the height to break the foot of the colossus?...If God wills that other persecutions follow, the Church is not afraid. On the contrary! In the persecution it will be purified, strengthened, and surrounded with new beauty.[21]

The Pope's remarks evoked a predictable reaction. Bismarck was understandably displeased. Everyone seemed to realize that the reference to

18. This simple and unqualified identification of Catholic with 'ultramontane' represents an extreme view.

19. *Frankfurter Zeitung*, February of 1875, as cited in Wallace, *The Papacy*, p. 193.

20. Ludwig Hahn, *Geschichte des Kulturkampf in Preussen* (Berlin, 1881), pp. 102-103. English translation by Wallace, *The Papacy*, p. 201.

21. Wallace, *The Papacy*, p. 201.

'the stone and the colossus' was to the German Empire and particularly to Bismarck himself. The Jesuits were banned and the *Kulturkampf* was now well underway.[22] This was the summer of 1872.

The following January, the first repressive laws were introduced into the Prussian legislature.[23] They can be summarized as follows:

> Priestly offices could only be conferred on candidates of German birth, who, after passing the school-leaving examination, had studied theology for three years in a German university, and had received a sound scientific training tested by the State. Certain exceptions notwithstanding, this rule was manifestly aimed at theological seminaries on whose behalf an outcry at once arose. Still more contentious…was the subjection of the appointment of candidates duly trained to the veto of the State…Appointments made without the approval of the State were null and void; and the making of such appointments or the leaving open of clerical offices beyond the period of a year, was to be punishable by fines. Heavy fines were also to be imposed on priests illegally appointed [even if they should only] exercise spiritual functions—a provision which had the effect of depriving a parish served by such a priest of the ordinary comforts of religion.[24]

These laws were passed by the lower legislative body by 245 votes to 110. After long debate and, finally, a speech by Bismarck alleging that it was 'the conviction of the King and the Government that the foundation of the state is in danger', this legislation was passed in the upper house on May 1 by 87 to 53. Thereafter these laws came to be known as the May Laws because it was in that month they came into effect. The Catholic bishops in response at once prepared for resistance, informing the government eleven days later that they were 'unable to cooperate in carrying out these enactments'.[25]

Six months later Pius IX issued an encyclical in which he lamented certain things, including the May Laws, which were causing Prussian Catholics so much suffering. He nonetheless advised courage and reminded everyone that the Church would be triumphant in the end. 'Heaven and earth may pass away, but my words will not pass away.'

22. Ward, *Germany*, pp. 63-64. A distinction should be borne in mind between the Imperial Parliament, the Reichstag, and the Prussian legislature, the Prussian Landtag. The 'May Laws' were Prussian, not Imperial. However, because of its enormous size, Prussia dominated the German Empire, exercising a virtual veto in the Reichstag.

23. January 9, 1873.

24. Ward, *Germany*, pp. 65-66.

25. Wallace, *The Papacy*, p. 215.

The Pope said that the words Jesus referred to were: 'Thou art Peter, and upon this rock I will build my Church.' Those who oppose the Church, history teaches us, have been defeated in the end, while the Church itself 'gleams brighter than the sun'.[26] Here can be seen one of these two protagonists publicly calling attention to what Yale historian Jaroslav Pelikan has designated as 'the charter of Roman Catholic Christianity'; that is, the passage in the Gospel of Matthew where Christ bestows on Peter the keys of the kingdom (Mt. 16.18-19), which passage undergirds Papal claims to universal jurisdiction and infallibility.[27] It would only be a matter of time before the other protagonist (Bismarck) would publicly level his counter charge to this Papal appeal to holy writ. Meanwhile, on the surface, these papal lamentations seem to have had no effect on developments in Germany. What reaction may have been going on behind the scenes, historians can only conjecture. In any case, the bishops were made to take an oath to keep the state's laws conscientiously, unconditionally and without reservations. Catholic legislators both in the Prussian and Imperial parliaments opposed these measures at every step and spat out their defiance at the Iron Chancellor and his government. On occasion they reduced their tormentors to silence. One day their chief spokesperson stood up in the Prussian parliament and said:

> You have power to torment us, to wound our hearts. You do not have the power to take our faith away from us. When you shall have closed all our churches we shall assemble in the forests, we shall imitate the Catholics of France during the [Reign of] Terror.[28]

Bismarck's campaign against the Catholic Church reached its highest point in 1874 with passage of the law on the 'internment or expulsion of recalcitrant priests'. With all Catholic bishops in Prussia either in prison or in exile, with hundreds of priests incarcerated, and several hundred parishes priestless, the Pope, on February 5, 1875, issued another encyclical in which he cried out against the May Laws and again lamented their damage to the Church. Because the Church no longer had control of the education of its priests and thus, for example, could not be sure that its 'charter' would be left intact, the Pope could hold that this anti-Catholic legislation overturned the constitution of the

26. Wallace, *The Papacy*, p. 216.
27. *The Riddle of Roman Catholicism* (New York: Abingdon, 1959), p. 79.
28. Wallace, *The Papacy*, p. 241.

Church and cut the ground from beneath the authority of the bishops. Catholic bishops who, because of their resistance to this oppressive legislation, were shut up in prison, he held up as martyrs.

> For it is not to the powers of this earth that the Lord has submitted the bishops of His Church, but to Peter to whom he has entrusted his sheep and his lambs. That is why no temporal power...has the right to despoil of their episcopal dignity those who have been named by the Holy Spirit to administer the Church...It is necessary to obey God rather than man.[29]

It followed that Bismarck was not contending with a mere human being but with the Prince of the Apostles who by faith was perceived by Catholics to be authoritatively present in the person and office of the Pope. It was this unending resistance of the Catholic bishops, urged on and supported by the ultramontane [read: Petrine] forces of other Catholic countries, that tormented Bismarck beyond endurance.[30]

This encyclical of the Pope evoked a response in a government newspaper:

> The fact of this open outspoken message leaves no doubt that the relations of the Papal See to secular government have been fundamentally altered through the newest development: [that is the appeal to scripture to justify resistance to the ultimate authority of the May Laws].

The Pope's message, the writer maintained, was a revolutionary confrontation of the state's authority which by virtue of its unmistakable purpose indicated the course the government must follow in combatting it; the Catholic Church must be made to learn who was sovereign in Prussia.[31]

---

29. Wallace, *The Papacy*, p. 241.
30. Wallace, *The Papacy*, pp. 241-42.
31. Wallace, *The Papacy*, p. 247. 'The consequences of the *Kulturkampf* were extremely serious for the Church. More than a million Catholics were deprived of the sacraments because thousands of priests were in exile or in prison. There were no bishops available to ordain new priests, because they had been relieved by the state of their sees after their failure to secure the approval of the prefects to their ordination; two archbishops (Cologne and Posen) had been exiled. The government forbade parish priests to visit other parishes than their own to give the sacraments. And, as a sort of crowning insult, priority in the use of the Churches was given to the handful of anti-Roman Old Catholics, and the government created a new bishopric which it bestowed upon the leader of that sect' (E.E.Y. Hales, *The Catholic Church in the Modern World: A Survey from the French Revolution to the Present* [London: Eyre & Spottiswoode in association with Burns & Oates, 1958], p. 235). This

As far as Bismarck was concerned there could be no question about the decisive role in all this of both the Vatican Council decree on Papal infallibility and of its basic ideological corollaries, Petrine primacy and Papal supremacy. Only two months after the Pope had last called public attention to his Petrine authority, on April 15, 1875, while the *Kulturkampf* was still at its height, Bismarck levelled a bitter counter attack against Pius IX. The [Catholic] Church, he said, is now nothing else but the Pope. Before the Vatican Council, German bishops exercised the right to at least think for themselves independently from what the Pope held. However, since the Vatican Council, they no longer, complained Bismarck, exercised this independence of the Pope. And now, going for the jugular [figuratively speaking] of his opponent, Bismarck juxtaposed Peter to the Pope saying that Pius IX was not really Peter's successor since the Apostle Peter had not been infallible: Peter had sinned, wept bitterly, and repented. Bismarck closed his attack with a touch of irony: 'From the Pope, I think, we need not expect that.'[32] This skillful use of Biblical exegesis strongly suggests, if it does not prove, that Bismarck and his advisors understood the role of Peter in the ongoing political struggle. It is clear that they would have understood the way in which state *Interesse* would be served by a university endorsed counter argument. Of course this counter argument could not be effective unless it was supported in most if not all influential universities of the realm. This certainly included the University of Berlin and universities like the newly reconstituted University of Strasbourg. Essential to this development would be a professorate that was sensitive (but not openly subservient) to the interests of the state, and a government that knew

---

undocumented summary paragraph represents how a twentieth century Catholic historian could look back on the *Kulturkampf* from a post-Third Reich perspective, and yet leave unnoted in his book how Bismarck paved the way for Hitler. Apparently because Bismarck 'believed in the value of the Church and was concerned to gain control over it, so as to make sure it gave support to his regime', whereas 'Hitler's personal standpoint was fundamentally antithetical to christianity as such' (p. 296), justified in this historian's mind not drawing his reader's attention to the way in which Bismarck's actions provided Hitler with legal precedents to consider. The fact that there are differences between Bismarck and Hitler that are decisive, does not justify a failure to take continuity seriously—as well as the discontinuity in the *modus operandi* of the leaders of the Second and Third Reich. A main difference between Bismarck and Hitler is their relationships with Jews. Bismarck chose for his personal banker a Jew. Hitler believed that Jews had stabbed Germany in the back.

32. *Provinzial-Correspondenz.*

how to work with local university officials.[33] Markan primacy clearly offered support for discounting the claims for a Papal authority which rested on the Peter passage in Matthew, absent in Mark. To have well placed professors in the universities whose publications supported Markan primacy would clearly serve the interests of the state. Conversely, any professor whose published work proceeded from the traditional position that the Gospel of Matthew is our earliest Gospel, would be out of step with the interests of the state, and could expect, under the new Reich, to wither on the vine. This is exactly what happened to the distinguished Hilgenfeld, whose negative review of Holtzmann's book did little to damage the growing support for the Markan Hypothesis. Protestant pastors caught up in the spirit of the times simply ceased to recommend to young theologians that they go to hear Hilgenfeld. It was deemed not necessary to take his views into account.[34]

And now I approach the point of the essay: Markan primacy, as Professor Bo Reicke has noted, became a German *theologumenon*. It was taught eventually to children in the schools without question. How did this happen? In 1870, the Markan Hypothesis was no more than an increasingly popular *wissenschaftliche Hypothese*. But certainly by 1914, probably by 1890, and possibly as early as 1880 this popular hypothesis implicitly converted into a German Protestant dogma. Why? I wish to suggest that in the cultural struggle between Church and state

33. The appointment of Bernhard Weiss as Professor in the University of Berlin in 1876 would have further strengthened the hand of Bismarck since he was an influential proponent of Markan primacy. The preliminary decisions leading to this important appointment would have been initiated while the *Kulturkampf* was still at its height. The realistic but subtle relationship between the professorate and state *Interesse* emerges clearly in two excellent books on the German universities. These are: C.E. McClelland, *State, Society, and University in Germany, 1700–1914* (Cambridge: Cambridge University Press, 1980), and F.K. Ringer, *The Decline of the German Mandarins: The German Academic Community, 1890–1933* (Cambridge, MA: Harvard University Press, 1969). For documentation of the anti-Catholic ethos of the Prussian controlled universities in the imperial period, see Konrad H. Jarausch, *Students, Society and Politics in Imperial Germany* (Princeton, NJ: Princeton University Press, 1982), and John E. Craig, *Scholarship and Nation Building: The University of Strasbourg and Alsation Society 1870–1939* (Chicago: University of Chicago Press, 1984).

34. This I learned from Emanuel Hirsch in an interview during the summer of 1958 arranged by his neighbor Professor Emeritus Friedrich Gogarten. By way of contrast young theologians were advised that Holtzmann was a professor whose views they needed to take into account, according to what I was told by Hirsch.

the ideas of Markan primacy and the existence of Q took on ideational and ideological roles. That is, they began to function canonically within the new university dominated Protestant Magisterium. In proposing this I wish to allow for the probability if not the certainty that this function of the Two-Source hypothesis was largely, if not wholly, unconscious. In any case, it cannot be denied that these university endorsed ideas served to undercut the canonical basis for the decrees of Vatican Council I. Moreover, in sociological terms, the theological achievements of Markan primacy and the existence of Q, correlate positively in results to the political achievements of the May Laws. In both cases the results achieved were anti-ultramontane [read: anti-Petrine], and were reached through state institutions under government influence. In both cases, parameters were set within which the Catholic minority was to find a viable place in the body politic of the Second Reich. (Not until they publicly accepted Markan primacy [following the appearance of Pope Pius XII's Encyclical Divino Afflante Spiritu in 1943] would Catholic exegetes be able to make significant headway in gaining acceptance by their Protestant colleagues).

The immediate reaction of the Catholic hierarchy was one of resistance to political aggression from the dominant Protestant majority. The symbolic centre of resistance within Germany was the tomb of Saint Boniface, the English Benedictine missionary who is venerated as 'The Apostle to Germany'. Catholic bishops assemble near this tomb in Fulda in times of peril and whenever they meet on matters of importance for all German Catholics. Bismarck, however, found a way around this resistance by going over the heads of German Catholics and negotiating with the new Pope an end to the *Kulturkampf*. The new Pope wanted to normalize relations between Germany and the Vatican. This eventually freed German Catholic liberals—who, in the first instance, in the face of state persecution, had joined forces with conservative Catholics—to resume their program of cultural assimilation through university sponsored German *Wissenschaft*. This, in turn, paved the way for German Catholic scholars to recommend Markan primacy and the existence of Q even in the face of the Vatican sponsored Biblical Commission's *responsum* of 1912, which at that time was still against this theory.

During the *Kulturkampf* the German universities were more unified in support of Bismarck's goals than was the Prussian legislature. There had been open opposition in the legislature to the May Laws. No such concerted opposition to Protestant shiboleths developed in the universities. It should be remembered that all professors at German universities, Catholics as well as Protestants, were appointed by the state. After 1875, for a brief period, any German scholar who would openly question the Markan Hypothesis, in however small a measure, would be perceived as endangering 'the foundation of the state'. They would have endangered the foundation of the state by denying it a decisive defensive weapon against Vatican inspired aggression manifest in the use the Jesuits and the Pope were making of the Peter passage, a Matthean passage notably absent in Mark.

This situation of intense conflict lasted only two or three years. When Pius IX died, his successor wanted to make peace, and upon learning this, Bismarck, as previously noted, went over the heads of German Catholic leaders and worked out a concordat with the Vatican directly, ending the *Kulturkampf* on terms favourable to a Protestant dominated German state. Persecution of Catholics in Germany abated, but by this time the die had been cast. The Gospel of Matthew was henceforth to be identified with ultramontanism. Matthean priority to Mark could hardly be advocated by a Protestant as a scientific solution without raising the suspicion that the scholar concerned was either 'pro-Catholic' or 'unpatriotic', or at least out of step with the rapidly growing scholarly consensus required by the Church's theologians. In this situation a critical mass of scholarly opinion certainly did form in favour of Markan primacy. But why? All careful histories show that this happened in the absence of convincing historical and literary evidence, and, indeed, in the face of compelling counter evidence. Therefore, the conclusion that other interests were exercising an influence is unavoidable. Some of these 'other interests' are discussed in the histories of Meyboom and Stoldt. To these may now be added state *Interesse*. While the conflict between Bismarck and the Vatican eventually subsided, anti-ultramontane feelings in Germany persisted, and remained strong throughout the life of the Second Reich.

The charge of 'Ultramontanism' can be translated into the charge of being 'subject to the Vatican'. A basis for this charge persisted after Bismarck had made peace with Leo XIII, and even after he was dismissed by the Kaiser in 1890. The source of continuing anti-Catholic feeling could be either theological or political.

And popular sympathy generally was a good deal estranged by the anti-Modernist campaign, which by emphasizing the supremacy of dogma over 'free enquiry', seemed an especial affront to the work of the German universities...The temperature of German nationalism was rising, and the violently anti-Catholic propaganda of the evangelical *Bund* served to fan the flames. It seemed increasingly intolerable that Germany's 'manifest mission in the world' should be restrained by a party (the Catholic Centre Party) in the Reichstag which was supposedly 'subject to the Vatican'.[35]

It may be argued that no German scholar would have allowed himself to be influenced by non-scientific considerations, like the fear of being regarded as one who wishes to limit 'free enquiry'. But is such an argument sociologically tenable? In any case, would these German scholars also be free from all national sentiment? For example, would Catholic professors during the Second Reich be immune from societal pressure emanating from a majority prejudice that a Catholic 'cannot love his Fatherland'? It is within this historical and sociological context that we are most likely to find the answer to the question: 'How did Mark displace Matthew as the foundational Gospel for Christian faith and find itself as the chief theological model for liberal Protestant, and eventually liberal Catholic theology?' I conjecture that once the Markan Hypothesis had become a popular alternative to the more radical Tübingen Hypothesis this transformation happened imperceptibly and unconsciously in response to the ideological need of the German state for a theological defense against a perceived Catholic threat. This perceived threat was triggered by Pius IX and his close advisers who were seen as having bulldozed through the Vatican Council, over the opposition of liberals from northern Europe and the United States, the decrees on Papal supremacy and Papal infallibility—decrees which were expected to rally a coalition of ultramontane forces against Protestant Prussia—decrees which proceeded from and depended upon the Peter passage found only in Matthew. Liberal Catholic losers at Vatican Council I, after the *Kulturkampf* was over, eventually regrouped, and in Vatican Council II, with assistance from various quarters, they became the winners. Meanwhile, however, they had learned an important lesson. By Vatican Council II, they had come to recognize who was sovereign in Germany. It was Mark, not Matthew.[36]

35. E.E.Y. Hales, *The Catholic Church in the Modern World: A Survey from the French Revolution to the Present* (London: Eyre & Spottiswoode with Burns & Oates, 1958), p. 241.

36. It should be noted that in contrast to Vatican Council I, none of the decrees issuing from Vatican Council II proceed from the Peter passage in Matthew. A very important contribution to Vatican Council II was made by French Patristic and

It is of the greatest importance to recognize that this reading of history does not require that the state exercise explicit pressure on university professors. Gordon A. Craig refers to *Selbst-Gleichschaltung*, by which he means 'the voluntary, pre-emptive acceptance of the conformity ordered or expected by the regime'. 'It signifies submission out of a whole range of motives...The regime had a calibrated sense of how to apply censorship and terror, which encouraged voluntary submission.'[37] Craig is writing about the Third Reich, and is referring, among other things, to the collapse of responsible resistance to Hitler in the German universities. But self imposed conformity operates at all levels in every society. And all that is required to explain the virtual collapse of all resistance to a critically dubious Markan primacy in the Second Reich on the part of almost all university professors is a common sense recognition on the part of the professoriate that state *Interesse* called for 'voluntary, preemptive acceptance of a conformity' that could be assumed to be expected. No one was asked to sign on the dotted line. No oath was required. Everyone was free to make up his or

Liturgical theological scholarship. With Vatican Council II behind them, contemporary Roman Catholic scholars can justifiably interpret their more favourable reception by Protestant colleagues as evidence that they are now more readily perceived as capable of being free of Vatican influence. It is not clear, however, whether they realize that this more favorable perception has been bought at a price, that is the apparent wholesale unquestioning academic acceptance of Markan primacy [read: 'anti-ultramontanism']. It is quite wrong however to think that contemporary liberal Catholic acceptance of Markan priority is due only, if at all, to concern over what Protestants might think. To most, if not all liberal Catholics, Markan priority is intellectually satisfying. It is with a genuine feeling of liberation that a liberal Catholic exegete can bring forth new insights from Mark, which insights somehow seem to be more difficult to derive from the more sophisticated (and ecclesiastically developed) Gospels of Matthew and Luke. Mark does not seem to represent freedom from Catholic dogma so much as a fresh start in the exciting quest for a putatively more valid faith, tested less by canon law or Church doctrine than by common Christian experience. For scholars who question Markan priority not to recognize this positive and liberating contribution of Markan priority to the ongoing life of liberal Catholicism, will only lead to further misunderstanding and miscommunication. Whether Mark in fact is less sophisticated or less ecclesiastically and/or theologically developed than the longer Gospels is another matter. But in learning from one another one must take seriously how the other perceives things and how the other feels about what she or he perceives to be the case.

37. G.A. Craig, *Germany: 1866–1945* (Oxford: Oxford University Press, 1988), p. 168.

her own mind, and to speak and act in accordance with his or her own conscience. But this did not preclude scholars from taking into consideration what might be their duty as servants of the state, and to exercise a voluntary self-censorship that would bring them into line with the majority of their colleagues and all higher authorities. Through the power to appoint, state *Interesse* would eventually prevail, in one way or another. It is true that once professors are appointed they are professionally free to follow their conscience. But in order to become a professor a discrete measure of *Selbst-Gleichschaltung* is a *sine qua non* in all universities.

The sovereignty of Mark in the Second Reich was quickly passed to all societies outside Germany which enjoyed a symbiotic relationship to the Second Reich through the agency of German *Wissenschaft*, whose currency through state supported research was ever on the rise.

It may be questioned whether Church of England scholars at the venerable British universities at Oxford and Cambridge would uncritically take over Markan primacy from their German Protestant colleagues. But that they did has been documented.[38] And that they did so is less surprising when it is recognized that the ideological needs of English society, with its Church of England anti-Roman Catholic majority and its Roman Catholic minority (and with its Christian majority and its Jewish minority), were not so very different from those of Bismarck's Germany.

Epilogue

The historian can seldom date with precision the exact beginning of any social phenomenon. But if there was a decisive moment when the social conditions prevailed which can account for when and why the tradition of the Church that Matthew is our earliest gospel became anathema for liberal Protestant theology, it would seem to have been that moment in June of 1871 when Bismarck decided to 'move vigorously' against recalcitrant priests of the Roman Catholic church. If Wallace is correct in suggesting that this decision was the result of a report from Rome that the papacy was assuming an 'anti-German attitude', we have what is essential to explain what happened. For the previous month, Bismarck had taken an action that forced the hand of the Pope. In May of 1871,

38. William R. Farmer, *The Synoptic Problem: A Critical Analysis* (New York: Macmillan, 1964), pp. 48-198.

Bismarck had told the Prussian legislators that the Prussian Cabinet was determined to take steps to make it 'impossible' for Catholic priests in Prussia to 'assert with impunity' that they would be guided by canon rather than by Prussian law. It is important to grasp the essential nature of the constitutional crisis that this juxtaposition of 'canon' and 'Prussian law' entailed. Canon law rests on the Bible. The New Testament is the norm of the Christian Bible. And within the New Testament the Gospels traditionally have given the norm for canon law since there is found the legislative voice of the son of God. Within this four-fold Gospel canon it is the first Gospel that has been foundational for the Church. There, Christ as the new Moses, reveals his law for his Church. 'All authority in heaven and on earth has been given to me. Go make disciples of all nations...teaching them to keep my commandments. And I will be with you until the close of the Age' (Mt. 28.18-20).

The Gospel of Matthew is the backbone of canon law. To break that back was to break the back of resistance to Prussian authority. Bismarck himself could hardly have thought consciously in these terms, since Matthew is scripture and Lutherans honour scripture. But 'canon law' could be attacked since that was identified as 'Catholic', and for the Protestant majority it could be construed as dispensable.

In any case let there be no mistake about it; it was ecclesiastical authority as it comes to its quintessential expression in the Gospel of Matthew that inspired the Pope and that stood in Bismarck's path. For in addition to the Peter passage, there is the Apostolic Discourse.

> You will be dragged before governors and kings for my sake, to bear testimony before them and to the nations. When they deliver you up, do not be anxious how you are to speak or what you are to say; for what you are to say will be given to you in that hour; for it is not you who speak, but the Spirit of your Father speaking through you...He who endures to the end will be saved...So have no fear of them; for nothing is covered that will not be revealed, or hidden that will not be known. And do not fear those who kill the body but cannot kill the soul; rather fear him who can destroy both soul and body in hell...He who does not take his cross and follow me is not worthy of me. (Matthew 10.18-38)

This Apostolic discourse of Jesus is what brought the Roman Empire to its knees and has steeled the martyrs of the Church ever since. The Second Reich with its Protestant Kaiser resurrected the spectre of Caesars of old. Bismarck's *Realpolitik* was bringing the crisis to a head. His successful move against canon law helped pave the way for the more blatant departure from traditional legal norms made by Hitler in 1933.

Sociologically speaking Markan primacy leads to a deconstruction of canonical authority based on the apostolic witness of the Church as traditionally understood. As most Lutherans think, however, it is not Matthew, but Paul who norms the New Testament. As many Lutherans in Bismarck's day believed, the apostle Paul teaches that Christians should be subject to the governing authorities.

> For there is no authority except from God, and those that exist have been instituted by God. Therefore, he who resists the authorities resists what God has appointed, and those who resist will incur judgment. For rulers are not a terror to good conduct, but to bad. Would you have been in fear of him who is in authority? Then do what is good, and you will receive his approval, for he is God's servant for your good. But if you do wrong, be afraid, for he does not bear the sword in vain; he is the servant of God to execute his wrath on the wrongdoer. Therefore, one must be subject, not only to avoid God's wrath but also for the sake of conscience (Rom. 13.1-5).

Traditionally the Church had always read these words in Romans in dialogue with the words of Jesus embodied in the Gospels which steel resistance against those unrighteous authorities who can kill the body but who cannot kill the soul. But in Lutheran circles where the authority of the Gospels, especially the canonical authority of Matthew, was under a cloud, this essential exegetical dialogue was suspended, and Rom. 13.1-5 was absolutised to serve state *Interesse*. This meant that Bismarck could count on the support of a Protestant dominated Prussian legislature in his move to fine, arrest, and imprison Catholic priests and bishops who resisted the authority of the German state. But such measures could only bring temporary relief. They would provide no long term solution for Church-state relations. To guarantee the German Catholic church the long term priestly and episcopal leadership essential to the required *modus vivendi*, Bismarck turned to the state controlled university system. By requiring all clerics to be educated in the state universities, he drafted into forces on his side, the German university professoriate. The end result of this move by Bismarck was to eradicate ultramontanism in German Catholicism.

There was no need for any official direction from Berlin to the university professoriate. Such open direction would have been counter productive in any case. Many Protestant German professors had courageously fought against princely government authorities on behalf of German unity in the first half of the nineteenth century. And now that Bismarck had brought about that German unity, these professors and their colleagues were more than willing to give their support to an Empire that respected and honored the German professor. These well paid servants of the state were perfectly capable of grateful self-censorship. One consequence of this was an ever increasing tendency to consent by silence to the Protestant shibboleth of Markan primacy. It is in this sense that it is possible for the historian to say with no small measure of confidence that Markan primacy won by default. This helps to explain how a critical mass of scholarly opinion, in spite of convincing evidence to the contrary, formed in favour of Markan primacy, so that during the first half of the twentieth century it became possible for almost all scholars to believe (what today many scholars have come to disbelieve) that the Two Source Hypothesis was an 'assured result' of nineteenth-century German scholarship.

If students of nineteenth-century Gospel criticism have learned anything in the second half of the twentieth century, it is this: broadly speaking, between the cosmopolitan scholarship coming from German universities at the beginning of the nineteenth century, and the malevolent influence of the state on the German universities during the Third Reich, stands the transitional second half of the nineteenth century. Much of Biblical scholarship (but of course not all) coming from the German universities in this period and much of twentieth century exegesis based on that legacy is misleading and sometimes downright wrongheaded.

Eugen Rosenstock-Huessy tried to get his colleagues on the Law faculty at the University of Breslau to resign in protest against the new laws Hitler was able to get passed in the German Reichstag which were aimed at reconstituting German society and instituting his New World Order. Rosenstock-Huessy failed. But in leaving his university position he set an example, which, had it been followed in sufficient numbers, would have averted the Holocaust. It is no accident that this prophetic theologian and legal scholar was one of the first to recognize the counterfeit character of the Two Document Hypothesis. When something goes wrong, the thoughtful person wants to know why. This led the legal historian Rosenstock-Huessy back from the Third Reich into the Second, and there he discovered that the idea of Markan priority had a dubious pedigree and was never critically established.[39]

---

39. For subsequent documentation of the fact that the notion is ill founded that the Two Document Hypothesis was firmly established by the careful linguistic work of Holtzmann, see David B. Peabody's 'Chapters in the History of the Linguistic

So far as has been established until now, Rosenstock-Huessy himself never made the connection that has been assumed throughout this paper, between Markan primacy and a breakdown in German society of traditional Christian solidarity with Jews. However, there is no doubt that German Christian theologians (certainly Emanuel Hirsch) were under the influence of the theory of Markan primacy, and that Markan primacy generally weakened the critical case that could be made for theological solidarity between Christians and Jews. In this sense Markan primacy weakened the Church not only in Germany but throughout the West in its efforts to protest against the portentous consequences of Hitler's heretical Arian clause. In any case it seems unlikely to have been an accident that the first German to publically pronounce his critical doubts about the university sponsored academic consensus on Markan primacy was himself a victim of consequent Christian enfeeblement.

After failing to persuade his colleagues on the law faculty of the University of Breslau to join him in protesting Hitler's illegal enactments, Rosenstock-Huessy, a Christian of Jewish ancestry, saw the writing on the wall. His actions in protesting both against Hitler and later against Markan primacy are sociologically consistent and morally coherent, even if he did not himself explicitly or even consciously connect the two.[40]

Argument for Solving the Synoptic Problem: The Nineteenth Century in Context', in *Jesus, the Gospels, and the Church* (ed. E.P. Sanders; Macon, GA: Mercer University Press, 1987), pp. 47-67. Peabody documents the fact that C.G. Wilke failed to distinguish between linguistic characteristics and linguistic peculiarities of each Gospel, thus contributing to a subsequent methodological confusion of decisive consequence. Holtzmann uncritically took over the ill conceived results of Wilke and passed on to all future generations of students nurtured in the Holtzmann-Kümmel critical tradition this misleading scholarship. Peabody, at the same time renders his readers the service of focusing critical attention on what he judges to be the reliable critical scholarship of Eduard Zeller, and shows that Zeller's work stands in a critical tradition that can be traced all the way back to Alexandrian text critical principles of the second century BCE.

40. It is an unfulfilled responsibility of Rosenstock-Huessy's Christian and Jewish colleagues to reflect together on the probabilities of the connection assumed in this paper. For it is an issue, the discussion of which could throw light on the yet unresolved question as to how it happened that German society could be the society in which the Holocaust was engendered and executed on a broad scale with unimaginable efficiency, while the university professorate, which knew what was happening, remained largely silent. Professor Joachim Jeremias once said with reference to what happened: 'They will say that we did not know what was happening. But we did know.'

Standing on his shoulders we can see more than he may have seen. And what we see (whether he saw it or not) is an inherent connection between hermeneutics and ethics: a connection, which, in this case, is yet to be explored and thus yet to be defined.[41]

A SELECT BIBLIOGRAPHY ON THE GERMAN UNIVERSITIES

Anrich, E. (ed.), *Die Idee der deutschen Universität* (Darmstadt: Wissenschaftliche Buchgesellschaft, 1964).

Asen, J., *Gesamtverzeichnis des Lehrkorpers der Universität Berlin*. I. *1810–1945* (Leipzig: Harrasowitz, 1955).

41. The point is not that Markan primacy contributed to Hitler's anti-semitism. This he came by initially through his Christian nurture in a church which inherited it from the middle ages. Hitler's inherited Christian bias against Jews was later transformed (in ways yet to be defined) into a more virulent anti-semitism that violated the sensibilities of many Christians, some of whom were faithful unto death in their opposition to Hitler's demonic and criminal anti-Jewish policies. Nor is the point that Marcan priority was anti-semitic in its origin. On the contrary, Markan priority served the ideological need of German society for a liberal form of Christianity which would diminish the scriptural grounds for anti-Jewish attitudes among Christians (see Part II). The point is, ironical as it may be, that this hypothesis which was serviceable in preparing the way for better relationships between Christians and Jews, ended up by serving a Marcionite function of separating the Old Testament from the New and paving the way for the liberal Harnackian denial that these Jewish scriptures deserve any place in the Church's canon. This extreme form of German Protestant liberalism was given state support when Harnack was put in control of dispensing funds for biblical research in the universities during the last years of the Second Reich. Liberal Protestant German theology under such social circumstances, was rendered theologically impotent in combating Hitler's Arian clause. It required a traditional theology to support a Roman Catholic witness unto blood, and a conservative Barthian reaction against Harnack to channel Protestant opposition to Hitler into the effective witness of the 'confessing' church. It is in this overall Catholic–Protestant context that we should begin the exploration of the connection between the hermeneutics of Markan primacy and ethical enfeeblement of the Church in its resistance to the persecution of Jews during the Third Reich. The less Jewish Jesus became, the less reason Christians had to experience theological and kinship shock over Hitler's treatment of Jews. The more mythical the role of Mary and legendary the role of Joseph, the more reason to dismiss the solidarity the Church had traditionally sensed between the Holy Family of the Christ Child, and the Jewish race of which it was a part. It is in this sense that we can say that Mark and Q helped pave the way for the Holocaust. The price that was paid for sanitizing the Gospels from anti-Jewishness, was a de-judaization of Jesus, which facilitated Christian toleration of the dehumanization and demonization of Jews under Hitler.

Beutler, K., and Henning, U. 'Der Professoren Geist und das Ministerium des Geistes', *Zur Rolle von Wissenschaft und Staat in Preussen–Deutschland unter dem 'System Althoff' 1882–1907* (Neue Sammlung; 17, 1977), pp. 2-26.

Bleuel, H.P., *Deutschlands Bekenner: Professoren zwischen Kaiserreich und Diktatur* (Munich: Scherz, 1968).

Boehlich, W. (ed.), *Der Berliner Antisemitismusstreit* (Frankfurt a.M.: Insel, 1965).

Brandt, H.-J., *Eine katholische Universität in Deutschland? Das Ringen der Katholiken in Deutschland um eine Universitätsbildung im 19. Jahrhundert* (Cologne: Böhlau, 1981).

Brock, K.-D., *Strukturgeschichte der Assistentur: Personalgefüge, Wert- und Zielvorstellungen in der deutschen Universität des 19. und 20. Jahrhunderts* (Düsseldorf: Bertelsmann Universitätsverlag, 1972).

Bruford, W.H., *The German Tradition of Self-Cultivation: 'Bildung' from Humboldt to Thomas Mann* (Cambridge: Cambridge University Press, 1975).

Busch, A., *Die Geschichte der Privatdozenten* (Stuttgart: Enke, 1959).

Craig, J.E., *Scholarship and Nation Building: The Universities of Strasbourg and Alsation Society 1870–1939* (Chicago: University of Chicago Press, 1984).

Delbrück, H., 'Akademische Wirren', *Preussische Jahrbücher*, CXXXIII, 1 (July, 1908), pp. 196-81.

Dahrendorf, R., *Society and Democracy in Germany* (Garden City: Doubleday, 1967), pp. 71-74, 99-106, 142-50.

Erman, W. and E. Horn, *Bibliographie der deutschen Universitäten* (3 vols.; Leipzig: Teubner, 1904–1905; repr. Hildesheim: Olms, 1960; and continued by O.E. Ebert and O. Scheuer, *Bibliographisches Jahrbuch für deutsches Hochschulwesen* (Vienna: E. Beyers, 1912).

Fallon, P.D., *The German University: A Heroic Ideal in Conflict with the Modern World* (Colorado: Colorado Associated University Press).

Fletcher, J.M. (ed.), *The History of European Universities* (Birmingham: The Department of Modern Languages, 1978).

Flexner, A., *Universities: American, English, German* (New York: Oxford University Press, 1930).

Fout, J.C., *German History and Civilization 1806–1914: A Bibliography of Scholarly Periodical Literature* (Metuchen, NJ: Scarecrow Press, 1974).

Hartshorne, E.Y., Jr, *The German Universities and National Socialism* (London: George Allen & Unwin, 1937).

Herrlitz, H.-G. and H. Titze, 'Überfüllung als bildungspolitische Strategie: Zur administrativen Steuerung der Lehrerarbeitslosigkeit in Preussen 1870–1914', *Die deutsche Schule* 68 (1976), pp. 348-70.

Humboldt, W. von, 'Über die innere und äussere Organisation der höheren wissenschaftlichen Anstalter zu Berlin', in *Die Idee der deutschen Universität* (ed. E. Anrich; Darmstadt: Wissenschaftliche Buchgesellellschaft, 1964), pp. 375-86.

Jarausch, K.H., *Students, Society, and Politics in Imperial Germany: The Rise of Academic Illiberalism* (Princeton: Princeton University Press, 1982).

Johanning, K., *Der Bibel-Babel-Streit* (Frankfurt a.M.: Lang, 1988).

Kahl, W., *Bekenntnisgebundenheit und Lehrfreiheit* (Berlin: Becker, 1897).

Kaufmann, G., *Die Lehrfreiheit an den deutschen Universitäten im neunzehnten Jahrhundert* (Leipzig: S. Hirzel, 1898).

Knoll, J.H., 'Vater der Universität: Zum 200. Geburtstag Wilhelms v. Humboldt', *Die Welt*, June 1967, pp. 16-17.

Lenz, M., *Römischer Glaube und Freie Wissenschaft* (Berlin: H. Walther, 1902).

—*Geschichte der Königlichen Friedrich-Wilhelms-Universität zu Berlin*, I (Halle: Verlag der Buchhandlung des Waisenhauses, 1910).

—*Freiheit und Macht im Lichte der Entwicklung unserer Universität* (Berlin: G. Schade, 1911).

Leussink, H., *et al.* (eds.), *Studium Berolinense, Gedenkschrift der Freien Universität Berlin zur 150. Wiederkehr des Gründungsjahres der Friedrich-Wilhelms-Universität zu Berlin* (Berlin: de Gruyter, 1960).

Lexis, W. (ed.), *Die deutschen Universitäten*, 25 (2 vols.; Berlin: A. Asher., 1893).

Leyen, F. von der, *Deutsche Universität und deutsche Zukunft: Betrachtungen* (Jena: Diederichs, 1906).

Luedicke, R., *Die preussischen Kultusminister und ihre Beamten im ersten Jahrhundert des Ministeriums 1817–1917* (Stuttgart: Weidmann'sche Buchhandlung, 1918).

Lundgreen, P., 'Quantifizierung in der Sozialgeschichte der Bildung', *VSWG* 63 (1976), pp. 433ff.

McClelland, C.E., 'A Step Forward in the Study of Universities', *Minerva* 14 (1976), pp. 150-61.

—*State, Society and University in Germany, 1700–1914* (Cambridge: Cambridge University Press, 1980).

Manegold, K.-H., 'Das "Ministerium des Geistes": Zur Organisation des ehemaligen preussischen Kultusministeriums', in *Die deutsche Berufs- und Fachschule* 63 (1967), pp. 512-24.

Mast, P., *Künstlerische und wissenschaftliche Freiheit im Deutschen Reich 1890–1901* (Reihe der Forschungen, 7; Diss. Munich, 1978; Rheinfelden: Schäuble, 1980).

Müller, D.K., *Sozialstruktur und Schulsystem: Aspekte zum Strukturwandel des Schulwesens im 19. Jahrhundert* (Göttingen: Vandenhoeck & Ruprecht, 1977).

Paulsen, F., *Geschichte des gelehrten Unterrichts*, I (Leipzig: Verlag von Viet, 1919).

—*Geschichte des gelehrten Unterrichts*, II (Berlin: Walter de Gruyter, 1921).

—*Geschichte des gelehrten Unterrichts* (3rd expanded edn by R. Lehmann; 2 vols.; Leipzig: Veit, 1919–21; reprinted Berlin: de Gruyter, 1965).

—*The German University and University Study* (New York: Charles Scribner's Sons, 1908) = *Die deutschen Universitäten und das Universitätsstudium* (Berlin: A. Asher, 1902; reprinted Hildesheim: Georg Olms Verlagsbuchhandlung, 1966).

—*An Autobiography* (New York: Columbia University Press, 1938), see esp. pp. 363-65.

Petry, L., 'Deutsche Forschungen nach dem zweiten Weltkrieg zur Geschichte der Universitäten', *VSWG* 46 (1959), pp. 145-203.

Preussen. Seine Wirkung auf die deutsche Geschichte: Vorlesungen...Bilanz-Kolloquium (Stuttgart: Klett–Cotta, 1985).

Riese, R., *Die Hochschule auf dem Wege zum wissenschaftlichen Grossbetrieb: Die Universität Heidelberg und das badische Hochschulwesen 1860–1914* (Stuttgart: Klett, 1977).

Ringer, F.K., *The Decline of the German Mandarins: The German Academic Community, 1890–1933* (Cambridge, MA: Harvard University Press, 1969).

Rogge, H., 'Affairen im Kaiserreich: Symptome der Staatskrise unter Wilhelm II', *Die politische Meinung* 81 (1963), pp. 58-72.

Rossmann, K., *Wissenschaft, Ethik und Politik: Erörterung des Grundsatzes der Voraussetzungslosigkeit in der Forschung* (Schriften der Wandlung, 4; Heidelberg: L. Schneider, 1949).

Sachse, A., *Friedrich Althoff und sein Werk* (Berlin: Mittler & Sohn, 1928).

Schleiermacher, F.E.D., 'Gelegentliche Gedanken über Universitäten im deutschen Sinn', in *Die Idee der deutschen Universität* (ed. E. Anrich; Darmstadt: Wissenschaftliche Buchgesellschaft, 1964), pp. 219-308.

Spranger, E., *Wilhelm von Humboldt und die Humanitätsidee* (Berlin: Reuther & Reichard, 1909).

—*Wilhelm von Humboldt und die Reform des Bildungswesens* (Berlin: Reuther & Reichard, 1910).

—*Der Sinn der Voraussetzungslosigkeit in den Geisteswissenschaften* (Berlin: Akademie der Wissenschaften, 1929).

—'Mein Konflikt mit der national-sozialistischen Regierung 1933', *Universitas: Zeitschrift für Wissenschaft, Kunst und Literatur* 10 (1955), pp. 457-73.

—'Gedenkrede zur 150 Jahrfeier der Gründung der Friedrich-Wilhelms Universität in Berlin', in *Berlin in Vergangenheit und Gegenwart: Tübinger Vorträge* (ed. H. Rothfels; Tübingen: Mohr [Paul Siebeck], 1961), pp. 61-74.

Steiger, G. and M. Straube, 'Forschungen und Publikationen seit 1945 zur Geschichte der deutschen Universitäten und Hochschulen auf dem Territorium der D.D.R.', *ZG* (Sonderheft, 1960), pp. 563-99.

Stirk, S.D., *German Universities—Through British Eyes* (London: V. Gollancz, 1946).

Schieder, T., 'Kultur, Wissenschaft und Wissenschaftspolitik im Deutschen Kaiserreich', in *Medizin, Naturwissenschaft, Technik und das zweite Kaiserreich* (ed. G. Man and R. Winau; Göttingen: Vandenhoeck & Ruprecht, 1977), pp. 9-34.

Steinmetz, M. (ed.), 'Geschichte der deutschen Universitäten und Hochschulen: Ein Überblick', *Studien zur Hochschulentwicklung* 25 (1971).

Tilman, K., *Die sogenannten Konkordatsprofessuren: Geschichtliche und heutige Rechtsproblematik* (Diss.; Freiburg, 1971).

Tompert, H., *Lebensformen und Denkweisen der akademischen Welt Heidelbergs im wilheminischen Zeitalter* (Lübeck: Matthiesen, 1969).

Van de Groff, J.H., *The Politics of German University Reform, 1810–1970* (PhD diss.; Columbia University, 1973).

Vogler, G., *Berliner Historiker: Die neuere deutsche Geschichte in Forschung und Lehre an der Berliner Universität* (Beiträge z. Gesch. d. Humboldt–Univ. Berlin, 13; Berlin, DDR, 1985).

Vom Brocke, B., 'Von der Wissenschaftsverwaltung zur Wissenschaftspolitik. Friedrich Althoff 19.2. 1839–20.10.1908', *Berichte zur Wissenschaftsgeschichte* 11 (1988), pp. 1-26.

Vom Bruch, R., *Wissenschaft, Politik und öffentliche Meinung: Gelehrtenpolitik im wilhelminischen Deutschland 1890–1914* (Diss.; Munich, 1977–78; Husum: Matthiesen, 1980).

Vondung, K. (ed.), *Das wilhelminische Bildungsbürgertum: Zur Sozialgeschichte seiner Ideen* (Göttingen: Vandenhoeck & Ruprecht, 1976).

Weber, C., *Der Fall Spahn: Ein Beitrag zur Wissenschafts- und Kulturdiskussion im ausgehenden 19. Jahrhundert* (Rome: Herder, 1980).

Weber, M., *Max Weber: Ein Lebensbild* (Tübingen: Mohr [Paul Siebeck], 1926).

Weber, Max, 'Die sogenannte "Lehrfreiheit" an den deutschen Universitäten', *Frankfurter Zeitung*, 20 September, 1908.

Wucher, A., *Theodor Mommsen: Geschichtsschreibung und Politik* (Göttingen: Musterschmidt, 1968).

Zahn-Harnack, A. von, *Adolf von Harnack* (Berlin: de Gruyter, 1951[2]).

A SELECT BIBLIOGRAPHY ON THE KULTURKAMPF

Andernach, N., *Der Einfluss der Parteien auf das Hochschulwesen in Preussen 1948–1918* (Göttingen: Vandenhoeck & Ruprecht, 1972).

Bachem, J., *Die Kirchenpolitischen Kämpfe in Preussen gegen die Katholische Kirche, insbesondere der 'grosse Kulturkampf' der Jahre 1871–1887* (ed. Julius Bachem and Karl Bachem; Freiburg im Breisgau: Herdersche Verlagshandlung, 1910).

Bar, L. von, *Staat und Katholische Kirche in Preussen* (Berlin: J. Springer, 1883).

Baum, W., *Johannes Janssen, 1829–1891. Persönlichkeit, Leben und Werk. Ein Beitrag zur Theologie- und Geistesgeschichte Deutschlands im 19. Jh.* (Diss.; Innsbruck, 1971).

Baumgart, P. (ed.), *Bildungspolitik in Preussen zur Zeit des Kaiserreichs* (Stuttgart: Klett-Cotta, 1980).

Bazin, G., *Windhorst, ses alliès et ses adversières; l'Allemagne catholique au XIX siècle* (Paris: Bloud & Barral, 1896).

Becker, J., *Liberaler Staat und Kirche in der Ära von Reichsgründung und Kulturkampf; Geschichte und Struktur ihres Verhältnisses in Baden, 1860–1875* (Mainz: Matthias-Grünewald-Verlag, 1973).

Bernard, P.S.J., *La persécution religieuse en Allemagne, 1872–1879* (Paris, 1907).

Borodziej, L., *Pruska polityka oswiatowa na ziemiach polskich w okresie Kulturkampfa* ([Oprac. graf. krzysztof Dobrowolski. Wyd. 1. Warszawa] Panstw. Wydawn. Naukowe, 1972 [with Russian and German summaries]).

Brück, H., *Die Culturkampfbewegung in Deutschland seit 1871 historisch dargestellt* (2 vols.; Münster: Aschendorff, 1901). Vol. I has title page reading: *Die Culturkampfbewegung in Deutschland 1871–1900* (Mainz: F. Kirschheim, 1901).

Bury, J.B., *History of the Papacy in the 19th Century: Liberty and Authority in the Roman Catholic Church* (aug. edn, New York: Schocken Books, 1964).

Butler, C., *The Vatican Council 1869–70, Based on Bishop Ullathorne's Letters* (Westminster, MD: The Newman Press, 1962).

Cathrein, V., *Actenstücke betreffend den preussischen Culturkampf, nebst einer geschichtlichen Einleitung* (ed. Nikolaus Siegfried [pseud.]; Freiburg im Breisgau: Herder, 1882).

Constabel, A. (ed.), *Staatliche Archivverwaltung: Die Vorgeschichte des Kulturkampfes; Quellen-Veröffentlichung aus dem deutschen Zentralarchiv* (with an introduction by F. Hartung; Berlin: Rütten & Loening, 1956).

Corrigan, R.S.J., *The Church and the Nineteenth Century* (Milwaukee: Bruce Publishing, 1938).

Dettmer, G., *Die ost- und westpreussischen Verwaltungsbehörden im Kulturkampf* (Heidelberg: Quelle & Meyer, 1958).

Eggers, K., *Rom gegen Reich: Ein Kapitel deutscher Geschichte um Bismark* (Stuttgart[2]: G. Trucken-Müller, 1937).

Evans, E.L., *The German Center Party 1870–1933: A Study in Political Catholicism* (Carbondale: Southern Illinois University Press, 1981) [especially valuable for her excellent treatment of the background to the *Kulturkampf*].

Feldenkirchen, T., *Die Bonner Deutsche Reichszeitung im Kulturkampf: Ein Beitrag zur preussisch-deutschen Geschichte im 19. Jahrhundert* (Cologne: Kleikamp, 1960).

Ferber, W., 'Der Weg Martin Spahns: Zur Ideengeschichte des politischen Rechtskatholizismus', *Hochland* 62 (1970).

Frantz, C., *Die Religion des Nationalliberalismus* (Leipzig: Rossberg'schen Buchhandlung, 1872).

Franz-Willing, G., *Kulturkampf: Staat und Katholische Kirche in Mitteleuropa von der Säkularisation bis zum Abschluss des preussischen Kulturkampfes* (Munich: D.W. Callwey, 1954).

Goyau, G., *Bismark et l'église: Le culturkampf, 1870–1887* (Paris: Perrin & cie, 1911–13).

Graue, G., *Nachwirkungen des Kulturkampfes: Zur tatsächlichen Berichtigung der weitverbreiteten abfälligen Urteile über O. von Bismarks Vorgehen gegen Rom* (Leipzig: M. Heinsius Nachfolger, 1907).

Groh, J.E., *Nineteenth Century German Protestantism: The Church as Social Model* (Washington, DC: University Press of America, 1982).

Hahn, L., *Geschichte des 'Kulturkampfes' in Preussen in Aktenstücken dargestellt* (Berlin: W. Hertz, 1881).

Hankamer, W., *Das Zentrum, die politische Vertretung des Katholischen Volksteils; die Geschichte seiner Entstehung und seiner Tätigkeit unter besonderer Berücksichtigung des kirchen-politischen Konfliktes* (Essen: Fredebeul & Koenen, 1927).

Hoefele, K.H., 'Sendungsglaube und Epochenbewusstein in Deutschland 1870–1871', *ZRGG* 15 (1963).

Holborn, H., *A History of Modern Germany* (4 vols.; New York: Alfred A. Knopf, 1951–1969), II & III.

Horstmann, J., *Katholizismus und moderne Welt: Katholikentage, Wirtschaft, Wissenschaft, 1848–1914* (Paderborn: Schöningh, 1976).

Huber, E.R., *Deutsche Verfassungsgeschichte seit 1789. IV. Struktur und Krisen des Kaiserreiches* (Stuttgart: Kohlhammer, 1969).

Kissling, J.B., *Geschichte des Kulturkampfes im deutschen Reiche, im Auftrage des Zentralkomitees für die Generalversammlungen der Katholiken in Deutschland. I. Die Vorgeschichte; II. Die Kulturkampfgesetzgebung, 1871–1874; III. Der Kampf gegen den passiven Widerstand: Die Friedensverhandlungen* (3 vols.; Freiburg im Breisgau: Herdersche Verlagshandlung, 1911–16).

Kolbeck, M.O., *American Opinion on the Kulturkampf (1871–1882)* (PhD thesis, Catholic University of America, 1941; Washington, DC: The Catholic University of America Press, 1941).

Krasuski, J., *Kulturkampf; katolicyzm; liberalizm w Niemczech XIX wieku* ([Poznan] Wydawn: Poznskie, 1963).

Lange, J., *Die Stellung der überregionalen katholischen deutschen Tagespresse zum Kulturkampf in Preussen (1871–1878)* (Bern: Herbert Lang; Frankfurt: Peter Lang, 1974).

Lehmann-Hohenberg, *Bismark's Erbe: Los von Rom gut deutsch allewege! Ein weckruf an das deutsche Volk zur Vollendung deutscher Reformation* (Munich: J.F. Lehmann, 1899).

Lescoeur, L., M. *de Bismarck et la persécution religieuse en Allemagne* (Paris: C. Douniol, 1879).

Lesmayoux, L.A., *Abbé, L'église évangélique de Prusse* (Paris: C. Douniol, 1869).

—*La persécution religieuse en Prusse* (Paris: C. Douniol, 1875).

Lill, R. (ed.), *Vatikanische Akten zur Geschichte des deutschen Kulturkampfes: Leo XIII. Im Auftrag des Deutschen Historischen Institutes in Rom* (Tübingen: M. Niemeyer, 1970). Compiled from documents in the archives of the *S. Congregazione per gli offari ecclesiastici Straordinari, the Nunziatura di Monaco, Nunziatura di Vienna*, and the *Segretaria di Stato*.

—*Die Wende im Kulturkampf: Leo XII, Bismarck u.d. Zentrumspartei, 1878–1880* (Tübingen: Niemeyer, 1973).

Loehde, W., *Das päpstliche Rom und das Deutsche Reich: Eine Dokumentation* (Hanover: Pfeiffer, 1964).

McCaffrey, J., *History of the Catholic Church in the Nineteenth Century*, I (St Louis: Herder, 1910).

McKnight, J.P., *The Papacy: A New Appraisal* (New York: Rinehart, 1952).

Majunke, P., *Geschichte des 'Culturkampfes' in Preussen-Deutschland* (Paderborn: F. Schöningh, 1886).

Nielsen, F., *The History of the Papacy in the XIXth Century* (trans. A.J. Mason; 2 vols.; London: John Murray, 1906).

Robolsky, H., *Geschichte des Kulturkampfes: Ursprung, Verlauf und heutiger Stand von H. Wiermann* [pseud.] 2ᵉ, *bis auf die Gegenwart fortgeführte Aufl.* (Leipzig: Rengersche Buchhandlung, Gerhardt & Wilisch, 1886).

Roux, X., *Les lois de persécution en Prusse* (Paris: J. le Clere, 1874) (covering the period from December 1873 to March 1874).

Rouy, H., *Le kulturkampf ou la lutte religieuse en Allemagne de 1870 à nos jours: Les progrés du catholicisme en Angleterre et aux Etats-Unis. A propos d'un livre du P. Sertillanges* (Charleville: A. Anciaux, 1904).

Ruhenstroth-Bauer, R. (von Hase), *Bismarck und Falk im Kulturkampf* (Heidelberg: C. Winter, 1944).

Sagarra, E., *A Social History of Germany, 1648–1914* (New York: Holmes & Meier, 1977).

Schmidt, E., *Bismarks Kampf mit dem politischen Katholizismus* (Hamburg: Hanseatische Verlagsanstalt, 1942).

Schmidt, H.J., *Der Kulturkampf* (Paderborn: F. Schöningh, 1926).

Schmidt-Volkmar, E., *Der Kulturkampf in Deutschland, 1871–1890* (Göttingen: Musterschmidt, 1972).

Schulte, F.X., *Geschichte des 'Kulturkampfes' in Preussen: In Aktenstücken dargestellt* (Essen: Fredebeul & Koenen, 1882).

Sperber, J., *Popular Catholicism in Nineteenth-Century Germany* (Princeton: Princeton University Press, 1984).

Trzeciakowski, L., *Kulturkampf w zaborze pruskim* (Germany summary; Poznan: Wydawn Poznanskie, 1970).

Wahl, A.E.A., *Vom Bismarck der 70er Jahre* (Tübingen: Mohr, 1920).

Weber, C., *Kirchliche Politik zwischen Rom, Berlin und Trier 1876 bis 1888: Die Beilegung d. preuss. Kulturkampfes* (Mainz: Matthias-Grünewald-Verl., 1970).

Wiermann, H., *Geschichte des Kulturkampfes: Ursprung, Verlauf und heutiger Stand. 2e bis auf die Gegenwart fortgeführte Aufl.* (Leipzig: Rengersche Buchhandlung, Gebhardt & Wilisch).

Windell, G.C., *The Catholics and German Unity, 1866–1871* (Minneapolis: University of Minnesota Press, 1954).

H.J. HOLTZMANN AND HIS EUROPEAN COLLEAGUES: ASPECTS OF THE NINETEENTH-CENTURY EUROPEAN DISCUSSION OF GOSPEL ORIGINS*

David Barrett Peabody

Introduction

I first became aware that studies by members of the so-called Strasbourg school might have importance for understanding the history of a paradigm shift that took place in Europe in the middle of the nineteenth century when I read an early version of an English translation of a Dutch doctoral dissertation. The paradigm shift to which I refer was the shift from the Griesbach explanation of gospel origins[1] to the theory of Markan Priority.[2] The dissertation was that by Hajo Uden Meijboom

*   An earlier version of this paper was invited for presentation at the symposium on 'Presuppositions, Paradigm Shifts, and Conveyance of Opinion to the Public in Biblical Studies 1850–1914' that was held at the Ruhr-Universität, Bochum, Germany, 20–24 July 1992. Here I wish to express my appreciation to Professor Dr H. Graf Reventlow and to his co-workers for planning and implementing this distinctive international and interdisciplinary symposium. I also wish to thank the Volkswagen-Stiftung, the Evangelische Landeskirch von Westfalen, and the Ruhr-Universität for the financial support which enabled scholars from both sides of the Atlantic to gather and share the results of their research, as these related to the theme of the conference. I also wish to thank Sheffield Academic Press for publishing the papers from this conference.

1.   The Griesbach Hypothesis holds that the Synoptic Gospels of Matthew, Luke and Mark were written in that order and that no Evangelist did his work in ignorance of that of his predecessor(s). That is to say, the Evangelist, 'Luke', utilized the Gospel attributed to Matthew as one of his sources in composing the Gospel according to Luke; and the Evangelist, 'Mark', utilized both the Gospel of Matthew and the Gospel of Luke in composing the Gospel attributed to Mark.

2.   By 'Marcan Priority', I include all theories of gospel origins which claim that some version(s) of the Gospel of Mark provided source material both for the author of the Gospel of Matthew and for the author of the Gospel of Luke. Variations in the

entitled *History and Criticism of the Markan Hypothesis* which was defended at Groningen, in the Netherlands, on Thursday, 27 September 1866, at noon.[3] The English translation was being prepared already in the early 1980s by John J. Kiwiet of the Southwestern Baptist Theological Seminary in Forth Worth, Texas. It was published by Mercer University Press in 1993, after more than ten years of work.[4]

I have chosen to begin this paper with an overview of Meijboom's dissertation and then to move to a closer examination of one chapter within it, namely, Meijboom's analysis of the development of the Markan Hypothesis in France.[5] The central section of my paper consists of a series of biographical sketches of Timothée Colani (1824–1888), Eduard Reuss (1804–1891), Edmond Scherer (1815–1889), Albert Réville (1826–1906) and Michel Nicolas (1810–1886), all members of the Strasbourg school.[6]

theory of 'Markan Priority', beyond this basic statement, remain numerous in the world today, as they were in the nineteenth century.

3.   So the title page of the dissertation indicates. See Hajo Uden Meijboom, *Geschiedenis en critiek der Marcushypothese* (Groningen: Proefschrift; Amsterdam: Gebroeder Kraay, 1866), 248 pp. The recently published English translation carries the title, *A History and Critique of the Origin of the Marcan Hypothesis 1835–1866: A Contemporary Report Rediscovered; a translation with introduction and notes of* Geschiedenis en critiek der Marcushypothese (*History and Critique of the Marcan Hypothesis*) *by Hajo Uden Meijboom at the University of Groningen* (trans. and ed. John J. Kiwiet; New Gospel Studies, 8; Macon, GA: Mercer University Press, 1993), xl + 236 pp. See the facsimile of the title page in the Kiwiet translation, p. 1.

4.   I have learned most of what I know about Meijboom from Professor Kiwiet's translation of this important Dutch dissertation and from a lecture he gave, putting Meijboom in the context of mid-nineteenth-century Dutch scholarship, at S.M.U. in Dallas, Texas, on November 11, 1983. Now see the 'Translator's Preface' and the 'Translator's Introduction' in Meijboom and Kiwiet, *History and Critique*, pp. xi-xxxiv; I also have learned some things about Meijboom from Bo Reicke's article, 'From Strauss to Holtzmann and Meijboom: Synoptic Theories Advanced during the Consolidation of Germany, 1830–70', *NovT* 29/1 (1987), pp. 1-21, esp. 2 and 19-21. I had the opportunity to hear an earlier version of this paper by Professor Reicke at a Colloquy on 'Nineteenth Century Gospel Criticism' held at S.M.U., 5–7 November 1985.

5.   Meijboom and Kiwiet, *History and Critique*, 'Chapter 2: The Development of the Marcan Hypothesis in France', pp. 45-63.

6.   For much of the biographical information on scholars in this paper, I have utilized the following standard reference works: *The New Schaff-Herzog Encyclopedia of Religious Knowledge, embracing Biblical, historical, doctrinal, and practical theology and Biblical, theological, and ecclesiastical biography from the*

With the exception of Eduard Reuss, these scholars are rarely included in twentieth century reviews of the history of the discussion of the Synoptic Problem. William Baird, however, did give some attention to some of these men and to Meijboom in his recently published history of post-Enlightenment, New Testament research. In a section devoted to Meijboom's work, Baird has concluded the following.

> Of special value is Meijboom's review of gospel studies in nineteenth-century France. There the key figure is Eduard Reuss of Strasbourg who favored Marcan priority but believed canonical Mark was preceded by an earlier edition of Mark—an *Urmarcus*. Reuss influenced other French scholars, like Albert Réville who referred to the earlier edition of Mark as 'Proto-Mark'. The preference for Marcan priority is seen finally in Ernst Renan, whose best-selling *Life of Jesus* presupposed a version of the two-document hypothesis.
>
> Meijboom's reading of the history also argues that the triumph of the Marcan hypothesis resulted in large part from reaction against Strauss and the Tübingen school, who had adopted the Griesbach solution.[7]

All five of the members of the Strasbourg school I will discuss— Colani, Reuss, Scherer, Réville, and Nicolas—believed in Markan priority. Yet all five called attention to literary data that were anomalous for that source hypothesis. Since they were all advocates of Markan priority, these men may be understood as hostile witnesses against the theory of Markan priority. At times, they even called attention to data that would rather support the Griesbach Hypothesis.

All five of these scholars were also associated with Ernest Renan's *Life of Jesus*. For that reason, I have included a brief section within this

---

earliest times to the present day...(12 vols; New York: Funk & Wagnalls Co., 1908–1914). This is an abbreviated version and English translation of the *Realencyklopädie für protestantische Theologie und Kirche*, founded by J.J. Herzog, third edn edited by Albert Hauck (22 vols.; Leipzig: J.C. Hinrichs, 1896–1909). Other biographical sources I have consulted have included Kurt Galling, Hans Freiherr von Campenhausen *et al.* (eds.), *Die Religion in Geschichte und Gegenwart: Handwörterbuch für Theologie und Religionswissenschaft* (7 vols.; Tübingen: Mohr, 3rd edn, 1957–1965) and *The Oxford Dictionary of the Christian Church*, second edn edited by F.L. Cross and E.A. Livingstone (Oxford: Oxford University Press, 1974). I have also consulted works cited in this paper by Beard, Meijboom, Schweitzer, Framer, Stoldt,and Baird for biographical information.

7.   William Baird, *History of New Testament Research. I. From Deism to Tübingen* (Minneapolis: Fortress Press, 1992), xxii + 450 pp.; The quotation is from pp. 308-309.

paper where I discuss this association and its effects on members of the Strasbourg school.

Perhaps because of their association with Renan's controversial book of 1863 and certainly because of other reasons to be discussed in this paper, members of the Strasbourg School contributed less and less to the discussion of the Synoptic Problem after 1863. By 1870 their voices were virtually silent in the discussion of the Synoptic Problem, four years before Heinrich Julius Holtzmann (1832–1910) was called to the theological faculty at Strasbourg.

To my discussions of these members of the Strasbourg school, I have added some comments on two other one-time members of the Strasbourg faculty. One of these was Heinrich Julius Holtzmann (1832–1910). The other was one of Holtzmann's most outstanding students, Albert Schweitzer (1875–1965).

I conclude with some comments on the more extensive debate about gospel origins taking place in Europe in the nineteenth century; draw some conclusions about circumstances that effected this debate; and speculate a bit about what might have altered the course of the debate, had some circumstances been different. There is no question that further research into the history of the discussion of the Synoptic Problem in the nineteenth century is needed and I would hope that readers will receive this paper as a preliminary report on research in progress.

Although the subject of the conference for which this paper was originally prepared was 'Presuppositions, Paradigm Shifts, and Conveyance of Opinion to the Public in Biblical Studies 1850–1914', from time to time I have needed to go beyond the boundaries of these dates in order to complete the story I want to tell.

Hajo Uden Meijboom (1842–1933)

I begin with a work that dates from the period set for consideration at the conference, the dissertation of Hajo Uden Meijboom that was defended in 1866. Meijboom's dissertation was a historical survey of the rise of the Markan Hypothesis in early to mid-nineteenth century Europe, followed by a critique of the Markan Hypothesis, in all of its forms prior to 1866, and arguments in favour of the Griesbach Hypothesis.

According to Bo Reicke, Meijboom had been a student of Abraham Dirk Loman, about whom Reicke has written the following:

Meijboom's support of Griesbach's theory met an interest of his main academic teacher, the Lutheran pastor and Amsterdam professor A.D. Loman (1823–1897). As a student Loman had paid visits to Strauss and Baur; since then he appreciated the Tübingen school and its application of Griesbach's hypothesis to different stages of religious ideas.[8]

From 1856, Loman was on the faculty of the Lutheran seminary in Amsterdam. In spite of being totally blind since 1874, Loman also became part of the theological faculty at the University of Amsterdam in 1877. Like Johannes Henricus Scholten and Albert Réville, to be discussed below, Loman belonged to the 'modern school' in the Netherlands. His publications included a volume on the Gospel of John and a series of articles on the Synoptic Gospels that were written after Meijboom defended his dissertation.[9]

In his dissertation, Meijboom suggested that 'Markan priority' in this period was not a single hypothesis, but rather something like a family of hypotheses. Meijboom writes in the opening pages of his dissertation:

> As a general description to be used for a guideline in this investigation I would like to propose the following formulation. The Marcan hypothesis attempts to use the second gospel as a key to the explanation of the origin and the interrelatedness of the Synoptic gospels…But priority in sequence alone is not sufficient to identify a scholar as a proponent of the Marcan hypothesis.[10]

Meijboom goes on to divide pre-1866 source-critical work on the gospels into two periods, the 'pre-Strauss' period (prior to 1835) and the 'post-Strauss' period (after 1835). In Meijboom's view, only scholars who wrote after Strauss should be considered advocates of 'the Markan Hypothesis'.[11] Meijboom continues,

---

8.   In support of the first sentence quoted here Reicke refers, in a footnote, to page viii of Meijboom's original dissertation. See Reicke, 'From Strauss to Holtzmann and Meijboom', p. 19. Kiwiet's translation does not seem to have included these prefatory pages from Meijboom.

9.   *Bijdragen ter inleiding op de Johanneische schriften des Nieuwen Testaments* (Amsterdam, 1865); 'Bijdragen tot de critiek der synoptische evangelien', *TT* 3–13 (Amsterdam: Loman & Verster, 1869–79). This journal was published in 53 volumes between 1857 and 1919. If Loman defended the Griesbach Hypothesis, this series of articles on the Synoptics would be a likely place to find such a defence.

10.   Meijboom and Kiwiet, *History and Critique*, pp. 3-4.

11.   In Meijboom's judgment, C.G. Wilke is a special case. 'Taking into consideration that [Wilke] invested more tha[n] ten years in his work and that its inception therefore preceded the new era [of Strauss after 1835] by more than seven

One would do injustice to the advocates of the Markan hypothesis if one would include all those who in an earlier era gave priority to Mark. At most one can speak of precursors, for almost any acceptable hypothesis had its antecedents a hundred or more years earlier. All the theories mentioned above[12] belong to the era of criticism which came to an end with David Friedrich Strauss.[13] Before his day there had been a period of abstract reasoning using methods of explanation for the interrelatedness of the gospels that were extraneous to the gospels themselves and alien to their historical content. When Strauss called the critics back to the concrete reality, however, the situation changed. Since that day scholars have studied the gospels increasingly from an historical perspective. Thus an earlier literary quest gradually changed into a historical quest.[14]

There is another watershed that should be added to the one Meijboom mentioned here relating to Strauss and I have already alluded to it. For the French at least, if not for all gospel critics, one needs also to take into consideration the 'pre-Renan' era (prior to the publication date of Renan's *Life of Jesus*, 1863) and the 'post-Renan era (after 1863).[15] Some of the most important works on the Synoptic Problem by members of the Strasbourg school belong to the 'pre-Renan' era. This paper includes some exploration of the fates of these 'pre-Renan' critics in the 'post-Renan' era.

In Part One of Meijboom's dissertation, which is his *Forschungsbericht* of studies on the Markan Hypothesis up to 1866, he takes up the following scholars in this order:

years, one must acknowledge that the publication of this work after Strauss was merely a coincidence. According to its form and content it belongs rather to an earlier era, since the whole procedure of study betrays a certain predisposition for the Ur-Gospel hypothesis in the form it took in [Johann Gottfried] Eichhorn. The question comes to mind, what connection Wilke has with the Marcan Hypothesis. Indeed, the connection is tenuous' (Meijboom and Kiwiet, *History and Critique*, p. 24).

12. Meijboom had mentioned the Oral Gospel Hypothesis, the Fragment Hypothesis, the Utilization Hypothesis, and the Ur-Gospel Hypothesis.

13. Meijboom marks the turn to this new era of criticism with the publication of Strauss's first *Life of Jesus* in 1835. David Friedrich Strauss, *Das Leben Jesu* (2 vols.; Tübingen, C.F. Osiander, 1835–36; reprint: Darmstadt: Wissenschaftliches Buchgesellschaft, 1969).

14. Meijboom and Kiwiet, *History and Critique*, p. 4.

15. Joseph Ernest Renan, *La vie de Jésus* (Paris: Michel Lévy Frères, 1863).

David Friedrich Strauss (1808–1874),[16]
Christian Hermann Weisse (1801–1866)[17]

with some discussion of Weisse's predecessors

Gottlob Christian Storr (1746–1805),
Johann Gottfried Herder (1744–1803),
Friedrich Daniel Ernst Schleiermacher (1768–1834),
Karl August Credner (1797–1857),
Karl Konrad Friedrich Wilhelm Lachmann (1793–1851),[18]
Christian Gottlob Wilke (1789–1854),[19]
Ferdinand Hitzig (1807–1875),[20]
Bruno Bauer (1809–1882),[21]
Ferdinand Christian Baur (1792–1860),[22]
Heinrich Ewald (1803–1875),[23]
Timothée Colani (1824–1888),[24]
Eduard Reuss (1804–1891),[25]
Edmond Scherer (1815–1889),[26]
Albert Réville (1826–1906),[27]
Michel Nicolas (1810–1886),[28]
Titus Tobler (1806–1877)
Heinrich August Wilhelm Meyer (1800–1873),[29]
Bernhard Weiss (1827–1918),[30]
Heinrich Julius Holtzmann (1832–1910),[31]
Karl Heinrich von Weizsäcker (1822–1899),[32]

16. Meijboom and Kiwiet, *History and Critique*, pp. 3-11.
17. *Ibid.*, pp. 12-20.
18. *Ibid.*, pp. 16-19.
19. *Ibid.*, pp. 20-26.
20. *Ibid.*, pp. 27-32.
21. *Ibid.*, pp. 32-34.
22. *Ibid.*, pp. 34-37.
23. *Ibid.*, pp. 38-43.
24. *Ibid.*, p. 52.
25. *Ibid.*, pp. 45-53.
26. *Ibid.*, pp. 53-55.
27. *Ibid.*, pp. 55-60.
28. *Ibid.*, pp. 61-63.
29. *Ibid.*, pp. 65-69.
30. *Ibid.*, pp. 69-71.
31. *Ibid.*, pp. 71-81.
32. *Ibid.*, pp. 81-83.

Gustav Volkmar (1809–1893),[33]
Albrecht Ritschl (1822–1889),[34]

and a list of the following supporters of the Markan Hypothesis in the
Netherlands by 1866,[35]

Johannes Jacobus Prins (1814–1898),[36]
Willem Hendrik van de Sande Bakhuyzen (b. 1831),[37]
Marinus Anne Nicolaas Rovers (1834–1898),[38]

33. Meijboom and Kiwiet, *History and Critique*, pp. 83-85.
34. Meijboom and Kiwiet, *History and Critique*, pp. 85-89.
35. Meijboom and Kiwiet, *History and Critique*, pp. 89-90.
36. Prins's publications included *Disputatio theologica inauguralis de locis Evangelistarum, in quibus Jesus baptismi ritum subisse traditur* (Amsterdam, 1838). From 1855–1876, Prins was professor of exegetical and practical theology at Leiden. During those years, he would have been a colleague of Scholten (see below). Meijboom [Kiwiet translation, p. 89 n. 71] refers to Prins's advocacy of Markan priority in an article published in *Godgeleerde bijdragen* (Amsterdam: Ten Brink & DeVries, 1858), p. 812. This journal was published twice a year between 1827 and 1879. It continued, *Bijdragen tot de beoefening en geschiedenis der godgeleerde wetenschappen*.
37. I do not yet know much about Bakhuyzen (born 1831), not even the year of his death. The publication date of the last monograph by him of which I am aware was 1907. Bakhuyzen's publications included *Het dogmatish karakter, dat aan het Evangelie van Lucas wordt toegekend, door W.H. van de Sande Bakhuyzen* (Verhandelingen der Koninklijke akademie van wetenschappen. Afdeeling Letterkunde; dl. 18 [no. 1]; Amsterdam: J. Mueller, 1889). *Over de toepassing van de conjecturaal-kritiek op den tekst des Nieuwen Testaments, door W.H. van de Sande Bakhuyzen* (Haarlem: F. Bohn, 1880). (Teylers godgeleerd genootschap; Nieuwe Serie; 2); *Evangelien buiten het Nieuwe Testament, bew. door W.H. van de Sande Bakhuyzen* (Oud-Christelijke geschriften in Nederlandsche vertaling; 1; Leiden: Sijthoff, 1907). None of these titles, of course, would have been available to Meijboom in 1866. Meijboom and Kiwiet (*History and Critique*, p. 89 n. 72) refer to Bakhuyzen's advocacy of Markan priority in another article in the *Godgeleerde bijdragen* (1865), p. 468.
38. Rovers's publications included *Apocalyptische Studien* (Leiden: S.C. van Doesburgh, 1888); and *Nieuw-Testamentische letterkunde/door M.A.N. Rovers* (Hertogenbosch: Gebroeders Muller, 1888). Prior to 1866, Rovers had published *Disquisitio de Paulo religionis christianae apologeta* (Traiecti ad Rhenum: T. de Bruyn, 1860). For Rovers's advocacy of Markan priority, Meijboom and Kiwiet (*History and Critique*, p. 89 n. 73) refer to *De synoptische Evangeliën* (n.p., n.d.), xi. I have not found this work in the lists of Rovers's publications to which I have thus far had access.

Dr Johannes Lambrechts,[39]
and Professor Johannes Hendricus Scholten (1811–1885).[40]

At the end of his dissertation, Meijboom also discusses works by three
other scholars,

Adolf Bernhard Christoph Christian Hilgenfeld (1823–1907),[41]

39.   Johannes Lambrechts, *Specimen exegetico-theologicum, quo e sermonis
narrationisque diversitate, Marcum inter et Lucam, hunc illius textu usum esse
colligitur..., quod...defendet Ioannes Lambrechts* (Lugduni-Batavorum: Apud
P. Engels, 1863): viii + 251 pp. What Meijboom says of Lambrechts is all that I
know about this scholar, too.

40.   Scholten was born (1811) and educated (1828–1835) in Utrecht. Following
some earlier appointments, he became a Professor at Leiden from 1843 until his death
in 1885. Scholten seems to have had a relationship with at least some members of the
Strasbourg school. Essays by Scholten appear in a collection with those by Réville
and other members of the Strasbourg school, like Colani and Scherer. Scholten also
contributed to the Strasbourg journal edited by Colani that became the main academic
journal of the Strasbourg school. At least one of Scholten's books was translated by
Albert Réville, another member of the Strasbourg school. Some of Scholten's views
on the gospels may be found in *Het Evangelie naar Johannes Kritisch historisch
onderzoek door J.H. Scholten* (Leiden: P. Engels, 1864), xii + 500 pp.; *Het oudste
Evangelie: critisch onderzoek naar de samenstelling, de onderlinge verhouding, de
historisch waarde en den oorsprong der evangelien naar Mattheus en Marcus, door
J.H. Scholten* (Leiden: Academische Boekhandel van P. Engels, 1868), translated into
German as *Das älteste Evangelium: Kritische Untersuchung der Zusammensetzung,
des wechselseitigen Verhältnisses, des geschichtlichen Werths und des Ursprungs
der Evangelien nach Matthäus und Marcus, von J.H. Scholten; aus dem
Holländischen mit Genehmigung des Verfassers übersetzt von Ernst Rud.
Redepenning* (Elberfeld: R.L. Friderichs, 1869); *Het Paulinisch evangelie: critisch
onderzoek van het evangelie naar Lucas en zijne verhouding tot Marcus, Mattheus
en de handelingen, door J.H. Scholten* (Leiden: Academische Boekhandel van
P. Engels, 1870), translated into German as *Das Paulinische Evangelium: Kritische
Untersuchung des Evangeliums nach Lucas und seines Verhältnisses zu Marcus,
Matthäus und der Apostelgeschichte, von J.H. Scholten; nach eigenhändiger Ueber-
arbeitung des Verfassers aus dem Holländischen übersetzt von E.R. Redepenning*
(Elberfeld: R.L. Friderichs, 1881); *De apostel Johannes in Klein-Azie* (Leiden:
S.C. van Doesburgh, 1871); also see Scholten's response to Renan, *Het Leven van
Jezuz door Ernest Renan: Toespraak bij de akademische lessen, September 1863,
door J.H. Scholten* (Leiden: P. Engels, 1863).

41.   Meijboom and Kiwiet, *History and Critique*, pp. 213-21. Hilgenfeld was a
German Protestant who taught for most of his career at Jena and who advocated a
modified form of the so-called 'Augustinian' Hypothesis, i.e. that the gospels were
written in the order Matthew, Mark, Luke and John and that no Evangelist did his

Gustave d'Eichthal (1804–1886),[42]
Karl Reinhold Köstlin.[43]

work as if in ignorance of that of his predecessor.

Hilgenfeld followed, with appreciation, the work of the Roman Catholic scholar, Johann Leonhard Hug (1765–1846) and edited, from 1858 until his death in 1907, the *Zeitschrift für wissenschaftliche Theologie* (Leipzig: D.R. Reisland, 1852–1908; Frankfurt a.M.: M. Diesterweg, 1908–1914). This journal continued to be published for only seven years after the death of Hilgenfeld who was both its founding editor and most prolific contributor.

42. Meijboom and Kiwiet, *History and Criticism*, pp. 222-24. Meijboom's discussion of d'Eichthal is the most extensive to which I have yet had access. See *Les evangiles*. I. *Examen critique et comparatif des trois premiers evangiles, par Gustave d'Eichthal* (Paris: Librairie de Hachette, 1863). Gustave d'Eichthal, like Hilgenfeld, advocated a form of the so-called 'Augustinian' Hypothesis. Schweizer (*Quest*, p. 189) mentions Gustave d'Eichthal among 'others of the [Strasbourg] school'. But this may be a mistake. In 1863, Adolf Hilgenfeld took quick note of the most recent release of d'Eichthal's book and was pleased that d'Eichthal like Hilgenfeld advocated a form of the so-called Augustinian Hypothesis. See Adolf Hilgenfeld, 'XIV. Die Evangelien und die geschichtliche Gestalt Jesu', *ZWT* 12 (1863), pp. 311-40. Hilgenfeld's brief discussion of this book by d'Eichthal is to be found on pp. 326-27. To my knowledge, none of the members of the Strasbourg school to be considered here (Colani, Reuss, Scherer, Réville and Nicolas) ever affirmed the priority of Matthew, as did d'Eichthal. Schweitzer's mistake in associating d'Eichthal with the Strasbourg school, if it is a mistake, is probably the result of his reading of Ernest Renan's *Life of Jesus*. There, Renan had associated d'Eichthal with other members of the Strasbourg school just prior to publishing his *Life of Jesus*. Strauss, who was also included in Renan's brief biographical list, was certainly not a member of the Strasbourg, but rather of the Second Tübingen, school. At the moment, it does not seem to me that d'Eichthal should be considered a member of the Strasbourg School either. Although it does not seem appropriate to list d'Eichthal as a member of the Strasbourg School, it would seem to be appropriate to include him among the members of what was sometimes called 'the French Critical School'. But John Hurst (*Rationalism*, pp. 394-409) includes only nine scholars in his discussion of the French Critical School, and d'Eichthal is not among them. In addition to Réville, Scherer, Colani and Renan, Hurst mentions P[atrice] Larroque (1801–1879), [Frederic de] Rougemont (1808–1876), [Felix] Pecaut (1828–1898), A. Grotz (a pastor at Nimes), and A[thanase Josue] Coquerel (1820–1875). Also see works by A.J. Coquerel's father, Athanase Laurent (Charles) Coquerel (1795–1868). The Coquerel brothers edited *Le Lien: Journal des eglises réformées de France* that was published weekly in Paris beginning in 1862.

43. Meijboom and Kiwiet, *History and Critique*, pp. 225-27. Karl Reinhold Köstlin, *Der Ursprung und die Komposition der synoptischen Evangelien* (Stuttgart: Mächen, 1853), 400 pp. Köstlin advocated an eclectic source theory that included elements of the Griesbach Hypothesis with elements of the Markan Hypothesis.

There has been more discussion of the German scholars in this list within twentieth century surveys of the history of the discussion of the Synoptic Problem than of scholars who worked in France, Switzerland and the Netherlands.[44] And I have commented elsewhere on works by some of the most important German scholars in this list—C.G. Wilke, B. Weiss, and H.J. Holtzmann—as their works related to how the linguistic characteristics of each of the Synoptic Evangelists might be of service in solving the Synoptic Problem.[45] It seems therefore appropriate to concentrate in this paper on the discussion of the Synoptic Problem among scholars in France, particularly among members of the Strasbourg School. I have included also within this paper some notes about scholars working in the Netherlands and Switzerland because of the relatively little attention these scholars have received in twentieth century surveys of the history of the discussion of the Synoptic Problem.

Before passing over most of the German advocates of Markan priority in this list I would just note that Meijboom's conclusions about the inadequacy of works by Wilke, Weisse, Ewald, B. Weiss, and Holtzmann in establishing the Markan Hypothesis have been confirmed in modern times by William R. Farmer,[46] Hans-Herbert Stoldt[47] and, within a more

---

44.   See the next three footnotes.

45.   David Barrett Peabody, 'Chapters in the History of the Linguistic Argument for Solving the Synoptic Problem: The Nineteenth Century in Context', in E.P. Sanders (ed.), *Jesus, the Gospels and the Church: Essays in Honor of William R. Farmer* (Macon, GA: Mercer University Press, 1987), pp. 47-68. I also discuss a work by Eduard Zeller (1814–1908), an advocate of the Griesbach Hypothesis, in this earlier article.

46.   William R. Farmer, *The Synoptic Problem: A Critical Analysis* (New York: Macmillan, 1964).

47.   Hans-Herbert Stoldt's twentieth-century analysis of works by C.G. Wilke, C.H. Weisse, Bernhard Weiss, H.J. Holtzmann and Paul Wernle on the question of gospel origins came to conclusions similar to those of Meijboom. See Hans-Herbert Stoldt, *Geschichte und Kritik der Markushypothese* (Göttingen: Vandenhoeck & Ruprecht, 1977); translated into English and edited by Donald L. Niewyk, introduction by William R. Farmer, *History and Criticism of the Marcan Hypothesis* (Macon, GA: Mercer University Press; Edinburgh: T. & T. Clark, 1980). It is interesting that the works of Stoldt and Meijboom carried such similar titles, although neither man knew the other and their works were published more than one hundred years apart. The outlines of their two works also have similarities, i.e., a historical survey of work by each man as it appeared, followed by a synthetic critique of major arguments shared by advocates of Markan priority, one by one.

limited perspective, by me.[48] The Markan Hypothesis was never established on truly scientific grounds in the nineteenth century.

If the independent judgments of Meijboom, Farmer and Stoldt, with support from my own work, are true; then one is forced to ask the following question. What was it, then, perhaps in the social history of the period, that did lead to the almost universal acceptance of the Markan Hypothesis in Europe by the end of the nineteenth century? And to this question, one could add a second. If the conclusions of Meijboom, Farmer, and Stoldt are true, then what is there about the context of the twentieth century that has led some current scholars to draw seemingly unwarranted conclusions about the work of our nineteenth century academic forebears? I do not attempt to address this second question here, but it is a question that also needs exploration.

Meijboom's critical survey of the history of the rise of the Markan Hypothesis prior to 1866,[49] led him to conclude that there was a consensus among scholars advocating Markan priority prior to that time on three major theses or presuppositions. First, the briefest gospel was, most likely, the earliest.[50] Second, the use of a particular kind of 'fresh and vibrant' literary imagery by an Evangelist revealed the early character of that gospel.[51] Third, the current texts of all of the canonical gospels, including Mark, had developed into their current forms from earlier forms. This third presupposition allowed scholars advocating Markan priority to appeal to a form of the text of Mark that was different from any manuscript or critical edition of the Greek New Testament in order to explain literary evidence within the Synoptics that was anomalous for Markan priority.[52] Having explored each of these three presuppositions, Meijboom found them all wanting.[53]

Meijboom then turned to consider arguments against Markan priority and favoring the Griesbach Hypothesis. These included arguments based on (1) Meijboom's perception of a more developed Christology in Mark than in Matthew and Luke,[54] (2) a comparison of the sequence of

48. Peabody, 'Chapters', in Sanders (ed.), *Jesus, the Gospels and the Church*, pp. 47-68.

49. Meijboom and Kiwiet, *History and Critique*, pp. 1-94.

50. Meijboom and Kiwiet, *History and Critique*, pp. 97-104.

51. Meijboom and Kiwiet, *History and Critique*, pp. 104-15.

52. Meijboom and Kiwiet, *History and Critique*, pp. 115-27.

53. Meijboom and Kiwiet, *History and Critique*, pp. 128-30.

54. Meijboom and Kiwiet, *History and Critique*, 'Chapter 5: Theological Assessment of the Gospel of Mark', pp. 131-48.

materials within the Synoptic Gospels,[55] (3) an examination of selected texts within Mark that are shared by the Gospels of Matthew or Luke or both[56] and (4) an examination of some of the sections of Mark that have no parallels in Matthew or Luke.[57]

Meijboom's research led him to the conclusion that a two-sided debate remained in 1866 between advocates of the Markan Hypothesis and advocates of the Griesbach Hypothesis. His discussions of the alternative source theories of Hilgenfeld,[58] d'Eichthal,[59] and Köstlin,[60] toward the end of his dissertation, were conducted for the purpose of dismissing these alternative source theories, and presumably all other alternatives. Meijboom wrote:

> With these last representatives [Hilgenfeld, d'Eichthal and Köstlin] I trust to have demonstrated that there is no adequate mediating position in the present state of canon criticism. The leading scholars have presented us with a dilemma concerning the Gospel of Mark. It is either the source [Markan Hypothesis] or it is a reworked edition of the two other Synoptic gospels [Griesbach Hypothesis].[61]

Meijboom expressed the major results of his research in these words.

> I have attempted to prove the weakness of the Markan Hypothesis. Together with Strauss, I cannot consider it anything else than the 'swindle of the century'. And, with Hilgenfeld, I would like to apply the old Roman dictum to this hypothesis: 'I am of the opinion Carthage has to be destroyed.'…The Gospel of Mark can best be understood as a document whose author used Matthew and Luke as his sources.[62]

With this brief overview of Maijboom's entire dissertation in view, I would now like to turn to a more detailed look at his discussion of the development of the Markan Hypothesis in France. But, in what follows, I have tried to supplement and complement what Meijboom said in

---

55. Meijboom and Kiwiet, *History and Critique*, 'Chapter 6: The Sequence of the Narrative Materials in Mark', pp. 151-74.

56. Meijboom and Kiwiet, *History and Critique*, 'Chapter 7: Text Studies in Mark', pp. 175-98.

57. Meijboom and Kiwiet, *History and Critique*, 'Chapter 8: The Uniquely Marcan Material', pp. 199-206.

58. Meijboom and Kiwiet, *History and Critique*, pp. 213-21.

59. Meijboom and Kiwiet, *History and Critique*, pp. 222-24.

60. Meijboom and Kiwiet, *History and Critique*, pp. 225-27.

61. Meijboom and Kiwiet, *History and Critique*, p. 227.

62. Meijboom and Kiwiet, *History and Critique*, pp. 227-28, 213.

several ways. First, I have provided some additional biographical and bibliographical information on the scholars Meijboom discussed in this chapter of his work, including some information about these scholars after 1866. Of course, Meijboom could not have known any of this latter information when his dissertation was published. Secondly, I have called attention to some of the political and social history of nineteenth-century Europe that may have had an effect on the course of the discussion of gospel origins in that period. Thirdly, I have provided reviews of articles dealing with the Synoptic Problem by Reuss and Scherer that are somewhat independent and more detailed than those that Meijboom could provide, given his larger task. Fourthly, I have sometimes correlated Meijboom's notes on the mid-nineteenth century discussion of gospel origins with the continuing discussion of this issue in the late twentieth century.

The Strasbourg School

Some members of the Strasbourg school were such gifted literary critics and acute observers of the details of the Biblical texts that even one of their harshest critics could not help but admire them. John Fletcher Hurst, a great detractor of Rationalism, wrote in 1865:

> The Critical School of Theology is beyond all comparison the greatest foe of orthodoxy in France. The English Rationalists exhibit but little scholarly depth, having borrowed their principal thoughts from Germany. The Dutch are too speculative to be successful at present, and the Germans have already grown weary of their long warfare. But the French School, claiming such writers as Scherer, Colani, Pecaut, Réville, Reuss, Coquerel, and Renan, is not to be disregarded, nor are its arguments to be met with indifference...
>
> The French Critical School numbers among its adherents many young and talented theologians, some of whom are already distinguished for profound learning and literary activity.[63]

---

63. John Fletcher Hurst, *History of Rationalism: Embracing a Survey of the Present State of Protestant Theology. With Appendix of Literature* (New York: Eaton & Mains, 1893 [1865]); the quotations are from pp. 391 and 409. Hurst's account of what he calls 'the French Critical School' constitutes most of his 'Chapter XVI, France: Rationalism in the Protestant Church—The Critical School of Theology', pp. 386-410. 'Chapter XVII, France Continued: Evangelical Theology Opposing Rationalism', pp. 411-24, covers the conservative response in France, with special attention to [Edmond Dehault] de Pressensé (1824–1891) and [M. Francois] Guizot

Timothée Colani (1824–1888)

Timothée Colani—like Eduard Reuss, H.J. Holtzmann and Albert Schweitzer—was, at one time, a member of the theological faculty at the state university in Strasbourg (Reuss, 1838–1891; Colani, 1864–1870; Holtzmann, 1874–1904, emeritus, 1904–1910; Schweitzer, 1902–1913). I have chosen to discuss Colani first, among members of the Strasbourg School, because important articles on the Synoptic Problem appeared within the academic journal that he edited at Strasbourg.

Born at Lemé near Sains, 190 m. northeast of Paris, Colani was the son of a Reformed minister. In 1840, at the age of sixteen, he went to Strasbourg to study theology, writing a thesis in 1845 on Kant, as did

(1787–1874). Hurst's 'Appendix: Literature of Rationalism', is a valuable collection of important contributions to the Rationalist-Supernaturalist debate prior to 1865.

Particularly helpful is Hurst's listing of 'Rationalistic Periodicals' for each of the three sections into which he divides this bibliography—I: Germany–Holland–Switzerland (pp. 590-95), II: France (pp. 595-98), and III: Great Britain–United States (pp. 599-606). These listings are followed by one on the 'Literature of Unitarianism and Universalism' (pp. 606-10).

It was here in Hurst's book that I first discovered that articles by Colani, Scholten, Réville, Scherer, and Renan appeared in English in a collection edited by John R. Beard, *The Progress of Religious Thought as Illustrated in the Protestant Church of France* (London: Simpkin, Marshall, 1861).

The opening sentences to the preface of Beard's volume say 'The following pieces (except the last) are translated from *La Revue de théologie et de la Philosophie Chrétienne*, the first volume of which appeared in the year 1850. Continued down to the present, that periodical now bears the title of *Nouvelle Revue de théologie*'.

Beard is here referring to the Strasbourg journal, edited by Timothée Colani, that was published between 1850 and 1869, discussed below. The contents of Beard's volume include: Albert Réville, 'Biographical Notices of the Contributors'. John R. Beard, 'Introductory Essay'. Timothée Colani, 'Views and Aims'. Johannes Henricus Scholten, 'On Modern Materialism and its Causes'. Albert Réville, 'Religion and Science'. Albert Réville, 'The Future Life: A Critique of the Chapter thereon in the "Dogmatik" of Strauss'. Albert Réville, 'The Authority of Jesus Christ'. A. Grotz, 'What is Revelation?' Edmond Scherer, 'Theological Conversations: 1. Catholicism is a Branch of Protestantism. 2. Protestantism is a Branch of Catholicism. 3. The Christ of the Popular Churches Offers no Medium of Reconciliation'. Edmond Scherer, 'The Errata of the New Testament'. Edmond Scherer, 'What the Bible Is'. Edmond Scherer, 'The Miracles of Jesus Christ'. Timothée Colani, 'What There is in the Bible'. Timothée Colani, 'The Simplicity of the Gospel'. Ernest Renan, 'Calvin'.

Albert Schweitzer later.[64] In 1847, Colani received his licentiate in Theology. Following his formal education, he remained in Strasbourg, preaching and acting as a private tutor.

While he was a theological student (1840–1845), Colani came to appreciate the work of the senior member of the Strasbourg school, Eduard Reuss. In 1850, encouraged by Reuss and assisted by Edmond Scherer who had recently left his teaching post in Geneva, Colani became the founding editor of the main academic journal of the Strasbourg School, the *Révue de Théologie et de Philosophie Chrétienne*. This journal was published from 1850–1869, although it had three different names during its run. Colani, however, was its editor throughout the course of its publication. In the very first article in the first issue of this journal, in July of 1850, Colani described the perspective the journal proposed to take. Selections from that article have been translated as follows:

> Two systems divide the minds of men—Orthodoxy and Rationalism; they do not satisfy us...Orthodoxy has the prestige of antiquity;...If however we survey its history, we cannot admit that it proceeds directly from the Gospel...Rationalism is a reaction called forth by the doctrine of salvation by magic—such as is taught by orthodoxy...But rationalism is not of Christian birth...We call around us those who are dissatisfied with the forms of an antiquated system of dogma, and fully admitting salvation by Christ alone, desire to labour in raising the new edifice which is to be built on the solid basis of him who is at once the Son of man and the Son of God. We ask you not to receive all the ideas we have propounded. Not a school, not a system, but a tendency is that which we represent. The device on our banner is *The True Development of Christian Thought*. We repeat the motto of the theologians of the sixteenth century: *In necessariis unitas, in dubiis libertas*; with us only one thing is necessary—The Gospel; for all the rest we demand the most complete liberty.[65]

Opposed to both Rationalism and Orthodoxy, the 'tendency' Colani describes here maintained a strong commitment to Christ, to the Protestant principle of 'justification by faith alone', to a developing theology, and to complete freedom in everything beyond what 'the gospel' may require. Rather than refer to 'a tendency', as he did in this

64. Timothée Colani, 'Exposé critique de la philosophie de la religion de Kant' (Thesis; Strasbourg: Berger-Levrult, 1845).

65. Timothée Colani, 'Avant-propos', *RTP* 1 (1850), pp. 1-9. The quotation is of selected passages from the translation entitled 'Views and Aims', in Beard (ed.), *Progress of Religious Thought*, pp. 1-9.

passage in 1850, by 1864 Colani was willing to speak 'in the name of those who belong to what is known as the new Protestant theology or the Strasbourg school'.[66]

At least since 1851, Colani had held pastorates in Strasbourg.[67] He was a popular, if controversial, preacher. Several volumes of sermons were published, some going into second or third editions and some being translated into German.[68] In 1861, in addition to pastoring a church, writing, publishing and editing a scholarly theological journal, Colani began to lecture on French literature at the Protestant Seminary in Strasbourg. From 1864, he also taught philosophy there. Between 1864 and 1870, Colani was also professor of homiletics on the theological faculty of the University of France in Strasbourg.[69]

In spite of opposition to his liberal views from some quarters, Colani became pastor of St. Nicolas' Church in Strasbourg on 15 May 1862. He resigned this pastorate four years later, in 1866, in order to devote more time to his responsibilities on two faculties.

It was in 1864, however, while Colani was still tending both to his teaching responsibilities and to a local church pastorate, that he was made Doctor of Theology at Strasbourg. This followed the publication of his work on *Jesus Christ and the Messianic Beliefs of his Time*, which was so popular that it went into a second edition even in the original year of its publication.[70] The second edition of this book allowed

66.   This phrase was used by Colani in his 1864 review of Renan's *Life of Jesus*. The quotation is part of that provided by Schweitzer in *Quest* (see n. 209, below), p. 189.

67.   So Schweitzer, *Quest*, p. 224.

68.   Timothée Colani, *Le sacerdoce universel: Sermon prononcé a l'eglise Saint-Pierre-le-vieux*[2] (Strasbourg, 1858) translated into German as *Predigten in Strasbourg gehalten*. Aus dem Französischen über. von August Victor Richard. Autorisirte deutsche Ausg. (Dresden: Verlagsbuchhandlung von K. Kuntze, 1858); *Sermons: Premier recueil*[3] (Strasbourg: Treuttel, 1860); *Sermons: Deuxième recueil*[2] (Strasbourg: Treuttel & Wurtz, 1860); *Quatre sermons prechés à Nimes* (Strasbourg: Treuttel & Wurtz, 1861), containing 1. Corneille, 2. David, 3. Les brebis errantes, and 4. La lettre et l'esprit; *Notre Père: Sermon preché au temple de l'oratoire a Paris, le 5 mai 1861* (Paris, 1861).

69.   Prior to 1872, when the Protestant Seminary in Strasbourg was absorbed into the theological faculty of the Kaiser-Wilhelm-Universität, these were separate institutions.

70.   Timothée Colani, *Jésus-Christ et les croyances messianiques de son temps* (2nd édn, rev. and augm.; Strasbourg: Treuttel & Wurtz, 1864), carrying the binder's title, *Réfutations de la Vie de Jésus* [v. 2, no. 5].

Colani to append a response to Ernest Renan's *Life of Jesus*, that had appeared in 1863.[71]

Schweitzer reviewed this book by Colani in 1906 and still thought the book was sufficiently important to comment on it again in his reflections on his life in 1931.[72] In Schweitzer's opinion, this work by Colani was just one more derailment of the train of New Testament research since Reimarus. It was one of the most influential books that challenged the 'eschatological, Messianic view of the life of Jesus'; the view that Schweitzer himself came to affirm.

In this work, according to Schweitzer, Colani argued that Mt. 10.23, 19.28, 23.39 and 26.29 were not authentic traditions from Jesus. In addition, much of Mark 13, Matthew 24 and Luke 21 was, in Colani's view, interpolated into the gospels from a Jewish-Christian apocalypse of the first century. These inauthentic materials were interwoven with supposedly authentic words of Jesus about the destruction of the Temple that were assumed to be original to the Synoptic Gospels.

Colani's agenda would seem to have been to reduce, if not to eliminate altogether, the material within the gospels that could be used to support a picture of an 'eschatological and Messianic' Jesus who was very much a Jew of his day. Colani seems to have wanted to remove the authoritative Scriptural basis for just the kind of picture of Jesus that Schweitzer was later to defend, but which enlightened scholars in the middle of the nineteenth century found 'offensive and incomprehensible'.

Of Colani's departure from Strasbourg and from the university, Schweitzer writes, 'The events of 1870 left him without a post'.[73] Schweitzer's oblique reference to 'the events of 1870' would seem to refer to the surrender of Strasbourg to the Prussians during the Franco-Prussian War of 1870–1871, but the exact circumstances leading to Colani's departure from the university in 1870 remain unknown to me.[74]

71.   Colani published two articles in response to this book by Renan in the *RT* (Troisième serie) 1 (1863), pp. 368ff. and 2 (1864), pp. 17ff.

72.   See Schweitzer's fuller review of this work by Colani in *Quest*, pp. 224-26; cf. Schweitzer, *Life and Thought*, pp. 58-61.

73.   Schweitzer, *Quest*, p. 244.

74.   It should be remembered that Schweitzer wrote *Von Reimarus zu Wrede* in Strasbourg with the aid of the archives there. Schweitzer tells us, 'Thanks to bequests from Edward [sic] Reuss and other Strasbourg theologians the University Library possessed a practically complete collection of the literature about the life of Jesus, and it had in addition to that nearly all the controversial writings which had been provoked by Strauss's and Renan's Lives. There was assuredly hardly a place in the world

After the University of Strasbourg was reconstituted by the Germans as the 'Kaiser-Wilhelm-Universität', following the Franco–Prussian war of 1870–1871, only five professors from the old theological faculty remained. Colani, of course, was not among them. Some of the members of the Protestant theological faculty at Strasbourg were transferred to Paris after the war, but Colani was not among these persons either.[75]

Leaving Strasbourg in 1870, Colani moved to Bordeaux where he devoted himself to politics. In 1876 he founded the Paris literary journal, *Le Courrier littéraire*, and later became a librarian at the Sorbonne and editor of *La République française*. In 1888, he was chosen to be the new editor of the Paris newspaper, *Le Temps*.[76] This paper had previously been co-edited by Colani's long-time friend and collaborator on the Strasbourg *Revue de théologie*, Edmond Scherer. The other founding editor of *Le Temps* was Auguste Nefftzer who had worked earlier in his life on another journal important to members of the Strasbourg School, the *Revue Germanique*.[77] Colani, however, died in Grindelwald, Switzerland on 2 September 1888, before he could accept the position of editor at *Le Temps*.

For students of social history and its influence on Biblical critics, an examination of some of Colani's posthumously published writings would be instructive. For instance, he wrote about his experiences during an extended visit to Prussia, on the revolution as judged by Taine, on Ollivier and the Vatican Council, on the politics of Napoleon in 1866, on the new religion, on the Catholic Party under the July Monarchy, on the

where circumstances were so favourable for studying the history of research on the life of Jesus'. Schweitzer, *Life and Thought*, p. 56.

The Strasbourg archives would probably also have contained records relating to Colani's departure from the university in 1870. No doubt, one would be able to find there a complete set of the journal Colani edited. Colani and Reuss would probably have seen that their library contained all of the important works of the school to which they both belonged, particularly since it was known, in some academic circles, as the *Strasbourg* School. Colani's journal and the archives relating to his dismissal from the University in 1870 deserve further research.

75.   Among those transferred to the Protestant faculty in Paris after 1871 was Auguste Sabatier (1839–1901).

76.   John Hurst, writing in 1865, included *Le Temps* as one of the publications that supported the 'French Critical School of Theology'. See n. 80.

77.   See below for a discussion of the *Revue germanique* and its importance to the Strasbourg School. Nefftzer also contributed to the French translation of Strauss's second Life of Jesus. A fuller note on this is also to be found below.

confessions of Renan, on Bismarck's plan, and on Wilhelm I, Emperor of Germany, King of Prussia.[78]

The Main Journals of the Strasbourg School

The new journal, that was originally published in Strasbourg, Geneva and Paris, under the general editorship of Timothée Colani, first appeared between 1850 and 1857 as the *Revue de théologie et de Philosophie Chrétienne*. In January of 1858 it became known as the *Nouvelle Revue de théologie*. Between 1863 and 1869 it was known simply as the *Revue de théologie*.[79] Beginning with a single volume for the year 1850, this journal produced two volumes a year thereafter, between January of 1851 and December of 1862. The journal produced just one volume a year in the last years of publication, 1863–1869. During its run, the Strasbourg *Revue de théologie* was the most important academic journal of the Strasbourg School.[80] When it ceased publi-

78.   Timothée Colani, *En Prusse il y a trente ans (1886–1888): Etudes, notes, impressions de voyage* (Paris: Librairie Fischbacher, 1920); *Essais de critique historique, philosophique et littéraire* (Preface by Joseph Reinach; Paris: L. Chailley, 1895 and 1895[2]). Contents: Victor Cousin jugé par ses contemporains— La correspondance de Sainte-Beuve—La révolution jugé par M. Taine—La Bible— M. Ollivier et le Concile du Vatican—La politique de Napoléon III en 1866—La religion nouvelle—Le parti catholique sous la monarchie de juillet—Les Rougon-Macquart—Les confessions de M. Renan—Le plan de Bismarck—Guillaume Ier, empereur d'Allemagne, roi de Prusse—Le caractère d'Hamlet—Encore Hamlet.

79.   *Revue de théologie et de Philosophie Chrétienne* (Première Série), ed. Timothée Colani, vols. 1–15 (Paris, Genève: J. Cherbulles; Strasbourg: Treuttel & Wurtz, July 1850–December 1857) (Table analytique to Première Série with vol. 15, 1857) continued as: *Nouvelle Revue de théologie* (Deuxième série), ed. Timothée Colani, vols. 1–10 (Paris, Genève: J. Cherbulles; Strasbourg: Treuttel & Wurtz, January 1858–December 1862) (Table analytique to Deuxième Série in vol. 10, 1862, pp. 361-84). Series 1 and 2 published monthly from 1850–1862; continued as *Revue de théologie* (Troisième Série), ed. Timothée Colani, vols. 1–7 (Strasbourg: Treuttel & Wurtz; Paris: J. Cherbulles, 1863–69) (Irregularly published, 1863–1869), 32 volumes in all. No more published after 1869.

80.   John Hurst (*Rationalism*, p. 392 n. 1) claims that the French Critical School had a number of organs for the publication of their views, both scholarly and popular. Hurst writes, 'For thinking circles, it issues the *Revue de théologie et de Philosophie Chrétienne*, founded fifteen years ago by Scherer and Colani [Hurst is writing in 1865]. It influences the general public by the daily political paper, *Le Temps*, and the *Revue germanique*. The Strasbourg *Revue* and Paris *Lien*, are for the special benefit of Protestants in general; while the *Disciple de Jesus Christ* and *Piéte-Charité* are

cation in 1869, some of the voices that raised questions about the Markan Hypothesis in the middle of the nineteenth century were muted. The second most important journal for the Strasbourg school also ceased publication in 1869.[81] Between the year of its first appearance, 1858, and February of 1861, this journal was known as the *Revue germanique*. From March of 1861 to December of 1861, it became known as the *Revue germanique, française & etrangère*, thus expanding the scope of the French journal's concerns to other countries besides Germany. Then, from January of 1862 until March of 1865 it became known as the *Revue germanique et française*, to reflect a renarrowing of focus, this time on literature from both France and Germany. Finally, from April of 1865 until it ceased publication in December of 1869, it became known as the *Revue moderne*. This final name change may have had something to do with increasing tensions between France and Germany, in the years leading up to the Franco-Prussian war of 1870–1871.

One of the original co-editors of the *Revue germanique* was Auguste Nefftzer (1820–1913). Nefftzer later joined Edmond Scherer as co-founder and co-editor of the Paris political newspaper, *Le Temps*, in 1860. It was Auguste Nefftzer and his co-editor at the original *Revue germanique*, Charles Dollfus (1827–1876), who translated Strauss's second *Life of Jesus* into French in the same year as the German original, 1864.[82]

---

designed for children and uneducated persons.' A. Nefftzer assisted with the editing of the *Revue germanique* from 1858–1861, prior to the founding of *Le Temps*, which he co-edited with Edmond Scherer.

81. *Revue germanique*, ed. Charles Dollfus with A. Nefftzer (Paris: A. Franck, etc., January 1858–January 1861); *Revue germanique*, ed. Charles Dollfus (Paris: A. Franck, etc., January 1861–February 1861); continued as *Revue germanique, française & etrangère*, ed. Charles Dollfus (Paris: A. Franck, etc., March 1861–December 1861); continued as *Revue germanique et française*, ed. Charles Dollfus (Paris: A. Franck, etc., January 1862–March 1865); continued as *Revue moderne*, ed. Charles Dollfus (Paris: A. Franck, etc., April 1865–December 1867); *Revue moderne*, ed. E. de Kératry (Paris: A. Franck, etc., February 1868–December 1869). Volumes 1–43 and 45–55 (vol. 43 ends with December 1, 1867 and vol. 45 opens with February 25, 1868; vol. 44 not published?; vol. 12 has two numbers only, October 31 and November 30). A total of 54 volumes were published under all names. No more published after 1869.

82. This information was reported by Maurice Goguel, *The Life of Jesus* (trans. Olive Wyon; New York: Macmillan, 1945), p. 53 n. 3; Strauss's second life of Jesus

Anyone interested in the history of the decline of the Griesbach Hypothesis and the rise of the Markan Hypothesis in mid-nineteenth-century Europe should also note that the leading journal of the Second Tübingen School, the Theologische *Jahrbücher*, was only published between 1842 and 1857. Some of the members of the Second Tübingen School, including the editors of this journal F.C. Baur (1792–1860) and Eduard Zeller (1814–1908), as well as Albert Schwegler (1819–1857), were liberal Griesbachians. The loss of this journal, no doubt, weakened their cause and the cause of the Griesbach Hypothesis after 1857.

Zeller was the only editor of the *Theologische Jahrbücher* when it began publication in Tübingen in 1842. But Zeller left Tübingen in 1847 to accept a call to a post in theology at Bern. This probably led Baur, who remained in Tübingen, to add his name to that of Zeller, as co-editor of this journal in 1847. Zeller and Baur then remained co-editors throughout the balance of the run of this publication. Zeller moved from Bern to Marburg in 1849, this time accepting a position in philosophy, rather than theology. Zeller's call to a post in theology at Bern had caused a stir in 1847. Zeller stayed at Marburg until 1862, when he accepted a call to Heidelberg and joined H.J. Holtzmann on that faculty. Since Zeller served as an editor of the *Theologische Jahrbücher* through its entire run (1842–1857), he worked on it not only in Tübingen, where the journal originated and was always published, but also from Bern and Marburg. But the journal had ceased its run in 1857, several years before Zeller joined Holtzmann on the Heidelberg faculty in 1862.

Albert Schwegler died in the same year this journal ceased publication, 1857. F.C. Baur, the leader of the Second Tübingen School, was also dead by 1860. Therefore, two of the most important liberal advocates of the Griesbach Hypothesis and the journal in which their views were often published ceased to be factors in the continuing nineteenth century discussion of the question of gospel origins after 1860. Zeller's increasing work within the discipline of philosophy must also have weakened the cause of the Griesbach Hypothesis after Zeller moved to Marburg in 1849.

The *Zeitschrift für wissenschaftliche Theologie* was founded at Jena in 1858. From its founding, an advocate of one form of the so-called 'Augustinian Hypothesis', Adolf Hilgenfeld (1823–1907) was its editor. Hilgenfeld continued as editor of this journal until he died in 1907. This

---

was entitled *Das Leben Jesu, für das deutsche Volk bearbeitet* (2 vols.; Leipzig: F.A. Brockhaus, 1864).

journal continued to be published and edited by Heinrich Hilgenfeld for seven years subsequent to the death of Adolf, the journal's founding editor and most prolific contributor (1907–1914). Hilgenfeld is sometimes labeled a member of the Second Tübingen School, even though he never attended the university at Tübingen nor taught there. Hilgenfeld's work was, rather, confined for most of his life to Jena where the *Zeitschrift* was published. Hilgenfeld did, however, share a belief in the priority of Matthew with F.C. Baur and other members of the Second Tübingen School and Hilgenfeld did utilize some of the same historical-critical methods that members of the Second Tübingen School advocated.

Hilgenfeld also was a frequent contributor to the *Theologische Jahrbücher* prior to 1857 when that journal ceased publication. At the moment, I can only wonder whether it is just a coincidence that the *Theologische Jahrbücher* ceased publication in 1857 and the *Zeitschrift für wissenschaftliche Theologie* began publication in 1858. Seven years after the death of Adolf Hilgenfeld, Heinrich Hilgenfeld reported in a closing word to the last issue of the *Zeitschrift* that the journal had been inaugurated as a part of the 300th Anniversary Celebration (1858) of the founding of the university in Jena (1558). Heinrich also said, in that context, that the principles which the journal had wanted to advocate (in the beginning) and had always advocated (throughout its run) were no longer distinguishing points of a particular school by 1914, but rather of Protestant theology in general, when correctly acknowledged.[83] It is, however, at least an interesting fact that an advocate of the so-called 'Augustian Hypothesis' began to edit and publish a journal in the year immediately following the cessation of publication of another journal that

---

83.   In the last volume of the *Zeitschrift für wissenschaftliche Theologie*, *ZWT* 55 (= Neue Folge 20) (1914), Heinrich Hilgenfeld included the following *Schlusswort*.

Im Jahre 1858 erschien der erste Jahrgang der Zeitschrift für wissenschaftliche Theologie, 'der Universität Jena zu ihrem 300 jährigen Jubiläum, diesem Feste des ganzen deutschen Volks, gewidmet'. Bis zum 50. Jahrgang hat sie der Begründer selbst [Adolf Hilgenfeld] herausgegeben. Da es unmöglich war, die nach seinem Tode [1907] eintretenden Schwierigkeiten verschiedener Art dauernd zu überwinden, kann die Zeitschrift leider nicht weiter erscheinen. Ich nehme also mit diesem Hefte Abschied von allen treuen Mitarbeitern und Lesern mit der Versicherung herzlichsten Dankes für ihre freundliche Unterstützung. Die Grundsätze, für welche diese Zeitschrift eintreten wollte und immer eingetreten ist, sind längst nicht mehr Kennzeichen einer bestimmten Schule, sondern von der protestantischen Theologie allgemein als richtig anerkannt. Die in 55 Jahrgängen geleistete Arbeit ist also nicht vergeblich gewesen.

was edited by two advocates of the Griesbach Hypothesis. One thing that the three editors of these two journals (Bauer, Zeller, and Hilgenfeld) had in common was their opposition to the Markan Hypothesis.

Eduard Reuss (1804–1891)

Eduard Reuss may be considered the patriarch of the Strasbourg school, not only because he was its senior member, but primarily because he was the teacher of most, if not all, of the other members.[84]

Reuss was a native of Strasbourg. Born 18 July 1804, he attended the gymnasium and began his university education there. After studying in Strasbourg until 1825, he traveled to Göttingen, Halle, Jena, and Paris, continuing his education. At the end of these educational travels, Reuss returned to Strasbourg in 1828 where he came a *privat-dozent*.[85] He completed his licentiate in theology in 1829 with a dissertation on the Protestant Old Testament Apocrypha.[86] He became extraordinary professor in 1834 and professor of New Testament in 1836. He also became professor of Old Testament at the Protestant Seminary in Strasbourg in 1864.

Reuss was advocating theses as early as 1833 that are sometimes labeled parts of the 'Graf–Wellhausen' theories, after Karl Heinrich Graf (1815–1869) and Julius Wellhausen (1844–1918). Graf had once been a student of Reuss and the two continued a considerable correspondence after Graf completed his studies at Strasbourg. Julius Wellhausen was not even born (b. 1844) when Reuss began advocating theories of the Pentateuch like those Wellhausen subsequently advocated (1833). Therefore, Reuss was at least a significant precursor of the 'Graf-Wellhausen'

---

84. Reuss certainly taught Colani, Scherer and Réville at Strasbourg. Although Michel Nicolas published two Strasbourg theses, it is not yet clear to me that he actually attended school in Strasbourg.

85. At Göttingen prior to 1828, Reuss may have already met Heinrich Georg August Ewald (1803–1875) who was himself a student at Göttingen before he became a part of the faculty there after 1827. The lives of Reuss and Ewald reveal that they shared many academic interests, including source criticism of books in both testaments. [But cf. J.M. Vincent, *Leben und Werk des frühen Eduard Reuss* (Munich: Kaiser, 1990), esp. p. 78—Addition of the editor.]

86. Eduard Reuss, 'Dissertatio Polemica de Libris V.T. Apocryphis Perperam Plebi Negatis' (Dissertation, Strasbourg, 1829).

source theory of the Pentateuch, if he was not, in fact, one of its originators.

By 1838, Reuss had also become a member of the theological faculty at the French state university in Strasbourg. When this university came under German control after the Franco-Prussian war of 1870–1871, and after the Protestant Seminary in Strasbourg was absorbed into the theological faculty of the new Kaiser-Wilhelm-Universität in 1872, Reuss became the first dean of that faculty.

Early in Reuss's academic career his publications focused on the New Testament. His major work on *The History of the Sacred Scriptures of the New Testament* first appeared in 1842 and eventually went through six editions.[87] Meijboom, who had access to the first four editions by 1866, traced a certain development in Reuss's thought from the first edition of 1842 through to the fourth of 1864.[88] Between the first and the sixth editions, the length of this book more than doubled, from 278 pages in 1842 to 686 pages by 1887.

While the Strasbourg journal that Colani edited was being published (1850–1869), Reuss contributed. Between 1855 and 1858, Reuss published a series of four articles on the Synoptic Problem.[89] These articles reflect some of Reuss's closest work with the texts of the Synoptics. In addition to what Reuss had to say about the Synoptic Problem in the several editions of his *History of the Sacred Scriptures of the New Testament*, he may have also returned to a discussion of the Synoptic Problem in a major work in 1876.[90]

---

87. Eduard Reuss, *Die Geschichte der heiligen Schriften Neuen Testaments entworfen von Eduard Reuss* (Halle: C.A. Schwetschke und Sohn, 1842; 1853²; 1860³; 1864⁴; 1874⁵; 1887⁶). English translation of the 5th edn by Edward L. Houghton, *History of the Sacred Scriptures of the New Testament* (2 vols.; Boston/New York: Houghton Mifflin, 1884).

88. Meijboom and Kiwiet, *History and Critique*, pp. 45-53.

89. Eduard Reuss, 'Etudes comparatives sur les trois premiers évangiles au point de vue de leurs rapports d'origine et de dépendance mutuelle', *RTP* (Première Série) 10 (Février, 1855), pp. 65-83; '[Second article]', *RTP* 11 (1856), pp. 163-88; '[Third article]', *RTP* 15 (Juillet, 1857), pp. 1-32; and 'Nouvelles études comparatives sur les trois premiers évangiles au point de vue de leurs rapports d'origine et de dépendance mutuelle', *NRT* (Deuxième série) 2 (1858), pp. 15-72.

90. Eduard Reuss, *Nouveaux Testament. I. Histoire evangelique. Synopse des trois premiers évangiles* (Paris, 1876). Like most of the works referred to in this paper, I have not had direct access to this one, so this may be no more than a reprinting of his earlier journal articles on the Synoptic Problem. This kind of

According to Meijboom, Reuss had announced himself to be an advocate of Markan priority in 1842, in the first edition of his *History*. This was four years after the publication of the works by Wilke and Weisse that are generally considered to be the most influential early German works advocating Markan priority.[91] Although Reuss advocated Markan priority, he also felt that it was necessary to modify this fundamental hypothesis as he gave increasing attention to the details of the gospel texts between 1842 and 1858.

In 1855, in the first of his series of four articles on the Synoptic Problem, Reuss included a synoptic chart.[92] Those of us who have been involved in the late twentieth century discussion of the Synoptic Problem are aware of the fact that how one presents the literary evidence within the gospels is a significant part of any argument for any source hypothesis. There is no unbiased, neutral, objective presentation of the evidence. Reuss was aware of the difference between his Synoptic Chart and that of Griesbach, and he called attention to it. For instance, Reuss noted that Griesbach's pericope divisions were different and more numerous than his own.[93] Reuss seems to have composed his chart, first, by applying the text of Luke to the text of Mark. He then seems to have inserted the text of Matthew into the chart as best he could, given what he had already established about the parallelism between the texts of Mark and Luke. There is nothing objective about this, or any other, procedure in constructing a synoptic chart, but few New Testament scholars are willing to admit the subjective nature of any synoptic arrangement of the gospels.[94] With the exception of a few scattered verses, enclosed in parentheses, Mark's order of narratives is never

republication was not unusual in the period. But it may, on the contrary, be a new work. One would have to examine several of Reuss's works first hand to decide.

91.   This perception of the works of Wilke and Weisse could be attributed to the fact that Albert Schweitzer only discusses these two scholars in his chapter on 'The Marcan Hypothesis' (*Quest*, pp. 121-36). See C.G. Wilke, *Der Urevangelist: Oder exegetisch-kritische Untersuchung über das Verwandtschaftsverhältnis der drei ersten Evangelien* (Dresden: Gerhard Fleischer, 1838), and C.H. Weisse, *Die evangelische Geschichte kritisch und philosophisch bearbeitet* (2 vols.; Leipzig: Breitkopf & Härtel, 1838).

92.   Reuss, 'Etudes comparatives', *RTP* 10 (1855), pp. 78-81.

93.   Reuss, 'Etudes comparatives', p. 82.

94.   One who does understand the subjective task of synopsis making is David L. Dungan. See his articles, 'Synopses of the Future', *Bib* 66 (1985), pp. 457-92; 'Theory of Synopsis Construction', *Bib* 61 (1980), pp. 305-29.

broken. Luke's order is also generally well preserved in this chart. The order of Matthew, however, has been broken up as necessary in order to accommodate the orders of the other two gospels. Reuss closed his first article with six points that included comments about what he wanted his readers to see in his synoptic chart.

The second article in this series by Reuss began with a reflection on the first. Having considered his synoptic chart in the first article, it was now time to take up details from the texts of the synoptic gospels. Early in this second article, Reuss commented on those texts in Mark that appear to be conflations of Matthew and Luke, but they did not seem to impress him very much.[95] It appears that the argument from omissions, which is less of a problem when Mark is placed first (Markan priority), than when it is placed last in the series of the three gospels (Griesbach Hypothesis), was enough, in Reuss's opinion, to counter-balance any weight one might give to possible evidence of conflations in Mark.

Then came a crucial move by Reuss. Specifically, Reuss chose to consider the details of the synoptic gospels by taking them up in a series of *pairs*. He first compared the text of Luke with the text of Mark. This constituted most of the balance of the second article.[96] For the third article, Reuss moved to a comparison of the text of Luke with the text of Matthew. Following his analysis, Reuss claimed that these two gospels did not stand in a relationship of direct literary dependence.[97] Finally, in the fourth article, Reuss compared the text of Matthew with the text of Mark.[98] There, he argued that Mark had served as a source for both Matthew and Luke,[99] including the passion narrative in the case of Matthew.[100] At the end of this last article in this series, Reuss drew his conclusions in fourteen points.[101] These may be summarized as follows.

The synoptic gospels that we now possess cannot, by themselves, explain all of the synoptic relationships. Among the synoptics, only one, which the tradition attributes to Luke, has come down from antiquity in its primitive form.

The original text of Mark, in Reuss's view, consisted only of

95. Reuss, 'Etudes comparatives', pp. 163-71, esp. 169-70.
96. Reuss, 'Etudes comparatives', pp. 171-88.
97. Reuss, 'Etudes comparatives', pp. 1-31.
98. Reuss, 'Nouvelles études', *NRT* (Deuxième série) 2 (1858), pp. 15-47.
99. Reuss, 'Nouvelles études', pp. 47-53.
100. Reuss, 'Nouvelles études, pp. 53-69.
101. Reuss, 'Nouvelles études, pp. 69-72.

Mk 1.21–13.37. Of that material, Mk 6.45–8.26 may not have been in the original of Mark. But Reuss did not want to press this point. He did argue, however, that this section of the early version of Mark was not in the copy that was known to Luke. This early text of Mark, in Reuss's view, was the book that the ancient and respectable tradition attributed to Mark, the disciple and interpreter of Peter.

This Petrine-Markan Ur-text was utilized by the author of the Gospel of Luke as one of several sources that Luke says he consulted in his prologue (Lk. 1.1-4). Other sources available to Luke, in Reuss's opinion, included oral tradition and sources whose origin Reuss found it difficult to specify. We can label these, Reuss's 'unknown sources'.

According to Reuss, the author of Luke used these unknown sources to begin his gospel from Lk. 1.1 through to Lk. 4.30. For Lk. 4.31–9.50, the author of Luke then used the Petrine-Markan Ur-Text (= canonical Mk 1.21–6.44 and 8.27–9.50). However, within this section of his gospel (Lk. 4.31–9.50), Luke substituted an alternate version of the call of the first disciples (Lk. 5.1-11, cf. Mk 1.16-20). At Lk. 6.19/ Mk 3.19, Luke inserted the following from his unknown sources: (1) the sermon on the Plain (Lk. 6.20–7.1; cf. Matt. 5.2–7.29), (2) the Healing of the Centurion's Son (Lk. 7.2-10, cf. Matt. 8.5–13.1), (3) the Healing of the Widow's Son at Nain (Luke 7.11-17), (4) material on John the Baptist and Jesus (Lk. 7.18-35; cf. Matt. 11.2-19), and (5) the Anointing of Jesus by the Sinful Woman (Lk. 7.36-50; cf. Matt. 26.6-13/ Mk 14.10-11).

Luke then returned to the Petrine-Markan Ur-text to compose Lk. 8.1–9.50 (cf. canonical Mk 4.1–6.44 and 8.21–9.50). From Lk. 9.51–18.14, Luke returned to oral tradition, and then, for Lk. 18.15–21.38 (= canonical Mk 10.1–13.37), back again to the Petrine-Markan Ur-text. Luke concluded his gospel, Luke 22–24, with more material from the oral tradition. In Reuss's view, at no time did Luke have access to Matthew's book.

After Luke made use of the Petrine-Markan Ur-text, a redactor of the latter added the 'Markan' account of the Passion (= canonical Mark 14.1–16.8) to the Ur-text. At the same time, this redactor may have added to the Gospel of Mark a series of brief passages that Reuss called 'historical elements', 'linking formulas', and 'some general resumes'. This first redaction of 'Mark' gave almost all of canonical Mark its current appearance of uniformity.

At about the time that the Petrine Markan Ur-text was composed,

Matthew, one of the twelve apostles, originally composed in Hebrew a collection of somewhat organized 'sentences of Jesus-Christ'. Reuss claimed that this document was never seen by either Mark or Luke even as he claimed that the authors of Matthew and Luke had never seen each other's work. With this 'collection of sentences of Jesus-Christ' in hand, and with the fuller, more orderly and unified, version of the Petrine-Markan Ur-Text (Mk 1.21–16.8), plus other sources that now make up Matthew 1–4; 8.5-13, 9.27-38, 11.2-30 and 17.24-27, a fourth (or fifth) writer composed the gospel now attributed to Matthew.

Once this first, canonical, Gospel of Matthew was complete, a still later redactor added Mk 1.1-20 to the beginning of Mark. Like the followers of Griesbach, Reuss argued that Mk 1.1-20 had been composed by a redactor who knew the canonical Gospels of Matthew and Luke and had conflated these earlier gospels in composing the first 20 verses of Mark. Mk 1.1–16.8 was then, in Reuss's view, the complete Gospel of Mark.[102]

The longer ending of Mark, Mk 16.9-20, was only one of several endings that were added to Mark by later scribes. This was what Reuss concluded from an examination of the manuscript evidence, the quotations of Mark by the early Church Fathers, and from evidence internal to Mk 16.9-20. Like the first twenty verses of Mark, Reuss claimed, these last twelve were also written by a conflating redactor. This redactor of Mk 16.9-20, in Reuss's view, made use of Luke–Acts and the Gospel of John, at least.[103]

---

102. To anyone who has followed the current discussion of the Synoptic Problem, at least since 1980, Reuss's theory will have a familiar ring. Reuss sounds something like Helmut Koester. See Helmut Koester, 'History and Development of Mark's Gospel (From Mark to *Secret Mark* and "Canonical" Mark)', in Bruce C. Corley (ed.), *Colloquy on New Testament Studies: A Time for Reappraisal and Fresh Approaches* (Macon, GA: Mercer University Press, 1983), pp. 35-37. For a response to Koester from the perspective of the Two Gospel or neo-Griesbach Hypothesis, see David B. Peabody, 'The Late Secondary Redaction of Mark's Gospel and the Griesbach Hypothesis: A Response to Helmut Koester', in Corley (ed.), *Colloquy*, pp. 87-132. A transcript of the seminar discussion on the Synoptic Problem is also included in the volume.

103. As a student of critical editions of the Greek New Testament and as one who studied the Greek manuscripts of the canonical gospels, Reuss could come to a critical judgment about the authenticity of Mk 16.9-20 that was, at least, more informed than many of his contemporaries. Cf. Reuss, *Bibliotheca Novi Testamenti graeci, cuius editiones ab initio typographiae ad nostram aetatem impressas,*

Thus, in Reuss's view, the Synoptic Gospels were to be explained by a kind of reciprocal dependence. Not only had 'Matthew' and 'Luke' made use of parts of Mark (Mk 1.21–16.8), but, in a somewhat reciprocal way, 'Mark' had also made use of Matthew and Luke (Mk 1.1-20, cf. Mk 16.9-20). The only direct literary relationship among the Synoptics that Reuss denied was one between the Gospels of Matthew and Luke.

Here the discussion was to stand in Colani's journal until Reuss's former student, Edmond Scherer, responded in 1861. But before leaving Reuss's series of articles on the Synoptic Problem, I would like to make some further observations.

1. In general, Reuss applies the criterion that 'when two Gospels are mutually dependent, the earliest date must be attributed to the least complete'.[104] This presupposition, which Meijboom sometimes called 'the quantitative maxim' leads to 'the problem of omissions'.[105] This principle, of course, had been used in synoptic source criticism at least since the time of Johann Gottfried Herder (1744–1803), but it is a principle whose validity has never been established and whose validity has been challenged.[106] This was the first of three presuppositions shared by advocates of Markan priority prior to 1866 that Meijboom demonstrated to be without merit.

2. Reuss produced his own synoptic chart in order best to display the evidence in accordance with his own thinking. Griesbach's earlier chart was explicitly noted by Reuss, but not used. If synoptic charts are neutral, why did Reuss not use the one already in the literature, created by Griesbach?

3. In his reconstruction of the history of the synoptic tradition, Reuss utilized the text of Luke in order to establish the more original form of the text of Mark. If something was missing in Luke, who *ex hypothesi*

---

quotquot reperiri potuerunt, collegit, digessit, illustravit *Eduardus Reuss* (Brunsvigae: C.A. Schwetschke & Sons, 1872); *idem, Notitia codicis quattuor Evangeliorum graeci membranacei viris doctis hucusque incogniti* (Cantabrigiai, Typis academicis: Excudebant C.J. Clay & filii, 1889).

104. 'Pour le moment, je n'insisterai sur ces témoignages que pour rendre plus plausible l'hypothèse d'après laquelle, en thèse générale du moins, de deux évangiles qui peuvent se trouver dans un rapport de dépendance l'un à l'égard de l'autre, le moins complet sera le plus ancien' (Reuss, *Etudes comparatives*, p. 76); cf. the reference in Meijboom and Kiwiet, *History and Critique*, p. 48.

105. Cf. Meijboom and Kiwiet, *History and Critique*, p. 49 and pp. 156-65.

106. Challenges are made in works cited by Stoldt, Farmer and Meijboom.

had copied Mark, then it was probable, in Reuss's opinion, that the missing material in Luke was also lacking in Luke's source, Mark. This method of synoptic analysis is valid, of course, only if the canonical gospels always grew by incremental gain. It is a corollary to Herder's notion that the briefer text must always be the older text. And like Herder's notion, this corollary can be demonstrated to be invalid in some cases where the direction of literary dependence between two documents is known.

4. Somewhat conversely, Reuss used the text of Mark in order to determine what Luke had added. As applications of methods for solving the Synoptic Problem, items (3) and (4) are clearly prejudicial. Not only is the validity of the assumptions behind these methods questionable, one must also already know the sequence and the relationships among the canonical gospels before one can apply these methods.

5. Beginning with his second article, Reuss considered synoptic relationships by focusing on pairs of gospels (Mark–Luke, Matthew–Luke, Matthew–Mark). This procedure, of course, hides from view some of the most important evidence in support of the Griesbach Hypothesis, that of alternating agreement between Mark and Matthew, on the one hand, and Mark and Luke, on the other. This applies both to alternating agreements in the sequence of pericopes as well as to alternating agreements in wording within pericopes.

6. Reuss did admit that the followers of Griesbach were correct, at least with respect to Mk 1.1-20. It appeared to Reuss that the literary evidence within this Markan unit was sufficient to support a view of Mark as a conflation of the texts of Matthew and Luke.

7. Reuss called attention to further literary evidence that is anomalous for an unmodified theory of Markan priority. This would be the fact that Mark's 'connecting formulas' (*formules de liaison*) were absent from the parallel text of Luke. Reuss apparently found it too incredible to imagine that an otherwise faithful copyist would always stop the faithful copying whenever that copyist came to some of the most fundamental structural features of his source. Apparently, in order to avoid such a reconstruction of the history of the synoptic tradition, Reuss preferred to postulate stages in the compositional development of Mark. Presumably Reuss reasoned that Luke, if he knew these Markan connecting formulas, could hardly have managed accidentally to omit them all and the copyist would have been a strange one if he intentionally omitted them. Reuss, therefore, seems to have reasoned that these formulas must

have been added to the text of Mark after Luke had made use of an earlier form of Mark. This is a position that Holtzmann was later to share with Reuss.

8. Reuss also affirmed that the longer ending of Mark, Mk 16.9-20, gave evidence of being a conflated text, where the author had made use of Luke–Acts and the Gospel of John, at least. Naturally, this section of Mark cannot have been earlier than the Gospel of Luke if its author made use of the Gospel of Luke in composing it. According to Reuss, these verses must have been added to the text of Mark by later scribes.

9. Reuss maintained that the authors of Matthew and Luke did not know each other's texts. Reuss, no doubt, realized that once one allows Matthew and Luke to stand in a direct literary relationship, Markan priority ceases to be a necessity.

To summarize, there is evidence in Reuss's analyses of the synoptic gospels that would have been welcomed by a mid-nineteenth-century advocate of the Griesbach Hypothesis, as both positive evidence, favouring the Griesbach Hypothesis, and negative evidence, arguing against Markan priority.

Edmond Scherer (1815–1889)[107]

Edmond Scherer was a third member of the Strasbourg School. Scherer was born in Paris, in the year of Napoleon's Waterloo, of a Swiss father and an English mother. He was, no doubt, brought up in a bilingual home and, early in his life, he was sent to England to live with Thomas Loader, a clergyman in Monmouth. During the Christmas season of 1832, at the age of sixteen or seventeen, he had a religious experience that marked him as an orthodox Christian during the earlier part of his life.[108] One of Scherer's biographers has written,

> Returning to Paris from his stay in England, Scherer studied law to please his family and philosophy to please himself (1833–1835). But he resolved to become a pastor, and in his twenty-first year (1836) he obtained permission to study theology at Strasbourg (1836–1839). He took his degrees, married early, and was ordained in April 1840, being then a pronounced and thorough believer in 'l'authorité de la Bible et de la Croix'. He tarried, however, for several years longer in Strasbourg (and

107. Meijboom and Kiwiet, *History and Critique*, pp. 53-55.
108. The standard biography is by Octave Gréard, *Edmond Scherer* (Paris: Hachett, 1890; 1891²).

Truttenhausen, 1840–1846), and he does not seem to have undertaken any directly pastoral work, though he preached and wrote hymns with much unction.[109]

Scherer's period of theological study (1836–1839) and his subsequent stay in and around Strasbourg (1839–1846) put him in contact with both Eduard Reuss who was one of his professors and Timothée Colani who pursued his theological studies in Strasbourg (1840–1845), while Scherer was still in the area (1836–1846). In 1846, Scherer moved to Geneva where he accepted a post in church history at the Ecole Libre de Théologie. A year later, he left this post in church history to become professor of Biblical exegesis at the same school.

Between 1846 and 1849 Scherer had something of a crisis of faith.[110] During that time, Scherer found that he could no longer accept a theory of verbal inspiration and infallibility of the Bible. From this time on, he came to doubt more and more of the orthodox tenets of the faith.[111] By 1849, Scherer could no longer continue to teach at the Geneva seminary in good conscience and resigned. Scherer stayed in Geneva, however, at least from June 1849 until February of 1850, giving private lectures. From those lectures, he issued a pamphlet on 'Criticism and Faith' which stirred sufficient interest in the Netherlands to be translated into Dutch.[112]

109. So, George Saintsbury, in his introduction to his translation of some of Scherer's literary critical essays. Edmond Scherer, *Essays on English Literature* (trans. George Saintsbury; New York: Charles Scribner's Sons, 1891); the quotation is from, p. xv.

110. Prior to 1846, Scherer's publications included *Dogmatique de l'église réformée* (Paris, 1843); *De l'état actuel de l'église réformée en France* (Paris, 1844) and *Esquisse d'une théorie de l'église Chrétienne* (Paris: L.R. Delay, 1845). These publications apparently led to his receiving a call to the seminary in Geneva.

111. In 1853, Scherer published *Alexandre Vinet, notice sur sa vie et ses écrits* (Paris: M. Ducloux, 1853). See also Edmond Scherer, 'Alex. Vinet', *RTP* 4 (1851), pp. 193-224, 257-76, 333-55 and 5 (1852), pp. 65-77 and 'La Théologie de Vinet', *RTP* 5 (1852), pp. 193-214. Alexandre Vinet (1797–1847) was a Swiss Reformed theologian who taught French language and literature at Basel where he came under the influence of W.M.L. de Wette (1780–1849). Did Vinet, like de Wette, advocate a modified form of the Griesbach Hypothesis or, at least, have problems with Markan priority? The biographical sketches that I have consulted suggest that Vinet and Scherer, at least by the late 1840s, did share several ideas. Was one of those a questioning of certain aspects if Markan priority? The relationship between Vinet and Scherer deserves further research.

112. Edmond Henri Adolphe Scherer, *La critique et la foi: Deux lettres par*

In 1850, Timothée Colani invited Scherer to join him in editing the new Strasbourg theological journal that he and Reuss were proposed to edit. The first issue of that journal appeared in July of 1850. Within that first volume for 1850, Scherer published an autobiographical account of his resignation from the seminary in Geneva and an article on the question of authority in matters of faith, the issue that first began to move Scherer away from his previously held orthodoxy.[113]

It is not yet clear to me whether Scherer returned to Strasbourg sometime after 1850, stayed in Geneva, or even lived in other places between 1850 and 1860.[114] I do know that Scherer had moved to Versailles by 1860 and that his important article on the Synoptic Problem was published in 1861. This article, therefore, appeared about a year after Scherer had re-established his residence in the regions of Paris where he had been born, and while he was sharing editorial responsibilities with Auguste Nefftzer at the Paris newspaper, *Le Temps*.

This article by Scherer in 1861 was a specific response to the four articles on the Synoptic Problem that had been contributed to Colani's journal by Eduard Reuss in the years, 1855–1858, discussed above.[115]

Edmond Scherer (Paris: M. Ducloux et comp, 1850); *De critiek en het geloof. Twee brieven. Uit het Fransch door S.A.J. de Ruever Groneman* (Leyden: P. Engels, 1851). It was also in 1851 that Albert Réville moved to Rotterdam. At the moment, I can only wonder whether there is a connection between Réville's move to the Netherlands and this translation of Scherer's work into Dutch in the same year. Also see *La question biblique: Trois documents* (Paris: Fischbacher, 1905). This volume includes 'La critique et la Foi' by Scherer, 'La parole et la foi' by Louis Bonnet and 'La Bible' by Frederic Godet.

113. See Edmond Scherer, 'Polémique touchant la démission de M. Scherer', *RTP* 1 (1950), pp. 49-55 and 'De l'autorité en matière de foi', *RTP* 1 (1850), pp. 65-87; cf. Scherer's 'La crise de la foi', *RTP* 3 (1851), pp. 98-110.

114. The first two series of the journal edited by Colani were published not only in Strasbourg and Paris, but also in Geneva (1850–1862). The third series (1863–1869) was not published in Geneva. This might indicate something about Scherer's residence between 1850 and 1860. He might have stayed in Geneva to help with the publication of the Strasbourg journal from there. A check of Gréard's biography of Scherer would probably clear up this uncertainty, but I have not yet done that.

115. Edmond Scherer, 'Quelques Observations sur les rapports des trois premiers évangiles', *NRT* (Deuxième série) 8 (1861), pp. 292-307. After the publication of this article, Scherer does not seem to have contributed to this Strasbourg journal again. But in contributions to this journal made one or two years earlier, Scherer had published, 'Notes sur les évangiles synoptiques', *NRT* 3 (1859), pp. 306-22, 371-84; *NRT* 4 (1859), pp. 36-61, 65-78, 329-50 and *NRT* 5 (1860), pp. 101-35. Holtzmann

Both Reuss and Scherer were advocates of the Markan Hypothesis, but neither could accept it without modifications.

Scherer began his response to Reuss by agreeing with him on the basic issue of Markan priority. He said that he did not want to dispute Reuss's basic findings, but rather to complete and correct them. For a complete synoptic analysis, Scherer believed that it was necessary to discuss three points: (1) the *elements* or contents of parallel synoptic gospels, including notes on omissions, additions and alterations that one Evangelist had made, relative to the test of another; (2) the relative *order* or sequence of pericopes in parallel gospels; and (3) the *redaction* or form of each gospel.[116]

Following his introduction, Scherer divided his article into two parts. In the first part, he concentrated on the Gospel of Luke and its relationship with Mark.[117] In the second part, he concentrated on the Gospel of Matthew and its relationship with Mark.[118] This format seems to follow that of Reuss to whom Scherer was responding.

In first comparing the contents of Mark and Luke, Scherer took note of Lukan additions, substitutions and omissions relative to Mark. Particularly striking for Scherer was Luke's alleged omission of Mk 6.45–8.26.[119] This omission, of course, had also been noted by Reuss who suggested that Luke did not have this unit in his copy of the Petrine-Markan Ur-Text. In Scherer's view, this omission, along with Luke's use of a passion narrative different from the one found in Mark (also observed by Reuss), provided stumbling blocks for advocates of Markan priority.

Then, comparing the relative sequences of materials in Luke and Mark, Scherer made some standard observations from a synopsis that need not be enumerated here. He did take particular note, however, that the two pericopes about Jesus' family (Mk 3.20-21 and 31-35) and the Beelzebul controversy (Mk 3.22-30), that constitute a single literary unit in Mark (Mk 3.20-35), were not only moved by Luke, on the Markan Hypothesis, but pieces of these stories were then also separated by Luke into three different literary contexts, none of which parallels the literary

referred to these articles by Scherer of 1869–1860 but he does not seem to have referred to Scherer's explicit response to Reuss of 1861.

116. Scherer, 'Quelques Observations...', pp. 292-93.
117. Scherer, 'Quelques Observations...', pp. 293-300.
118. Scherer, 'Quelques Observations...', pp. 300-307.
119. Scherer, 'Quelques Observations...', pp. 293-94.

context in Mark (cf. Lk. 8.19-21, 11.14-23 and 12.20). These changes of order in Luke relative to Mark seemed to provide further doubts in Scherer's mind about an unmodified theory of Markan priority.[120]

Scherer's notes relating to his third concern, the form or the redaction of each gospel, are his most impressive ones.[121] His sophistication as a student of the linguistic characteristics of the gospels shows through this section of his work in ways that only Eduard Zeller (1814–1908) had surpassed in this period.[122] Scherer said that what he had observed in this type of comparative analysis of the synoptic gospels was 'rather unexpected'.

Within this section of his article Scherer noted, as had Reuss before him, that Luke, if he had copied canonical Mark, had managed to leave out almost all of what Reuss had called Mark's connecting formulas (*formules de liaison*). In his work, Scherer sometimes referred to transition formulas (*formules de transition*) as well as to connecting formulas (*formules de liaison*), as had Reuss before him. At the moment, I do not think that Scherer had two different collections of formulas in mind when he used these variant phrases, but I do think that a gifted literary critic like Scherer would have recognized that a transition formula is a more sophisticated literary device than a linking formula.

When Scherer discussed these and other literary characteristics of Mark, he sometimes wrote about Mark's 'redaction', but he also often described these as 'the colour' of the author. This metaphor is similar to one that was used by an ancient Christian literary critic of the Greek New Testament, Dionysius of Alexandria.[123] Scherer wondered how a copyist, as Luke is alleged to have been by the Markan Hypothesis, can have managed to 'take the colour out of his model', Mark. That is, Scherer wondered how Luke had managed to avoid almost all of Mark's literary characteristics in the process of copying Mark. Scherer is careful to note, however, that a few of Mark's literary characteristics are to be found in parallel passages in Luke, such as the use of

120. Scherer, 'Quelques Observations...', pp. 294-95.

121. Scherer, 'Quelques Observations...', pp. 295-300.

122. See Eduard Zeller, 'Studien zur neutestamentlichen Theologie 4: Vergleichende Uebersicht über den Wörtervorrath der neutestamentlichen Schriftsteller', *TJ* 2/2 (1843), pp. 443-543.

123. See, for instance, Dionysius of Alexander's use of the Greek word χρώς in his discussion of the literary characteristics he isolated in the canonical books attributed to the apostle John, as quoted in Eusebius, *Hist. eccl.* 7.24-25.

περιβλεψάμενος at Lk. 6.10 and a number of parallel uses of Mark's εὐθέως.

Scherer then rehearsed Reuss's reconstruction of the history of the development of the synoptic gospels, taking particular note of the fact that Mark is supposed to have developed through several stages, at the hands of different authors. Although Scherer admitted that Reuss had taken account of some of the relevant data in his work, Scherer believed that Reuss's hypothesis was not reconcilable with other facts. Scherer than proceeded to discuss these.

Scherer observed that Matthew's gospel was clearly a composite document. It, therefore, should be expected to reflect the several different literary styles of Matthew's sources. He also noted that the prologue of Luke provided evidence for that Evangelist's use of several sources. Therefore, one would also expect the different literary styles of the different authors of Luke's sources to appear within the Gospel of Luke.

By contrast, Scherer noted that the gospel of Mark contains 'numerous characteristics of redaction that distinguish it from one end to the other'. And these literary characteristics most distinguish the text of the Gospel of Mark from the text of both the other synoptic gospels. Mark has 'its own literary colour' (*sa couleur littéraire*). Unlike the Gospels of both Matthew and Luke, the Gospel of Mark appears to be the product of a single hand.

To make explicit what he had in mind in referring to Mark's own literary colour, Scherer enumerated the peculiarities of the redaction of Mark that characterize that gospel, such as (1) precise numbers, (2) the use of proper names, (3) Hebrew terms accompanied by translations, (4) the explanations of Jewish practices, and (5) the repetition of favourite words. But what was most characteristic of Mark's text, in Scherer's opinion, was (6) Mark's habit of padding[124] and paraphrasing what was expressed more simply in the narratives of one or both of the other synoptic Evangelists. Scherer added that Mark's narrative was also characterized by (7) the insertion of a host of descriptive details, strokes of the pen that (8) depict emotions, (9) provide situation indicators, and (10) give a certain liveliness to the narrative. Scherer said that the value and originality of each of these distinctive, often unique, literary characteristics of Mark were still matters of debate in 1861 but they seemed to him to be 'arbitrary additions'.[125]

124. Scherer uses the French verb, *délayer*, here, 'diluting'.
125. Scherer wrote in 1861 that these characteristics of Mark had been recognized

Scherer had observed that these characteristics, including such basic structural features as linking and transitional formulas, are found throughout the Gospel of Mark. Scherer, therefore, found the same literary characteristics in Mk 1.21–6.44 and 8.27–13.37, which was Reuss's Petrine-Markan Ur-text, as he found in Mk 6.45–8.26, which Reuss had suggested was not available to Luke when he made use of that Petrine-Mark Ur-text. Scherer found this same literary style in Mk 14.1–16.8, which Reuss had claimed to be an addition to the Petrine-Markan Ur-text after Luke had made use of it.

Adding insult to injury, Scherer even pointed out that this same literary style, Mark's distinctive 'literary colour' was even present in Mk 1.1-20. Reuss had claimed that Mk 1.1-20 was a conflated text, created by a later redactor of 'Mark', who made use of the canonical Gospels of Matthew and Luke as sources for his composition. Scherer then asked, in effect, 'How is one to explain these identities in literary style among diverse authors?' Reuss's theory of Markan development did not conform with the facts to be found in the texts of the gospels, according to Scherer.[126]

Within his work, Scherer emphasized something that Reuss had not. Specifically, Reuss concluded at the end of his four articles on the Synoptic Problem that Mark's linking formulas were absent from the parallel text of Luke. But Scherer took prominent note of the fact that 'the colour of Mark', including Mark's transitional formulas, was absent not only from Luke, but also from Matthew. Since Reuss had tended to analyze the gospels in a series of pairs, he was perhaps not impressed by these facts in the way that Scherer was.

To these facts, Scherer added some discussion of what advocates of Markan priority today would label the 'minor agreements' between Matthew and Luke. These consist of both positive agreements and negative agreements. Positive agreements would include those places where Matthew and Luke agree on some wording alternative to that in Mark or on some wording in addition to that found in Mark. Negative

for a long time. One wonders whether Scherer's own research revealed these traits of Mark to him or whether he had read some recognized expert on this subject. If the latter, it would be interesting to know who the expert(s) might have been. Scherer provides no note on this comment.

126. Reading the Reuss–Scherer exchange in the French literature from 1855–1861 was like reliving the Koester–Peabody exchange of 1980. See Corley, *Colloquy*, cited above.

agreements include those places in which Matthew and Luke agree in omitting something from Mark.[127] For Scherer, these data confirmed that something was wrong with the theory of Markan priority and with Reuss's source theory in particular. Reuss had claimed that neither Luke nor Matthew ever had access to the text of the other and the minor agreements do not seem to be consistent with that claim.

From his examination of the literary evidence, Scherer concluded that Reuss's theory about the development of the gospels was 'a critical dream' (*le rêve critique*), even if it was a dream that Scherer himself had once shared. Reuss thought he had provided a solid foundation for his reconstruction of the history of the synoptic tradition, but, in Scherer's view, the texts of the gospels would not support the super-structure of the source theory that Reuss had built upon them.

At the end of this first section of his article, Scherer made some suggestions alternative to those that had been made by Reuss. First, Scherer suggested that Ruess's later additions to the text of Mark might also be explained as deliberate omissions from Mark by Matthew and Luke. Presumably, Scherer thought that this thesis better explained the unity of style present throughout the Gospel of Mark than did Reuss's theory of multiple redactions of Mark at the hands of different authors.

Secondly, continuing work with the text of the synoptic gospels led Scherer to conclude that the minor agreements of Matthew and Luke against Mark did not always seem to him to provide a reading that was more primitive than that in canonical Mark. If this were true, then Scherer could conclude, on the basis of this type of evidence as well, that Reuss's various editions of Mark were not necessary.

Thirdly, Scherer repeated his observations that some, even if only a few, of Mark's literary characteristics did appear within the parallel text of Luke. A similar observation had been made by Eduard Zeller in the German literature, in 1843. That is, the direction of literary dependence indicated by the presence or absence of the literary characteristics of one Evangelist within the text of another was not consistent. Sometimes the evidence supported Mark's use of Luke and, at other times, the evidence supported Luke's use of Mark. And so it was, Zeller had found, for every possible direction of literary dependence between any

---

127. For a record of the most recent discussion of the minor agreements among experts on the Synoptic Problem, see Georg Strecker (ed.), *Minor Agreements. Symposium Göttingen 1991* (Göttinger Theologische Arbeiten, 50; Göttingen: Vandenhoeck & Ruprecht, 1993).

two of the synoptic gospels. However, on the basis of an examination of this type of literary evidence that was much more thorough than that Scherer provided, Zeller concluded that, in balance, this type of literary evidence weighed in favour of the Griesbach Hypothesis.[128]

Fourthly, and perhaps most importantly, Scherer confessed that he had trouble imagining a redactor acting in the way that Reuss's later redactor(s) of Mark supposedly acted; that is, deleting a word here, adding one there, interspersing the text of his predecessor with a multitude of favourite words, picturesque expressions, formulas of transition, chronological details, etc.

The main usefulness of Reuss's source theory and of Scherer's own alternatives to parts of that theory, in Scherer's opinion, was in helping to pose the question of gospel origins better, rather than in providing answers to it. As Scherer had wisely said, in introducing his article, 'Nothing more resembles the answer to a question than the well asked question.' If Reuss and Scherer had better asked the question of gospel origins, they would have been more likely to get the right answer. This, at least, is the implication of the proverbial affirmation, quoted here by Scherer himself.

Scherer concluded part one of his article by noting two points that, for him, remained certain. First, there was evidence of a direct literary relationship between Mark and Luke. Scherer accepted Reuss's view that the direction of this literary dependence ran from Mark to Luke. He, therefore, did not argue the case for that in this article. But there were also differences between the texts of Mark and Luke that Scherer believed could not be reconciled with the assumption that Luke had used Mark. These facts created a dilemma for Scherer that remained unresolved for him. He only hoped that these apparently incompatible facts would be addressed by future scholars who sought to solve the problem of gospel origins.

In Part II of his article, Scherer turned to a consideration of the relationships between the texts of Matthew and Mark. As with his analysis of Luke's relationship to Mark, Scherer first noted certain differences in content when the text of Matthew was compared to that of Mark. He noted passages where Matthew agreed with Luke in omitting material from Mark, passages where Matthew omitted material that Luke had shared with Mark, passages where Matthew had modified Mark and many passages where Matthew had supplemented Mark.

128. Zeller, 'Wörtervorrath', *TJ* 2/2 (1843), pp. 443-543.

Most of Scherer's discussion of the relationships between Mark and Matthew, however, dealt with differences in their orders of pericopes. In Scherer's opinion, this was the most difficult aspect of Matthew's relationship to Mark to explain on the Markan Hypothesis. For this second part of his article, Scherer prepared and published a synoptic chart, as had Reuss before him. Scherer's was a chart of some of the opening chapters of Mark and Matthew (Mk 1.1–6.29/Matt. 3.1–14.12). In this chart, Scherer left Luke out of consideration altogether. If Scherer's discussion of the relevance of the literary characteristics of the synoptic Evangelists for solving the Synoptic Problem was superior to that of Reuss, then Scherer's synoptic chart was clearly inferior to that of Reuss. Reuss's chart was, at least, a more complete view of all three gospels, whereas Scherer's chart was only a partial view of two gospels. Scherer's discussion of the different orders of pericopes within limited sections of the Gospels of Matthew and Mark is not too enlightening. One expects more after the illuminating notes in Part I of this article.

While Scherer discussed the contents and orders of Matthew and Mark in Part II of his article, he never turned to an analysis of the redactions of Matthew and Mark after the close of Part I. One assumes that Scherer thought his discussion of these matters in Part I of his article made it unnecessary for him to repeat parts of that discussion in Part II or even to elaborate upon it there. Scherer's article, therefore, comes to a close with his discussion of the differences in the order of pericopes in Matthew and Mark. Scherer concluded that the composition of each of the canonical gospels, like the subsequent composition of the New Testament canon, should not be explained by a single principle, but rather by several, complex and interrelated, principles. 'This', concluded Scherer, 'is what we must never forget in the study that occupies us'.

This article has provided good evidence of Scherer's sensitivity to matters of literary style that marked his life as a literary critic. And here again is some interesting evidence within the synoptic gospels laid out in a way that should have given an advocate of Markan priority reasons to rethink his or her position. Scherer was such an advocate of Markan priority and the evidence he himself marshalled did give him pause.

Within Colani's journal, Reuss never rebutted this article by Scherer; but further research is required in order to find out whether Reuss took account of Scherer's article in works by Reuss that appeared after 1861.

As was mentioned above, Edmond Scherer moved to Versailles in 1860, but he rejected a call to the newly established chair of religious

science at the Ecole de Hautes Etudes in Paris. Unfortunately for gospel
criticism, during the mid-1860s Scherer left behind most of his theological interests[129] and subsequently became a distinguished literary
critic,[130] a journalist[131] and, toward the end of his life, a politician.

129. Saintsbury (*Essays*, p. xvii) writes, 'He had, as it were, at once summed up
and said good-bye to his interest in religious subjects proper in his *Mélanges
d'histoire réligieuse*' [Paris: Michel Lévy frères, 1864, 1865²]. Also see *Mélanges de
critique réligieuse* (Paris: Michel Lévy frères, 1860).

130. Edmond Scherer, *Essays on English Literature* (trans. George Saintsbury;
New York: Charles Scribner's Sons, 1891) being a translation of selections from
Etudes sur la littérature contemporaine (10 vols.; Paris: C. Lévy, 1873–1891), vol. 1,
1885; vol. 2, 1886; vol 3., 1885; vols. 4-5, 1886; vol. 6, 1886; vol. 7, 1882; vol. 8,
1885; vol. 9, 1889; vol. 10, 1895.

Contents of this English translation include the translator's 'Preface', vi-x;
'Contents', xi; the translator's 'Introduction', which includes some interesting
historical material on Scherer, pp. xii-xl; and English translations of the following
reviews of English literature by Scherer: I. George Eliot—'Silas Marner', pp. 1-12
(A Review of 'Silas Marner, the Weaver of Raveloe', published in 1861) [the French
original is found in Scherer's *Etudes sur la littérature contemporaine*]; II. John
Stuart Mill, (A Review of *Representative Government* by J. Stuart Mill, translated and
preceded by an introduction by Dupont White, 1851), pp. 13-35 [French original =
Etudes, I]; III. Shakespeare (A Review of *Prédécesseurs et contemporains de
Shakespeare. Shakespeare, ses œuvres et ses critiques: Contemporains et
successeurs de Shakespeare*, A. Mézières, 2nd édn, 3 vols.), pp. 36-50 [French
Original = *Etudes*, III]; IV. George Eliot—'Daniel Deronda' (A review of this work
published in 4 vols. in 1876), pp. 51-69 [French Original = *Etudes*, V]. [Scherer's
review is dated January, 1877]; V. Taine's *History of English Literature* (3 vols.;
Paris: Hachette, 1863), pp. 70-95 [French Original = *Etudes*, VI]; VI. Shakespeare
and Criticism (A Review of *Œuvres Complètes de Shakespeare*. Translated by Emile
Montégue, 10 vols.), pp. 91-110 [French Original = *Etudes*, vol. VI); VII. Milton and
"Paradise Lost", pp. 111-49 (French Original = *Etudes*, vol. VI); VIII. Laurence
Sterne, or The Humorist (A Review of *Laurence Sterne: His Person and his
Writings*, by Paul Stapfer, 1870), pp. 150-73 (French Original = *Etudes*, VI) [the
Review is dated May, 1870]; IX. Wordsworth (and Modern Poetry in England),
pp. 174-225 (French Original = *Etudes*, VII); X. Thomas Carlyle, pp. 226-35 (French
Original = *Etudes*, VII) [the Review is dated February, 1881]; XI. 'Endymion',
pp. 236-50 (French Original = *Etudes*, VII) [the Review is dated December, 1880];
XII. George Eliot, pp. 251-309 [French Original = *Etudes*, VII] [the Review is dated
March, 1885].

131. Along with Auguste Nefftzer (1820–1913), Scherer became co-editor of the
Paris newspaper, *Le Temps*, from the time of its first appearance in 1860. George
Saintsbury writes, 'To return to the course of M. Scherer's life, the last thirty years
[i.e. 1859–1889], or nearly so, give us Paris for scene, and literature and politics for

Scherer's departure from publishing explicitly theological works seems
to have happened around 1864, about a year after Renan's *Life of Jesus*
was published. As we will note below, Scherer, Colani and Reuss were
all implicated in the controversy that followed the publication of this
book by Renan. With these events, one of the best, mid-nineteenth century, literary critics of the gospels, who also had problems with certain
aspects of the Markan Hypothesis, left the field. After 1864, Scherer's
energies were never again directed towards the Synoptic Problem, so far
as I have yet discovered.

Given an interest in the influence of social history on the course of literary criticism, some comments by George Saintsbury on Scherer's
later life at Versailles are noteworthy.

> During the [Franco-Prussian] war he was called upon to play a most
> difficult part, and played it in a manner which cannot be too much admired,
> especially when we remember that he was a literary recluse, fifty-five years
> old and with very little experience of business. He, who never feared any-
> thing, was the last man likely to be a *pantouflard*, and to complete the
> agony of France from the safe seclusion of Geneva or London. But it
> could scarcely have been anticipated that he would take up and discharge
> to admiration the hard and hateful duty of administering the affairs of
> Versailles [his place of residence] during the German occupation [1871].
> He seems to have done this necessary and odious work with the most
> admirable good sense and fortitude, standing between his countrymen and
> the invaders and being proof alike against the unreasonable sensitiveness
> of the former (Frenchmen) and the inconsiderate roughness of the latter
> (Prussians). Such work is not always rewarded, but it speaks much for
> M. Scherer's townsmen and the inhabitants of the department of Seine-et-
> Oise generally that when the peace came they at once selected him to rep-
> resent them. He very soon became a life Senator and retained the position
> till his death [in 1889].[132]

subjects. The 'Revue des deux Mondes' was not shut to M. Scherer, but almost the
whole of his work in both departments was given to the 'Temps', then under the
direction of M.[essieur, Auguste] Nefftzer, who was akin to him in race and general
sentiments. The character of this paper was very mainly formed and settled by
M. Scherer's collaboration' (*Essays*, p. xvii).

132. Saintsbury, *Essays*, pp. xviii-xix. Some of Scherer's political writings would
also be interesting to explore. See especially *Edmond Scherer on the Franco-
Prussian war*; nine letters written anonymously to the *New York World* (with an
introduction by N.J. Tremblay; Arizona University, Social Science bulletin, no. 11;
University of Arizona bulletin, vol. VII, no. 4; Tucson: University of Arizona Press,
1936); 'The French Republic and the Catholic Church', in *The Library Magazine*, 4
(New York, 1880), pp. 1-18; *La révision de la constitution par Edmond Scherer*

Albert Réville (1826–1906)[133]

A fourth member of the Strasbourg School, Albert Réville, was born in Dieppe in Normandy on 4 November 1826, the son of a liberal Protestant pastor. Réville was educated in his home town and in Geneva where his father had attended school before him. Like three other members of the Strasbourg School—Reuss, Scherer and Colani—Réville studied at the University of Strasbourg. He served as the assistant pastor at Nimes (1847–1848) and, as pastor at Luneray (1848–1851).

Assuming that Réville studied at Strasbourg prior to accepting his responsibilities as assistant pastor at Nimes in 1847, I infer that Réville had been a student of Eduard Reuss. Reuss had been part of the

(Paris: Librairie nouvelle, 1882); *La démocratie et la France: Etudes par Edmond Scherer*...(Paris: Librairie nouvelle, 1883, 1884[2]); *El sufragio universal y la democracia: Versión castellana de la segunda edición francesa por Eduardo Sanz. y Escartín* (Madrid, 1888); even some of Scherer's 'literary studies' hold interest for the student of the history of gospel research. Scherer regularly reviewed literature in the English language and maintained a particular interest in the work of George Eliot [the pen name of Mary Ann Evans], who, as her first literary work, translated David Friedrich Strauss's first *Life of Jesus*. David Friedrich Strauss, *The Life of Jesus Critically Examined* (trans. from the 4th German edn by George Eliot [i.e. Mary Ann Evans]; 3 vols.; London: Chapman Brothers, 1846). A rather more readily available English translation is that of the 4th edn (by Eliot), but including notes from the 3rd edition, and translations of the prefaces of all four editions (ed. with an introduction by Peter C. Hodgson; trans. George Eliot; Lives of Jesus Series; Philadelphia: Fortress Press, 1972). When asked which of his literary essays he wished to be presented in translation to an English-speaking audience, Scherer chose twelve of his essays previously published in French. He chose three dealing with works by George Eliot, but only two on Shakespeare and only one on each of the other authors in this collection. In one of these essays on 'George Eliot' Scherer wrote, 'Miss Evans was by no means utterly unknown in the literary world. She had worked on a very serious periodical, the "Westminster Review". She had written theological articles in it. A translation of Strauss's celebrated work on the Life of Jesus was hers. What a mixture of contradictions and surprises! It was not enough to have to acknowledge a woman as the first novelist of England; more than that, this woman combined faculties which had never been associated in the memory of man. She was at once a savant and a poet. There was in her the critic who analyzes and the artist who creates. Nay, the pen which had interpreted Strauss—the most pitiless adversary of Christian tradition that the world has produced—this very pen had just drawn the charming portrait of Dinah, and had put on the lips of this young Methodist girl the inspired discourse at Haysloope and the touching prayer in the prison' (Saintsbury, *Essays*, p. 5).

133. Meijboom and Kiwiet, *History and Critique*, pp. 55-60.

theological faculty at the state university in Strasbourg since 1838 and had been teaching at the Protestant Seminary there for ten years prior to that. I may infer also that Réville was a student colleague of Colani who studied in Strasbourg between 1840 and 1845. Réville may also have known Scherer prior to 1847, because Scherer was still in Strasbourg until 1846, when he accepted a teaching post at a seminary in Geneva. It may be remembered, however, that Scherer had completed his theological studies in Strasbourg by 1839.

Having served earlier pastorates in France, Albert Réville moved to the Netherlands in 1851 where he became the pastor of the Walloon church in Rotterdam from 1851 to 1873.[134] With Réville's move to Rotterdam, a significant connection was made between the scholars of the Strasbourg School and those in the Netherlands. Perhaps, Réville knew Abraham Dirk Loman (1823–1897), the friend and mentor of Meijboom.[135] Maybe Réville even knew the young Hajo Uden Meijboom (1842–1930).

One of the Dutch scholars with whom Réville certainly became acquainted was Johannes Henricus Scholten (1811–1885) at Leiden. Réville translated one of Scholten's books from Dutch into French and the translation was published in 1861.[136] Some of Scholten's other works were translated into other languages by other people. His book on Mark, for instance, where he advocated the Markan Hypothesis (Dutch original, 1868), was translated into German (1869),[137] as was a

134. Albert Réville, *Discourse d'adieu, prononcé le 27 Avril 1873, dans l'Eglise Wallonne de Rotterdam* (Rotterdam: Nijgh & van Ditmar, 1873).

135. Meijboom co-authored a series with Loman: Abraham Dirk Loman, Willem Christiann van Manen and Hajo Uden Meijboom, *Nalatenschap* (Gröningen: J.B. Wolters, 1899). One volume in the series was Loman's work on Galatians. After Loman's death, Meijboom wrote some biographical pieces about him. See the Dutch journal, *De Gids* 2 (1898), pp. 80-117, and *Levensberichten der afgestorven medeleden van de Maatschappij der Nederlandische Letterkunde* (1898), pp. 26-28 and 69-72.

136. Johannes Henricus Scholten, *Manuel d'histoire comparée de la philosophie et de la religion* (trans. from the Dutch by A. Reville; Paris: Treuttel & Wurtz, 1861). Other works by Scholten appeared in German and English translation.

137. See J.H. Scholten, *Het oudste Evangelie: critisch onderzoek naar de samenstelling, de onderlinge verhouding, de historische waarde en den oorsprong der evangelien narr Mattheus en Marcus* (Leiden: Academische Boekhandel van P. Engels, 1868) = *Das älteste Evangelium: Kritische Untersuchung der Zusammensetzung, des wechselseitiges Verhältnisses, des geschichtlichen Werths und des Ursprungs der Evangelien nach Matthäus und Marcus, von J.H. Scholten*

later book by Scholten on Luke (Dutch original, 1870; German translation, 1881).[138] In a biographical sketch of Scholten, published in 1861, Réville wrote,

> As to Dr Scholten I must refer for everything relating to his ideas to my article in the *Revue des Deux Mondes* upon the religious schools of Holland. He is without any doubt at the present moment the most distinguished theologian of that country, and he exercises an immense influence upon the young by his zeal and by his philosophic depths of thought. He is a man of ripe age (Scholten was 50 in 1861), the son of a pastor liberal according to the old meaning of the word, and very well acquainted with the German philosophy. It is to him I owe my comprehension of it. Constantly exposed to the violent attacks of the orthodox and of the old liberals, he defends himself with a boldness and a success which disconcert his adversaries. Supported by his colleague (Abraham) Kuenen (1828–1891), who is a younger man, and whose special duty is criticism, strengthened also by the recent addition of one of his pupils, Professor Raunenhoff, for ecclesiastical history, he finds his position becoming stronger from day to day. He is in other respects a man of very simple tastes and in every sense lovable.[139]

Born in Utrecht in 1811, Scholten was also educated there (1828–1835). Following earlier appointments, he became a professor at Leiden from 1843 until his death in 1885. Scholten was a member of 'the modern school' in Holland and seems to have had some relationship

(trans. E.R. Redepenning; Elberfeld: R.L. Friderichs, 1869).

138. J.H. Scholten, *Het Paulinisch evangelie: Critisch onderzoek van het evangelie naar Lucas en zijne verhouding tot Marcus, Mattheus en de handelingen* (Leiden: Academische Boekhandel van P. Engels, 1870) = *Das Paulinische Evangelium: Kritische Untersuchung des Evangeliums nach Lucas und seines Verhältnisses zu Marcus, Matthäus und der Apostelgeschichte, von J.H. Scholten* (trans. E.R. Redepenning;Elberfeld: R.L. Friderichs, 1881).

139. Albert Réville, 'Biographical Notices of the Contributors', in Beard (ed.), *Progress of Religious Thought*, p. vi. If Scholten was as dynamic as Réville claims here and he advocated Markan priority, it seems likely that his work would have contributed significantly to the rise of Markan priority in the Netherlands. Of the early Dutch advocates of the Markan Hypothesis mentioned by Meijboom—Prins, Bakhuyzen, Rovers, Lambrechts and Scholten—it seems that Scholten became the most important, at least in the area of gospel studies. (Cf. Meijboom and Kiwiet, *History and Critique*, pp. 89-90.) The translations of several of Scholten's works speak to his international reputation and yet also to the need for such translations of Dutch works in nineteenth-century Europe. The obscurity of Meijboom's dissertation until today speaks in another way to the importance of such translations.

with the Strasbourg school, at least through Réville, if not through others.

In the same 1861 volume in which Réville's biographical sketch of Scholten appeared, Reville wrote the following about himself.

> I have not much to report respecting myself. I was born at Dieppe, in Normandy, the son of a pastor there, whose recent loss I am still mourning. My father brought me up in his own liberal ideas, as they were taught at Geneva. Whilst very heretical in matters of doctrine, I was quasi-orthodox in matters Biblical. My own reading, my knowledge of German, and the *Revue de théologie* have brought me to the point at which I now am. Desirous, as far as might be in my power, of assisting in the revival of the Theology of French Protestantism, and in rectifying the common notions of Christianity I accepted a pastorship offered me at Rotterdam, in 1859 [sic], although out of my native land, in the hope that I might find there some time and more opportunities than in most of the churches in France, to devote myself to this work. My hope has not been disappointed. I have succeeded in gaining for myself a certain name in connection with French Protestantism, and even beyond that limit. My writings in the *Lein, le Disciple de Jésus Christ*, the *Revue de Strasburg*, etc., etc., have contributed to propagate what I believe to be the truth, and have even drawn upon me the attentions of readers whom I little expected; I mean men like [Ernest] Renan, [Edouard Rene Lefebre de] Laboulaye [1811–1883], etc. who have opened to me the door of extensive Parisian publicity. I have entered in, and I quite hope to remain inside. I have made an opening through which better men than I am will pass, and I am well pleased at having been able to make it. Just now there is in the press at Leyden, a treatise of mine, on the Origin and Composition of the Gospel of Matthew, a treatise which I wrote in answer to a question professed by a Theological Society of this country. My answer received the prize offered for competition, and has procured me the degree of Doctor of Theology. Four or five years ago, I was all but appointed professor at Montauban. Happily I was spared that misfortune. Montauban being the seat of authority where four or five ignoramuses set themselves up to lay down the law for the world, I should have been stifled in such a stove. From the seclusion of my Dutch study, I send forth my shafts against orthodoxy, when and how I will; four French Protestant Journals are at my disposal, the *Revue des Deux Mondes* and the *Revue Germanique* are open to me: what would I have more?[140]

140. Réville, 'Biographical Notices', in Beard (ed.), *Progress in Religious Thought*, pp. vi-viii. The date of Réville's move to Rotterdam published here (1859) is at odds with that given in the biographies of him I have consulted, i.e. 1851. More importantly, p. 5 of the index volume to the first series of the Strasbourg *Revue de Theologie* (1852–1857) already describes Réville as 'pasteur à Rotterdam' by 1857.

In addition to these biographical sketches of Scholten and himself, Réville also contributed biographical sketches on the remaining contributors to this volume, Timothée Colani, A. Grotz, Ernest Renan, and Edmond Scherer. These provide interesting windows into the lives of these men before 1861.

In 1862, Réville's study of the Gospel of Matthew to which he makes reference in this sketch of his own life was published in Leiden where Scholten was teaching.[141] By 1866, Meijboom could refer to this work by Réville as 'a well-known book'.[142] According to Meijboom, within this study Réville defended the theory of Markan priority, but, like others from the Strasbourg school, not without reservations.[143] Like Reuss, Réville appealed to an alternative form of the Gospel of Mark as part of his explanation of data within the synoptic gospels. But unlike Reuss, Réville's reconstruction of an early form of Mark included passages from Matthew and Luke that are not to be found in canonical Mark. In this way, Réville's reconstruction of an early form of Mark was more like the early form of Mark to be reconstructed by Holtzmann a year later in 1863. Meijboom said, 'We owe to Réville the current name of "Proto-Mark" for the document preceding Mark'.[144]

Réville, like Scherer, also noticed that the transition formulas in Mark did not appear in either Matthew or Luke. Meijboom says of Réville,

> His opinion was that the few features which, dispersed throughout Mark, are of later origin, and the few transition formulas, which occasionally take

Therefore, I take the date given here (1859) as a misprint and currently accept the earlier date, 1851, as the correct one.

141. Albert Réville, *Etudes critiques sur l'Evangile selon St Matthieu* (Leiden: D. Nothoven van Goor, 1862), 'Ouvrage couronné par la Société de La Haye pour la défense de la religion chrétienne'. This work included an appendix of 15 pages entitled 'Troisième partie du traité sur la composition de l'Evangile selon St Matthieu, de m. Eduard de Muralt [1808–1895]'.

142. Meijboom and Kiwiet, *History and Critique*, p. 53. The book was reviewed in the same year it was published by Charles Dardier (1820–1893), who was, at the time, a pastor in Nimes. See *NRT* (Deuxième série) 10 (1862), pp. 272-88. Meijboom says, 'it was received enthusiastically by Dardier'.

143. Unlike my comments on Scherer and Reuss, some of whose work on the Synoptic Problem I have consulted directly, most of what I say about Réville is from Meijboom and Kiwiet, *History and Critique*, pp. 55-60. Meijboom's comment, p. 55, 'I would do an injustice to Réville if I did not specifically indicate that there is hardly a trace of dependence on the theologian Eduard Reuss', needs to be tested.

144. Meijboom and Kiwiet, *History and Critique*, p. 56.

the place of a loose connection, would suggest a gospel not much different from our present Gospel of Mark. The only significant difference would be that the canonical Mark has omitted the following stories from the Proto-Mark which are still recorded in Matthew. They include the story of the Roman officer at Capernaum (Matthew 8.5-13/Luke 7.2-10), the messengers sent by John the Baptist (Matthew 11.2-19/Luke 7.18-35), Jesus' appearance in Galilee (Matthew 28.9-10, 16-20) and perhaps the indecisive followers of Jesus (Matthew 8.18-22/Luke 9.57-62), which sections can be found in Mt. 8.5-10, 11.2-6; 28.9-10, 16-20; and 8.19-20. This divergence from Reuss is certainly not completely accidental.[145]

It may be remembered that Reuss had consigned the stories of the Roman officer at Capernaum and the messengers sent by John the Baptist to Luke's unknown sources. At the same time, Reuss had claimed that these stories had come to Matthew from his other sources.

Within his synoptic chart, Reuss had paralleled Mt. 8.18-27, that includes Matthew's version of the indecisive followers of Jesus, with Mk 4.35-41. Reuss labeled this §35 of his chart. When Reuss came to §58 of his chart, which was, for Reuss, a unit composed of Lk. 9.57-62 that includes Luke's version of the indecisive followers of Jesus, Reuss inserted a reference back to §35 of his chart in the column dedicated to Matthew, while leaving the column dedicated to Mark with no entry. Since Reuss denied that Luke and Matthew had access to one another's gospels, Reuss had to conclude that the story of the indecisive followers of Jesus came to Luke from his unknown sources while it came to Matthew from his other sources.

Even though these stories are told in many of the same ways and even in many of the same words in Matthew and Luke, Reuss had claimed that neither Matthew nor Luke had access to the other's gospel. And Reuss went even further in his claims, by affirming that Matthew and Luke did not even have access to a common source for these three non-Markan stories.

Réville claimed, as had Reuss, that neither Matthew nor Luke had access to the other's gospel. But Réville preferred to explain the presence of these non-Markan stories in Matthew and Luke as the result of their independent use of a common source, what Réville called Proto-Mark, in contrast to Reuss. In Réville's view, both Matthew and Luke had copied these three stories from Proto-Mark, though each had edited them somewhat differently. The redactor of canonical Mark, however, in

Réville's reconstruction, had omitted all three stories from Proto-Mark.

Réville also chose to assign Mt. 28.9-10, 16-20 to his Proto-Mark. The authenticity of the intervening verses, Mt. 28.11-15, which contain part of the uniquely Matthean story of guards set at the tomb to prevent the body of Jesus from being stolen, had been questioned long before the time of Réville.[146]

According to Meijboom, one of Réville's distinctive contributions to the on-going discussion of the Synoptic Problem was the articulation of new criteria for distinguishing earlier from later traditions. Meijboom quoted Réville as follows:

> The irrefutable thesis is that, when two narratives agree in general, the most obscure and contradictory account betrays the closest familiarity with the narrated facts. After a certain lapse of time objections had to be raised from a theological or pragmatic point of view. The relation of the original to the corrected narrative becomes then that of text to paraphrase, of the unclear passage to its interpretation, of the reading to the gloss, of the prolix enumeration to its resumeé—in any case the obscure passage is the oldest and cannot be held to have been derived from the clear passage.[147]

These criteria, outlined by Réville in 1862, may be compared with those of Ernest de Witt Burton, outlined in 1904.[148] Burton regarded the following as evidences of the secondary character of one narrative when compared to another:

> (1) manifest misunderstanding of what stands in one document on the part of the writer of the other; (2) insertion by one writer of material not in the other, and clearly interrupting the course of thought or symmetry of plan in the other; (3) clear omission from one document of matter which was in the other, the omission of which destroys the connection; (4) insertion of matter the motive for which can be clearly seen in the light of the author's general aim, while no motive can be discovered for its omission by the author if he had it in his source; (5) vice versa omission of matter traceable

146. See, for instance, Friedrich Andreas Stroth, 'Von Interpolationen im Evangelium Matthaei', in *Repertorium für biblische und morgenländische Literatur* 9 (ed. J.G. Eichhorn; Leipzig; Weidmann, 1781), pp. 99-156 and my discussion of Stroth in 'Chapters in the History of the Linguistic Argument for Solving the Synoptic Problem', in Sanders (ed.), *Jesus, the Gospels and the Church*, pp. 54-56.

147. Réville, *Matthieu*, pp. 129ff. as quoted in Meijboom and Kiwiet, *History and Critique*, p. 58.

148. Ernest de Witt Burton, *Some Principles of Literary Criticism and their Application to the Synoptic Problem* (Chicago: University of Chicago Press, 1904), reprinted from vol. 5 of the Decennial Publications of the University of Chicago.

to the motive natural to the writer when the insertion (of the same matter in the other Gospel) could not thus be accounted for; (6) alterations of other kinds which confirm the matter to the general method or tendency of the author.[149]

From 1880 until his death in 1906, Réville was professor of the history of religions in the Collège de France in Paris where, after 1884, he also served as the president of the section for religious sciences in the Ecole Pratique des Hautes Etudes.[150] Therefore, after 1880 and perhaps as early as his departure from Rotterdam in 1873, Réville's interests were focused away from New Testament studies generally and synoptic source criticism more specifically and toward the study of the world's religions.[151]

149. Burton, *Principles*, as quoted in Farmer, *Synoptic Problem*, p. 229. I have not yet had direct access to either Réville or Burton. It would be interesting to see if Burton knew Réville's work.

150. I have yet to discover what Réville was doing between 1873, when he left the Waloon Church in Rotterdam, and 1880, when he took up his duties at the Ecole Pratique des Hautes Etudes in Paris. His farewell sermon to the Church in Rotterdam in 1873, cited above, could be revealing.

151. There is a trail leading from Réville that I cannot follow now, but I mention here only some of its scenery. First Réville wrote a book about Theodore Parker (1810–1860), a liberal clergyman, scholar, and leader of the abolitionist movement in the United States. See Albert Réville, *Théodore Parker: sa vie et ses oeures: Un chapitre de l'histoire de l'abolition de l'esclavage aux Etats-Unis* (Paris: C. Reinwald; J. Cherbuliez, 1865). This book appeared in English translation in 1865 as *The Life and writings of Theodore Parker. By Albert Réville* (Authorized translation, revised by the author; London: Simpkin, Marshall & Co., 1865), and in German translation in 1867 as *Theodor Parker, sein Leben und Wirken: Ein Kapitel aus der Geschichte der Aufhebung der Scaverei in den Vereinigten Staaten...*(trans. Paul Deussen; Paris: Reinwald, 1867). A second English edition appeared in 1877, published by the British and Foreign Unitarian Association. Part of Parker's work for abolition included speeches relating to the state of Nebraska being a free state, rather than a slave state. And among Parker's theological work was an English translation of de Wette's *Introduction to the Old Testament*. See *A Critical and Historical Introduction to the Canonical Scriptures of the Old Testament: From the German of Wilhelm Martin Leberecht DeWette. Translated and Enlarged by Theodore Parker* (Boston: C.C. Little & J. Brown, 1843). De Wette, of course, was an advocate of a modified form of the Griesbach Hypothesis. Parker's theological writings also included a response to Strauss's first *Life of Jesus*. See *The Critical and Miscellaneous Writings of Theodore Parker* (Boston: J. Munroe & Co., 1843). Perhaps this is sufficient information to allow someone to see why I, a liberal clergyman with a social conscience, a teacher-scholar, an advocate of the Two Gospel

Michel Nicolas (1810–1886)

Michel Nicolas was a fifth member of the Strasbourg school and the last to be discussed here. Born on 22 May 1810 in Nimes, Nicolas studied theology in the city of Geneva (1827–1832) and in Germany (1832–1834). Early in life he also published two Strasbourg theses; one for his Bachelors degree in theology, on the form of Hebrew poetry (1833) and one on Hermeneutics (1838).[152] Nicolas briefly served as assistant pastor in Bordeaux, then, as pastor in Metz (1835–1838). From Metz, Nicolas returned to southern France in 1939 where he was appointed to the philosophy faculty at Montauban.[153] In 1860 he moved from philosophy to theology, where his interests included issues of introduction and Church history. Nicolas remained at Montauban from 1839 until his death on 28 July 1886.

While at Montauban, Nicolas published an introduction to the study of the history of philosophy (1849–1850) and essays on philosophy and religious history (1863).[154] In 1858, he began to introduce German Biblical criticism to French readers of the *Revue germanique*, with an article in the first volume of that literary journal.[155] In this same journal, in 1859, he discussed critical works on the formation of

or Neo-Griesbach Hypothesis, a current resident of the state of Nebraska and the author of this paper, might be interested in following this trail from a member of the Strasbourg School to Theodore Parker.

152. Michel Nicolas, *Dissertation sur la forme de la poésie hébraïque* (dissertation for the BTh at Strasbourg, University of France; Strasbourg: Silbermann, 1833); *Essai d'herménitique* (Thesis; Strasbourg: G. Silbermann, 1838).

153. At the moment, I do not think Réville would have included Nicolas among those 'four or five ignoramuses' at Montauban between 1856 and 1861 who 'set themselves up to lay down the law for the world'. Réville could have read Nicolas's work both in the Strasbourg *Revue de théologie* and in the *Revue germanique* to which they both contributed. I assume that Réville would have appreciated the work of Nicolas which had a liberal bent as did that of Réville, but Réville's attitude toward Nicolas is another matter that remains for further research.

154. *Introduction à l'étude de l'histoire de la philosophie par Michel Nicolas* (Paris: Librairie philosophique de Ladrange, 1849–1850); *Essais de philosophie et d'histoire religieuse* (Paris: M. Lévy frères, 1863).

155. Michel Nicolas, 'De la critique biblique in Allemagne', *RG* 2/5 (1858), pp. 242-75.

the Pentateuch.[156] In 1860, this journal carried articles by Nicolas on German Biblical criticism of the Prophets[157] and, in 1862, he published two articles on the formation of the canon of the New Testament.[158] These were followed by a series of four critical studies of the gospels, the last two of which focused on the Gospel of John (1862–1863).[159]

In 1860, Nicolas published a volume on selected Jewish ideas in the first two centuries before the common era.[160] His interest in this range of issues, however, had already been expressed several years earlier through a series of articles for the *Revue de théologie*, the first of which had appeared in 1856.[161] After 1860, Nicolas brought out two collections of critical essays on the Bible, beginning with a volume dedicated to Old Testament studies, in 1862, and followed by a collection of New Testament studies, in 1864.[162] The former volume included some of Nicolas's earlier essays that had appeared in the *Revue germanique*.

In his *Etudes critiques sur la Bible, Ancien Testament* of 1862, Nicolas is said to have provided essays 'in the Graf-Wellhausen spirit'. This biographical note should probably be corrected to read 'in the *Reuss* spirit', since both Nicolas and Graf were students of Eduard Reuss. But it was in Nicolas's companion volume of 1866, *Etudes*

156. Michel Nicolas, 'Des travaux critiques sur la formation du Pentateuque', *RG* 6/4 (1859), pp. 5-31.

157. Michel Nicolas, 'La critique biblique en Allemagne: Les Prophètes (first article)', *RG* 10/6 (1860), pp. 497-533; (second article) 11/7 (1860), pp. 52-88.

158. Michel Nicolas, 'De la formation du canon du Nouveau Testament', *RG* 16/3 (1861), pp. 321-49 (first article); 16/4 (1861), pp. 481-522 (second article).

159. Michel Nicolas, 'Etudes critiques sur les Evangiles', *RG* 23/1 (1 September, 1862), pp. 5-33 (first article); 24/1 (1 December, 1862), pp. 5-48 (second article); 'Etudes critiques sur les Evangiles: l'Evangile de saint Jean', *RG* 25/2 (1 April, 1863), pp. 255-74; continued in 26/1 (1 June, 1863), pp. 43-67.

160. Michel Nicolas, *Des doctrines religieuses des Juifs pendant les deux siècles anterieurs à l'ère chrétienne* (Paris: M. Lévy frères, 1860, 1867²).

161. Michel Nicolas, 'De l'origine et de la forme des croyances apocalyptiques chez les Juifs', *RTP* 11 (1856), pp. 193-216; 'De l'origine de la doctrine du Logos chez les Juifs', *RTP* 12 (1856), pp. 339-62, 'De l'origine des doctrines de l'immortalité de l'ame et de la résurrection des corps chez les Juifs', *RTP* 14 (1857), pp. 356-77; 'De la doctrine de Dieu chez les Juifs pendant les deux siècles antérieurs à l'ère chrétienne', *NRT* (deuxième serie) 3 (1859), pp. 49-62; 'Les Thérapeutes', *RT* (troisième série) 6 (1860), pp. 25ff.

162. Michel Nicolas, *Etudes critiques sur la Bible, Ancien Testament* (Paris: M. Lévy frères, 1862); *Etudes critiques sur la Bible, Nouveau Testament* (Paris: M. Lévy, 1864). Includes two articles previously published in *RG*.

critiques sur la Bible, Nouveau Testament that Nicolas made contributions to the discussion of the Synoptic Problem.[163] Like Reuss and Réville, Nicolas also reconstructed a version of Mark different from canonical Mark in order to explain data within the synoptic gospels that were anomalous for an unmodified theory of Markan priority. Nicolas argued that the author of canonical Mark had used this earlier form of Mark and other special sources in composing his gospel. In addition to this early form of Mark, the author of canonical Mark had utilized a second source for Mk 6.45–8.26 and a third source for the Markan passion narrative, Mark 14–16. Nicolas postulated yet a fourth source from which the author of canonical Mark had got the miracle stories now found in canonical Mk 7.31-37 and 8.22-26.

The author of Matthew, in Nicolas's view, also made use of the early form of Mark in constructing his gospel. In addition to this early form of Mark, Matthew also used the passion narrative source, now found in Mk 14.1–16.8. Further, according to Nicolas, Matthew had also utilized Mark's source for Mark 6.45–8.26. The early form of Mark which Matthew utilized did not include the miracle stories of canonical Mk 7.31-37 and 8.22-26, so Matthew did not omit them. He just did not ever have access to them, in Nicolas's view.

Like Reuss and Réville, Nicolas also believed that the absence of Mark's literary characteristics from the parallel texts of the other synoptics suggested a later date for these parts of canonical Mark. According to Meijboom, Nicolas tried to avoid suggesting that any evangelist omitted sections from his source material.

Following the publication of his collection of essays on the New Testament, Nicolas went on to publish studies of the apocryphal gospels (1866)[164] and the Apostles' Creed (1867),[165] before his interests

---

163. Again, for what I say about the details of Nicolas's book, I am dependent upon Meijboom and Kiwiet, *History and Critique*, pp. 61-63.

164. Michel Nicolas, *Etudes sur les évangiles apocryphes* (Paris: Michel Lévy frères, 1866); cf. 'Des origines du gnosticism', *NRT* (deuxième série) 5 (1860), pp. 324-51; 7 (1861), pp. 65-88.

165. Michel Nicolas, *Le symbole des apôtres: Essais historiques* (Paris: M. Lévy frères, 1867); cf. 'Le Symbole des Apôtres', *RM* 32/1 (1 January, 1865), pp. 5-30 (first article); *RM* 33/3 (1 June, 1865), pp. 428-51 (second article); 'La résurrection des corps et l'immortalité de l'ame', *RM* 36/1 (1 February, 1866), pp. 290-304; 'De la formation des dogmes Chrétiens (première partie)', *RM* 42/2 (1 August, 1867), pp. 277-96.

returned to the history of his native region in southern France.[166] Like
other members of the Strasbourg school, Nicolas's interests seem to
have moved away from the synoptic gospels sometime in the mid-
1860s.

Joseph Ernest Renan (1823–1892)

Joseph Ernest Renan's life is probably better known than those of the
other scholars reviewed above and he was not a member of the
Strasbourg school, so I will not spend time rehearsing his life here.
Schweitzer devoted an entire chapter to Renan's life and work[167] and
Renan's most famous book, *La Vie de Jésus*,[168] also needs no intro-
duction. All that I wish to note here is the fact that Renan began this
famous book of 1863 with an introductory chapter, 'In Which the
Sources of this History are Principally Treated.' Within that chapter,
Renan included the following note:

> The plan followed in this history has prevented the introduction into the
> text of long critical dissertations upon controverted points. A continuous
> system of notes enables the reader to verify from the authorities all the
> statements of the text. These notes are strictly limited to quotations from
> the primary sources; that is to say, the original passages upon which each
> assertion or conjecture rests. I know that for persons little accustomed to
> studies of this kind many other explanations would have been necessary.
> But it is not my practice to do over again what has been already done well.
> To cite only books written in French, those who will consult the following
> excellent writings will there find explained a number of points upon which
> I have been obliged to be very brief:
>   *Etudes Critiques sur l'Evangile de saint Matthieu*, par M. Albert
> Réville, pasteur de l'église Wallonne de Rotterdam.

---

166. Michel Nicolas, *Histoire littéraire de Nimes et de localités voisines qui
forment actuellement le département du Gard* (3 vols.; Nimes: Ballivet & Fabre,
1854); *Histoire des artistes: Peintres, sculpteurs, architectes et musiciens—
compositeurs nés dans le Département du Gard* (Nimes: Imp. Ballivet, 1859);
*Histoire de l'ancienne académie protestante de Montauban (1598–1659) et de
Puylaurens (1660–1685) publiée sous les auspices de la faculté de théologie
protestante de Montauban* (Montauban: E. Forestie, 1885).

167. Schweitzer, *Quest*, pp. 180-92.

168. Joseph Ernest Renan, *La vie de Jésus* (Paris: Michel Lévy frères, 1863); *The
Life of Jesus by Ernest Renan* (Introduction by John Haynes Holmes; Modern
Library; New York: Random House, 1927). All references to page numbers in
Renan's book are to this English translation.

Histoire de la théologie Chretienne au Siecle Apostolique, par M. Reuss, professeur à la Faculté de Théologie et au Séminaire Protestant de Strasbourg.

Des Doctrines Religieuses des Juifs pendant les Deux Siécles Antériers à l'Ere Chrétienne, par M. Michel Nicolas, professeur à la Faculté de Théologie Protestante de Montauban.

Vie de Jésus par le Dr Strauss; traduite par M. Littré, Membre de l'Institut.

Revue de théologie et de Philosophie Chrétienne, publiée sous la direction de M. Colani de 1850 à 1857.—*Nouvelle Revue de théologie*, faisant suite à la precédénte depuis 1858.[169]

In footnotes, Renan gives full bibliographical information for each work, including names of publishing houses, dates and places of publication, but he also adds a substantive footnote on this same page. It reads:

> While this work was in the press, a book has appeared which I do not hesitate to add to this list, although I have not read it with the attention it deserves—*Les Evangiles*, par M. Gustave d'Eichthal. Première Partie: *Examen Critique et Comparatif des Trois Premiers Evangiles*. Paris, Hachette, 1863.[170]

A few pages later, the following sentence appears,

> Leaving aside all which belongs to the portraiture of the apostolic times, we will inquire only in what degree the data furnished by the Gospels may be employed in a history formed according to rational principles.[171]

In the footnote to this sentence, Renan wrote,

> Persons who wish to read more ample explanations, may consult, in addition to the work of M. Réville, previously cited, the writings of Reuss and *Scherer* in the *Revue d'Theologie*, vol. x, xi, xv; new series, ii, iii, iv; and that of Nicolas in the *Revue Germanique*, Sept. and Dec., 1862; April and June, 1863.[172]

In this note, Renan directed his readers to the articles by Reuss on the Synoptic Problem because these articles were contained in *Revue de théologie*, vols. 10, 11, 15 and 'new series' vol. 2.[173]

---

169. Renan, *The Life of Jesus*, pp. 27-28.
170. Renan, *The Life of Jesus*, p. 27 n. 1.
171. Renan, *The Life of Jesus*, p. 33.
172. Renan, *The Life of Jesus*, p. 33 n. 1, italics are mine.
173. Reuss's contributions to the '*Revue* vols. x, xi, xv and new series ii, iii, iv', included the following: 'Etudes comparatives sur les trois premiers évangiles au point de vue de leurs rapports d'origine et de dependance mutuelle', *RTP* 10 (1855),

Scherer's response to Reuss on the Synoptic Problem did not appear until 1861 in vol. 8 of the 'new series', but Scherer had published a series of 'Notes on the Synoptic Gospels' in 1859 in vols. 3 and 4 of the 'new series'. Renan might have had these articles by Scherer in mind here, although Scherer had also contributed a number of articles related to method in Biblical research within these volumes of the *Revue* that Renan might also have invited his readers to consult.[174]

The articles by Michel Nicolas to which Renan makes reference here must be his four 'Critical Studies on the Gospels', (1862–1863), because Nicolas published no other articles in these particular issues of *Revue germanique*.[175] It is interesting that Renan could refer to an article by Nicolas that was published as late as June of 1863 when Renan's own book was also published in 1863.

It is virtually certain that Renan wished to express his appreciation to these scholars for his indebtedness to their works and/or to marshal their authority for his own. Little did Renan know what a storm his book was going to cause. And little did he realize, that, for good or ill, the names of these scholars would be eternally linked with his most controversial work.

pp. 65-83, 11 (1855), pp. 163-88 and 15 (1857), pp. 1-32; 'Bibliographie des sciences bibliques', *RTP* 15 (1857), p. 262; 'Article de critique', *RTP* 10 (1855), p. 162; 'Nouvelles études comparatives sur les trois premiers évangiles', *NRT* 2 (1858), pp. 15-75; 'La Conférence de Jérusalem', *NRT* 2 (1858), pp. 324-49, and 3 (1859), pp. 62-93; 'Flavius Josèphe', *NRT* 4 (1859), pp. 253-320.

174. Scherer's contributions to the '*Revue*, vols. x, xi, xv and new series ii, iii, iv', included the following: 'La critique externe et la critique interne dans leur application au Nouveau Testament', *RTP* 10 (1855), pp. 129-52; 'De la formation du canon du Nouveau Testament', *RTP* 10 (1855), pp. 193-217; 'Due mouvement théologique en Angleterre', *RTP* 5 (1855), pp. 282-301; 'Etudes sur la première épitre de Paul aux Corinthiens', *RTP* 11 (1855), pp. 129-62; 'Les procédes de la critique interne', *RTP* 11 (1855), pp. 299-319; 'L'apologétique en Angleterre', *RTP* 11 (1855), pp. 321-42; 'De la dogmatique en Allemagne', *RTP* 11 (1855), pp. 358-64; 'Les épitres de Pierre', *RTP* 15 (1857), pp. 33-42; 'Quelques questions d'apologétique', *NRT* 2 (1858), pp. 103-26; 'Conversations théologiques (IV Montaigu) *NRT* 2 (1858), pp. 275-97; 'Notes sur les évangiles synoptiques', *NRT* 3 (1859), pp. 306-22, 371-84; 4 (1859), pp. 36-61, 65-78, 329-50; 'Le monothéisme sémitique', *NRT* 4 (1859), pp. 361-71.

175. Michel Nicolas, 'Etudes critiques sur les Evangiles', *RG* 23/1 (1 September, 1862), pp. 5-33 (first article); *RG* 24/1 (1 December, 1862), pp. 5-48 (second article); 'Etudes critiques sur les Evangiles: L'Evangile de saint Jean', *RG* 25/2 (1 April, 1863), pp. 255-74 and *RG* 26/1 (1 June, 1863), pp. 43-67.

To a degree at least, Renan's reputation, following the publication of his *Life of Jesus* in 1863 would be shared by the seven other scholars whom Renan had named in prominent places in the first chapter of this book—Colani, Reuss, Scherer, Réville, Nicolas, Strauss and d'Eichthal. Renan's references to the works of these seven scholars early in his book become even more prominent, given the fact that there are almost no other references to the secondary literature elsewhere in Renan's book. Renan not only provided the titles of scholarly works of these men. He also provided his readers with the professional affiliations of Nicolas, Réville, and Reuss. Of course, anyone who read the *Revue de théologie et de philosophie Chrétienne* would have been able to write to Colani, since his name, as journal editor, and the addresses of the journal's publishers in Strasbourg, Paris and Geneva were printed in every issue. Contributors to this journal, including Scherer, could probably also be contacted through the published house address.

The storms of responses that reached Renan from conservatives and liberals, rationalists and supernaturalists, the educated and the not so educated, must also have sometimes reached the desks of Colani, Reuss, Scherer, Réville, and Nicolas. Published responses to Renan came directly from members of the Strasbourg school in the persons of Réville,[176] Colani,[177] and Scherer.[178] Reuss made an indirect negative response, if Maurice Goguel's source is accurate.[179]

176. Albert Réville, 'La Vie de Jésus de M. Renan', *RG* 27/1 (1 December, 1863), pp. 577-624, and *La Vie de Jésus de Renan devant les orthodoxes et devant la critique* (Paris, 1864). One of Réville's responses to Renan was translated into Dutch as *Het leven van Jezus van Ernest Renan: Vedediging en kritiek* (trans. A.G. van Anarooij; Haarlem: A.C. Krueman, 1864). See also Réville's own, *Jésus de Nazareth: Etudes critiques sur les antécédents de l'histoire évangélique et la Vie de Jésus* (Paris, 1897, 1906²). Schweitzer (*Quest*, p. 189) says that Réville, in his review of Renan, 'claims recognition for Renan's services to criticism'.

177. Colani, 'La *Vie de Jésus* de M. Renan (1er article)', *RT* 1 (1863), pp. 369ff.; (2nd article), *RT* (1864), pp. 17-58.

178. Edmond Scherer and Athanase Coquerel the Younger, *Zwei französische Stimmen über Renans Leben Jesu: Ein Beitrag zur Kenntnis des französischen Protestantismus* (Regensburg, 1864). See also Scherer's 'Vie de Jésus', in *Mélanges d'histoire réligieuse* (Paris: Michel Lévy frères, 1864, 1865²), pp. 61-137. Schweitzer (*Quest*, p. 188) says that Scherer wrote five articles on Renan's book for *Le Temps*.

179. Maurice Goguel provides the following information: '"In the circle of the intimate friends of Reuss", we learn from A. Causse (review of *La bible de Reuss et la renaissance des études d'histoire réligieuse en France* [Cahiers de la Revue

Colani's review for the *Revue de théologie* described Renan's picture of Jesus and the Strasbourg school's judgment about Renan's book in the following words.

> This is not the Christ of history, the Christ of the Synoptics, but the Christ of the Fourth Gospel, though without His metaphysical halo, and painted over with a brush which has been dipped in the melancholy blue of modern poetry, in the rose of the eighteenth-century idyll, in the grey of a moral philosophy which seems to be derived from La Rochefoucauld...In expressing this opinion, I believe I am speaking in the name of those who belong to what is known as the new Protestant theology, or the Strasbourg school. We opened M. Renan's book with sympathetic interest; we closed it with deep disappointment.[180]

Whether this comment was sufficient to distance Colani, if not others within the Strasbourg school, from Renan requires further research. For the moment, however, we can refer to Albert Schweitzer's conclusion about this matter.

> The Strasbourg school had good cause to complain of Renan, for he had trampled their growing crops. They had just begun to arouse some interest, and slowly and surely to exercise an influence upon the whole spiritual life of France. [Charles Augustin] Sainte-Beuve [1804–1868] had called attention to the work of Reuss, Colani, Réville, and Scherer. Others of the school were Michel Nicolas of Montauban and Gustave d'Eichthal. [Auguste] Nefftzer, the editor of the *Temps*, who was at the same time a prophet of coming political events, defended their cause in the Parisian literary world. The *Revue germanique* of that period, the influence of which upon French literature can hardly be over-estimated, was their sworn ally. Then came Renan and threw public opinion into a ferment of excitement. Everything in the nature of criticism, and of progress in religious thought,

d'histoire et de philosophie religieuses, 19]; Paris: Felix Alcan, 1929), in *Revue d'histoire et de philosophie religieuses* 10 [1929], p. 27 n. 64), people did not speak very kindly of Renan, and he quotes a passage from a letter of Scherer to Reuss of March 22, 1886, which passes a very severe criticism on the author of the *Vie de Jésus*. "We are assured", he says, "that Reuss quoted it more than once with great approval"' (Maurice Goguel, *The Life of Jesus* [trans. Olive Wyon; New York: Macmillan, 1945], pp. 53 n. 1). It appears that Goguel is, in turn, quoting himself in this footnote, *Critique et histoire: A propos de la Vie de Jésus* (Paris, 1928), pp. 20ff. So what we seem to have is Goguel quoting Goguel quoting A. Causse who quoted Scherer's letter to Reuss and who reported on Reuss's use of Scherer's letter (from oral tradition?).

180. Colani, 'Examen de la vie de Jésus de M. Renan', *RT* (issued separately, Strasbourg–Paris, 1864, 74 pp.), as cited and quoted by Schweitzer, *Quest*, p. 189.

was associated with his name, and was thereby discredited. By his untimely and over-easy popularisation of the ideas of the critical school he ruined their quiet work. The excitement roused by his book swept away all that had been done by those noble and lofty spirits, who now found themselves involved in a struggle with the outraged orthodoxy of Paris, and were hard put to it to defend themselves. Even down to the present day (Schweitzer was writing in 1906), Renan's work forms the greatest hindrance to any serious advance in French religious thought.[181]

Eduard Reuss and Heinrich Julius Holtzmann's Call to Strasbourg[182]

Heinrich Julius Holtzmann (1832–1910), of course, was not a member of what Colani called 'the Strasbourg School' in his response to Renan's *Life of Jesus* in 1864. But Holtzmann did join Eduard Reuss on the theological faculty of the Kaiser-Wilhelm Universität at Strasbourg in 1874. It is, therefore, appropriate to discuss Holtzmann along with other scholars related to the university at Strasbourg who contributed to the history of the discussion of gospel origins. In fact, Holtzmann is probably the best known contributor to the discussion of Synoptic Problems who ever taught at Strasbourg.

Born at Karlsruhe in Germany on 17 May 1832, Heinrich Julius Holtzmann was educated at the universities of Heidelberg and Berlin. Following his formal education, he served as a pastor in Baden from 1854–1857. In 1858, having been a student there himself, Holtzmann became a *privat-dozent* at Heidelberg. In 1861, he became extraordinary professor and, in 1865, was advanced to the rank of professor. In the period between his last two promotions at Heidelberg (1861–1865), Holtzmann published his most famous contribution to the discussion of the Synoptic Problem, *Die synoptischen Evangelien* (1863).[183]

A year earlier, in 1862, Eduard Zeller had moved for a second time to a position in philosophy; this time, to Heidelberg, where he became a faculty colleague of Holtzmann. And these two remained together at Heidelberg from 1862, when Zeller arrived, until 1872, when Zeller

181. Schweitzer, *Quest*, pp. 189-90.

182. See the discussion of Holtzmann in Meijboom and Kiwiet, *History and Critique*, pp. 71-81. Also see the discussions of Holtzmann in Farmer, *Synoptic Problem*, pp. 36-47; Stoldt, *History and Criticism*, pp. 69-93 and Peabody, 'Chapters', in Sanders (ed.), *Jesus the Gospels and the Church*, pp. 57-58.

183. Heinrich Julius Holtzmann, *Die synoptischen Evangelien: Ihr Ursprung und geschichtlicher Charakter* (Leipzig: W. Engelmann, 1863).

accepted a call to the university in Berlin.

I have argued elsewhere that Holtzmann, in his famous book of 1863, had misunderstood Zeller's method for making the linguistic characteristics of the synoptic evangelists of service in solving the Synoptic Problem. I argued further that Holtzmann also misused the linguistic characteristics that Zeller had compiled for one of his contributions to the *Theologische Jahrbücher* in 1843.[184] How could Holtzmann have made this mistake with Zeller right there on the Heidelberg faculty with him? The answer to that question, if it can be provided, would contribute a significant note in the history of the demise of the Griesbach Hypothesis and the rise of Markan priority in the last decades of the nineteenth century.

There is also evidence within Holtzmann's book of 1863 of his knowledge of work done by members of the Strasbourg school including works by Réville, Reuss and Scherer.[185] In his foreword, Holtzmann noted the work of Albert Réville on the Gospel of Matthew.[186] References to Reuss are found throughout Holtzmann's work and many of the references to Scherer are made in contexts where the views of

184. Peabody, 'Chapters', in Sanders (ed.), *Jesus, the Gospels and the Church*, pp. 47-68; Eduard Zeller, 'Studien zur neutestamentlichen Theologie 4: Vergleichende Uebersicht über den Wörtervorrath der neutestamentlichen Schriftsteller', *TJ* 2/2 (1843), pp. 443-543; Holtzmann's major response to Zeller is to be found in *Die synoptischen Evangelien*, pp. 346-58, following section XV, entitled 'Gegen die Griesbach'sche Hypothese'. Holtzmann's response to Zeller is probably to be understood as a continuing counter to the Griesbach Hypothesis since Zeller used his linguistic argument and the linguistic characteristics of the several synoptic evangelists to demonstrate, in balance, the validity of that hypothesis. Chapter 4 of Holtzmann's book, entitled 'Proben', concludes with two further sections. These are (1) 'XVII. Einfluss des Styls von L auf Matthäus und Lucas' in which Holtzmann refers only to the work of Lekebusch, and (2) the last section, entitled 'XVIII. Neutrales Gebiet'. There Holtzmann only refers to the work of Gersdorf, who consulted with Griesbach in preparing his book that isolated literary characteristics of the synoptic gospels. Footnotes to works by Credner and Weiss are also found within this concluding section to ch. 4 of Holtzmann's book.

185. Bo Reicke needs to be corrected, at least in the case of Holtzmann, when he writes, 'In the eyes of many academic citizens there was nothing like a German professor. An interesting expression of this self-confidence is the fact that all scholarly contributions to the synoptic question, published in Germany during the period 1830–1870, were restricted to a discussion with German colleagues'. See Reicke, 'From Strauss to Holtzmann and Meijboom', pp. 4-5.

186. Holtzmann, *Die synoptischen Evangelien*, xiii.

Reuss are being discussed by Holtzmann. Like Reuss, Holtzmann reconstructed an Ur-Marcus in order to explain data that were anomalous for his two-source theory. Scherer was more reluctant to reconstruct hypothetical sources.

Although Scherer's response to Reuss, discussed above, was published in 1861 and thus was available to Holtzmann prior to 1863, I did not find any reference to that article by Scherer in Holtzmann's book of 1863. Rather, Holtzmann's notes on Scherer's work seem to be limited to his articles on the synoptic gospels that are found in earlier issues of the *Nouvelle Revue*, specifically volumes III and IV of 1859. Did Holtzmann somehow miss Scherer's explicit response to Reuss of 1861 or did Holtzmann intentionally ignore it?

Holtzmann himself, like Reuss, gave evidence at the outset of his book of 1863 that canonical Mark could not have been the original gospel used by Matthew and Luke.[187] As the last of five sets of evidence for coming to this conclusion, Holtzmann notes that 'Matthew and Luke are united, often in the same places in the narrative, in excluding individual formulas and sentences, with which the historical report of Mark is woven together (*unterwebt*)'.[188] If Holtzmann had paid attention to Scherer's response to Reuss, this would have been an appropriate context to footnote it.

Zeller's work on the linguistic characteristics of the synoptic evangelists was certainly more detailed than Scherer's. And Holtzmann did give a considerable, though sometimes inappropriate, response to Zeller. But Zeller had not described the facts of synoptic relationships in quite the way that Scherer did. Specifically, Zeller did not observe that either the linking formulas (Reuss and Scherer) or the transition formulas (Scherer) are missing from the parallel texts of Luke (Reuss and Scherer) and Matthew (Scherer).

Two years after Zeller accepted a call to Berlin (1872), Holtzmann accepted a call to Strasbourg to become professor of New Testament exegesis (1874). Presumably this was the same position at Strasbourg that Ritschl had refused a few years earlier. If one compares the environment for the study of theology in Strasbourg in 1874 to what that environment was like between 1830 and 1870, much had changed. Siege had been laid to the city of Strasbourg by the Prussian army in 1870 and the city surrendered in the same year. A peace treaty was

---

187. Holtzmann, *Die synoptischen Evangelien*, pp. 60-63.
188. Holtzmann, *Die synoptischen Evangelien*, pp. 62-63.

negotiated a year later, but the Germans did not completely leave French territory until 1873. As a part of the post-war settlement, the city of Strasbourg and the whole of Alsace-Lorraine was ceded to Germany. And with that, of course, the control of the university in Strasbourg also changed from French to German hands.

Of the members of the theological faculty at Strasbourg prior to the war, only five remained after the war. Eduard Reuss was among them. He was the only Biblical scholar who kept his position through the change of administrations and, by 1872, Reuss had become dean of the theological faculty at Strasbourg. Four years after he arrived in Strasbourg, in 1878, Holtzmann also became an administrator.[189]

Reuss published his fourth and final article in his series on the Synoptic Problem in Colani's journal in 1858. Between that time and 1874, when Holtzmann joined Reuss on the faculty in Strasbourg, at least three other events took place that may have effected Holtzmann's call.

The first was the publication of Renan's *Life of Jesus* in 1863 and the subsequent controversies that this book provoked throughout Europe. As was suggested above, the appearance of Reuss's name within the highly selective list of secondary works at the beginning of Renan's *Life of Jesus* may well have got Reuss caught up in a controversy from which he would have been glad to have been extricated.

The second was the publication of Holtzmann's own discussion of the Synoptic Problem, in the same year that Renan's book appeared, 1863. The storm created by Renan's *Life of Jesus* after 1863, particularly in the wake of Strauss's first *Life of Jesus* of 1835 and in combination with Strauss's second *Life of Jesus* in 1864, must have kept some scholars from giving too much detailed attention to Holtzmann's book of 1863.

Although Renan's *Life of Jesus* received a two-part review by Colani in the volumes of the Strasbourg *Revue de théologie* for 1863–1864, Holtzmann's 1863 study of the synoptic gospels was never reviewed in that journal.[190] The only work by Holtzmann that was ever reviewed in this Strasbourg journal was a work that Holtzmann co-authored and that

---

189. Heinrich Julius Holtzmann, *Über fortschritte und rückschritte der theologie unseres jahrhunderts und über ihre stellung zur gesammtheit der wissenschaften* (*Rede gehalten am 1. mai 1878 bei übernahme des rectorats der Kaiser-Wilhelm-Universität Strasbourg, 1878*).

190. See 'La *Vie de Jésus* de M. Renan (1er article), par M. Colani', *RT* (troisième série) 1 (1863), pp. 369ff. and '(2e article)', 2 (1864), pp. 17ff.

appeared in 1866.[191] Holtzmann's own contribution to the Strasbourg *Revue* seems to have been limited to a single article on the Acts of the Apostles, published in 1868, just a year before this journal ceased publication.[192]

The third event that may have effected Holtzmann's call to Strasbourg was Albrecht Ritschl's refusal to accept a call to Strasbourg between 1870 and 1874. Had Ritschl not declined this call, it is probable that Holtzmann would not have become part of the faculty at Strasbourg, at least not as early in his career as he did.

I do not know why Holtzmann was called to the Kaiser-Wilhelm-Universität in Strasbourg in 1874. Perhaps I will never know. But I do know that Holtzmann was called and, unlike Ritschl before him, he accepted the call. It is difficult to imagine that Reuss would not have had an influential voice in Holtzmann's call to Strasbourg. Reuss was, at the time of Holtzmann's call, the senior Biblical scholar at Strasbourg and the only Biblical scholar who remained at Strasbourg through the transition of 1870–1872. Not only did Reuss keep his academic post at Strasbourg when his colleague, Timothée Colani, was losing his, he even became a dean within the reconstituted German state university.

Reuss might have thought that, with someone else in synoptic studies at Strasbourg, he could become further removed from the controversy that was created by the association of his name with Renan's *Life of Jesus*. It may also be remembered that Reuss was made professor of Old Testament at the seminary in Strasbourg in 1864. What, if anything, did this new title have to do with Reuss's involvement in the Renan controversy?

But whatever those realities might have been, someone else on the Strasbourg faculty in synoptic studies would allow Reuss to redirect his attention to what seems to have been his first love, the Old Testament. He would finally be able to write the Old Testament companion volume to his earlier *History of the Sacred Scriptures of the New Testament*, published in 1842. Reuss is said to have 'projected his work on the history of the Old Testament as early as 1834', as much as eight years before the companion volume on the New Testament was published

191. Bluntschli, Holtzmann, Rothe and Schenke, *Aufgaben des Christenthums in der Gegenwart* (M. Schwalb, reviewer]) (Elberfeld, 1866), *RT* (troisième série) 5 (1867), pp. 108ff.

192. 'Les Actes des Apôtres, par M. Holtzmann', *RT* (troisième série) 6 (1868), pp. 283ff.

(1842). But it was only in 1881, four years after Holtzmann arrived in Strasbourg, that the first edition of Reuss's *History of the Sacred Scriptures of the Old Testament* finally appeared.[193]

Prior to Colani's departure from Strasbourg in 1870, Reuss contributed regularly to the Strasbourg *Revue*, including of course his series of articles on the synoptic gospels that were reviewed above. He published books on the history of Christian Theology in the Apostolic Period (1852),[194] on the Book of Hebrews (1862)[195] and on the history of the Christian canon (1863).[196] He wrote studies about literary and critical fragments relative to French translations of the Bible (1866) that complemented an earlier work on German translations (1855).[197] He published a booklet on Job (1869)[198] and contributed to an edition of Calvin's *Institutes of the Christian Religion* (1869)[199] and to a complete edition of Calvin's works (1863–1900).[200]

With the exceptions of translations of books of the Bible, critical editions of it and a history of the canonization of the Bible, Reuss does not seem to have worked much in the area of New Testament studies after 1863. Later editions of Reuss's earlier works on New Testament issues did, however, appear after 1863.

In the interim between Colani's departure (1870) and Holtzmann's

---

193. Eduard Reuss, *Die Geschichte der Heiligen Schriften Alten Testaments* (Braunschweig: C.A. Schwetschke, 1880, 1890²).

194. Eduard Reuss, *Histoire de la theologie chrétienne au siècle apostolique* (2 vols.; Strasbourg: Treuttel & Wurtz, 1852, 1860², 1864³, 1864⁴).

195. Eduard Reuss, *L'Epître aux Hébreux: Essai d'une introduction nouvelle* (Strasbourg: Treuttel & Wurtz, 1862).

196. Eduard Reuss, *Histoire du canon des Saintes-Ecritures dans l'eglise Chretienne* (Strasbourg: Treuttel & Wurtz, 1863²).

197. Eduard Reuss, *Die deutsche Historienbibel vor der Erfindung des Bücherdrucks* (Jena: F. Mauke, 1855).

198. Eduard Reuss, *Das Buch Hiob: Vortrag gehalten in der Nicolaikirche, den 8 Februar 1869* (Strasbourg: Treuttel & Wurtz, 1869).

199. Eduard Reuss, Johann Wilhelm Baum, Eduard Cunitz (eds.), *Ioannis Calvini Institutio religionis christianae; ad fidem editionum principum et authenticarum additis prolegomenis literariis et annotationibus criticis triplici forma ediderunt* (2 vols.; Braunschweig: C.A. Schwetschke, 1869).

200. Wilhelm Baldensperger, *et al.* (eds.), *Ioannis Calvini Opera quae supersunt omnia: Ad fidem editionum principum et authenticarum ex parte etiam codicum manu scriptorum, additis prolegomenis literariis, annotationibus criticis, annalibus Calvinianis indicibusque novis et copiosissmis* (59 vols.; Corpus reformatorum vols. 29-87; Braunschweig: C.A. Schwetschke & filium, 1863–1900).

arrival in Strasbourg (1874), my record of Reuss's publications gets slim. This is not surprising since the university had experienced the effects of a war during this period and had then gone through a major reorganization under the control of a new government. If Reuss became a dean under this new administration, he would, no doubt, have had heavy administrative duties in the years 1871–1872, and further administrative duties after that.

After Holtzmann arrived in Strasbourg, Reuss seems to have concentrated on the Old Testament. After 1874, in addition to Reuss's companion volume on *The History of the Sacred Books of the Old Testament* (1881), Reuss made a new French translation of the Bible (1874–1879), gave speeches on the academic study of theology (1878, 1879),[201] and wrote on the Song of Songs (1879)[202] and the Pentateuch (1879).[203] After Reuss took emeritus status at Strasbourg (1888), he published a list of codices of the gospels (1889).[204]

Reuss died on 15 April 1891, still in Strasbourg where he was born and where he had lived and worked for most of his life. Following his death, Holtzmann wrote a biographical sketch of Reuss for the *Protestantische Kirchenzeitung*.[205] Reuss's translations of books of the Bible accompanied by critical studies (1892–1894)[206] and an edition of Calvin's Bible by Reuss (1897)[207] were published posthumously.

In 1904, when Holtzmann himself accepted emeritus status at Strasbourg, he used some of his time to assist K. Budde in editing

201. Eduard Reuss, *Reden an Theologie studirende im akademischen Kreise gehalten* (Leipzig: Breitkopf & Härtel [1878]) (Braunschweig: C.A. Schwetschke & Sohn, 1879²).

202. Eduard Reuss, *Le Cantique des Cantiques dit de Salomon: Recueil de poesies érotiques traduites de l'Hébreu avec introduction et commentaire* (Paris: Librairie Sandoz & Fischbacher, 1879).

203. Eduard Reuss, *L'histoire saint et la loi: introduction, critique au Pentateuque et au livre de Josué* (Paris: Librairie Sandoz & Fischbacher, 1879).

204. Eduard Reuss, *Notitia codicis quattuor Evangeliorum graeci membranacei viris doctis hucusque incogniti*...(Typis academicis; Cambridge: C.J. Clay & filii [1889]).

205. (1891), pp. 385-93.

206. Eduard Reuss, *Das alte Testament: Übersetzt, eingeleitet und erläutert* (7 vols.; Braunschweig: C.A. Schwetschke, 1892–1894).

207. Jean Calvin, *La Bible Française de Calvin: Livres des Saintes Ecritures traduits ou revises par le reformateur tirés de ses œuvres et accompagnés de variantes d'autres versions du 16ème siècle* (ed. Eduard Reuss; Paris: Librairie Fischbacher, 1897).

and publishing Reuss's correspondence with Graf.[208] Holtzmann died in 1910.

Albert Schweitzer's Evaluation of Holtzmann's Work

Like Colani and Reuss, Albert Schweitzer (1875–1965) was also once a student at the University of Strasbourg who later became a member of its faculty. It was, in fact, while Schweitzer was teaching at Strasbourg as one of Holtzmann's younger colleagues that he came to write his famous book, *Von Reimarus zu Wrede: Eine Geschichte der Leben-Jesu-Forschung.*

Students of the history of the discussion of the Synoptic Problem sometimes take note of the following comment by Schweitzer about Holtzmann's source theory within that book.

> The [Two-Source] hypothesis has a literary existence, indeed it is carried by Holtzmann to such a degree of demonstration that it can no longer be called a mere hypothesis,...[209]

This quotation, taken out of context, might give the impression that Schweitzer was convinced in 1906 of the correctness of the Two Source Hypothesis as worked out by Holtzmann.[210] It should be noted, however, that Schweitzer never made reference, so far as I can tell, to the Two Sources, A (Ur-Marcus) and L (Ur-Matthäus), that were reconstructed by Holtzmann in chapters two and three of his famous book of 1863.[211] Schweizer typically preferred to make reference to 'the two

---

208. *Briefwechsel mit...K.H. Graf* (Giessen, 1904).

209. See, for instance, a similar excerpt from Schweitzer (*Quest*) in Hans-Herbert Stoldt, *Geschichte und Kritik der Markushypothese* (Göttingen: Vandenhoeck & Ruprecht, 1977); *History and Criticism of the Marcan Hypothesis* (trans. Donald L. Niewyk; Macon, GA: Mercer University Press; Edinburgh: T. & T. Clark, 1980), p. 69. See Albert Schweitzer, *Von Reimarus zu Wrede: Eine Geschichte der Leben-Jesu-Forschung* (Tübingen: J.C.B. Mohr [Paul Siebeck], 1906) (*The Quest of the Historical Jesus: A Critical Study of its Progress from Reimarus to Wrede* [trans. W. Montgomery, first printing in England by A.C. Black, 1910; repr. edn, New York: Macmillan, 1948], p. 202). All quotations from this work by Schweitzer within this paper are from this English translation.

210. Heinrich Julius Holtzmann, *Die synoptischen Evangelien: Ihr Ursprung und geschichtlicher Charakter* (Leipzig: W. Engelmann, 1863).

211. Holtzmann, *Die synoptischen Evangelien*, pp. 67-242.

oldest gospels'. In his view, these were the gospels of Matthew and Mark.[212] Schweitzer's point also becomes clearer when the whole of the relevant sentence is quoted.

> ...but it does not succeed in winning an assured position in the critical study of the Life of Jesus. It is common-land not yet taken into civilization.

With this more extensive quotation from Schweitzer, one might also compare a few words from Schweitzer's first chapter on 'The Problem' in Life of Jesus research. This passage would also seem to be important in evaluating Schweitzer's attitude toward the Markan Hypothesis in 1906 and Holtzmann's role in advancing it. In his first chapter, Schweitzer wrote

> Reimarus had drawn attention to the contemporary eschatological views; Hase, in his first Life of Jesus (1829), had sought to trace a development in the self-consciousness of Jesus.
>
> But on this point a clear view was impossible, because all the students of the subject were still basing their operations upon the harmony of the Synoptics and the Fourth Gospel; which means that they had not so far felt the need of a historically intelligible outline of the life of Jesus. Here, too, Strauss was the lightbringer. But the transient illumination [of Strauss's outline which presupposed the validity of the Griesbach hypothesis] was destined to be *obscured by the Markan hypothesis*, which now came to the front. The necessity of choosing between John and the Synoptists was first fully established by the Tübingen school [more advocates of the Griesbach hypothesis]; and the right relation of this question to the Markan hypothesis was subsequently shown by Holtzmann.[213]

Schweitzer could be making one of two points about Holtzmann here. Neither point requires Schweitzer to be praising Holtzmann's source theory. Schweitzer's claim that a moment of 'transient illumination' in life of Jesus research was 'obscured by the Markan Hypothesis' can hardly be taken as praise for that hypothesis.

One point Schweitzer might be making would be that Holtzmann had managed to '*relate* his historically intelligible outline of the life of Jesus' to his Markan Hypothesis, but that need not mean that Holtzmann's

---

212. For references to 'the two oldest gospels' in Schweitzer, see, for instance, *Life and Thought*, pp. 49, 59 *et passim*, and Schweitzer's comment in the preface to *Quest* in 1950, discussed in a footnote below.

213. Schweitzer, *Quest*, p. 10, emphasis added.

outline of the life of Jesus was *derived from* Holtzmann's source theory. Schweitzer's alternative point—which seems to me to be the one he is more likely making here—would be that Holtzmann had been able to relate his Markan Hypothesis to the question of 'choosing between John and the Synoptists'.

Schweitzer's view of Holtzmann's role in the discussion of this latter issue was made clear later in Schweitzer's book within a passage that provides a good outline of Schweitzer's whole view of the history he recounted. There Schweitzer wrote

> [Johannes Weiss] lays down the third great alternative which the study of the life of Jesus had to meet. The first was laid down by Strauss: *either* purely historical *or* purely supernatural. The second had been worked out by the Tübingen school and Holtzmann: *either* Synoptic *or* Johannine. Now came the third: *either* eschatological *or* non-eschatological.[214]

Schweitzer seems to have had little interest in the details of either Holtzmann's or Wilke's 'linguistic arguments' for solving the Synoptic Problem. Schweitzer refers to Wilke as 'the "mathematician" of the Synoptic Problem' and criticizes Wilke's historical work (what Schweitzer could find of it in Wilke's book).[215]

Some of Schweitzer's comments on Holtzmann echo what he had to say about Wilke.

> Holtzmann did not work out the [Markan] hypothesis from the historical side, but rather on literary lines, recalling Wilke—as a kind of problem in Synoptic arithmetic.[216]

As may already be seen from these quotations, Schweitzer's interest lay more in reconstructing an historically intelligible outline of the life of Jesus and less in working out the Synoptic Problem, particularly 'as a problem in Synoptic arithmetic'. Nevertheless Schweitzer tells us that he was doubting both Holtzmann's outline of the life of Jesus and his solution to the Synoptic Problem[217] even when he was a first year

---

214. Schweitzer, *Quest*, p. 237.
215. Schweitzer, *Quest*, p. 113.
216. Schweitzer, *Quest*, p. 202.
217. Few scholars in the nineteenth century would have separated the Synoptic question from the question about the life of Jesus. Perhaps Wilke would have made such a distinction, but he, as Hajo Uden Meijboom suggested, belonged to an earlier period of biblical studies, i.e., the 'pre-Strauss' as opposed to the 'post-Strauss' period. See Meijboom and Kiwiet, *History and Critique*, pp. 9-11, 20-26.

student at the University of Strasbourg (1893–1894).[218]

> During my remaining years at the University I occupied myself, often to
> the neglect of my other subjects, with independent research into the
> Synoptic question and the problems of the life of Jesus, coming ever more
> and more confidently to the conviction that the key to the puzzles that are
> awaiting solution is to be looked for in the explanation of the words of
> Jesus when he sent out the disciples on their mission (Matthew 9.35–11.1;
> cf. Mark 6.7-13 and Luke 9.1-6), in the question sent by the Baptist from
> his prison (Matthew 11.2-19/Luke 7.18-35), and, further, in the way Jesus
> acts on the return of the disciples (Luke 9.10ff. and parallels).[219]

Schweitzer's major concern in reconstructing the life of Jesus was
whether or not Jesus and his ministry were eschatological and Messianic.
In preparation for an exam to be administered by Holtzmann on the
synoptic gospels, Schweitzer took his Greek New Testament with him,
even when he had to go on military manoeuvres during the fall of 1894.
Schweitzer explains,

> It was to avoid disgracing myself in the eyes of a teacher whom I respected
> so much as I did Holtzmann by my performance in his subject, that I took
> my Greek Testament with me to the manœuvres, and being then so robust
> that I did not know what fatigue was, I was able to get through some real
> work in the evenings and on the rest-day. During the summer I had gone
> through Holtzmann's commentary. Now I wanted to get a knowledge of
> the text, and see how much I remembered of his commentary and his
> lectures. This had for me a remarkable result. Holtzmann had gained
> recognition in scientific circles for the Markan hypothesis, that is, the
> theory that Mark's gospel is the oldest, and that its plan underlies those of
> Matthew and Luke. That seemed to justify the conclusion that the activities
> of Jesus can be understood from Mark's Gospel only. By this conclusion
> I felt to my astonishment, sorely puzzled when on a certain rest-day which
> we spent in the village of Guggenheim, I concentrated on the tenth and
> eleventh chapters of Matthew, and became conscious of the significance of
> what is narrated in these two chapters by him (i.e. Matthew) alone, and not
> by Mark as well.[220]

At that early point in his theological studies (1893–1894), Schweitzer
had already concluded that at least chapters 10 and 11 of Matthew
should be used in reconstucting the life of Jesus, in addition to whatever

---

218. See particularly Schweitzer, *Life and Thought*, pp. 17-21.
219. Schweitzer, *Life and Thought*, p. 20, bracketed material added.
220. Schweitzer, *Life and Thought*, pp. 17-18.

material one might use from Mark.[221] Schweitzer continued,

> Thus was I, at the end of my first year at the University, landed in per-
> plexity about the explanation then accepted as historically correct of the
> words and actions of Jesus when He sent out the disciples on their
> mission, and as a consequence of this about the wider question of the con-
> ception of the whole life of Jesus which was then regarded as history.
> When I reached home after the manœuvres entirely new horizons had
> opened themselves to me. Of this I was certain: that Jesus had announced
> no kingdom that was to be founded and realized in the natural world by
> Himself and the believers, but one that was to be expected as coming with
> the almost immediate dawn of a supernatural age…
> I should of course have held it an impertinence to hint to Holtzmann in my
> examination which came on shortly afterwards that I distrusted the con-
> ception of the life of Jesus which he maintained, and which was universally
> accepted by the critical school of that time.[222]

In 1931, Albert Schweitzer gave the world an autobiographical
account of the first 56 years of his life. He lived another 34 years, dying
at the age of 90. Less than two thirds of the way through a most
impressive life, Schweitzer took time to look back on his career from the
vantage point of Lambaréné and his African hospital. In the course of
this autobiography, Schweitzer revealed to his readers three of his debts
to Heinrich Julius Holtzmann. First, he said that Holtzmann was instrumental in securing for him a prestigious Goll scholarship.[223] Secondly,
he attributed the publication of his dissertation in philosophy, *Die
Religionsphilosophie Kants*, by Mohr and Siebeck 'to a warm recom-
mendation of it from Holtzmann'.[224] Thirdly, he considered his securing
an appointment to teach at the University of Strasbourg (1902–1913) to
have been due, at least in part, to Holtzmann's efforts.[225] Schweitzer

221. A detailed summary of Schweitzer's thoughts on this is contained on pp. 18-
19 of *Life and Thought*.

222. Schweitzer, *Life and Thought*, p. 20.

223. The Goll scholarship 'was administered by the S. Thomas's Chapter and the
Theological Faculty jointly. Its value was £60 (1,200 marks) a year and it was
awarded each time for six years. The scholar was under an obligation either to take,
within six years at the longest, the degree of Licentiate in Theology at Strasbourg, or
to repay the money he had received'. Albert Schweitzer, *Aus meinem Leben und
Denken* (1931) (= *Out of my Life and Thought: An Autobiography* [trans.
C.T. Campion; New York: Henry Holt & Co., 1933], p. 29). All quotations from this
work by Schweitzer within this paper are from this English translation.

224. Schweitzer, *Life and Thought*, p. 36.

225. Schweitzer wrote, 'On March 1, 1902, I delivered my inaugural lecture before

owed a good deal to Holtzmann and he was reluctant, at least as a young man, to criticize him.

Albert Schweitzer is one late-nineteenth–early-twentieth century scholar who had private doubts about Holtzmann's form of the Markan Hypothesis as early as 1894; but he was willing to publish those doubts, in any clear way, only in 1931, when Holtzmann had been dead for almost a quarter of a century. And Schweitzer expressed those doubts again, along with a suggestion of his own alternative view, only in 1950. By 1950, when Holtzmann had been dead for some forty years, Schweitzer was willing to admit that F.C. Baur and other members of the Tübingen school had probably been right all along, at least in giving preference to Matthew![226]

As a first year theological student, Schweitzer said that he had too much respect for Holtzmann to challenge his views.[227] Schweitzer's reluctance to challenge his teacher at that stage of life is certainly understandable, but was Schweitzer's treatment of Holtzmann in his book of 1906 on *Leben-Jesu-Forschung* also less critical of Holtzmann than it might have been? If so, was this reluctance caused (1) by Schweitzer's three personal debts to Holtzmann, (2) by Schweitzer's great respect for

the Theological Faculty at Strasbourg on the Logos doctrine in the Fourth Gospel. I learnt later that protests against my acceptance as a University Lecturer had been lodged by two members of the Faculty. They expressed disapproval of my method of historical investigation and a fear that I should confuse the students with my views. They were impotent, however, in face of the authority of Holtzmann, who took my part' (Schweitzer, *Life and Thought*, p. 55). The index to the English translation of this work by Schweitzer is inadequate and will not lead one to 'Holtzmann' on any one of the three pages just utilized, pp. 27, 36 or 55.

226. See the reference to Schweitzer's views by 1950 in William R. Farmer, *The Synoptic Problem: A Critical Analysis* (New York: Macmillan, 1964), p. 42 n. 7, which reads, in part, 'In the preface to the latest edition of his book [in 1950], Schweitzer writes: "The decisive point in the quest of the historical Jesus is not which of *the two oldest Gospels* (Matthew and Mark) is a trifle older than the other. That, moreover, is a literary question which is scarcely possible to answer. The historical problem of the life of Jesus cannot be recognized, much less solved, from the fragmentary record of Mark. The differing narratives of the two oldest Gospels are equally valuable, but Matthew's fullness gives it greater importance, and [F.C.] Baur and his school rightly gave it preference"' (*The Quest for the Historical Jesus* [London, 1950], p. xi [= *Geschichte der Leben-Jesu-Forschung* (Tübingen, 1951), p. xii] [emphasis mine]).

227. Farmer also took note in 1964 of Schweitzer's reluctance to challenge Holtzmann (*The Synoptic Problem*, p. 57).

Holtzmann and (3) by the fact that, by 1906, the two had been faculty colleagues at Strasbourg for four years? In the last two years, 1904–1906, Holtzmann had taken emeritus status, which he held until his death in 1910.

Those within the English speaking part of the world could be misled by a reading of Schweitzer's history of *Leben-Jesu-Forschung* under the English title, *The Quest for the Historical Jesus: A Critical Study of Its Progress from Reimarus to Wrede.* The potentially misleading word is 'progress', an Enlightenment ideal. Schweitzer's translator, W. Montgomery, and perhaps also Francis Crawford Burkitt (1864–1935), who provided the introduction to the English translation in 1910, might have thought of Schweitzer's history of nineteenth century research as 'progress', but for Schweitzer, in 1906, his history of research from Reimarus to Wrede was mostly a series of derailments of the train of scholarship that he wished to get back on track.[228] And it should be remembered that one of the cars on that train was 'The Markan Hypothesis', to which Schweitzer had devoted an entire chapter.[229] It should also be noted that within this chapter of Schweitzer's book, he only discusses the works of Weisse and Wilke. Holtzmann's book of 1863 is not listed in the bibliography with which Schweitzer is accustomed to begin each chapter.

Holtzmann's book of 1863 does not appear until the opening bibliography for chapter fourteen of Schweitzer's book. There it appears as one of what Schweitzer labels 'The "Liberal" Lives of Jesus'.[230] When Schweitzer does speak about Holtzmann in his book of 1906, it tends to be either in connection with Holtzmann's views on the authenticity of

---

228. The pictures of Jesus created throughout the nineteenth century which were false in Schweitzer's opinion, are contrasted with Schweitzer's own on pp. 48-54 of *Life and Thought.* On this question cf. David Dungan, 'Albert Schweitzer's Disillusionment with the Historical Reconstruction of the Life of Jesus', *PSTJ* 39/3 (Spring, 1976), pp. 27-48, esp. pp. 28-28 where Dungan concludes, 'Without sparing anyone, Schweitzer had carefully traced the entire life of Jesus movement from its earliest manifestations in post-Reformation Germany, step-by-step, to his own time 200 years later, and showed how the entire process was riddled with inconsistencies, arbitrary conclusions, politically motivated denunciations, theological muddle-headedness, blind alleys, one-sided attacks answered by equally narrow responses and—much truly brilliant insight'.

229. Schweitzer, *Quest*, ch. 10, pp. 121-36.

230. Schweitzer, *Quest*, pp. 193-222.

the Gospel of John or, thereby, on the usefulness of John's Gospel in reconstructing a Life of Jesus.

Schweitzer evaluated Holtzmann's own reconstruction of the Life of Jesus as follows:

> The ideal life of Jesus at the close of the nineteenth century is the Life which Heinrich Julius Holtzmann did not write—but which can be pieced together from his commentary on the Synoptic Gospels and his New Testament Theology.[231]

Schweitzer's history began with Reimarus, who not only attempted to write the first critical history of the life of Jesus but who also had, in Schweitzer's view, the correct view of the eschatological, Messianic character of Jesus. From the beginning of the 'Quest', in Schweitzer's view, the history of *Leben-Jesu-Forschung* after Reimarus had got off on the wrong track. Schweitzer says,

> Of the attempt made by Reimarus to understand the preaching of Jesus from the standpoint of the eschatological Messianic doctrine of late Judaism, no one of that period takes any notice at all.[232]

And by the time New Testament critics had meandered through the nineteenth century with one wrong notion about the gospels and Jesus after another, they were confronted with a choice in 1906 between 'Thoroughgoing Skepticism (Wrede)' and 'Thoroughgoing Eschatology (Schweitzer)'.[233] Schweitzer continues,

> The question whether Jesus thought eschatologically or not resolves itself, therefore, into the one point, whether he held Himself to be the Messiah, or not. Anyone who admits that he did so must also admit that His ideas and expectations were of the eschatological type of late Judaism. Anyone who refuses to recognize this element in his thought must also refuse to attribute to him any consciousness of being the Messiah.
>
> That is the way in which William Wrede in his work *The Messianic Secret of the Gospels* (1901) preserves consistency. He works throughout on the assumption that Jesus appeared in public simply as a teacher, and only after His death, that is in the imagination of His followers, became Messiah. Into the original tradition about the appearance in public and

---

231. Schweitzer, *Quest*, p. 295; see also *Quest*, pp. 203-204, quoted in Farmer, *Synoptic Problem*, p. 56.

232. Schweitzer, *Life and Thought*, p. 59.

233. Schweitzer, *Quest*, ch. 14, pp. 330-97.

the activity of 'Jesus the Teacher', this later view, says Wrede, was incorporated in such a way as to represent him as not confessing his Messiahship, but keeping it to Himself as a secret.[234]

Like some of his rationalist and liberal predecessors in the eighteenth and nineteenth centuries, Schweitzer did not find this eschatological, Messianic Jesus relevant to modern times. But that, according to Schweitzer, is who Jesus was, so Christians must meet him in modern times, not so much as 'who he was', but rather as 'Who He Is'.[235] And if this historical picture of Jesus causes problems for the Church, then so be it.[236]

But Schweitzer also remarked that this dilemma about the relevance of such an eschatological Jesus for the modern world was already recognized in the latter half of the nineteenth century. He wrote,

> But as early as 1860 separate investigations into the problems of the life of Jesus began to make it clear that the view which represents Him as trying to spiritualize the eschatological, Messianic expectations of his time, cannot be sustained, because in a series of passages he speaks in a quite realistic way of the coming of the Son of Man and the Messianic Kingdom when this world comes to an end. If the attempt is given up to reinterpret or to discredit these passages, there remain two alternatives: either to recognize and admit that Jesus did really live with a belief in the ideas of late-Jewish eschatology, or assert that only those sayings are genuine in which he speaks in a truly spiritual way of the Messiah and the Messianic Kingdom, the remainder having been attributed to Him by a primitive Christianity which had fallen back into the realistic views of late Judaism. Faced by these alternatives, research decides at first for the second. That Jesus should be thought to have shared the Messianic ideas of late-Judaism, which are so alien to our ideas (in 1906 and for at least half a century before) seems to it so incomprehensible and so offensive, that it prefers to doubt to some extent the trustworthiness of the two oldest Gospels, and to deny the genuineness of a portion of the sayings which they report, on account of their strange content. But when it goes on, as it does in the works of Timothy [sic] Colani (*Jésus Christ et les croyances messianiques de son temps*, 1864) and Gustave Volkmar (*Jesus Nazarenus*, 1882), to establish this distinction between genuine 'spiritual messianic' and spurious 'eschatological Messianic' pronouncements, it

---

234. Schweitzer, *Life and Thought*, p. 61.

235. Quoting the last three words of *Quest*, p. 403, which Schweitzer himself repeats in *Life and Thought*, pp. 71-72.

236. See Schweitzer, *Life and Thought*, Chapter 6: 'The Historical Jesus and the Christianity of Today', pp. 65-75.

becomes clear that it must go on to deny that Jesus ever believed Himself to be the Messiah at all. For the passages in which he entrusts to His disciples the secret that he is the Messiah are, one and all, 'eschatological messianic', in that he, according to them, holds Himself to be the person who at the end of the world will appear as the Son of Man.[237]

And so, with Schweitzer's reference here to Timothy (i.e. Timothée) Colani I have come full circle back to where I began my discussion of the Strasbourg school.

Conclusions

What happened to the voices of dissent from the Strasbourg school that were raised against certain aspects of the Markan Hypothesis after Meijboom published his dissertation in 1866? According to Schweitzer, 'the events of 1870' led Timothée Colani away from his academic base at the University of Strasbourg. He came upon hard times, and, in desperation, became a librarian.

But even before Colani left Strasbourg, the *Revue de théologie*, the most important academic journal of the Strasbourg school, had already ceased publication in 1869. With its demise, other journals had to be sought in which to continue the discussion of the Synoptic Problem. It was in the *Revue de Theologie* that the interesting debate between Eduard Reuss and Edmond Scherer over the history of the development of the gospels had been found between 1855 and 1861. But one of the protagonists in this debate, Edmond Scherer, had left the teaching of theology by 1850. Although he was in Paris by 1860 and continued to publish in Colani's journal until 1861, Scherer had probably published his last specifically theological piece by 1864.

Scherer's theological interests are still visible in his secular literary criticism, but he did not find the occasion, nor the journals after 1869, in which to publish detailed analyses of the gospels. By 1860, he had settled in Versailles and Paris, where he became a successful literary critic, reviewing literature in English, French and German. In 1860 he helped to found and edit with Auguste Nefftzer the Paris newspaper, *Le Temps*, to which he was also a frequent contributor. Pressed into the service of his country at Versailles when the hostilities of the Franco-Prussian war came to an end, his skill in negotiating the peace led him into politics and a concluding lifetime as a French Senator.

237. Schweitzer, *Life and Thought*, pp. 60-61.

Who would then question Reuss's theories about the Synoptic Gospels after 1861, with Scherer out of the picture? And who, besides Scherer, was a skilled enough observer of the linguistic characteristics of the several synoptic authors to be able to use those characteristics in the service of solving the Synoptic Problem? One might appoint Eduard Zeller (1814–1908). It is certain that Zeller could have done what Scherer did, and perhaps better. In 1843, in fact, Zeller had already published the most adequate scientific research on how the linguistic characteristics of the several synoptic evangelists might be of service in solving the Synoptic Problem. But Holtzmann misused Zeller's data in his book of 1863 and, by then, Zeller had turned to philosophy, rather than theology. Within the discipline of philosophy, Zeller flourished. His books are standards in the field of the history of philosophy to this day. Zeller did manage to maintain his hand in theological matters after 1863. In addition to a number of journal articles on New Testament themes after 1863, Zeller wrote a small book on David Friedrich Strauss and Ernest Renan (1866),[238] a second book on Strauss (1874),[239] and collected, edited, and published letters and other writings by Strauss (1895).[240] Zeller also provided a foreword to the eleventh German edition of Strauss' *The Old Faith and the New*.[241] For some, of course,

238. Eduard Zeller, *Strauss und Renan*, an extract from *HZ* 12 (Munich 1864), pp. 70-130 [= ET *Strauss and Renan An Essay by E. Zeller: With Introductory Remarks by the Translator* (London: Trübner, 1866)]; cf. *Vorträge und Abhandlungen geschichtlichen Inhalts* (Leipzig: Fues, 1865). Zeller's essay on 'Strauss and Renan' is also included in this collection, as well as essays on the Tübingen School and F.C. Baur.

239. Eduard Zeller, *David Friedrich Strauss in seinem leben und seinen schriften* (Bonn: E. Strauss, 1874) = ET *David Friedrich Strauss in his Life and Writings* (London: Smith, Elder, 1874).

240. *Gesammelte Schriften von David Friedrich Strauss. Nach des verfassers letzwilligen bestimmungen zusammengestellt. Eingeleitet und mit erklärenden nachweisungen versehen von Eduard Zeller* (12 vols.; Bonn, 1876–1878); David Friedrich Strauss, *Poetisches Gedenkbuch: Gedichte aus dem Nachlass* (ed. Eduard Zeller; Bonn, 1878); *Ausgewählte Briefe von David Friedrich Strauss, hrsg. und erläutert von Eduard Zeller* (Bonn: E. Strauss, 1895).

241. David Friedrich Strauss, *Der alte und der neue Glaube: Ein Bekenntnis von David Friedrich Strauss* (11 Aufl. mit einem Vorworte von Eduard Zeller; Bonn: E. Strauss, 1881); an English translation of the sixth edition, without Zeller's foreword, is available as *The Old Faith and the New: A Confession by David Friedrich Strauss* (authorized trans. from the sixth edn by Mathilde Blind, American Edition; 2 vols. in one; Revised and partly rewritten, and preceded by an American version of

these activities relating to Strauss's work by Zeller would not heighten his prestige nor increase admiration for him, either within certain academic circles or among the general populace.

I have also noted that the *Revue germanique* ceased publication in 1869. This journal carried numerous articles by Albert Réville and Michel Nicolas. In 1862 and 1863, Michel Nicolas published four articles on the gospels that caught the eye of Ernest Renan. It also carried Réville's response to Renan's *Vie de Jésus* in the issue for 1 December 1863. The demise of both the *Revue de théologie* and the *Revue germanique* in 1869 can probably be indirectly, if not directly, related to the Franco-Prussian War of 1870–1871. Note that the name of the *Revue germanique* was changed to the *Revue moderne* between 1865 and 1869, when publication ceased. Perhaps this was also due, at least in part, to increasing tensions between France and Germany during that time.

The demise of these two journals, where challenges to the theory of Markan priority had once been published in the 1850s and 1860s, even by persons who were mostly sympathetic to the Markan Hypothesis, must have led authors to look to other journals to publish research on the Synoptic Problem. But, I have also noted above that the chief periodical of the advocates of the Griesbach Hypothesis in Tübingen, the *Theologische Jahrbücher*, had already ceased publication in 1857. One of the editors of this journal, who was also one of the chief defenders of the Griesbach Hypothesis in the nineteenth century, F.C. Baur, was dead in 1860. And even before the end of this journal's run in 1869, the founding editor, Eduard Zeller, had turned his major attention to philosophy, rather than theology (c. 1849).

A thorough review of the contents of nineteenth-century theological journals is needed, to see what might be discovered within them about the continuing nineteenth-century discussion of the Synoptic Problem. Meijboom has pointed to four interesting articles by Reuss and a response by Scherer on this topic. There are probably more contributions like these to be found.

After the decade of the 1860s, Michel Nicolas's research interests seem to have shifted back to the history of his native region in south-western France, in and around Nimes and Montauban. The demise of the *Revue germanique* and the *Revue de théologie* in 1869 may have left Nicolas with no regular outlet for detailed Biblical scholarship. This

the author's 'Prefatory Postscript'; New York: Henry Holt, 1874).

may even have encouraged him to pursue other research interests.

I have not yet traced out where Albert Réville went after leaving the pastorate of the Walloon church in Rotterdam in 1873. But when Réville appears for me again, in Paris in 1880, his research interests have moved to the history of religions and it was to that assignment that he was appointed.

After 1870 and until his death in 1891, Eduard Reuss, the senior member of the Strasbourg school upon whom all of the other members were in some way dependent, continued his teaching as a member of the theological faculty at the Kaiser-Wilhelm-Universität in Strasbourg. In 1874, Heinrich Julius Holtzmann joined him on the faculty there and became the faculty member most responsible for synoptic studies. Reuss's duties included those of an administrator after 1872 and his scholarly attention was directed to Old Testament studies after Holtzmann arrived in Strasbourg in 1874.

More research is also needed into what, if any, relationship there may be between Colani's departure from the University of Strasbourg in 1870 and Holtzmann's arrival there in 1874. Colani, as a Frenchman, would have had more problems with the political fortunes of Strasbourg and Alsace-Lorraine, than Holtzmann, the native German, would have had. Perhaps there is something to these thoughts, relating to this changing of the guard. And in the interim, 1870–1874, why did Albrecht Ritschl choose to decline a call to Strasbourg?

Finally, we have considered the witness of Albert Schweitzer. Even in 1894, Schweitzer was not happy with either Holtzmann's reconstruction of the Life of Jesus or with his synoptic source theory. Did Schweitzer's debts to Holtzmann get in the way of the former's academic honesty? Did he portray Holtzmann as a better scholar than he knew him to be, at least while Holtzmann was still living? What difference would it have made to Holtzmann's career at Strasbourg and to the growth of acceptance of the Markan Hypothesis, if Schweitzer had said in 1894 or written in his book of 1906, what he eventually put in writing in 1950?

Schweitzer suggested in 1906 that Holtzmann's picture of Jesus was the ideal for liberal, German, Protestant, New Testament scholars. But Schweitzer demonstrated that this picture of Jesus was not a picture that was grounded in a truly historical-critical analysis of the gospel texts.

Schweitzer described Holtzmann's work with the texts of the synoptic gospels in 1906 as 'synoptic arithmetic', after the manner of Wilke. But the master of this type of 'maths' was Eduard Zeller and, by 1863, he was no longer a force in synoptic criticism. What if Zeller had continued to devote himself to theology, instead of philosophy? Would he have demonstrated the weaknesses of Holtzmann's book of 1863? Would he, or could he have influenced the opinion of the larger academic community in Germany in the middle decades of the nineteenth century? Adolf Hilgenfeld gave Holtzmann's book of 1863 such a negative review that he felt constrained to express his sorrow for its negativity in a footnote.[242] But Hilgenfeld's negative review and the absence of any review of Holtzmann's book of 1863 in the Strasbourg *Revue de théologie* did not seem to have any effect on his career. These certainly did not stand in the way of Holtzmann being promoted to the rank of professor at Heidelberg in 1865 nor called to Strasbourg in 1874.

What if Meijboom's history and critique of the Markan Hypothesis, which included another strong critique of Holtzmann's book of 1863, had been anything but a doctoral dissertation? What if it had been written later in his life, after he had established himself as a significant church historian? Would it have received more attention then? What if it had been written in German or French (or even English), rather than Dutch? Would he have gained more readers before now? Or what if it had been translated into one of these languages, as it now has been? But the translation of doctoral dissertations then, as now, is only slightly less rare than the readers of dissertations. The old claim that most dissertations are read by 1.3 people—the dissertation advisor and the author's mother who had good intentions but could not finish it—may have applied to Meijboom's dissertation for one hundred years. Meijboom himself seems to have been even less hopeful about the readership of his dissertation when he wrote in his conclusions, 'I will feel richly rewarded for my efforts if, in addition to my doctor's degree, I will have gained at least one reader who has carefully read my exposition up to the last page'.[243]

---

242. Adolf Hilgenfeld, 'Die Evangelien und die geschichtliche Gestalt Jesu', *ZWT* 7/3 (1863), pp. 311-40, esp. 311-27. Hilgenfeld's feeling about his review are expressed on p. 362 n. 1. 'Es thut mir aufrichtig leid, die sonst von Freisinnigkeit und sprachlichen Forschungen zeugende Arbeit des Heidelberger Theologen so ganz bestreiten zu müssen, was aber nur um der Sache willen, nicht wegen einer frühern Anzeige meines Buchs über den Paschastreit in Schenkel's "Allgemeiner kirchlicher Zeitschrift", deren Verfasser wohl Holtzmann sein wird, geschieht. Die gennante Zeitschrift hat sich in der letzten Zeit oft billiger und freundlicher über mich ausgesprochen.'

243. Meijboom and Kiwiet, *History and Critique*, p. 228.

Perhaps the doctrine of Markan priority flourished in Europe in the second half of the nineteenth century and the Griesbach Hypothesis floundered, by default. By a seemingly unrelated series of circumstances, most of the voices favouring the Griesbach Hypothesis or challenging the Markan Hypothesis had been silenced by 1864; some, it seems, in the waves of responses following the storm created by Renan's book on Jesus. Even Hajo Uden Meijboom turned to Church history after 1866, rather than continue with his synoptic criticism.

By 1863, when Renan's book was published, F.C. Baur was already dead (d. 1860). Zeller had turned to philosophy (c. 1849–1854). Eduard Scherer had gone into literary criticism and service in French politics (c. 1861). Albert Réville was still in Rotterdam in 1863, but, by 1873, he had left. Where was he? Was he traveling the world during that period (the Americas, Peru, Mexico, China?) developing his later academic interests in world religions? If so, these are not places in which a nineteenth-century European academic is likely to be writing scholarly articles on the Synoptic Problem.

By the latter decades of the nineteenth century, Nicolas's research interests had returned to the history of his old home in southwestern France. Renan was in deep trouble because of his book on Jesus and, by 1870, Colani was looking for work.

After 1863, Adolf Hilgenfeld was still in Jena, valiantly protesting the Markan Hypothesis, at every turn.[244] Was Hilgenfeld, at the turn of the

---

244. Hilgenfeld's reviews of gospel studies in the Jena *ZWT* were numerous after 1863. The following are just some of the articles by Hilgenfeld that appeared there relating to gospel study: 'Baur's kritische Urgeschichte des Christenthums', 7 (1864), pp. 113-45; 'Das Marcus-Evangelium und die Marcus-Hypothese', 7 (1864), pp. 287-333; 'C. Weizsäcker's Untersuchungen über die evangelische Geschichte', 7 (1865), pp. 171-212; 'Marcus zwischen Matthäus und Lucas', 9 (1866), pp. 82-113; 'Das Matthäus-Evangelium', 10 (1867), pp. 303-23, 366-447, 11 (1868), pp. 22-76; 'Die neueste Evangelien-Forschung', 13 (1870), pp. 151-88; 'Volkmar und die Evangelien', 13 (1870), pp. 347-77; 'Die neueste Evangelien-Forschung', 20 (1877), pp. 1-48; 'Der gegenwärtige Stand der Evangelienforschung', 25 (1882), pp. 189-226; 'Neutestamentliche Forschungen. I. Die neueste Marcus-Hypothese. II. Der Christus des Philipperbriefes', 27 (1884), pp. 484-505; 'Papias und die neueste Evangelienforschung', 29 (1886), pp. 257-91; 'Die neueste synoptische Evangelienforschung' (C. Holsten und C. Weizsäcker)', 30 (1887), pp. 1-42; 'Das Urevangelium', 32 (1889), pp. 1-42; 'Paul Ewald's Lösung der Evangelienfrage', 34 (1891), pp. 80-95; 'Die synoptische Zweiquellen-Theorie in neuester Fassung', 36 (1893), pp. 1-36; 'W. Brandt's evangelische Geschichte', 37 (1894), pp. 1-33; 'Drei Evangelienforscher der Gegenwart (W. Beyschlag, A. Harnack, J. Weiss)', 41

century, like Elijah crying out and saying, 'Oh Lord, I am the only prophet of Matthean priority still left, but there are four hundred and fifty prophets of Markan priority. I alone am left, and they seek to take even my life?'

(1898), pp. 137-49; 'Die synoptische Zweiquellen-Theorie und Papias von Hierapolis', 44 (1901), pp. 151-56; 'Review of H.J. Holtzmann, Die Synoptiker. 3. Aufl. 1901', 45 (1902), pp. 144-45; 'Der Evangelist Marcus und Julius Wellhausen. Erster Artikel', 47 (1904), pp. 180-228; 'Der Evangelist Marcus und Julius Wellhausen. Zweiter Artikel', 47 (1904), pp. 289-331; 'Der Evangelist Marcus und Julius Wellhausen. Dritter Artikel', 47 (1904), pp. 462-524; 'J. Wellhausen und die synoptischen Evangelien', 49 (1906), pp. 193-238.

Review articles, particularly reviews of developments in the study of the gospels, by Hilgenfeld began already in the Tübingen *Theologische Jahrbücher*. One of the first articles of this type by Hilgenfeld was his response to the work of F.C. Baur. See the following by Hilgenfeld in the *Theologische Jahrbücher*: 'Der Paschastreit und das Evangelium Johannis, mit Rücksicht auf Weitzel's Darstellung', 8/2 (1849), pp. 209-80; 'Neue Untersuchung über das Markus-Evangelium, mit Rücksicht auf Dr Baur's Darstellung', 11/1 (1852), pp. 108-32, 11/2 (1852), pp. 259-92; 'Das marcionitische Evangelium und seine neueste Bearbeitung', 12/2 (1853), pp. 192-244; 'Der Ursprung der pseudoclementinischen Recognitionen und Homilien, nach dem neuesten Stande der Untersuchung', 13/4 (1854), pp. 483-535; 'Die Evangelienfrage und ihre neuesten Behandlungen von Weisse, Volkmar und Meyer', 16/3 (1857), pp. 381-440. With the fourth issue in the volume for 1857 the *Theologische Jahrbücher* ceased publication.

THE ROLE OF THE OLD TESTAMENT IN THE GERMAN LIBERAL PROTESTANT THEOLOGY OF THE NINETEENTH CENTURY

Henning Graf Reventlow

For an adequate understanding of the role of the Old Testament in German Liberal Protestant Theology in the second half of the Nineteenth Century, it is indispensable to glance at the various ideological movements which had their impact on liberal thinking in that period and which were rooted mostly in the previous century. Well-known key words are: Enlightenment and rationalism, romanticism, idealism; each of them comprising a great variety of individual standpoints, partly also overlapping or intermingling in the multifarious thinking unfolding in the so-called liberal movement of the period. The attitudes of the famous thinkers towards the problem of the Old Testament are a useful scale allowing us a deeper insight into the subconscious motivations that formed the theological systems of the century. Even though they were not outspoken or though they hid behind well-sounding public declarations they render useful hints regarding the intellectual climate among the liberals.

As prominent names among the founder-generation should be mentioned: G.E. Lessing, J.G. Herder, J.P. Gabler, F. Schleiermacher and G.F. Hegel. I deliberately do not include specialists in the scholarly field of the Old Testament, as my interest is not in reformulating the well-known history of exegesis over and over again, but in learning more about the general feeling regarding the Bible and revelation. I do not dwell either upon the conservative groups which were never lacking in the period: pietists, confessional Lutherans and some Reformed communities. Their influence on public opinion was restricted. But public opinion as typified in the feeling and thinking of the educated class in the Second Reich is the field of this research. From the journalistic pen of Lessing the utterance is well known (which he wrote down in his struggle against the orthodox admirers of the Bible), that 'accidental verities of history can never become the proof of necessary verities of reason'.[1] The sentence differentiates, in the way of thinking typical of the Enlightenment, between the simple facts and a timeless form of truth to be gained by human reason. In a way, this model never died out and played a significant role throughout the nineteenth century. But Lessing had another approach, typical of which is the place he gave to the Old Testament. In his late essay 'The Education of the Human Race'[2] he treated the history of revelation as a history of education in which humankind as a whole, beginning with a small part of it, but aiming at the perfection of each human being, would be guided through different succeeding stages to a moral standard of self-motivation for good acts similar to the categorical imperative described by Kant. In this development the Old Testament plays the role of an elementary schoolbook (§§47–52)—useful for a time of childhood, but to be thrown away as the child grows older (§55) and needs a better teacher. 'A better teacher must come and tear away the exhausted elementary book from the child's hands (§53).' History as moral—equivalent to religious—development: this is a further central topic in the popular creed of the nineteenth century.

Herder, the romantic, but still partly Enlightenment-orientated theologian, was influential in his remarkably high regard for the Old Testament; a place that seems at a first look opposite to the transitory place the Old Testament occupies for Lessing.[3] He is close to Lessing in his theory of a universal education of humanity, but he regards that as based upon the hidden plan of God. Outer nature, inner conscience, language as a means of communicating God-given experiences in nature and history, and language as a gift of God itself, all this is included in the panorama of the world that Herder approaches with feeling and knowledge. This founds the high regard in which Herder holds the great personalities of the Bible, for instance the prophets; the poetry of the

---

1. G.E. Lessing, 'Über den Beweis des Geistes und der Kraft', in Göpfert (ed.), *Werke*, VIII (Darmstadt: Wiss. Buchgesellschaft, 1979), p. 12.

2. I used the edition in *Werke* (ed. Göpfert, VIII), pp. 489-510, and L.F. Helbig (ed.), *Die Erziehung des Menschengeschlects: Historisch-kritische Edition mit Urteilen Lessings und seiner Zeitgenossen: Einleitung, Entstehungsgeschichte und Kommentar* (Frankfurt a.M.: Lang, 1980).

3. Cf. Herder, *Auch eine Philosophie der Geschichte zur Bildung der Menschheit* (Riga, 1774) now in Bernhard Suphan *et al.* (eds.), *Sämtliche Werke*, V (Berlin: Weidmann, 1891), pp. 474-586.

Bible; the Old Testament as 'the oldest document of mankind'.[4] For the romantic thinker, history is not a one-way development from lower to higher stages, but there is also a paradise in the beginning to be regained by grasping at the half-forgotten traditions.

In a way, the otherwise barely explicable antinomies in the evaluation of the Old Testament during the later parts of the nineteenth century originate with Herder's influence upon the educated upper class in Germany, which held its classical thinkers in high regard. Romanticism in the wake of Herder could not overlook the aesthetic values of the Old Testament, the glamour of its personalities; whereas moral evaluation—a heritage of the Enlightenment—tended to devalue it as insufficiently Christian and morally worthless.

When I mentioned Gabler, I did not intend to place him on the same level as Lessing and Herder. But he is important insofar as he laid the foundation for the subject 'Biblical Theology' and formulated the maxims it followed during the century and even later.[5] His distinction between Biblical Theology as a historic and Dogmatic Theology as a systematic topic[6] is fundamental. This limited the endeavours of biblical theologians throughout the century to historic reconstructions and prevented dogmatics from taking into consideration its theological foundations in the Bible. This resulted in the general view that Israel's belief as laid down in the literature of the Old Testament was to be regarded as part of the religious history of humankind—despite the protests uttered from orthodox circles that such a treatment would completely misunderstand the importance of this part of the Christian Bible for the belief of the Church.

The intellectual climate at the beginning of the century is represented by the utterances of the influential thinkers F. Schleiermacher and G.F. Hegel. Schleiermacher—later representative theologian of the newly

4.   *Aelteste Urkunde des Menschengeschlechts* (1774–76), now in Suphan *et al.* (ed.), *Sämtliche Werke*, VI, pp. 193-97, 172.

5.   On Gabler, cf. 'Gabler, Johann Philipp (1753–1826)', *TRE*, XII (1984), pp. 1-3 (lit.); M. Saebo, 'Johann Philipp Gablers Bedeutung für die biblische Theologie', *ZAW* 99 (1987), pp. 1-16.

6.   Cf. his famous utterance: 'Est vera theologia biblica e genere historica, tradens, quid scriptores sacri de rebus divinis senserint; theologia contra dogmatica e genere didactico, docens, quid theologus quisque...ratione super rebus divinis philosophetur' (Oratio de justo discrimine theologiae biblicae et dogmaticae regundisque recte utriusque finibus [Altdorfii, 1787] = *id.*, *Opuscula Academica*, II [Ulmae: Stettin, 1831], pp. 179-94).

founded Berlin university and spiritual guide of a whole epoch, but above all the one who on the eve of the century in his early essay 'On Religion: Speeches to the Educated among its Despisers'[7] opened the gate to the new romantic understanding of religion—had already expressed his disdain of the Bible as a whole. For the adherers of a religion based on feeling and the contemplation of the universe[8] the belief in scriptures is superfluous: 'Every holy scripture is just a mausoleum of religion, a monument that great spirit once existed which does not exist any more'.[9] Late in his life, when he was looking back on his dogmatics and was still engaged against the orthodox standpoint regarding the messianic prophecies of the Old Testament as announcing the coming of Jesus Christ, in expressing his firm conviction, 'that those predictions do not fit upon Jesus', he expanded his negative sentiment to the very formulation: 'The belief in a special inspiration or revelation of God in the Jewish people continued to a certain moment is so little to be expected of everybody that one has to abandon the whole theory.'[10] He adds the personal remark: 'This conviction that living Christianity in its progress does not need a stronghold in Judaism is as old in me as my religious consciousness as such.'[11] Statements claiming a different level of piety in both testaments or a 'legal form of thinking' in the Old point back to Enlightenment standards.[12] The result is formulated concisely: 'To include the Jewish codex into the canon means looking upon Christianity as a continuation of Judaism and is contrary to the idea of canon.'[13]

---

7. 'Über die Religion. Reden an die Gebildeten unter ihren Verächtern (1799)', in H.J. Birkner *et al.* (eds.), *Kritische Gesamtausgabe*, I, II, (Berlin: de Gruyter, 1984), pp. 185-326 [= *On Religion: Addresses in Response to its Cultured Critics* (trans. T.N. Tice; Richmond, VA: John Knox Press, 1969)].

8. Cf. especially the second speech in 'Über die Religion', in Birkner (ed.), *Kritische Gesamtausgabe*, pp. 206-47.

9. 'Über die Religion', in Birkner (ed.), *Kritische Gesamtausgabe*, p. 242.

10. 'Zweites Sendschreiben an Lücke', *Kritische Gesamtausgabe*, I.10 (Berlin: de Gruyter, 1990), pp. 337-94, 353.

11. 'Über die Religion', in Birkner (ed.), *Kritische Gesamtausgabe*, p. 354.

12. Cf. 'Der christliche Glaube', §132 in Birkner (ed.), *Kritische Gesamtausgabe*, VII.2 (Berlin: de Gruyter, 1980), p. 236 [= *The Christian Faith*; ed. H.R. Mackintosh and J.S. Stewart; Edinburgh: T. & T. Clark, 1928)].

13. 'Kurze Darstellung des theologischen Studiums', §15 in H. Scholz (ed.), *Kritische Ausgabe* (Darmstadt: Wiss. Buchgesellschaft, 1969) (= unveränd reprograf. Nachdr. d. Ausg. Leipzig, 1910), p. 6 [= *Brief Outline on the Study of Theology* (trans. T.N. Tice; Richmond, VA: John Knox Press, 1966)].

Less strong is the impact of Hegel on the theological thinking in the second half of the century. The very negative judgment of his youth on the Old Testament is well known since the publication of his early manuscripts in 1907,[14] but could not have had any impact at all before that date. However it is an indicator of the very incendiary feeling against this part of the Bible in the group of young theologians who were Hegel's friends in the *Stift* of Tübingen. In his fully developed system of a philosophy of history Hegel was less radical. In his 'Lectures on the Philosophy of Religion',[15] in which he constructed a three-step scheme of types of religion, ascending from the religion of nature through 'the religion of spiritual individuality' to the height of absolute religion, Israel's religion receives its place on the second level as 'the religion of sublimity'.[16] But that means it is no more than a passing stage on the way to absolute religion which is to be identified with Christianity. Even if Hegel's idealistic philosophy did not find a broad following after his death in 1832 in the strict form of his dialectical system, the idea of religious development maintained a central place in the thinking of the century. In this conception the place to be conceded to Israel's religion and the Old Testament as its documentation is but a transient one; it cannot receive the same acknowledgement as the New Testament in the way it is enjoyed as a part of the Christian canon.

The intention of the following considerations will be to gain—on the basis of a choice of different publications belonging to the period we are interested in at this symposium—some insight into the general theological climate reigning in the Second Reich. Looking upon the esteem the Old Testament enjoyed or failed to enjoy seems to supply a touchstone against which to check how not only well-known theological thinkers, but also the educated class interested in theological problems formed their image of 'Christian religion', as a popular phrase of the period put it. To reach both aims it seemed convenient to adduce, first,

---

14. *Hegels theologische Jugendschriften* (ed. H. Nohl; Tübingen: Mohr, 1907; reprinted Frankfurt a.M.: Minerva, 1966). Cf. especially the quotations in H.J. Kraus, *Geschichte der historisch-kritischen Erforschung des Alten Testaments* (Neukirchen: Neukirchener Verlag, 1982³), pp. 189-90.

15. *Vorlesungen über die Philosophie der Religion, Sämtliche Werke.* H. Glockner (ed.), *Jubileumsausgabe*, XV-XVI (Stuttgart: Frommann-Holzboog, 1959³), pp. 46-95.

16. Cf. the Contents, Hegel's *Lectures on the Philosophy of Religion*.

some characteristic utterances in periodicals directed to a broader public. The periodicals I choose are 1. The *Protestantische Kirchenzeitung für das evangelische Deutschland*, published between 1854 and 1896 by the Protestant Union (followed by the *Protestantische Monatshefte* between 1897 and 1921). 2. The *Christliche Welt*, edited by M. Rade, organ of the Friends of the Christian World to which belonged the best known liberal theologians of the time. Their expressed aim was to write for the educated of the communities[17] and to fight against secularisation in modern society. 'Education and Christianity shall not be compatible? We do not believe that as long as we are working on ourselves and in ourselves at being both: an educated human being and a Christian.'[18]

To begin with, I shall look at those contributions which are listed in *CW* in the Contents under the rubric 'Biblical and Edifying'. Take for example volume three (1889). Here we have meditations on thirty four New Testament passages, three on the Old Testament. In volume two (1888), fifty five on the New Testament, one on the Old. This one, on Amos,[19] is mainly a short description of Amos's work as a prophet, the time in which he worked, his criticism of Israel's behaviour, the disastrous results announced and his final hope for the future. Edifying traits are lacking. But there is at least one article, continued through several numbers, on 'The New Investigations in the Orient and the Old Testament' by the renowned Professor H. Guthe.[20] Its tenor is to show that whatever Israel might have borrowed from the surrounding cultures of the Ancient Near East—'It possessed in its religion a property that raised it far over them and prevented its being mixed under them'.[21] The story of the flood (Gen. 6–8) shows how Israel adopted the material—'but Israel's belief in God has purified it'.[22] But Guthe was also a believer: he saw God's spirit working in this intellectual achievement.[23] These glances at typical contributions to one of the leading journals of German popular protestantism (one could accumulate the examples from other volumes) gives two insights. First, the role of

17. *Die christliche Welt (CW)* 1 (1887), foreword to the specimen copy, p. 1.
18. *CW* 1, p. 1.
19. *CW* 1, pp. 322-24, by a certain cand. min. V. Weichelt.
20. 'Die neuen Forschungen im Morgenlande und das Alte Testament', in *CW* 2 (1889), pp. 10-11, 18-19, 26-27, 38-39.
21. *CW* 2, p. 27.
22. *CW* 2, p. 39.
23. *CW* 2, p. 39.

the Old Testament in the practical use of the Bible in Protestantism is comparatively small. For the usual edifying meditation the practitioner in the parish would normally choose a text from the New Testament. Secondly, when the Old Testament is considered, it is mainly the task of the specialist. The usual approach would be a historical-descriptive one, including an evaluation which sees Israel's religion as a progressive stage in the development of religious thinking, compared with other Ancient Oriental religions. If the Professor of Old Testament is pious, he or she could even see God's spirit at work in this development. More often a sort of mental reservation comes across or even the express utterance that the Old Testament is not to be seen on the same level as the New. As an example, I quote from the short meditation on Ps. 62.6,[24] which the author closes with the remark: '"My soul is quiet before God who helps me", the whole depth of this old holy message is first revealed to the Christian heart...What peace really means and how God is...the Saviour first revealed.'[25] Whereas this utterance, which could be multiplied with similar ones, seems to deny to Israel's belief an independent religious value, we can also read popular articles in which a high esteem of Israel's religion is mixed with passages criticizing the low moral standard to be met with in parts of the Old Testament in a way typical of the moralism of the Enlightenment period. For instance, a contribution of a pastor F. Gleiss in the same volume as the one cited before[26] begins with a panegyric praising Israel's religion: 'Israel's importance for world history lies in its religion. Its religion, that means, the highest, best, noble in it...is the heritage which it transferred to the world.'[27] Then the author mentions for the early period he is treating Moses and Elijah as the outstanding personalities who represent in their work decisive stages of national and religious development in ancient Israel. After having described the role of Jehovah in the frame of Israel's henotheistic—not yet monotheistic—faith as national god, leader of its wars and guardian of justice he continues by stressing the moral deficiencies which are visible in the behaviour of such leading figures as Jacob the deceiver, Samuel the butcher (1 Sam. 15.33), Jehu the murderer (2 Kgs 9.24ff.)

---

24. *CW* 6 (1892), p. 709.

25. *CW* 6 (author Johanna Lang).

26. 'Israel's Gottesglauben in der ältesten Periode seiner Geschichte', *CW* 6 (1892), pp. 716-22.

27. *CW* 6, p. 716.

and Israel as a whole in numerous stories told in the Old Testament. But his conclusion is positive

> in the later periods Israel let itself be 'purified by its historical experience and be deepened in the perception of its faith...This is the clearest proof for the vigour of faith of this people and the singularity of divine education under which the history of Israel developed'.[28]

The concept of history as religious and moral education, the importance of the great personalities, the moralistic sentence on certain events narrated in the Old Testament: this specimen shows how the ideological topics inherited from the beginning of the century and before had been internalized in the judgment a normal parishioner would utter when asked for an opinion of the Old Testament.

Whereas, from 1887, the *Christliche Welt* under the editorship of Martin Rade (1857–1940) was the organ of an undogmatic, open liberalism and of the Ritschlians who had inherited from Ritschl the theological approach of the biblical-historical person of Jesus as the revealer (and even a high regard for Luther), the *Protestantische Kirchenzeitung (PKZ)* was the voice of the Protestant Union, implying a more consequent form of 'free protestantism'. We know that Holtzmann was a member of the editorial board, as was the systematic theologian R.A. Lipsius (1830–1892), professor in Jena since 1871. He was the author of a lecture on 'The Idea of God'[29] that contains some remarks of interest. In this short paper Lipsius formulates his basic religious conviction which he developed in a more detailed way in his main works:[30] that religious knowledge is no matter of the intellect but must be restricted to personal religious experience and inner feeling.[31] In this context he formulates:

> The highest expression of the religious idea of God is found in the Christian faith in the heavenly father. Christianity has replaced the God of

28. *CW* 6, pp. 721-22.

29. R.A. Lipsius, 'Die Gottesidee: Ein Vortrag', *PKZ* 24 (1877), pp. 309-19.

30. On Lipsius, cf. H. Hohlwein, 'Lipsius, Richard Albert', *RGG*[3], IV, pp. 385-86 (lit.).

31. Cf. Lipsius, 'Die Gottesidee', p. 318: 'God is to be known as far as he reveals himself, to be known from the inner processes and facts of religious life itself in which the pious immediately experiences the present acting of God'. 'In the personal spirit of man God manifests himself as a person, as a holy Thou in front of the human I, as living intelligence, as holy power of will, as eternal love revealing itself in human mind.'

the covenant of Israel by the loving father of all believers. It has brought the religious relation to its most accomplished expression imaginable. Also the Greeks call their Zeus occasionally father of gods and men, and the Old Testament religion can tell about the many proofs of paternal care which Israel's God of covenant...had shown.—But no sooner than in Christianity has the name of father been raised to the standing name of God.[32]

In these utterances it is not the historic connection between the two religions attested in the two Testaments, but the free comparison between the levels of any religions which results in the evaluation of Christianity as the supreme form of religion.

To what consequences such a position can lead becomes visible in the theses which the systematic theologian C. Holsten published in the PKZ in 1881.[33] Holsten characterized the official Church governments as a repressive system trying to ban free theological scholarship not only from the pulpits, but also from the universities. In his opinion, the reason was the protest of modern free theology against the traditional forms of confession coming down from the sixteenth and seventeenth centuries. The main points of protest include, among others: 1. The Bible is not inspired and the revealed word of God, but the revelation of God in Christ is mediated in human conscience and developing in human conscience. 2. Revelation is not an established fact, having come to its close in the New Testament after having been prepared in the Old Covenant. Rather, it is 'a spiritual principle' 'having created its realization in Christian conscience and life'.[34] 3. This principle or 'the gospel of Jesus Christ' in the Bible and in the confession of the Church is expressed in the forms of thinking of the respective times; therefore we have the right to reformulate it according to forms of thinking belonging to our own time—which is coined as the 'Christian and Protestant conscience of the individual'.[35] It is 'faith alone which raises the certainty of God's revelation in Christ in free action to the power of life over the self in the mind'.[36] 4. The idea of development and religious progress has replaced the traditional concept of depravation from the height of Biblical faith, which must be regained by reform. This

32. Lipsius, 'Die Gottesidee'.

33. C. Holsten, 'Thesen über die Aechtung der protestantischen Theologie in den Glaubensgerichten der protestantischen Kirche', *PKZ* 28 (1881), pp. 563-59.

34. Holsten, 'Thesen', p. 565.

35. Holsten, 'Thesen', p. 566.

36. Holsten, 'Thesen'.

development is not a movement restricted to the relation between the Testaments, but is going on in the history of the Christian Church understood as a kind of spiritual progress.

It is not hard to imagine what a role the Old Testament could maintain in such a global programme in which even the New Testament is just the starting point of a religious movement going forth in post-biblical times and coming to a culmination in the present. That Jesus sought a confirmation of his mission in the Old Testament seeing in it a type of the New Covenant could occasionally be mentioned as a historic observation. But P.W. Schmidt (1845–1917), a systematic theologian in Basel, saw in the fact the starting point for subsequent allegoric interpretation of the Bible, the source of all dogmatic errors.[37] Thus it cannot astonish that now a picture of Christianity is sketched which starts with the 'Gospel of Jesus'. To begin with, I shall look at the popular expression of this standpoint in the paper of a certain Wilhelm Brückner: 'The Gospel of Jesus as Basis for Evangelical Christianity.'[38] The paper is useful in this context because Brückner includes considerations about the Old Testament. 'The Gospel of Jesus' is, for him, the basis of evangelical Christianity. He defines the expression as 'the gospel which he himself proclaimed'.[39] At first it is remarkable that Brückner observed the close connections between the historical Jesus and his Old Testament heritage. But this heritage is, in his opinion, divided between two different streams: the prophetic and the nomistic.

> What the prophets communicated from the depth of their religious thought-world, lent to the piety of Israel the strong faith in the one omnipotent holy God...But the law with its many statutes and its priesthood caused a stiffening of this piety into fixed forms...[40]

Here Wellhausen's impact is clearly observable, whose *Prolegomena*[41] belonged to the most influential books in the field of Old Testament

37. 'Die Theologie als historische Wissenschaft', *PKZ* 23 (1876), pp. 581-91, 583.

38. 'Das Evangelium Jesu als die Grundlage des evangelischen Christentums', *PKZ* 43 (1896), pp. 1215-24.

39. 'Das Evangelium Jesu', p. 1215.

40. 'Das Evangelium Jesu', p. 1216.

41. Wellhausen, *Prolegomena zur Geschichte Israels* (Berlin: Reimer, 1905[6]) [*Prolegomena to the History of Israel* (trans. J.S. Black and A. Menzies; Edinburgh: A. & C. Black, 1885)].

study. His arrangement of Israel's religious history into the three epochs of early religious freedom, the advance of the law with the appearance of Deuteronomy and the late hierocracy as the end of true religious life,[42] itself a product of the prevailing intellectual climate, impressed a large public. According to Brückner, Jesus assumed a clear position in the struggle between these two positions:

> Whereas the religious life of his time and of his people stood on the side of the law with its externals, its service of work...he placed himself...with full determination on the side of the prophetical faith in God and concluded from this faith the same spirituality and inwardness.[43]

But the high esteem of the prophets does not mean that their message, taken for itself, has an immediate value for Christian faith. Later on, Brückner—after having described some details of Jesus's work—came to the conclusion: 'Therefore we can, we will keep to the gospel of Jesus as the sufficient, as the only basis of evangelical Christianity.'[44] The Old Testament, in spite of the religious value of the prophetic utterances, is just the prehistory; Jesus' message alone is the fundament of Christianity.

What we meet here, in a popular form, can be observed to be the leading principle of some of the best known theological programs of the period. I want to draw your attention especially to two of the best known publications. One is a comparatively small book of the famous Ernst Troeltsch of which Trutz Rendtorff in the introduction to a paperback reprint[45] could write: 'The...essay represents a pivot in the scientific work of Ernst Troeltsch'.[46] It is his essay, 'Die Absolutheit des Christentums und die Religionsgeschichte' (1902 [= 'The Absoluteness of Christianity and the History of Religions'[47]]). The other is A. Harnack's 'The Essence of Christianity' (1900), a series of lectures, the printed form of which was spread in about one hundred thousand copies in Germany and abroad. Both can be taken as representative of the period. It is not my intention to dwell upon the manifold work of both scholars, which has been the subject of a widespread discussion

---

42. Wellhausen, *Prolegomena*, pp. 402ff.
43. Brückner, *Evangelium*, p. 1216.
44. Brückner, *Evangelium*, p. 1220.
45. *Siebenstern-Taschenbuch* 138 (Munich/Hamburg, 1969).
46. Rendtorff in *Siebenstern-Taschenbuch* 138, p. 8.
47. Introduced by J.L. Adams, trans. by D. Reid (Richmond, VA: John Knox Press, 1971).

especially in recent years,[48] but I take the two programmatical essays as representative of the prevalent mood in liberal theology at the turn of the century.

Harnack's *Essence of Christianity*, if measured on its popularity, represents an understanding of Christianity widespread in the protestant middle classes of the Wilhelmine Empire. Therefore we can see in it more than the private opinion of its author. Even at a short glance the arrangement shows that the Old Testament does not play any positive role in Harnack's systematics. His starting point, in the first part superscribed 'The Gospel', is the message of Jesus. He divides it into three topics: 1. The kingdom of God and its coming; 2. God as father and the unlimited worth of the human soul; 3. better justice and the commandment of love. In all three topics, it is one of Harnack's approaches to stress the contrast between Jesus' message and the traditional religion of his people: 1. As regards the kingdom of God, in the message of Jesus it is already come and no longer expected in a distant future; 2. The proclamation of God as father 'and human soul so ennobled that it can unify itself with Him and does unify' shows that the gospel is not at all a positive religion as the other (religions), that it has nothing statuary and particularistic, that it is therefore *religion itself*;[49] 3. Jesus' ethics are characterized by the sharp separation from all forms of cult, laying their foundation in the inner conscience and the motive of love. That means he has disengaged ethics from religion except in the motive of humility as a leading stimulus.[50] It is well known that Harnack later formulated his strict disapproval of the Old Testament as part of the Christian Bible in his book on Marcion:[51]

> to reject the Old Testament in the second century was a mistake which the mainstream church rightly rejected; to retain it in the sixteenth century was a fate which the Reformation was still unable to avoid; but to retain it as a

48. For Troeltsch, see E. Apfelbacher, 'Frömmigkeit und Wissenschaft: Ernst Troeltsch und sein theologisches Programm', *Beiträge zur ökumenischen Theologie* 18 (Paderborn, e.a., 1978). For Harnack, F.W. Kantzenbach, 'Harnack, Adolf von (1851–1930)', *TRE* 14 (1985), pp. 450-58.

49. *Das Wesen des Christentums: Neuauflage zum fünfzigsten Jahrestag des ersten Erscheinens mit einem Geleitwort von R. Bultmann* (Stuttgart: Klotz, 1950), p. 38—last words in italics in the original. This edition was also reprinted as a *Siebenstern-Taschenbuch* (Munich, 1964).

50. Harnack, *Das Wesen des Christentums*, pp. 43-44.

51. *Marcion: Das Evangelium vom fremden Gott* (Leipzig: Hinrichs, 1924²; repr. Darmstadt: Wiss. Buchgesellschaft, 1960).

canonical document in Protestantism after the nineteenth century is the consequence of a crippling of religion and the church.[52]

After Harnack, I shall glance at Troeltsch and his essay 'The Absoluteness of Christianity and the History of Religions'.[53] It is not my intention to enter into the intricate debate about Troeltsch and his very various work. I want to stress that the title of this essay is misleading insofar as it was not Troeltsch's opinion that the absoluteness of Christianity could be proven.[54] That was impossible for him, as he mistrusted the metaphysical background of Hegel's program, in which the term was coined. To be a Christian was his personal choice.[55] But the History of Religion as a scholarly program is connected with this decision: the person who is a Christian—and Troeltsch saw himself as one who was deeply rooted in this religion—'will originate in the strongest and deepest and will assume from the others only that what may be developed by them in an especially impressing way'.[56] Christianity as a 'historical whole' comprises 'Israelite prophetism, the preaching of Jesus, the mysticism of Paul, the idealism of platonism and stoicism, the melting of European cultural unity in the middle ages, the Germanic individualism of Luther, the conscientiousness and activity of Protestantism'.[57] What is striking in this enumeration is that it describes Christianity as an amalgam of contrasting ideological influences without differentiating between the essential in which Christian faith consists and the forms of thinking in which it might have expressed itself through the centuries. This form of idealism, which has cast off its metaphysical foundation, leads to an aesthetic approach to the Old Testament as seen in the work of Hermann Gunkel, for instance in his contribution to the volume which was intended to inform a broader interested public about the 'situation of religion in present life'[58]: *Beiträge zur Weiterentwicklung der christlichen Religion.*[59] Though Gunkel's essay is soberly entitled 'The Old Testament in the

---

52. *Marcion*, p. 217.
53. *Die Absolutheit des Christentums und die Religionsgeschichte* (Tübingen: Mohr, 1902[2]; 1929[3]). Cf. above, n. 45.
54. For the problem, Apfelbacher, 'Fömmigkeit und Wissenschaft', esp. pp. 220-38.
55. Troeltsch, *Absolutheit*, pp. 74, 84.
56. Troeltsch, *Absolutheit*, p. 74.
57. Troeltsch, *Absolutheit*, p. 85.
58. Gunkel, *Beiträge*, III (Munich, 1905).
59. Gunkel, *Beiträge*, III.

Light of Modern Research'[60] it contains nearly hymnic praises of Israel's religion which for Gunkel is, above all, the soil of religious personality. 'There rise powerful, demonic men, moved in their innermost marrow, full of passion...Such men are at that time the prophets; next to them the poet of Job...lastly the psalmists...'[61] Neo-romanticism forms the utterances, for example: 'One has to read[62] such majestically roaring speeches of Isaiah to understand how unjustified it is that nowadays some who are less informed about the Old Testament are denying to Israel any creative power in religion'.[63] Using aesthetic measures, this standpoint is rather subjective and open to criticism from everybody who is not ready, for instance, to believe in the idea of personality or to whom poetic beauty is not a scale on which to measure religious truth. Therefore Gunkel's approach, though very popular for a time, did not possess the strength to resist the criticism against the Old Testament coming from different sides during his lifetime.

My last duty in the frame of this short paper is to inquire into the impact which anti-semitism might have had on the view of the Old Testament. After many discussions on the role of anti-semitism in the German Second Empire,[64] it is surprising to hear that the importance of anti-semitism for the judgment of the Old Testament is less central than one might guess. Take for instance the utterance of A. Harnack which he published in 1890:[65]

> There may exist a Jewish problem in a national and economic sense—I do not know that and am not competent for it—but this do I know that to write anti-semitism on the banners of Evangelical Christianity is a sad scandal.

60. Gunkel, *Beiträge*, III, pp. 40-76.
61. Gunkel, *Beiträge*, III, pp. 70-71.
62. 'lesen' for 'lasen'.
63. Gunkel, *Beiträge*, III, p. 71.
64. Cf. for example, the handbook *Kirche und Synagoge* (ed. K.H. Rengstorff and S. von Kortzfleisch; 2 vols.; Stuttgart: Klett, 1970), esp. ch. 10: 'Protestantismus nach 1848' by F.-H. Philipp, II, pp. 280-357; H. Greive, 'Zu den Ursachen des Antisemitismus im deutschen Kaiserreich von 1871', *Judaica* 27 (1971), pp. 184-92; S. St Lehr, *Antisemitismus—Religiöse Motive im sozialen Vorurteil: Aus der Frühgeschichte des Antisemitismus in Deutschland 1870–1914* (Munich: Kaiser, 1974).
65. 'Der Evangelisch-soziale Kongress zu Berlin', *PJ* 65 (1890), pp. 566-76, 574.

This is written by the same Harnack who frankly denied any importance of the Old Testament for the Christian faith! Indeed, anti-semitism in the Second Empire was not mainly a religious, but a nationalistic and economic, syndrome, though partly nourished by religious arguments from the side of its protagonists.[66] Organized anti-semitism came from a comparatively unimportant political force, represented by the group of five members of the German Social party in the Reichstag of 1890. Better known is the anti-semitism of the Berlin court-preacher, A. Stoecker, which originated in the first decade of the period and for a while gained a large following among people who were searching for a scapegoat for the economic problems following the deep depression in the second half of the seventies. They found it in the Jews, some of whom were visibly in influential positions in economic management and the press. Stoecker followed the prejudices of his adherents and delivered anti-semitic speeches to a large audience in the gatherings of his Christian Social Party, founded 1878.[67] Lacking ability in organization prevented his success on the political platform, but the influence of his thought was far-reaching in deepening the vulgar anti-semitism of many. The same Stoecker, however—and this is the observation I want to emphasise—published a collection of his popular sermons on Old Testament texts which show him as a conservative theologian seeing the standing importance of the Old Testament in the traditional scheme of prediction and fulfilment.[68] The apparent contrast disappears with the insight that reading the Old Testament as part of the Christian canon— explicit or not—denies the claim of current Judaism to any right of its own to the text. For a just judgment it must be added that the German Jewish community in the second half of the nineteenth century had passed through emancipation and many Jews wished assimilation instead of claiming their special religious identity. Even Zionism was a political, not a religious movement. It should also be mentioned that there were other voices than Harnack's who courageously voted against the

66. For details, see for example the volume, W.E. Mosse and A. Paucker (eds.), *Juden im Wilhelminischen Deutschland* (Tübingen: Mohr, 1976); U. Tal, *Christians and Jews in Germany: Religion, Politics, and Ideology in the Second Reich, 1870– 1914* (Ithaca, NY: Cornell University Press, 1975).

67. Cf. A. Stoecker, *Christlich-Sozial. Reden und Aufsätze* (Berlin: Buchhandlung der Berliner Stadtmission, 1890²).

68. *Verheissung und Erfüllung: Ein Jahrgang Volkspredigten über alttestamentliche Texte* (Berlin, n.d. [1897]).

popular anti-semitism from the standpoint of a Christian conscience. One of them was the young Erich Foerster (1865–1945), a pupil of Harnack,[69] to whom Rade opened the pages of the *Christliche Welt* for a lengthy article, in which he refuted the alleged justifications diffused by a tendentious public.[70]

Indirectly however, the growing subconscious anti-semitism had an impact on judgment about the Old Testament. Curiously enough, the alleged results of scholarly research played an important part in it. One gets an impression of this connection by perusing Houston Stewart Chamberlain's book *Die Grundlagen des neunzehnten Jahrhunderts* (The Fundaments of the Nineteenth Century).[71] This work, that became very popular in the anti-semitic movement, and after his death (in 1927) also with the *Deutsche Christen*, was not at all a primitive ideological pamphlet, but the work of a man who tried to present himself as being up to date and well informed about the scholarly discussion in the different fields he was discussing. It is striking to see that for the history of the Jews he uses such Jewish authors as Heinrich Graetz,[72] Ludwig Philippson[73] and C.G. Montefiore,[74] but also the Christian scholars of his time, such as E. Renan, H. Gunkel, W. Robertson Smith and—most of all—J. Wellhausen. The three stage model of the history of Israel's religion that Wellhausen had made popular, in which the earliest period fitted to the Protestant ideal of religious freedom and the latest, post-exilic period was the stage of Jewish torpid legalism,[75] formed the

69. On him, K.G. Steck, 'Foerster, Erich', *RGG*[3], II, pp. 986-87.

70. E. Foerster, 'Evangelische Gedanken zur Judenfrage', *CW* 5 (1891), pp. 313-21, 368-75, 387-93.

71. I used the 16th edn (Munich: F. Bruckmann, 1932) ('Ungekürzte Volksausgabe').

72. On Graetz (1817–1891), M. Graetz, 'Graetz, Heinrich', *TRE* 14 (1985), pp. 112-15. Chamberlain quotes Graetz's *Volkstümliche Geschichte der Juden* (3 vols.; Leipzig: O. Leiner, 1887–89); Graetz, *Gnostizismus und Judentum* (Krotoschin, 1846).

73. *Israelitische Religionslehre* (Leipzig: Baumgärtner, 1861).

74. He quotes the author's *Religion of the Ancient Hebrews: Lectures on the Origin and Growth of Religion as Illustrated by the Religion of the Ancient Hebrews* (London: Willliams & Norgate, 1892, 1893[2]; repr. New York: AMS Press, 1979).

75. Chamberlain quotes Wellhausen's *Israelitische und jüdische Geschichte* (1894; repr. Berlin: de Gruyter, 1958) and his *Prolegomena zur Geschichte Israels* (Berlin, 1905[6]), in which the scheme is most clearly developed. Also Hans Liebeschütz, *Das Judentum im deutschen Geschichtsbild von Hegel bis Max Weber* (Tübingen: Mohr, 1967), pp. 245-68, does not seem to know the impact of

common picture of the Old Testament for a long time. It returned as late as 1940 in M. Noth's *Die Gesetze im Pentateuch: Ihre Voraussetzungen und ihr Sinn*.[76] This construction allowed praise to the prophets as models of religious personalities and gave modern Protestants as their legitimate heirs, without being forced to meditate on the importance of the Torah for Biblical thinking. In the margin, it might be of interest that Chamberlain had his own racist theory which allowed him to differentiate between the Jews—as a race to be found in the present diaspora and already mentioned in the Bible—and the Israelites.[77] Israelites were for him, just the inhabitants of the Northern Kingdom, whom he regarded as a different race. In his opinion, all really important religious personalities were members of this population, including Jesus himself who, being a Galilean, was treated as a stranger by the Jews in Jerusalem. Taken to the extreme these racist theories lead to the terrible consequences of the later holocaust. Before they became preponderant, baptism was the usual way of assimilation and prevented being regarded as a Jew any more, at least in the second generation.

What I wanted to stress in this part of my paper is that one has to be careful to avoid over-simplification. Though partly connected with one another, the question of the evaluation of the Old Testament in German Protestantism and the problem of anti-semitism are two different matters and cannot be lumped together, if one wants to get a clear picture.

To sum up, it seems to me that the evaluation of the Old Testament in German Protestantism which I reflected on, in the main, with the representatives of so-called liberal theology, is a fitting yardstick by which to measure the deeper convictions that lay behind the utterances of the leading scholars of the period, and the typical ways of thinking of the educated middle classes. For these, the contributions to the popular theological periodicals (which I selected) are representative. It remains to ask how much these convictions are still alive: what has survived the Nazi period, the collapse of that ideology, the period of Dialectic Theology and so on? Perhaps we recognize some of these judgments in ourselves? The conclusion are open to debate.

Wellhausen's construction upon the popular view of the so-called 'late Judaism' in the biblical period after the exile.

76. Reprinted in his *Gesammelte Studien zum Alten Testament* (Munich: Kaiser, 1957), pp. 9-141.

77. *Grundlagen*, pp. 409ff.

THE NOTION OF HISTORICISM AND 19TH CENTURY THEOLOGY*

Gunter Scholtz

Introduction

The notion 'historicism'[1] counts among those which contemporary scholars in the humanities either cannot or do not want to renounce. At the same time, the notion creates a lot of misunderstanding due to its various use. Some reference books mention in their bibliographies under the heading 'historicism' Karl R. Popper's well-known title *The Poverty of Historicism*, as if Popper wanted to criticize what one usually called historicism, namely, that form of scientific history fixed to the notions of individuality and development. Hermann Lübbe then made clear that Popper's philosophy, on the contrary, has justified this kind of historicism and laid its theoretical foundation.[2] In short: 'historicism' is an important notion which presents difficulties. This is why, in 1972, Wesley Morris was absolutely right in beginning his book *Toward a New Historicism* with the statement: 'The meaning of the term historicism, according to a distinguished historian, has become so broad as to make the word useless for the philosophy of history. It does not take long to discover why he reached this conclusion; there is little agreement as to

---

* For the translation of this article I am grateful to Dr Reiner Hülsewiesche.

1. In the English language we find today only the word 'historicism'. In German there are two forms: *Historismus* and *Historizismus*. The second one always has a pejorative sense and is a term of criticism; the first one can be used in very different meanings, to characterize, to criticize, and to name programmes. This is a source of misunderstandings and difficulties of translations. See for example: Hayden White, *Auch Klio dichtet oder Die Fiktion des Faktischen: Studien zur Tropologie des historisichen Diskurses* (Stuttgart: Klett-Cotta, 1986), p. 123 (note of the translator, and note 1). To the change of the word from 'historism' to 'historicism' in America see Dwight E. Lee and Robert N. Beck: 'The Meaning of "Historicism"', *AHR* 59 (1953/54), pp. 568-77.

2. Hermann Lübbe, *Geschichtsbegriff und Geschichtsinteresse: Analytik und Pragmatik der Historie* (Basel: Schwabe, 1977), pp. 120ff.

what the term means and less to its origins.'[3]
It was Ernst Troeltsch, who eventually made historicism a well-known
notion. In his treatise *The 19th Century*, an article written for the
Realencyklopädie für protestantische Theologie und Kirche of 1913, he
applied the notion to characterize the century: 'Historicism constitutes
one of the outstanding elements of this century's spiritual state
(*Seelenverfassung*).'[4] Historicism here denotes 'historical relativism',
which, like 'naturalistic determinism', created 'paralysing' and 'enervating
effects'. Historicism, so he went on, is the 'completely relativistic
rediscovery of any arbitrary past formations with the burdening and
tiring impression of general historical knowledge and skeptical non-
productivity for the present'. One may assume that this notion of
historicism had already inhaled Nietzsche's criticism of the historicising
nineteenth century.[5] At any rate, Nietzsche's criticism of culture was
given broad treatment in this 1913 treatise.[6]

This meaning of historicism is just one, beside others. Before Troeltsch
the notion was already in use in various, quite different, senses. In the
course of the nineteenth century, which the contemporaries called 'the
historical' century, to mark its difference to the eighteenth, the
'philosophical' century, the notion of historicism was used in manifold
ways: for individual programmes, for the criticism of opponents and for
the characterization of important tendencies.[7] So I will state the central

3.   Wesley Morris, *Toward a New Historicism* (Princeton: Princeton University
Press, 1972), p. vii.
4.   Ernst Troeltsch, 'Neunzehntes Jahrhundert', *RE*[3], XXIV, p. 250. *Aufsätze zur
Geistesgeschichte und Religionssoziologie* (= *Gesammelte Schriften*, IV) (Tübingen:
J.C.B. Mohr [Paul Siebeck], 1925), p. 628.
5.   Friedrich Nietzsche, *Vom Nutzen und Nachtheil der Historie für das Leben:
Unzeitgemässe Betrachtungen. Zweites Stück* (Leipzig: E.W. Fritzsch, 1874).
6.   Troeltsch, *Aufsätze*, p. 642.
7.   Concerning the history and use of the term historicism, see: Karl Heussi, *Die
Krisis des Historismus* (Tübingen: J.C.B. Mohr, 1932); D.E. Lee and R.N. Beck,
'The Meaning of "Historicism"'; G. Scholtz, 'Historismus', *Historisches Wörterbuch der Philosophie* (ed. Joachim Ritter; Basel: Schwabe & Co, 1974), III,
pp. 1142-47; Otto Gerhard Oexle, '"Historismus": Überlegungen zur Geschichte
des Phänomens und des Begriffs', *Braunschweigische Wissenschaftliche
Gesellschaft: Jahrbuch, 1986* (Göttingen, 1986), pp. 119-55. In the following I will
try to aply the differentiation of the notion (given in a former work of mine) to the
realm of theology. Cf. *Zwischen Wissenschaftsanspruch und Orientierungsbedürfnis:
Zu Grundlage und Wandel der Geisteswissenschaften* (Frankfurt a.M.: Suhrkamp,
1991), pp. 131ff.

meanings of the notion and will then show that all of them can also represent important tendencies of nineteenth-century theology. I will do this for three reasons: first of all, this makes clear that theology is completely embedded in the development of all the other humanities and hence does not lead a separate existence. Secondly, I hope to discover in this way paradigm shifts or at least dislocations in the history of theology. And thirdly, I am convinced that those problems and tendencies which the notion of historicism contained then are also effective during the twentieth century and in an open or more hidden way even determine the discussion of contemporary theology.

The five basic meanings which historicism received in the nineteenth century are as follows:

1. Historicism as broadening of the historical, genetical view, to all phenomena of culture, in short, the universal historical view of the human world, also including reason. (This is the meaning of the term which was presumably introduced into German first by Novalis and Friedrich Schlegel around 1800.[8])

2. Historicism as that kind of philosophy of history which presumes to understand the order and rationality of all history in its course, or at least seems to have an idea of it— that is, metaphysics of history (this is the usage in the middle of the nineteenth century: be it programmatically, as used by the late idealistic philosopher C.J. Braniss, or be it critically or indifferently, as used for example by R. Haym and R. Zimmermann with regard to Hegel's philosophy[9]).

3. Historicism as a glorifying retrospect of the past and an adherence to the old values, while simultaneously criticizing everything new: romanticism, traditionalism and conservatism (for

---

8. Novalis, *Schriften* (ed. P. Kluckhohn, R. Samuel), III (= *Das philosophische Werk*, II) (Stuttgart: W. Kohlhammer, 1960), p. 446; *Kritische Friedrich-Schlegel-Ausgabe* (ed. Ernst Behler), vol. XVI, pp. 35, 37, 38, 41; XVIII, pp. 91, 484, 490; XIX, p. 184.

9. Christlieb Julius Braniss, *Die wissenschaftliche Aufgabe der Gegenwart als leitende Idee im akademischen Studium: Hodegetische Vorträge* (Breslau: L.F. Maske, 1848), pp. 116ff.; Rudolf Haym, *Hegel und seine Zeit* (Berlin: Gaertner, 1857; repr. Darmstadt: Wiss. Buchges., 1962), pp. 354, 467; Robert Zimmermann, *Geschichte der Ästhetik als philosophischer Wissenschaft* (Vienna: Wilhelm Braunmüller, 1858), pp. 607ff.

example L. Feuerbach[10] in 1839 in his criticism of the historian H. Leo, or R. Haym in his critical remarks about Hegel).

4. Historicism as a restriction of historical research to the collection and securing of facts along the guidelines of philological or historical methods, for example historical positivism and objectivism (like R. Eucken, K. Lamprecht, and later Troeltsch on the unfruitful tendencies in the history of the ending of the nineteenth century[11]).

5. Historicism as the relativity of all value and orientation systems which makes them mere transitory phenomena in the incalculable flow of history; that is, historical relativism (as used by I.H. Fichte[12] in respect of the Historical School of law and later predominantly by E. Troeltsch in respect of the nineteenth century as a whole).

These five basic meanings—(1) the universal historical view, (2) the metaphysics of history, (3) romanticism and traditionalism, (4) objectivism and positivism, (5) relativism—roughly reflect the passing of the dispositions of consciousness of history or historical consciousness from the end of the eighteenth to the end of the nineteenth century. It was typical of the time around 1800 and the first half of the nineteenth century to develop a material history of philosophy and to reconstruct history in general as a reasonable process of development, as an evolution of spirit (if you remember, for example, the philosophies of history created by Schelling and Hegel and their followers). It was typical of the romantic tendencies beginning at the same time, to turn toward the past and to trace the cultural ideals in it which were superior to contemporary culture and could serve as their ideal model (let me remind you of

10. Ludwig Feuerbach, *Erläuterungen und Ergänzungen zum Wesen des Christenthums, Sämtliche Werke* (ed. Wilhelm Bolin and Friedrich Jodl; Stuttgart–Bad Cannstatt: Frommann, 2nd edn, 1960), pp. 1-2, 43-44.

11. Rudolf Eucken, *Geistige Strömungen der Gegenwart* (Leipzig: Veit, 1904³), p. 259; Karl Lamprecht, *Moderne Geschichtswissenschaft* (Freiburg i.B.: Heyfelder, 1905), p. 12.

12. Immanuel Hermann Fichte, *System der Ethik: Erster kritischer Theil: Die philosophischen Lehren von Recht, Staat und Sitte in Deutschland, Frankreich und England von der Mitte des achtzehnten Jahrhunderts bis zur Gegenwart* (Leipzig: Dyk'sche Buchhandlung, 1850), pp. 465ff.; cf. Heinrich Moritz Chalybäus, *System der speculativen Ethik, oder Philosophie der Familie, des Staats und der religiösen Sitte* (Leipzig: Brockhaus, 1850), II, pp. 42ff.

Novalis's title *Die Christenheit oder Europa* [Christianity or Europe] or the Historical School of law which was founded by F.C. v. Savigny). It was typical of the second half of the nineteenth century, however, to concentrate on the indubitable facts in history, to obtain from history knowledge which is just as positive as that which the sciences obtained from nature (this is illustrated by the positivist currents, for example T. Buckle, and in the new methodologies of history, E. Bernheim). At the same time, the appearance of historical relativism is equally typical of the end of the nineteenth century.

Because the central meanings of the notion of historicism denote mainstreams of historical thought and principal attitudes to history, these five basic meanings can also be applied to nineteenth-century theology. Theology, as I am going to show, used that notion of historicism even before Troeltsch. It can be expected from historical research, that this notion can be traced in further theological contexts. In the next step I will try to explain ways in which the notion was applied, and I intend to show which positions in the history of theology might be co-ordinated with them. It should be borne in mind that the notion could be used affirmatively or critically, and evaluation was a question of conception: what was a desirable historicism for the one standpoint was bad historicism for the next.

Historicism 1: The Universal Historical View

When F. Schlegel and Novalis used the term 'historicism' for the first time, around 1800, they demanded—as far as we can discern from their fragments—that we no longer look at the human world as a realm of static relations, but as a changing and developing world, in a word, that we look upon it as history. Today we still have the same broad notion of historicism: historicism as the observation of the human world as a whole in its variety and its steady development.

This historicism, which expresses itself clearly at the end of the eighteenth century, can be interpreted as an unintended result of modern science and of the Enlightenment. First, because these two had created a new situation which brought into consciousness that humanity was living in a world which was separated from Greek and Roman antiquity by an epochal break (Francis Bacon and, around 1700, the French Academy, had already discussed this new situation). Secondly, the Enlightenment had opened an unprejudiced view over the wide field of the human through the destruction of established concepts of Christian salvation or universal history. Richness of experience and, combined with this, experiences of divergence and an abundance of new empirical knowledge, were the basic conditions and constituent elements of this historicism.

Although a result of the new science, historicism, especially in Germany, could adopt a theological character; this is true at least for its self reflection, its own theory. For the new colourful abundance of culture was in this case interpreted and affirmed with the help of a theological model: the revelation of God. Herder, who certainly laid the path of historicism for Schlegel and Novalis, as well as for us, made revelation, following Shaftesbury's lead, a notion in his metaphysics:[13] everything existing from the realms of nature and history is a revelation of God. Herder's historicist theory of history, which encourages the study of the manifold human world, thus clearly has a theological disposition. The new historical abundance of reality, which was wrenched off from traditional theology, was theologically interpreted in a new way.

Naturally this thought especially changed people's relation to the different religions. The Enlightenment had understood the historical variety of religions simply as a source of dispute and so as a testimony for the mere human origin of religions and therefore proclaimed—in deism—a general religion of reason. But this solution soon seemed insufficient. The deist God either was completely indeterminate and void, or showed elements derived from a historical religion. Under the auspices of historicism one can, therefore, overcome the problem of the plurality of religions in a completely different way: they are states of God's revelation or branches of God's revelation. This solution is hinted at or even presented in different possible ways by Lessing, Herder and Hamann, whereas Schleiermacher in his *Reden über die Religion* in 1799 put it forward as a principle.[14] And this solution to the problem shows many advantages. One can accept divergent forms of religion because they are willed by God: the manifold religions do not oppose God's unity; and in this way systematical theological ground is prepared for the history of religion. All the human discourses about God, all the

13. Johann Gottfried Herder, *Metakritik zur Kritik der reinen Vernunft* (1799). *Sämtliche Werke*, XXI (ed. B. Suphan; Berlin: Weidmannsche Buchhandlung, 1881), pp. 62ff., 68, 142.

14. Friedrich Schleiermacher, *Über die Religion: Reden an die Gebildeten unter ihren Verächtern* (Berlin: J.F. Unger, 1799).

for the history of religion. All the human discourses about God, all the anthropomorphisms, are finally God's own acts, forms of God's condescendence, revelation. The historical character and the 'positive' in the different religions are not the unreasonable any more, a matter of arbitrariness, the 'statuary', as Kant called it, but, on the contrary, the specifically religious.

This results in a first thesis: with historicism as an insight into the divergence and changeability of the human world, the notion of revelation, still strictly abhorred in deism, advances to become a central term of theology and religious philosophy. This notion, then, comes to terms with the multitudinous forms of religion and even favours their historical exploration, because theology now has to deal with different forms of God's revelation, everywhere. At the time when the science of language became the history of language, when aesthetics integrated the history of art, and when in law a Historical School began to emerge, simultaneously theology became foremost theology of revelation and so laid a systematic foundation enabling it to turn toward a divergent history.

Historicism 2: Metaphysics and Theology of History

This is not a different historicism in substance, but only in form: it is historicism 1 brought into a systematic or dogmatic shape. R. Haym called Hegel this kind of historicist. And Hegel himself and his theological disciples represent this kind of historicism in the history of theology, too, the first and foremost exponent being P. Marheineke. His dogmatic cannot make God conceivable except as a self-revealing God, and it comprises God's 'inner self-revelation' (the logos), and the 'outer revelation': creation, preservation, providence, epiphany of Christ, hence the whole world.[15]

The so-called Catholic Tübinger School accepted this broad notion of revelation, too. J.S. Drey and F.A. Staudenmaier looked at revelations not only as 'supernatural communications' which humans require because of human reason's weakness; but the whole 'universe', world and humanity, are God's revelations.[16] The doctrine of revelation is

15. Philip Marheineke, *Die Grundlehren der christlichen Dogmatik als Wissenschaft* (Berlin: Duncker & Humblot, 1827²), §§115, 206ff.

16. Johann Sebastian Drey, *Kurze Einleitung in das Studium der Theologie, mit Rücksicht auf den wissenschaftlichen Standpunct und das katholische System* (Tübingen, 1819; repr. Frankfurt a.M.: Minerva, 1966), p. 10; *Die Apologetik als*

then, too, as Staudenmaier titled a book in 1837, 'Science of the Principles of History'.[17] To my knowledge, neither Herder nor Schleiermacher, nor the Hegelians and the representatives of the Tübinger School, called themselves historicists. Nevertheless, they might certainly have been characterized as such, for example by R. Haym, and it is more suitable a label for them than for Hegel himself.

Staudenmaier, for example, emphasized that the true conception of the world (*die wahre Weltanschauung*) is based on Christian revelation and that it is a *historical* one: 'Christendom...is the *system of God's activities*. God's activities cannot but be conceived historically, and that is whence the historical conception of the world (*die historische Weltanschauung*) of Christendom generates itself.'[18] And because for Staudenmaier theology explains and illustrates a historical conception of the world, it cannot take the form of a 'construction *a priori*', like philosophy, but rather it has to be a 'reconstruction *a posteriori* and *a priori* at the same time'.[19] Why should we not be allowed to call this a historicism in the sense of a speculative theology of history? The historical speculation which a short time later Braniss programmatically called historicism is certainly not very far from this theology, especially as regards its principles.

Historicism as metaphysics of history is thus not only traceable in philosophy but in theology as well. Here especially, it receives a systematic shape, different to the science of law, for example, where Savigny and Puchta were satisfied with mere allusions concerning an organically developing national spirit (*Volksgeist*) (nevertheless, this is metaphysics of history, too). Philosophy and theology draw together under the sign of that metaphysical, speculative historicism. Philosophy accepts the theological notion of revelation and widens it: revelation then is God's manifestation in nature and history (Hegel);[20] and theology in

Erscheinung. I. *Philosophie der Offenbarung* (Mainz, 1838; repr. Frankfurt a.M.: Minerva, 1967).

17. Franz Anton Staudenmaier, *Geist der göttlichen Offenbarung, oder Wissenschaft der Geschichtsprincipien des Christenthums* (Giessen, 1837; repr. Frankfurt a.M.: Minerva, 1967), cf. pp. 14-15.

18. Staudenmaier, *Geist der göttlichen Offenbarung*, pp. 118, 119.

19. Staudenmaier, *Geist der göttlichen Offenbarung*, p. 119.

20. G.W.F. Hegel, *Enzyklopädie der philosophischen Wissenschaften im Grundrisse* (1830), §§383-84. Cf. F.W.J. Schelling: 'the history as a whole is a progressive gradually developing revelation', (*Sämtliche Werke*. I.3. *System des transzendentalen Idealismus* [Stuttgart, Augsburg: Cotta, 1858 (1800)], p. 603).

return joins in this. Metaphysical or historico-theological historicism is thus nothing but a historicism of the first kind, explicitly founded in speculation and theology.

Historicism 3: Traditionalism and Romanticism

This third version of historicism existed during the nineteenth century, to my knowledge, only in a critical sense. The word is used quite early by the theologian W.M.L. de Wette. In 1816 he characterized Schleiermacher's learned student, the classical scholar August Boeckh, thus: he, Boeckh, 'seems to have returned from the unphilosophical historicism (*Historizismus*), at least, he expressed lately that one soon wouldn't dare to think for oneself, but would only ruminate old wisdom'.[21] This is the kind of historicism with which Feuerbach later reproached the historian H. Leo: he meant the burden of history, a conservatism and traditionalism which only looks backwards, and which, as Troeltsch was to say later, makes the present unproductive and paralyzes it. It is possible that this critical version of historicism was already formed for theology and applied in the nineteenth-century, for example by liberal theologians who campaigned against what they called restoration. Among the theological restoration trends of the nineteenth century Troeltsch counted for example Methodism and the Oxford Movement, the new pietist groups and Neo-Scholasticism;[22] and in Germany the Hengstenberg party, Neo-Thomism and the Old Lutherans (*Altlutheraner*) also belonged to these circles. For the liberal or progressive minded and for the Hegelians, too, all those were historicists in the sense of traditionalists or, at least, could have been called such.

Ferdinand Kattenbusch used the notion similarly in 1908 in his entry in the *Realencyklopädie für protestantische Theologie und Kirche* entitled 'Theologie'. Here he stated that, compared with modern psychologism, Albrecht Ritschl's theology 'could be perceived to be mere historicism', because Ritschl spoke of a 'fixed, closed revelation',

transzendentalen Idealismus [Stuttgart, Augsburg: Cotta, 1858 (1800)], p. 603).

21. Max Lenz, *Geschichte der Königlichen Friedrich-Wilhelms-Universität zu Berlin* (Halle a.d.S.: Verlag der Buchhandlung des Waisenhauses, 1910), I, p. 1910 (note).

22. Ernst Troeltsch, 'Die Restaurationsepoche am Anfang des 19. Jahrhunderts' (1913), *Aufsätze zur Geistesgeschichte und Religionssoziologie* (= *Gesammelte Schriften*, IV), pp. 587-614.

obedience. 'From this point onwards dogma receives a character of mastership over the individual, which scientifically assigns dogma a strong religious meaning'.[23] Historicism in this case amounts to 'positivism of revelation'; a theology that declares New Testament revelation to be the sole historical authority and carries a strongly confessional feature.

The notion of revelation serves to demonstrate most clearly the difference between conservative and speculative universal historicism: whereas the Catholic Tübinger School conceived the notion of revelation so broadly that nature and history were founded in it, the counter movement, namely neo-scholasticism, restricted it to an orthodox sense. For H. Denzinger and J. Kleutgen, revelation was the 'disclosure [of Godly truth and intentions] through the word or by allowing the object of revelation itself to be immediately beheld (*Schauenlassen*)'.[24] For traditionalism, speculative historicism was no longer theological enough: it was diluted, as it were, by philosophy—whereas conservative historicism was for the speculative universal view too narrow and too strictly hostile towards modernity; in a conservative perspective, the world as a whole could not be understood theologically. In this way, the third meaning of historicism sets itself clearly apart from the first and second meanings.

Troeltsch gave a sociological explanation for this kind of conservatism in theology and religion. According to him, through the differentiation of modern life, religion dissociated itself from public life and the sphere of economy and, consequently, lost its relevance, but beside these sectors it found a niche, so to speak. Restorative theology was too weak to shape the whole society, but it would be strong enough to hold its ground.[25] According to the new functionalist theory of religion,[26] Troeltsch's critical remarks concerning restorative theology are valid for every

23. Ferdinand Kattenbusch, 'Theologie', *RE³*, XXI, p. 912; cf. F.K., *Von Schleiermacher zu Ritschl: Zur Orientierung über die Dogmatik des neunzehnten Jahrhunderts* (Giessen: J. Ricker'sche Verlagsbuchhandlung, 1903³), pp. 60ff.

24. Heinrich Denzinger, *Vier Bücher von der religiösen Erkenntniss* (Würzburg, 1856; repr. Frankfurt a.M.: Minerva, 1967), I, p. 116. Cf. Josef Kleutgen, *Die Theologie der Vorzeit* (Münster: Theissing'sche Buchhandlung, 1854), II, pp. 61ff., 342ff.; III (1860), pp. 386ff., 444ff.

25. Troeltsch, 'Die Restaurationsepoche', p. 613; 'Das Neunzehnte Jahrhundert', p. 647.

26. Hermann Lübbe, *Religion nach der Aufklärung* (Graz: Styria, 1986); cf. Niklas Luhmann, *Funktion der Religion* (Frankfurt a.M.: Suhrkamp, 1977).

religion. In the modern, secularized society, religion is shut out of most sectors of public life and so loses social influence and power. But for this theory of religion, that is not a sign of the weakness and decline of religion and theology, but this development only means that religion in modern times is completely limited to its own sphere: that of overcoming contingency, the contingency of everything the human being can neither calculate nor have power over. To speak of restoration and conservatism in theology is probably only possible for one who, like Troeltsch, is convinced of a progressing evolution of Christendom or at least calls for it.[27]

Historicism 4: Historical Positivism

To my knowledge, this version of the notion was not used until around the end of the nineteenth century: R. Eucken, K. Lamprecht and shortly thereafter E. Troeltsch, expressed with its help a general criticism of the newer historically oriented humanities, which took science as their methodological ideal and only accumulated historical facts. For how long will the mind and nerves of the human being be able to bear, Troeltsch asks, the constantly expanding mass of data?[28]

This variation, historicism as historical positivism, is prominently formed by theology at the end of the nineteenth century, and for modern theology this meaning of historicism is without any doubt the most important. For this notion aimed at the historico-philological scientific orientation of theology, which was looked upon as a danger.

In 1892 Martin Kähler published a book entitled *The So-Called Historical Jesus and the Real Biblical Christ*. In that work Kähler calls modern life of Jesus research 'historicism' and criticizes it sharply. According to him it is justifiable neither as a scholarly nor as a theological undertaking, because 'we don't possess any sources for a life of Jesus which a scientific historian might accept as reliable and sufficient'.[29] This is why, for lack of a solid basis, all results of the life of Jesus research are mere constructions of a history which alienates the biblical world from its meaning and destroys faith.

---

27. Troeltsch, *Glaubenslehre* (Munich: Duncker & Humbolt, 1925).
28. Troeltsch, 'Das Neunzehnte Jahrhundert', p. 625.
29. Martin Kähler, *Der sogenannte historische Jesus und der geschichtliche, biblische Christus* (Leipzig: A. Deichertsche Verlagsbuchhandlung, 1913²), pp. 49, 118.

The historical Jesus of a modern writer conceals the living Christ from us. The Jesus presented by the life of Jesus research is just a modern degenerated species of the productions of human creative art, not better than the discredited dogmatic Christ of Byzantine christology; both are just as distant from the real Christ. Historicism in this respect is as arbitrary, as humanly arrogant, as faithlessly gnostic as dogmaticism, which was also modern in its time.[30]

Historicism is for Kähler that historico-philological positivism, which in life of Jesus research surrenders to illusions concerning the security of its basis and so has destructive consequences.

Nevertheless, Kähler did not want to excommuniate philologico-historical research, he only attacked the modern gullibility vis-à-vis science: one lives in general, he says, in 'idolatry of infallible science'.[31] In theology this has led to the view that every dogma only contains arbitrary assertions, whereas statements about reality solely are expected from history.[32] In 1897 Kähler described this conflict between historicism and dogmatics in an article entitled 'Biblical theology'.[33] Here he discussed the difficulty of obtaining a systematic dogmatic from the canon in the face of a historico-critical biblical science, because 'the "unprejudiced critic" is confronted by a field covered with ruins of single traditions'.[34] So Kähler drew the following conclusion:

> Every attempt to bring the essence of the Bible down to one expression or into one system necessarily leads to a modern mixed and so deformed version which is dependent on ecclesiastical dogma, a version which can only temporarily be recommended as an antidote to an overstrained historicism and which will be recommended again and again.[35]

By 'overstrained historicism' (this becomes clear from the context), he meant the complete delivering up of theology to history and philosophy and the splitting of the canon into divergent positions.

---

30. Kähler, *Historische Jesus*, p. 44.
31. Kähler, *Historische Jesus*, pp. 38-39.
32. Kähler, *Historische Jesus*, p. 67.
33. Kähler, 'Biblische Theologie', *RE³*, III, p. 198.
34. By the same word Wilhelm Dilthey characterized the result of the historical consciousness: 'We are looking back to a field covered with ruins (*Trümmerfeld*) of religious traditions, metaphysical statements, demonstrated systems...' (*Die Typen der Weltanschauung und ihre Ausbildung in den metaphysischen Systemen: Gesammelte Schriften*, VIII, p. 76). History as *Trümmerfeld* is the bad historicism they try to overcome.
35. Kähler, 'Biblische Theologie', p. 198.

The question of where this historicism, this historical positivism, has its origin cannot be answered easily. Even Hegel had already seen a danger in the biblical studies inaugurated by the Enlightenment and therefore tried to save the substance of Christianity with the help of speculative philosophy.[36] Schleiermacher, on the other hand, demanded that the biblical writings be studied with the same methods which were valid in philology. At the same time, Schleiermacher required an 'interest in Christianity' from the theologian and asked him to look at the biblical sources for the common origin and core.[37] This changed radically when D.F. Strauss demanded the same 'unChristian neutral presuppositions' of the biblical scientist as of all other scientists.[38] Today it is immediately recognizable that this is a new form of presupposition which a historian already possesses. Strauss expressed this presupposition, which is orientated toward the ideal of modern science, as follows: 'There is no purely historical consciousness without the insight into the unbreakable chain of final causes and into the impossibility of miracle'.[39] Strauss himself called this presupposition the core of his lack of all presuppositions: 'Lack of presuppositions (*Voraussetzungslosigkeit*) means that the same presuppositions are made everywhere: everything in the world always happens in the same way'.[40]

Strauss took it for granted that we are separated from the biblical world. The new endeavours of a mystical, that means speculative, philosophy 'to make the past become present and to render thinkable that which is unthinkable' are, in his opinion, completely hopeless, mere 'desperate undertakings'.[41] It is this supposed distance that he himself raised into consciousness and thus increased. An awareness was reached of the biblical world as absolutely past and gone, an estranged world.

This was presumably the starting point of Franz Overbeck's criticism of modern biblical scholarship. After science started to criticize Christianity and its sources, scientific theology itself became subject to

36. *Die Flucht in den Begriff: Materialien zu Hegels Religionsphilosophie* (ed. Friedrich Wilhelm Graf and Falk Wagner; Stuttgart: Klett-Cotta, 1982).

37. G. Scholtz, 'Herméneutique et dogmatique chez Schleiermacher', in *La naissance du paradigme herméneutique* (ed. André Laks and Ada Neschke; Presses Universitaires de Lille, 1990), pp. 279-98.

38. David Friedrich Strauss, *Das Leben Jesu kritisch bearbeitet* (Tübingen: Osiander, 1838[3]), (praef. 1835), I, p. ix.

39. Strauss, *Das Leben Jesu*, I, p. 86.

40. Strauss, *Das Leben Jesu*, I, p. 97, n. 5.

41. Strauss, *Das Leben Jesu*, I, pp. viii, IXix

criticism. It is a pure fantasy, Overbeck said, for theologians to believe it is possible to ascertain true Christianity in a historical way, by historical interpretation; history makes clear, rather, that all knowledge, especially theological knowledge and that of historico-critical theology all the more, only destroys religion.[42] This criticism is the ground for a critical polemic notion of historicism in the sense of historical positivism such as can be found in M. Kähler. Historicism is now that form of critical historical research which makes the biblical canon unsuitable as a basis of dogmatics and of preaching. This version of the term historicism is therefore a part of criticism of science. Gadamer's philosophical hermeneutic would later try to surmount exactly this form of historicism, too. The ground for this criticism was obviously prepared when neither a theology of feeling (as in Schleiermacher) nor a speculative theology (as in Hegel) stood at the side of historical research and formed a counter-balance. E. Hirsch[43] said that in the nineteenth century A.E. Biedermann and O. Pfleiderer were the last to support their dogmatics with metaphysics. But such undertakings could no longer claim to be scientific at the end of the nineteenth century.

Historicism 5: Historical Relativism

If all phenomena of the human world become subjects of factual sciences, then value standards, meaning orientations, interpretations of being will be reduced to mere facts, too, and their validity cannot be proved. Relativism is thus far a consequence of that historical positivism.[44] So it is hardly a coincidence that hand in hand with this criticism of positivism, around 1900, the notion 'relativism' took its seat in the language for the first time.[45] There were, already however,

---

42. Franz Overbeck, *Über die Christlichkeit unserer heutigen Theologen* (1873) (Leipzig, 1903²; repr. Darmstadt: Wissenschaftl. Buchges., 1963).

43. Emanuel Hirsch, *Geschichte der neuern evangelischen Theologie* (Gütersloh: C. Bertelsmann, 1964³), V, pp. 560-71.

44. In Troeltsch's opinion the relativism is surely a result of the Enlightenment and romantic subjectivism. Therefore he recognized historicism (in the sense of relativism) since Schleiermacher's early philosophy of religion, 'Das Wesen des modernen Geistes' (1907), *Gesammelte Schriften*, IV, p. 318. 'Die Restaurationsepoche des 19. Jahrhunderts' (1913), *Gesammelte Schriften*, IV, pp. 593-94. But to relativism belongs the feeling of uncertainty and the lack of orientation, therefore the application of the term to Schleiermacher seems to be problematical.

45. Gert König, 'Relativismus', *Historisches Wörterbuch der Philosophie*

attempts to apply the notion of historicism for a critique of historical relativism around the middle of the nineteenth century.[46] Only later, at the beginning of the twentieth century, did historicism as 'historical relativism' become a central notion of this criticism, not only for Troeltsch but for Husserl, Rickert and others, too.

Troeltsch, like Husserl, referred with this notion especially to Dilthey, the 'philosopher of historicism', who was finally driven about 'rudderless in the wealth of history'. In the sphere of theology Troeltsch always thought of Ernest Renan as a prototype for this historical relativism, one who, like Strauss, had to leave institutional theology. The big problem of Renan's book about the life of Jesus lies, according to Troeltsch,

> in a historical scepticism and relativism which, in light of a mass of apperceptions (*Anempfindung*) of thousands of past religious feelings and opinions, does not find the courage to present its own position, in the fragmentation of a religious feeling, which perceives in all phenomena of religious history the deep mysterious voice from beyond but melancholically eschews hearing any unity or any aim in these flittering voices. Historical knowledge and variety stifles the human being through the reminiscence of what has—a thousand times—been and so takes away the courage and power for his own productions. The reality of everything historical, playing to and fro, where everything has its advantages and disadvantages and all just depends on its time, obstructs all nutrition or consolidation from history. Only a religion and an intellectual life which you took part in faithfully and then overcame and left behind can be understood scientifically.

Renan for Troeltsch illustrates that history kills theology; what is left is 'that spirit of fatigue and ennui' which has 'worked seductively and destructively enough'.[47]

I have quoted abundantly here to make clear: historicism in the sense of historical relativism is not, for Troeltsch, a theological position—and could not be—but it is the consequence of a theology made historical and scientific, of a theology which has become history. And this version of historicism, according to Troeltsch, formed the convictions of all the historically educated and the whole culture at the turn of the twentieth century. He saw a spirit of skepticism spreading and the fragmented

(ed. Joachim Ritter and Karlfried Gründer; Basel: Schwabe, 1992), VIII, pp. 613-22.

46. See n. 12.

47. 'Die theologische und religiöse Lage der Gegenwart' (1903), *Gesammelte Schriften*, II, p. 11.

culture acquiring a character of 'non-perspicuity' (*Unübersichtlichkeit*).[48]

Troeltsch wanted to overcome this historical relativism, this burdening heritage of the nineteenth century. This service was to be fulfilled by his great opus *Historicism and its Problems* published in 1922. Here Troeltsch opposed 'bad historicism', namely relativism and positivism, to a good historicism: modern historical thought which understand culture and humanity in its coming into being and which we cannot forego in our self-reflection and the shaping of our future; because only by working through our past do we recognize our place in history and our tasks for the future. Taking a closer look, you will find a lot of hints in this book that Troeltsch came close to the old metaphysics of history and theology (historicism 1 and 2). He wrote, for example, that historical phenomena root in an 'inner impulse and impetus of reason' and the task is 'to lead this reason back to its divine ground, to the inner movement of the divine spirit in the finite'.[49] Culture and all its various forms as manifestations, self-presentations of the absolute seemed to be a thought for the twentieth century too, with the help of which you could accept and come to terms with the plurality and the changes of culture. Friedrich Meineke's works also contain such elements of a historico-metaphysical historicism.[50] It is certainly significant that neither Troeltsch nor Meineke brought this thought into the shape of an explicit philosophical or theological system. Apparently, a historicism as metaphysics of history can only determine historical research in the twentieth century in a very weakened form, as a figure of 'cultural religion' (*Kulturreligion*).[51] And so, one may critically ask how Troeltsch was able to overcome historical relativism with the help of such a pallid *theologoumenon*. Dialectical theology soon reproached liberal theology with a historicism in the sense of historical relativism. In

---

48. 'Das Neunzehnte Jahrhundert', pp. 618, 625. Today the word *Unübersicht-lichkeit* has got a new use. See Jürgen Habermas, *Die neue Unübersichtlichkeit* (Frankfurt a.M.: Suhrkamp, 1985). The 'postmodern age', it has been said, has a divergent and splintering character.

49. Troeltsch, *Der Historismus und seine Probleme* (Tübingen: Mohr, 1922) (= *Gesammelte Schriften*, III), pp. 172-73.

50. See e.g. Friedrich Meinecke, 'Deutung eines Rankewortes' (1942), *Zur Theorie und Philosophie der Geschichte* (= *Werke*, IV) (Stuttgart: K.F. Koehler, 1959), pp. 117-39.

51. Hermann Lübbe calls by the term *Kulturreligion* secularized religious attitudes (*Religion nach der Aufklärung*), pp. 281-97.

its crusade against all forms of historicism, dialectical theology can be called an 'anti-historicistic revolution'.[52]

Conclusions

Books on historicism today mainly treat subjects like philosophy, history, art, philology, sometimes law (if they consider the Historical School), but hardly ever theology.[53] So it might seem that theology is strictly apart from those human sciences and that it has not been touched by historicism. This is why I tried to indicate that this notion was indeed used in theology and that all the central meanings of the notion as it was used in the nineteenth century can be related to theological positions. Since the nineteenth century, 'historicism' has been used in a predominantly critical or even polemic sense, so it always reveals clearly the view of those who use it. Nearly every position could be called historicism, if seen from a different standpoint. Those who were confined to historical research were historicists (in the sense of historical positivism) for the dogmatists; those who kept strictly to orthodox revelation doctrines were historicists for the liberal theologians (a historicist in the sense of traditionalism); those who declared the complete history of religions a work of God's revelation were historicists for traditional theology (in the sense of metaphysics of history or of relativism) and so on. This reflects

52. Emil Brunner, *Die Mystik und das Wort* (Tübingen: J.C.B. Mohr [Paul Siebeck], 1924), pp. 206, 332. Historicism in Brunner's mind is the form of historical thinking 'behind which the idea of a developing soul of world or mankind is standing' (pp. 206-207). This historicism is a 'historicism of evolution' (p. 308). Criticizing such a historicism in Schleiermacher's thought, Brunner is looking to Troeltsch too, who continued the way of Schleiermacher (pp. 8-9). Concerning the anti-historicism of the 'dialectical theology', see Friedrich Wilhelm Graf: 'Die "antihistoristische Revolution" in der protestantischen Theologie der zwanziger Jahre', in *Vernunft des Glaubens: Wissenschaftliche Theologie und kirchliche Lehre. Festschrift zum 60. Geburtstag von Wolfhard Pannenberg* (ed. Jan Rohls and Gunther Wenz; Göttingen: Vandenhoeck & Ruprecht, 1988), pp. 377-405.

53. Fulvio Tessitore, *Introduzione a lo storicismo* (Rome: Laterza, 1991), Friedrich Jaeger and Jörn Rüsen, *Geschichte des Historismus* (Munich: C.H. Beck, 1992). Annette Wittkau regards, e.g., the term historicism of M. Kähler; but the problem of her books is that the beginning of historicism is fixed only in the end of the 19th century (A. Wittkau, *Historismus: Zur Geschichte des Begriffs und des Problems* [Göttingen: Vandenhoeck & Ruprecht, 1992]). You will find in Heussi, 'Die Krisis', and Oexle, '"Historismus"', and Graf, 'Die "antihistoristische Revolution"', some remarks concerning twentieth-century theology.

the fact that the correct treatment of history became contested. And if historicism is used to designate an epoch, that must certainly mean an epoch which had collected a huge amount of historical knowledge, but in which the use of this knowledge and the relation to history in general was disputed, so that these different notions of historicism could be formed.

I have presented these notions and forms of historicism so that they show a succession, and this is justified to a certain extent by the findings of history. If one asks about breaks and paradigm shifts, it seems to me that a caesura can best be shown where the effort to gain status against rationalist deism provoked a turn towards history, thus giving rise to a historicism of the first and second form. Whereas before, reason had distanced itself from revelation in every way, it now became partly integrated into the process of revelation. A further caesura can be presumed, where theology became historico-philological research. But this shift is less obvious—who could assert that F.C. Baur worked less historico-philologically, or less scientifically, than D.F. Strauss? Nevertheless, Baur's historical work stands in a theologico-philosophical framework. Therefore one may assert a transition to a new phase primarily in those cases, where theology—like D.F. Strauss's—professed the principle of research without presuppositions (*Voraussetzungslosigkeit*). A very clear turning point is marked later by the anti-historicism of the dialectical theology of K. Barth, E. Brunner *et al*. But it is debatable, whether (natural) science indeed developed in the way Thomas S. Kuhn schematized it. It is even more under question, if there are paradigms in Kuhn's sense in any of the humanities. This is why I restricted my arguments to the thesis that it is typical for the beginning of the nineteenth century to work out a metaphysics of history or to take one as a presupposition for one's own work, and typical for the end of the nineteenth century to restrict itself to supposedly unprejudiced, empirical research.

Even if the problems and positions discussed in the nineteenth century, and thus the different meanings of historicism, are partly relevant today, a new situation seems to have come about. The process of civilization makes the world more uniform, civilization implies levelling. But we can recognize reactions against this: the stressing of individual culture, tradition, religion, nationality and so on. These reactions can be witnessed in two different ways: in a human way, as a preservation and development of those factors which make human life meaningful and which, at the same time, guarantee the liberty of others or at least leave them in peace. And there are barbaric ways, like chauvinism and religious fanaticism. How we predominantly understand historicism and how we judge it in the future may well depend on the development of these two opposing movements.

HISTORY AS A CASE-STUDY OF THE RELATIONS BETWEEN UNIVERSITY PROFESSORS AND THE STATE IN GERMANY*

Christian Simon

Introduction

My topic is the relationship of professors of history in Germany to their Nation State. This is an area which can serve as a useful basis of comparison with a discipline such as theology. Certainly, the methodological problems posed are similar, if the relationship of professors to the state is seen in terms not only of the actual relationship of the state to university teachers, but also of state and nation as the subject of pronouncements in the works of professors themselves. This involves looking for connections between their situation as professors at state universities and the topic of the state in their utterances. In this manner, an approach can be found to the pre-scholarly and non-scholarly influences on a discipline's development, and the balance between external compulsions and immanent tendencies is more easily evaluated. My theses concern the second half of the nineteenth century; where not otherwise stated, I am focusing primarily on Berlin, occasionally on Munich.[1] I will commence with some observations on the relation of the German university to state and society. By doing so I am attempting to point out the connection between the disciplines, history and theology; namely, considering the university as framework which brings individual subjects into contact with each other and thus facilitates interdisciplinary study. The following observations are not intended to bring any new aspects to light, but rather to present the state of research as of around 1990 in a manner suitable for the requirements of this symposium.

* Translated by Stephen Tranter (Basel, Switzerland).

1. Christian Simon, *Staat und Geschichtswissenschaft in Deutschland und Frankreich: Situation und Werk von Geschichtsprofessoren an den Universitäten Berlin, München, Paris* (State and Historical Science in Germany and France: Situation and Work of Professors of History at the Universities of Berlin, Munich, Paris) (Berne: Lang, 1988).

Part One: University, State, Society and Nation

The concept of the university in nineteenth-century Germany can be outlined as follows:[2] scholarship should find its primary home in universities, rather than in academies, special schools, research institutes or among private scholars. Teaching and research therefore were combined in the single person, the professor, in a single institution, the university, designed to create knowledge and disseminate it. The appropriate medium for this was the seminar, in its double sense of a form of teaching and of the building in which this was carried out. Scholarship[3] was regarded as a process towards truth, not directed towards specific practical applications, but towards knowledge for its own sake. Since Germany had no private universities worthy of mention, the institutions mentioned above had in practice a monopoly of control over higher qualifications, including those of higher-ranking teachers,[4] the senior civil service and the professions. The university thus combined elements of the corporation with those of the state institution.

It was a corporation in the minds of its full members (chair-holding professors) inasmuch as it was self administering through faculty boards and the Vice-Chancellor's office and possessed its own sources of income, fees and revenues from university estate. The corporate character was evident in the fact that the faculty itself decided its

2. Charles E. McClelland, *State, Society, and University in Germany 1700–1914* (Cambridge: Cambridge University Press, 1980); Hans Herzfeld, 'Der Nationalstaat und die deutsche Universität', in *Nationalsozialismus und die deutsche Universität* (Universitätstage, 1965); *Veröff. der Freien Universität Berlin* (Berlin, 1966), pp. 8-23; Helga Romberg, *Staat und höhere Schule: Ein Beitrag zur deutschen Bildungsverfassung vom Anfang des 19. Jhs. bis zum Ersten Weltkrieg* (Studien und Dokumentationen zur deutschen Bildungsgeschichte 11; Weinheim: Beltz, 1979); Rüdiger vom Bruch, Universität, Staat und Gesellschaft. Neuere sozial- und personengeschichtliche Beiträge zum deutschen Hochschulwesen vorwiegend im 19. und frühen 20. Jahrhundert', *Archiv für Sozialgeschichte* 20 (1980), pp. 526-44.

3. Translator's note: orig. *Wissenschaft*, a term that embraces the pursuit of knowledge in a broader sense than either 'science' or 'scholarship' and combines these two terms. I translate the term throughout as 'scholarship'.

4. The university was in close communication with the élitist section of secondary education; cf. Fritz Ringer, *Education and Society in Modern Europe* (Bloomington: Indiana University Press, 1979); Detlef K. Müller, Fritz Ringer and Brian Simon (eds.), *The Rise of the Modern Educational System: Structural Change and Social Reproduction 1870–1920* (Cambridge: Cambridge University Press, 1987).

successors by appointing professors, though *de jure* the state had final control over appointments to the corporation. The pre-modern character of the university was furthermore evident in its liberties: right of discipline over students, freedom of learning and teaching and the right of the faculty over appointments and examinations.

On the other hand, each university was a state institution because the state had final control over appointment and remuneration of professors; in Prussia this was explicitly termed 'crown right'. Their remuneration and the basic prerequisite for their work, the institute, with its books, staff, rooms and apparatus, were largely financed by the state. In addition, the university was a state training institution for producing qualified state servants. Because of this and the appointment of professors by royal decree, the monarch regarded the university as his own institution, an attitude sometimes manifest in his desire to define the frame of reference of the university in terms of its loyalty and suitability to the court.

The universities' monopoly over the qualifications of senior civil servants and teachers was not only one of the foundations of the state's claim to control over the universities, but also a means whereby the universities made their influence felt in the state and helped to shape the culture of the educational and bureaucratic élite.[5]

State administration of scholarship in universities developed towards the end of the century into an educational policy.[6] This opened a new and often discordant chapter in the relations between state and university. The notes of strife can be heard in the texts of the time, in the professors' opposition to the so-called 'Althoff-System' and in the

---

5. The same applies in the case of the churches. McClelland concludes: 'In most parts of Germany the clergy was better trained than its counterparts in other European countries, thanks in part to government pressure for such training and to the high standards of theology faculties from the late eighteenth century onward. The close ties between churches and states in Germany since the Reformation involved the universities, as well. The struggle against domination by church orthodoxy is a major element in the history of German universities; but even when this struggle was won, the interests of the churches continued to be represented in the universities' (McClelland, *State, Society and University*, p. 7).

6.   Bernhard vom Brocke (ed.), *Wissenschaftsgeschichte und Wissenschafts-politik im Industriezeitalter: Das 'System Althoff' in historischer Perspektive* (Hildesheim: Ed. Bildung und Wissenschaft, 1991) (also listing earlier literature on the subject).

renewed discussion of 'scholarly freedom'.[7] The state's influence was felt in the following areas: control of information and appointment in the filling of vacant chairs; granting of state funds for building, furnishing and maintenance of institutions; the creation of new institutes of further education parallel to the universities and the founding of research institutes for utilitarian purposes in direct contradiction of the aims and ethics of the universities.[8]

With increasingly systematic state intervention in personnel appointments, an issue was made of the rights of the faculties, as evinced by three statements from 1884, 1891 and 1905.

I commence with the discussion between Bismarck and the Minister for Ecclesiastical Affairs, Gossler, in 1884.[9] Bismarck considered that faculty consultation in the question of appointments was purely a matter of courtesy and that recognition of the faculties' claims was equivalent to 'republicanizing state control'. The Minister for Cultural Affairs emphasized that the faculties were responsible for maintaining a complete curriculum, and that this was the sole justification for consulting them when vacancies were to be filled. A true right of nomination did not exist. When faculties presented their shortlists[10]

7.   Peter Mast, *Künstlerische und wissenschaftliche Freiheit im Deutschen Reich 1890–1901* (Rheinfelden: Schäuble, 1980); Kurt Rossmann, *Wissenschaft, Ethik und Politik: Erörterung des Grundsatzes der Voraussetzungslosigkeit in der Forschung* (Heidelberg, 1949); Max Weber, 'The Power of the State and the Dignity of the Academic Calling in Imperial Germany: The Writings of Max Weber on University Problems' (ed. E. Sils), *Minerva* 11.4 (Oct. 1973); Georg Kaufmann, *Die Lehrfreiheit an den deutschen Universitäten im 19. Jahrhundert* (Leipzig: Hirzel, 1898). The legal situation is discussed in Ernst Rudolf Huber, *Deutsche Verfassungsgeschichte seit 1789, Band 4: Struktur und Krisen des Kaiserreichs* (Stuttgart: Kohlhammer, 1969). Viktor Naumann, *Die deutschen Universitäten in ihrem Verhältnis zum Staat, ihre Verfassung und Verwaltung* (Graz: Styria, 1909).

8.   Frank R. Pfetsch, *Zur Entwicklung der Wissenschaftspolitik in Deutschland 1750–1914* (Berlin: Duncker & Humblot, 1974); Lothar Burchardt, *Wissenschaftspolitik im wilhelminischen Deutschland* (Göttingen: Vandenhoeck & Ruprecht, 1975); Reinhard Rürup (ed.), *Wissenschaft und Gesellschaft* (Berlin: Springer, 1979); vom Brocke, *Wissenschaftsgeschichte und Wissenschaftspolitike*; McClelland, *State, Society and University*, p. 282, with an example from theology: the creation of an Institute for Missionary studies in Halle in 1897.

9.   Simon, *Staat und Geschichtswissenschaft*, p. 122.

10.   Translator's note: *Dreierliste*, lit. 'list of three'; appointing bodies in German universities, then as now, submitted a shortlist of three acceptable candidates in order of their preference to the Ministry responsible for the appointment.

they were merely acting on behalf of the Ministry.

In the Prussian *Landtag* Althoff, a lawyer himself, set the tone as follows: 'investigations and recommendations of the faculties should not be presented as if these constituted legal rights of the faculties in which the right of the crown might be diminished in any manner.'[11] The influential civil servant's[12] position is further clarified by the case of the economist Ludwig Bernhard (1908): 'the university faculties had acquired a customary right to a hearing in all questions of professorial appointments. The Government were empowered to make exceptions when there were serious grounds for doing so, but should seek contact with important members of the faculty concerned before doing so.'[13]

Discussion of the threatened liberties of the universities centred on themes such as: civil servant status (and disciplinary rights); the politically motivated endowment of 'punitive chairs'[14]; the appointment of Catholic professors for considerations of religious policy; the weakening of the universities by means of the Althoff System; which was considered a loss of influence and dignity (reactions in which South German attitudes to Prussian hegemony sometimes played their part). The argument was in full swing at a time in which state disregard of university wishes had become much rarer than previously (before 1860).[15] The discussion was provoked above all by the complaints of certain industrialists against 'Lecture-hall socialists'[16] in the 'Stumm Era' (1895–1899), by the proceedings against Arons in 1896,[17] and the Spahn case

11.   As quoted by Bärbel Boschan in vom Brocke, *Wissenschaftsgeschichte und Wissenschaftspolitik*.

12.   Orig. *Ministerialdirektor* (translator's note).

13.   Althoff to Schmoller 1908, quoted by Simon, *Staat und Geschichtswissenschaft*, p. 124.

14.   Orig. *Strafprofessuren*: appointments made to ensure that state policy was followed when this had hitherto not been the case (translator's note).

15.   Figures for Prussia up to 1895 in McClelland, *State, Society and University*, p. 185.

16.   Orig. *Kathedersozialisten*, lit. 'professor's chair socialists', *Katheder* designating the chair on a raised platform used by the university professor or schoolteacher (translator's note).

17.   Rüdiger vom Bruch, *Wissenschaft, Politik und öffentliche Meinung: Gelehrtenpolitik im wilhelminischen Deutschland 1890–1914* (Husum: Mathiesen, 1980), p. 333. It should be borne in mind that this conflict did not centre merely on the defence of scholarly freedom, but also on the perception of the relationship between state and Social Democracy represented by Schmoller. Furthermore it should be noted that the *Lex Arons* was only applied in one case (that of Arons himself), so

of 1901 (in which a Catholic professor was nominated to a chair of History parallel to Meinecke at Strasbourg).[18] As an answer to this state of affairs, Brentano urged the convening of a Conference of German University Teachers in 1907, on the grounds that scholarship was losing respect because it was no longer free.[19] However, a contributory factor was protest against moves toward structural modernisation coming from the state and certain colleagues. This was to some extent a crisis caused by universities' problems with adaptation to the demands of an expanding capitalist economy, seen as the encroachment of management and industry into the universities, and was at the same time a protest against educational policies which appeared to be abandoning Humboldt's libertarian principles in favour of utilitarian considerations.[20]

Althoff's administration clearly demonstrates an attempt on the part of the administration to come to terms with a new situation, which had arisen since 1860 through problems of integration and growth, by means of state educational policy. The state was becoming increasingly interested in the results of scholarship and was therefore prepared

> to invest considerable resources in a loss-making enterprise for the production of public knowledge. In contrast to the 'ideals of 1809', the separation of state and scholarship (Humboldt), the 'ideals of 1882' (Althoff) combine what had in practice fused long before, forming, in the literal sense, a process of compound growth.[21]

According to Humboldt's idealistic theory the university stood detached from society. His concept of the university revolved around the wish to see an area of freedom in the hierarchical state, from which the regeneration of Prussia after 1806 could proceed. The faculties'

that the affair was the vehement conclusion of an epoch of increasing repression rather than the start of it.

18. Christoph Weber, *Der Fall Spahn: Ein Beitrag zur Wissenschafts- und Kulturdiskussion im ausgehenden 19. Jahrhundert* (Rome: Herder, 1980); Walter Ferber, 'Der Weg Martin Spahns. Zur Ideengeschichte des politischen Rechtskatholizismus', *Hochland* 62 (1970), pp. 218-29.

19. See Rüdiger vom Bruch's stimulating comments in *Wissenschaft, Politik und öffentliche Meinung*, pp. 16-17.

20. McClelland, *State, Society and University*, pp. 282-83. Cf. vom Brocke in Charles McClelland, *The German Experience of Professionalization: Modern Learned Professions and their Organizations from the Early 19th Century to the Hitler Era* (Cambridge: Cambridge University Press, 1991), p. 18.

21. H.F. Spinner, in vom Brocke, *Wissenschaftsgeschichte und Wissenschaftspolitik*, p. 514 (transl.).

claims to autonomy were repeatedly given legitimacy by invocation of this theory. As Helmut F. Spinner puts it:

> Not only as a point of departure in the history of ideas, but also as a timeless objective, the 'ideals of 1809' represent an idealistic philosophical basis for an autonomous republic of learning in a society of a completely different character, not to mention a sharply antirepublican state.

The same author has spoken of the 'Four Great Separations', which characterized this desired isolation:

1. Separation of the commerce of ideas from the commerce of goods, since knowledge becomes, by being published, common property of the research community.
2. Separation of ideas from vested interests, the search for truth without extraneous influence.
3. Separation of theory and practice, not depoliticisation but the removal of political pressures and of compulsion to take actions or make decisions.
4. Separation of the scholarly province from the normal social environment in the form of a separation of scholarship and state, providing a free area of scholarship autonomous from the state.[22]

Nonetheless, the university had an important function in nineteenth-century German society. This was not merely because the universities alone, by means of courses and academic titles, conferred the signs of status and of cultural and professional qualification.

> More than in the relatively open societies to the west and the closed ones to the east, the German universities served as the breeding ground for a peculiar social stratum, an academic bourgeoisie (*Bildungsbürgertum*), the recruiting pool for both cultural and administrative élites.[23]

However, the significance of the administrative groups was increasing concomitantly with the increasing significance of the state and its administration in society. A further extension of the universities' sphere of interest within society must be noted towards the end of the century. With the professionalisation of many occupations, acquisition of qualifications invariably led to the university, and the representatives of

---

22. Spinner, in vom Brocke, *Wissenschaftsgeschichte und Wissenschaftspolitik*, p. 513 (transl.).
23. McClelland, *State, Society and University*, p. 3.

these occupations were increasingly concerned to ensure that the universities served the interests of their class—their social status depended on this. The universities reproduced status boundaries, but in individual cases they could confer higher status, or endorse the achievement of higher status by conferring a title. This plays a less important part in the case of history, than for example in the medical and technical professions.[24]

Observers from Western Europe and from overseas will be struck by the reluctance of German universities to engage in positive relations with the middle classes, the classes of riches and industrial success. The faculties acted as élitists, despising higher secondary schools, technical high schools and the practical application of knowledge to an equal degree; and by calling in the aid of the state against the industrial middle classes, strengthened its influence on the university yet further.[25]

In the minds of those concerned, the explanation lay in the idea that state and intelligence should govern society, not the reverse, and that society had no right of influence in those spheres in which the fate of the nation was to be decided. In other words, scholarship was an autonomous moral and cultural force detached from society. Seen in practical terms, this meant that scholarship would be more prepared to subject itself to state control than to social, economic, party-political or ecclesiastical interests.[26] Seen materialistically, the grounds for this decision probably lay in the wish to defend the 'irrelevant' courses of pure scholarship which effectively form one of the strengths of the German university. Thus Harnack said 'It is the parliamentary parties (to which the synods also belong) which are oppressing the freedom of scholarship, not the Government'. He mentions by name the National Liberals (*Nationalliberale*) and Empire Party (*Reichspartei*), who were demanding punitive appointments[27] against the 'lecture-hall Socialists', and the desire of the centralists to nominate Catholic professors. As Max

24. McClelland, *State, Society and University*, pp. 8-9; for the professions and their interests see the same author's *The German Experience of Professionalization*.

25. 'Although the universities were benefiting from the new prosperity begotten by the German industrial revolution, they were largely unable or unwilling to cement an alliance with the industrial middle class that would have acted as a counterweight to state control. By posing itself between the burgeoning Germany economy and the universities, the state was able to heighten its control' (McClelland, *State, Society and University*, p. 288).

26. McClelland, *State Society and University*, p. 314.

27. Cf. note 14.

Lenz points out in his history of the universities in Berlin 'In this respect [attacks against the corporate rights of the faculties] we have less to fear from the government than from the parties or from capitalist lobbies'.[28] Before examining the universities' attitude to the nation, I should draw attention to the concept of 'professorial politics' (*Gelehrtenpolitik*)[29] as made familiar by Meinecke and used in empirical research nowadays in the sense of 'attempts by professors *qua* professors to gain and use political influence'. Determinated thus, the concept

> concentrates on a small group of university teachers of arts and humanities who were in close agreement on their assessment of the political objectives and possible influence of scholarship, on the desirability of its remaining closely-tied to the political decision-making élite, in the conviction that scholarship should retain an ultimate function of guidance and arbitration above and between parties and factions, and in a wish to represent these aims in their publications.[30]

In contravention of one of the 'Four Great Separations', the separation of theory and practice, political conceptions in a present-day sense were evolved as, for example, a solution to the class problem or concerning the correct attitude of the state to the Social Democrats. The same was true of topics from cultural, foreign and defence policy, all claiming to present the state with conclusions drawn directly from theoretical analysis without regard to party political considerations.[31] This

---

28. In Simon, *Staat und Geschichtswissenschaft*, p. 131 (transl.); Konrad Tilmann, 'Die sogenannten Konkordatsprofessuren: Geschichtliche und heutige Rechtsproblematik' (Diss., Freiburg, 1971).

29. Friedrich Meinecke, 'Drei Generationen deutscher Gelehrtenpolitik', *HZ* 125 (1922), pp. 248-83.

30. Vom Bruch, *Wissenschaft, Politik und öffentliche Meinung*, p. 20 (transl.).

31. The most well-known forms of this were *Kathedersozialismus*, so-called, and the fact that professors engaged in propaganda on behalf of the Navy and in pan-German educational and linguistic politics. See Abraham Ascher, 'Professors as Propagandists: The Politics of the Kathedersozialisten', *Journal of Central European Affairs* 23 (1963), pp. 282-302; Felix Gilbert, 'Political Power and Academic Responsibility. Reflections on Friedrich Meinecke's "Drei Generationen deutscher Gelehrtenpolitik"', in L. Krieger and F. Stern (eds.), *Responsibility of Power* (Garden City: Doubleday, 1967), pp. 405-15; Gustav Schmidt and Jörn Rüsen (eds.), *Gelehrtenpolitik und politische Kultur in Deutschland 1830–1930: Referate und Diskussionsbeiträge* (Bochum: Brockmeyer, 1986); Wolfgang Marienfeld, 'Wissenschaft und Schlachtflottenbau in Deutschland, 1897–1906', in *Marine-Rundschau* (Supp. 2, April, 1957); Roger Chickering, *We Men who Feel Most*

professorial politics should not be confused with the direct political
involvement of professors prior to 1870, which frequently brought them
into opposition to the German states, as in the orbit of the 1830
revolution, and of the Vormärz and the Prussian constitutional conflict
of the 1860s.

However, in this context the universities—in particular in History, but
I shall examine this in detail in Part Two—made a decisive impact on the
development of the concept of nationality and of national consciousness.
In the early nineteenth century, in some cases even in the eighteenth,
university professors had formed a structure of communication which
widened the horizons of the young élite from the dimensions of the
region and the individual state to that of the nation; they were the
centres of a national discourse and of a *religion civile* of national
integration. This discourse constituted an opposition, as long as German
states insisted on individual sovereignty under their rulers' control and
rejected nationalistic tendencies as the subversive inheritance of the
revolution. The liberal professors of the mid-century saw themselves as
the spokespersons and conscience of the nation; given this legitimation,
they exploited their freedom until removed from office. They did this in
the conviction that scholarship had the answer to the problems of the
nation. In addition, from 1840 on, they aimed at a minimal individual
consensus: liberal policy, which in essence meant a constitution,
guarantees for citizens' rights and liberties, budgetary consultation and
ratification of taxation by Parliament and academic freedom, in return
for the renunciation of revolution and of direct attacks on bureaucratic
forms of government and for a concept for the unity of the nation.

In this respect, university professors, in particular, played a decisive
part. Between 1840 and 1860 they were leaders of political opinion outside the universities as well, 'virtually the most articulate and influential
"loyal opposition" to reigning political ideas', but the state rarely
considered them loyal, usually thinking them subversive. They were only
acting loyally in their own eyes, in that they were seeking the best for
the monarchal state and for the élite-led nation. Thus by invoking state
and nation they were acting as potentially critical citizens as well as
performing an exercise of nationalistic piety.[32]

German: A Cultural Study of the Pan-German League 1886–1914 (Boston: Allen &
Unwin, 1984).

32. McClelland, *State, Society and University*, p. 152. Cf. pp. 217, 220-21. 'With
few exceptions, the professors active in politics were loyal monarchists, asking at

Germany, as a Nation State, came into being only through the success of Prussian armaments. The State was imposed from above, preserving the sovereignty of individual rulers in the constitutional compromise of the 1871 Empire. Thus the state appeared to produce the nation itself; the liberal élite assisted as reserve officers. From 1871 onwards, the academic élite could only celebrate the accomplishment and keep alive the memory of the historical moment of 1870; the prophets had become the guardians of the memorial. Nonetheless, this transformed rôle still allowed them to form a sort of 'loyal opposition', a standpoint from which the real existing nation state could be criticized by the keepers of the Grail themselves. By virtue of this function, they assumed that they were entitled to point out and discuss the problems that had arisen with the new Empire. To the external view it was the boundaries of loyal opposition that had to be emphasized, that is, its subjection to the imposed and historical framework of constitution and society; to the internal view, it was the continuance of the liberal claim to far-reaching critique of rulers, governments and prevailing tendencies in policy, culture, industry and society.

The trends of development effective in the late nineteenth century and which determined the state university relationship are relevant for the history of all university disciplines, including history and theology.

a. Universities were extended and the numbers of students increased; the real wave did not, however, start until 1870. In addition the number of professors increased as a result of subject specialization and the founding of new disciplines. The numbers of teaching staff doubled between 1870 and 1905, whereas the numbers of those studying trebled. In particular, within the medical and philosophical faculties, the number of non-chair holding professors increased.[33]

b. Institutes were being extended and funded by the state from the 1860s onwards, so that expenditure for institutes and seminars had overtaken the wages of professors as the largest

most that the royal government yield the principle of taxation with real representation' (p. 227).

33. Total numbers of teaching staff at universities in Germany (*Privatdozenten, ausserordentliche Professoren, Ordinarien*), 1835: 1200; 1860: 1200; 1870: 1500; 1880: 1800; 1890: 2300; 1900: 2700; 1905: 3000; as in McClelland, *State, Society and University*, pp. 234, 259.

budget item.[34] This was not the consequence of a thirst for power on the part of the state, but of individual professors' wishes to see state financing of private seminars and libraries, and of administrators such as Althoff, who granted such wishes in order to entice first-rate scholars to Berlin.[35] Professors were and had to be willing to co-operate more closely with the state bureaucracy to secure funding of their research projects. As a result they became more dependent on the state and were prepared in the case of conflict to renounce such traditional concepts as 'liberty of the faculty'. This did not simply mean that the faculties were being outflanked, but also presented opportunities for innovation.

c. The political framework in which the professors' liberalism operated shifted in comparison to the time in which professors could still have played an active part. In the Empire, the decisive factors were the relationships between parties and organized lobbies on the one hand and the state on the other. The 'public' no longer consisted of the better educated, and professors were no longer the leading group within it; it was the electoral masses who set the tone, and issues no longer revolved around ideal postulates such as the constitutional state, but around socio-economic problems. Finally the state withdrew from its conflict with the Church (*Kulturkampf*), so that one of the last themes in which the Protestant professors felt truly at home was rendered obsolete.

d. In this political constellation, conditions were favourable for right-wing pressure to be effective against the universities; for example the 'Anti-Provocation Bill' (*Umsturzvorlage*, 1894/5) or Heinze's Law (1900), designed to submit all public discourse

34. McClelland, *State, Society and University*, p. 212; for Berlin, see Max Lenz, *Geschichte der königlichen Friedrich-Wilhelms-Universität zu Berlin* (4 vols.; Halle: Buchhandluug des Waisenhauses, 1910–1918).

35. McClelland, *State, Society and University*, p. 282. For the benefit of those not entirely familiar with the German university system it should be pointed out that the conventional credit allocation pattern for a German university consists of individual salaries on the one hand and overheads for the institute on the other, and that these are specific non-transferable allocations; in other words, universities or faculties have no say as to the use of the funding they manage to persuade the state to grant them and the state holds them accountable as to the exact deployment of professors or heads of institutes. Cf. McClelland, *State, Society and University*, p. 212.

to state ideological control; the concept of the state civil servant and his intra- and extramural duties were to be extended to the university teacher. In this manner, enemies of the state, (i.e. Social Democrats and possibly further groups that might be designated such by sovereign and government) could be removed from or denied admittance to the universities (*Lex Arons*[36]).

What became of the right to liberalism and loyal opposition under these circumstances? What was the trend of development of a common consensus, or even conformity, among the professors? In Berlin in particular, they had the chance of forming direct relationships with high-ranking civil servants and members of the government, to the Chancellor (Bülow, Bethmann Hollweg)[37] and finally to the Kaiser himself.[38] It was always more important for professors to have contact with high-ranking administrators than with party politicians. They agreed that scholarship was a third power between government and society, but tended nonetheless to adopt the standpoints of the civil service and the government in theory and practice, analysing current problems from the perspective of the state and its administration[39]—a fact that seems obvious by German standards, but which is a particularity worthy of mention for the external observer.

As much as was possible, the state furthered this attitude, finding help and even active encouragement from members of the faculties. Schäfer, the historian, was praised as a second Treitschke, herald of national ideals and leader of the professorial naval propaganda, and this, in the eyes of certain colleagues within the discipline (and of the ministry) made him specially suitable for appointment to a chair in Berlin. Schiemann's career is characterized by different attitudes; as a specialist on Russia and an advisor of the Kaiser, he was made professor against the concerted resistance of the university.[40]

---

36. Law instituted as an instrument of policy in the Arons case (translator's note).

37. Vom Bruch, *Wissenschaft, Politik und öffentliche Meinung*, pp. 100-101, pp. 253ff.

38. Christian Simon, 'Kaiser Wilhelm II. und die deutsche Wissenschaft', in John C.G. Röhl (ed.), *Der Ort Kaiser Wilhelms II. in der deutschen Geschichte* (Schriften des Historischen Kollegs, *Kolloquien*, 17; Munich: Oldenbourg, 1991, pp. 91-110.

39. Vom Bruch, *Wissenschaft, Politik und öffentliche Meinung*, pp. 98ff., 195.

40. On Schäfer's appointment in 1903, see Simon, *Staat und Geschichtswissenschaft*, pp. 102-103; on Schiemann, see pp. 116ff.

Unequivocally, the state demanded loyalty from its professors. Bosse, in 1898, formulated his expectations clearly: professors had a duty to teach the young respect for the monarchy, for the constitution and for other state institutions, and were in this respect to be an example to the young. This principle was not a matter of dispute between the state and the body of professors; the question was how much practical freedom of movement this left to the initiative and sense of responsibility of the individual professor. The national élite reserved for itself the right as loyal opposition to utter on scholarly grounds opinions differing from those prevailing in court and government. 'Most professors at German universities appear to have agreed with this vision of loyalty to God, king, and country, which for them was above politics'.[41] In accordance with this, processes leading to a development of consensus among the body of professors were a more significant factor in ensuring relative conformity than external correction, which was on the whole seldom imposed. However, it should be borne in mind that achievement of internal consensus was influenced by specific groups' perceptions of the trends of the age, and of the intentions, anticipated or imputed, of external authorities.

The term 'political' requires definition. On the one hand, the standards of the professors and the ideas of those in government coincided more or less, but not completely; on the other, the choices of the professors, whether measured by the standards of individual parties of the age or, to a greater extent, by post 1918 analyses, show a clear conservative political tendency.[42] The best example of the exertions of scholarship on behalf of conformity to the ideals of state and nation was the campaign for the Army and Navy Bills.[43] Two hundred and seventy professors spoke or published in favour of strengthening the navy and thus acquired the name Navy Professors (*Flottenprofessoren*), among them thirty seven historians and twenty nine theologians, twenty three

41. McClelland, *State, Society and University*, p. 294.
42. Vom Bruch quotes and in places criticizes Charles McClelland, 'Berlin Historians and German Politics', in Walter Laqueur and G.L. Mosse (eds.), *Historians in Politics* (Beverley Hills: Sage, 1974), pp. 191-221. Vom Bruch is aware of the cases of Schäfer, Delbrück and Schiemann, in whose university careers political considerations played a part. See on Schäfer, Hans-Thomas Krause, 'Dietrich Schäfer, vom Schüler Treitschkes zum ideologischen Wegbereiter des ersten Weltkrieges' (Diss. Halle/Wittenberg, 1968), pp. 198-213.
43. For details, see vom Bruch, *Wissenschaft, Politik und öffentliche Meinung*, pp. 66-67, for the 1897–1898 and 1899–1900 pro-Navy campaigns.

Protestant and six Catholic. In 1900 their commitment ceased abruptly with the passing of the Naval Act. Their arguments were: 'trade jealousy' of other nations, the necessity of a navy to protect the colonies, the external threat to Germany. An analysis according to the principles of ideological criticism perceives this as a veiling of the internal division of labour between agriculture and heavy industry in terms of ideology and of the national policy to secure the policy of collectivity. The commitment of the professors 'could at best be seen as a sporadic and externally imposed partial politicisation, of the German professors. In their own consciousness, however, there was no question of politicisation, a conviction that became evident in their continued rejection of 'aims dictated purely by political interest'. Due to the effect of this commitment one can nonetheless see a 'deepening of the conviction of the necessity of national power-politics which exerted an influence on their mentality'.[44] This was combined with openness to pan-Germanic considerations, such as support of German cultural communities abroad and language policy in the East, which were considered national and therefore neither party nor political.

A combination of social institutional factors and group attitudes led in short to a *relatively* conformist professorial body. They were liberal nationalists or (if loyal oppositionists) conservative in attitude, nationalistic, Protestant and never Jewish by belief or descent if this could be avoided.[45] Definite hopes and fears conditioned their world

---

44. Vom Bruch, *Wissenschaft, Politik und öffentliche Meinung*, p. 68: 'mentalitätsbeeinflussende Verfestigung der Überzeugung erforderlicher "nationaler Machtpolitik"'.

45. See Bärbel Boschan's chart, in vom Brocke, *Wissenschaftsgeschichte und Wissenschaftspolitik*, p. 282: *Ordinarien* in Berlin belonged to the following denominations:

```
1870 prot. 24
     RC    1
     jew.  0
     NC    0    NC = 'nonconformist'
1880 prot. 32
     RC    6
     jew.  0
     NC    0
1890 prot. 41
     RC    4
     jew.  1
     NC    0
```

view at a level only partially accessible to rational analysis which can be regarded as their mentality. It comprised the following elements:

a. *A sense of crisis reflecting loss of influence in policies determined by parties and lobbies.*[46] This combined with anxiety concerning the liberties of their particular group, threatened not only by industry, parties and the Church but also, incomprehensibly to them, by the state through its own prospective educational policy and politically motivated concessions for social and denominational reasons.[47] Even the Kaiser could not be relied upon in the end; on the contrary. Although he was the Prussian sovereign and the embodiment of the nation, and should have been revered as such, as a person actively interfering in politics he was often despised by the professors, who played off the old and experienced Bismarck against the young Kaiser. The deepening of this world view led to

b. *An exacerbation of the existing rift separating the professors from capitalism and parliamentarianism.* The professorial mentality thus clung for support, despite growing mistrust, to a state whose authoritarian nature they considered essential, since it alone was able to protect the liberty of scholarship and stood or should have stood above party politics. According to this view, the universities' close relationship with the state was a pre-requisite for state protection, so that readiness to serve state interests was temporarily weakened by the conflicts over corporate liberties, but remained unbroken in the long term. A certain measure of subservience to the state thus resulted from

---

46. Fritz Ringer, *Die Gelehrten: Der Niedergang der deutschen Mandarine 1890–1933* (Munich: Klett-Cotta [= *The Decline of the German Mandarins* (Cambridge, MA: Harvard University Press, 1969)], 1987]).

47. Explicitly proclaimed as maxims by Bosse in the *Landtag*, defending himself against accusations of having appointed too many professors from the opposition: he claimed that the Ministry was following a policy of balance and compensation (quoted in McClelland, *State, Society and University*, p. 295). For the support of Catholic professors by the Government against the wishes of the Faculties, see Ulrich Sieg, in vom Brocke, *Wissenschaftsgeschichte und Wissenschaftspolitik*, p. 295, based on the example of philosophy appointments under Althoff ('[…]charakteristische Elemente der Althoffschen Bildungspolitik, welche im ganzen auf die Integration der katholischen Bevölkerung und ihrer Gelehrtenwelt abzielte').

a multiplicity of converging factors: the professorial body, core of the educated citizenry,[48] which the state created as it also created the Civil Service; the idea of the state as overriding power-structure above society as possessing universal validity;[49] the notion that objective scholarship should adopt a viewpoint prescribed by the state in order not to judge subjectively and in isolation; and the expectation that the state alone would be in a position to offer protection against a new order perceived as inimical to culture and education. In the face of these factors direct state intervention in selection and replacement of members of the universities assume second place as an explanation of the relative conformity of professorial decisions and mentality.

Part Two: History as an Example

Why mention the experience of history at the universities of the Empire in this context? Four propositions should serve to answer this question.

First Proposition

There are clear relationships with theology, since history, too, must be regarded as one of the leading disciplines of the nineteenth century (*Leitwissenschaft*),[50] other subjects being forced into the historical mode. Both subjects sought for truth and administered it, the one in the form of Christian articles of belief, the other in the form of a *religion civile* which displayed the true character of the nation in origin and development. Both employed the same methods of textual exegesis and hermeneutics, both were fundamental to the state and were regarded as sufficiently important by the Prussian monarchy to be given their special personal attention.

Second Proposition

Historians regarded themselves as interpreters not only of the past, but also of the present, and as prophets of the future—these latter in conjunction with the newly arising political and social sciences. Attitudes to

---

48. Orig. *Bildungsbürgertum* (translator's note).
49. In the sense of the Hegelian concept of the *Allgemeine* (translator's note).
50. Gangolf Hübinger, 'Geschichte als leitende Orientierungswissenschaft im 19. Jahrhundert', *Berichte zur Wissenschaftsgeschichte* 11 (1988), pp. 149-58.

state, nation and policy were at the centre of their research. This was self-evidently true of those who specialized in post-reformation German and European history. Topics from mediaeval and ancient history (concepts of Empire, eastward colonialism, Rome and Carthage, Athens and Sparta) were also highly susceptible to topical interpretation. All the same, there was always a strong component of scholarly life to which access cannot be gained using an approach of presentism and of topicality.[51]

> History, in imparting sense to a historical development perceived as contingent by transmitting knowledge concerning connections of sense and significance between present and past, created, by transmitting a specific content of interpretative fact, a historical consciousness in Germany according to which history consisted for the most part in political actions performed within the framework of the nation state and in which the creation of historical identity was aligned on the perception of the state.[52]

51. Cf. for ancient history: Karl Christ, *Römische Geschichte und deutsche Geschichtswissenschaft* (Munich: Beck, 1982); Christ, *Römische Geschichte und Wissenschaftsgeschichte. III. Wissenschaftsgeschichte* (Darmstadt Wiss. Buchgesellschaft, 1983); Christ, *Von Gibbon zu Rostovtzeff: Leben und Werk führender Althistoriker der Neuzeit* (Darmstadt, 1972); D. Flach, 'Der sogenannte römische Imperialismus. Sein Verständnis im Wandel der neuzeitlichen Erfahrungswelt', *HZ* 222 (1976), pp. 1-42; Beat Näf, *Von Perikles zu Hitler? Die athenische Demokratie und die deutsche Althistorie bis 1945* (Bern: Lang, 1986); William M. Calder III and Alexander Demandt (eds.), *Eduard Meyer: Leben und Leistung eines Universalhistorikers* (Leiden: Brill, 1990). On mediaeval studies: H. Hostenkamp, *Die mittelalterliche Kaiserpolitik in der deutschen Historiographie seit von Sybel und Ficker* (Berlin: Ebering, 1934); G. Koch, 'Der Streit zwischen Sybel und Ficker und die Einschätzung der mittelalterlichen Kaiserpolitik in der modernen Historiographie', in Joachim Streisand (ed.), *Studien über diedeutsche Geschichtswissenschaft*, I (Berlin: Akademie-Verlag, 1965), pp. 311-36; Thomas Kleinknecht, 'Mittelalterauffassung in Forschung und politischer Kontroverse: Zu den Beiträgen von James Bryce und Georg Waitz', in H. Dollinger *et al.* (eds.), *Weltpolitik, Europagedanke, Regionalismus: Festschrift für Heinz Gollwitzer* (Münster: Aschendorff, 1980), pp. 269-86; Elisabeth Fehrenbach, *Wandlungen des deutschen Kaisergedankens 1871–1918* (Munich: Oldenbourg, 1969); Simon, *Staat und Geschitswissenschaft*, pp. 57ff.

52. Gustav Schmidt, 'Gelehrtenpolitik und politische Kultur in Deutschland—Zur Einführung', in Schmidt and Rüsen (eds.), *Gelehrtenpolitik und politische Kultur*, p. 5 (transl.).

Third Proposition
Historians considered themselves justified in this role firstly because they presided over the history of the nation, knew the nation's characteristics and therefore knew what was good for it; secondly because the correct perception of history was considered a prerequisite for correct civil attitudes, so that historians were obliged to intervene to rescue the state; thirdly because only a strong state could guarantee the freedom of the nation and of scholarship and the flourishing of law and culture. Recognition of this forced historians to speak not only for the nation, but also for the state, and for a definite form of state suitable to Germany's position in the world.[53]

Fourth Proposition
Finally, the potential direct effect of history must be considered:

> History, not being able to impart directly applicable morals from the past, is effective not as a set of direct instructions but as habitual practice on the part of the academic élite in the use of politico-social patterns of orientation.[54]

There was a common denominator in German historians' perception of state and nation. Despite all individual differences, I can see a basic conviction shared to a certain degree by all representatives of the discipline.[55] Rejection of Western European models—of government responsibility to Parliament in the British pattern and of a republic with

---

53. This results in an assignment of rôles for politicians and historians; in the words of vom Bruch, summarizing an essay of Oncken's (Oncken, 'Politik', and idem, Bruch, 'Historiker und Politiker', *Preussische Jahrbücher 60* [1897], p. 426): 'Hieraus ergibt sich eine Abstufung, indem der Politiker von seiner höheren Warte aus überlegen die Teilinteressen innerhalb der Nation am Massstab des nationalen Wohls zu beurteilen und dementsprechend zu beeinflussen und lenken, indem der Historiker—aber auch nur der Historiker—kraft seiner universalistischen Perspektive eben diese nationalen Interessen aufzuzeigen und so einen Bewertungsmassstab für die Staatspolitik zu finden vermag' (vom Bruch, *Wissenschaft, Politik und öffentliche Meinung*, p. 224).

54. Gustav Schmidt, *Gelehrtenpolitik und politische Kultur*, p. 15 (transl.).

55. Franz Schnabel, 'Die Geschichtswissenschaft und der Staat in den letzten hundert Jahren', in Schnabel, *Abhandlungen* (Freiburg: Herder, 1970), pp. 330-43. Fritz Ringer suggests, for the purpose of comparative study, analysing basic ideas and directions of this sort interdisciplinarity in terms of 'intellectual fields'; cf. Ringer, *Fields of Knowledge: French Academic Culture in Comparative Perspective, 1890–1920* (Cambridge, 1992).

democratic tendencies in the French—was widespread even before the 1914 war, strengthened by the experience of victory in 1871, which appeared to have vindicated their own Prussian form of state and refuted the general concept of strict liberalism as in the Prussian constitutional conflict.[56] The entitlement of state power to pursue policies determined purely by pragmatic considerations (*Realpolitik*) became a topos as a result of the events of 1870, though similar ideas had been used to come to terms with the dashed hopes of 1848. The ideas of 1813 (and later of 1914) were played off against those of 1789, though arguments such as these did not achieve canonical status until the wartime journalism of 1914–18 and of the period of the struggle against the Versailles Settlement and the Weimar Republic; that is, until after the period presently under discussion.[57]

As detailed in Part One, the state had to have an authority independent of the popular majority, since only thus could it protect scholarship, law and culture, and lead the nation successfully in international struggle. Historians played a leading part in developing this creed.[58] Naturally one can demonstrate that for discriminating authors, the power of the state was justified only inasmuch as it defended cultural values. However, the relationship of state to culture in the arguments of the historians must be discussed in more detail.

Gustav Schmidt sees it as follows:

56. Karl-Georg Faber, 'Realpolitik als Ideologie: Die Bedeutung des Jahres 1866 für das politische Denken in Deutschland', *HZ* 203 (1966), pp. 1-45; Elisabeth Fehrenbach, 'Die Reichsgründung in der deutschen Geschichtsschreibung', in Theodor Schieder and Ernst Deuerlein (eds.), *Reichsgründung* (Stuttgart: Seewald, 1970), pp. 259-90; Wolfgang Hardtwig, 'Von Preussens Aufgabe in Deutschland zu Deutschlands Aufgabe in der Welt. Liberalismus und borussisches Geschichtsbild zwischen Revolution und Imperialismus', *HZ* 231 (1980), pp. 265-324; Birgit Knorr, 'Autorität und Freiheit. Das Liberalismusverständnis des Bildungsbürgertums im Kaiserreich und in der Weimarer Republik im Spiegel der Historiographie über den Frühliberalismus' (Diss. Tübingen, Frankfurt, 1977); Leonard Krieger, *The German Idea of Freedom. History of a Political Tradition, from the Reformation to 1871* (Boston: Beacon Press, 1957).

57. Cf. Bernd Faulenbach, *Ideologie des deutschen Weges: Die deutsche Geschichte in der Historiographie zwischen Kaiserreich und Nationalsozialismus* (Munich: Beck, 1980).

58. Volker Dotterweich, *Heinrich von Sybel: Geschichtswissenschaft in politischer Absicht (1817–1861)* (Göttingen: Vandenhoeck & Ruprecht, 1978); Simon, *Staat und Geschichtswissenschaft*, pp. 3ff.

Assuming that individuals obtain their socialization and acculturation in organisations of second degree, that is in received forms of cultural context on the one hand and forms of socialization (state, industry, law) on the other, they [the 'historian philosophers' of the *Historismus* movement, especially Dilthey and Troeltsch] seek to determine the correct balance between the two typical structures of communication (state and culture). The overemphasis of the rôle and significance of the state of which German historic thought is often accused thus appears in the context of a primary concern for the preservation of the 'European cultural synthesis' in the face of the danger, proceeding from the French Revolution, of the 'politicisation' of all areas of life. Using the rhetorical trick of asking the question as to whether any of the human spheres of existence which characterize social organization could have any permanence outside the state or of the system of law and security established by political association, they attempt to ensure that culture is an integral concern of politics. It is important to note that the state, like any other organization of second degree, (industry, law, associations) is basically only a frame to retain cultural cohesiveness by means of a voluntarily agreed political structure. With regard to their early recognition of the significance of socialisation and of the tasks of 'national education' one realizes why it is precisely those critics of imperial German nationalism such as Dilthey or Troeltsch who provided the justification and made use of the *topos* that no area of national life could have any permanence outside the legal system created and maintained by the state. This did not signify sublimation of the state, but a reminder that the relationship between state and culture must be repeatedly reassessed and renewed.[59]

However, no matter how correct it may be on the one hand to reject generalizing statements about 'German thought', we are on the other hand, justified in doubting how representative was the discriminating derivation of the concept of state in the two historians mentioned from among the many historians within the German State. How easily the threshold to adulation of state power could be crossed, could be seen in numerous speeches on the Kaiser's birthday or the anniversary of Sedan.

Historians were fond of repeating their conviction that Germany occupied a central geographical position in Europe and was therefore especially threatened and thus could not afford too many civil liberties or allow free rein for divergent opinion. This argument was repeatedly used in comparisons with the British political system and served to promote the view that hopes for a development of the imperial constitution towards government accountability before parliament were dangerous

59. Schmidt, 'Gelehrtenpolitik und politische Kultur', pp. 33-34 (transl.).

and unjustified. The view that permanency of German national unity was considered basically undesirable by other powers and was only to be achieved by war (against France) led historians to the conclusion that it must be defended above all by military preparedness. The logical development to a position in the world appropriate to Germany's potency had to be secured by rearmament, a moral drawn from the history of national unification.

On the other hand, professors of history almost always clung to professorial liberalism. Thus, to continue the points I made in Part One, Law and Constitution must never be renounced; both property-owing *and* academic élites must be involved in decisions on budget and taxation; free discussion among scholars must never be prevented by censorship—scholarship and methodology were the only acceptable means of regulating this discussion. This was compounded in most cases with the idea that the state owed its members a minimum of social justice or security, a conservative definition of welfare in other words, which came into conflict with economic *laissez faire* and might, in those days, polemically and deceptively, be termed 'Socialism'.

The thesis that 'non-liberalism' or 'non-liberal behaviour'[60] dominated German society as a whole, needs critical examination. It is clear that for most professors of the period, liberalism and democratic thought were mutually exclusive, but their perception of liberalism was not thereby non-liberal. There is a German historical liberalism, as I have described above, and there is a normative concept of liberalism sharpened on ideas of human and civil rights and other achievements of Western European development. Although German professorial liberalism at the close of the nineteenth century does not fully live up to this latter concept, it has historical affinities with it. This makes it difficult to name and assess the phenomenon adequately. Their liberalism and their emphasis on adherence to the nation as a powerful Nation State were reciprocal functions, however, since the idea of the nation lay at the core of this form of liberalism. The idea was liberal, because these professors saw themselves as the heart of the nation, as witness such terms as 'conscience of the nation' or 'natural representatives of the people' as descriptions of the university.

60. E.g. Fritz Stern, *Das Scheitern illiberaler Politik: Studien zur politischen Kultur Deutschlands im 19. und 20. Jahrhundert* (Frankfurt a.M.: Propyläen, 1974). Konrad H. Jarausch, *Students, Society, and Politics in Imperial Germany: The Rise of Academic Illiberalism* (Princeton: Princeton University Press, 1982).

The tendency, justly denigrated by modern liberals (and democrats of the period, for example, Ludwig Quidde[61]), to adore authority, can once more be explained by the attitude that the German nation could only be realized in a powerful state not hindered by any disloyal opposition. It is a question of finding the right sense of scale, and for an analysis which does not make use of comparisons with other Nation States, it seems appropriate to emphasize the professors' relative liberalism. However, a due sense of scale can only be gained from a perspective of comparison with other nations.

After all, this liberal basic attitude did not exclude the fact that a whole series of groups were considered undesirable within the universities: Jews, on account of latent anti-semitism and sometimes open discrimination (only Christians were considered able to understand German history correctly, German national patterns of thought were assumed to be incomprehensible to Jews, there were allegedly so many Jews in the intelligentsia that they were driving true Germans out of the universities); Social Democrats (because they were considered enemies of the state); Democrats (for the same reason); Catholics to some degree (because it was assumed that for them scholarship had only limited validity in matters of faith and because they were believed to be subject to a foreign authority, the Pope; they did not enjoy the liberty of thought brought by Luther). In all this there were significant nuances. The open promulgation of anti-semitism on racist principles was not generally accepted (although this did little to alter their practical exclusion from leading positions, for example, chairs).[62] Individual professors

---

61. Reinhard Rürup, 'Ludwig Quidde', in Hans-Ulrich Wehler (ed.), *Deutsche Historiker*, III (Göttingen: Vandenhoeck & Ruprecht, 1972), pp. 124-74; Utz-Friedebert Taube, *Ludwig Quidde: Ein Beitrag zur Geschichte des demokratischen Gedankens in Deutschland* (Kallmünz: Lassleben, 1963); Roger Chickering, *Imperial Germany and a World without War: The Peace Movement and German Society 1892–1914* (Princeton: Princeton University Press, 1975).

62. See Boschung's figures in vom Brocke (above, note 45). A good example of this attitude among historians in Berlin is the Bresslau case: cf. Simon, *Staat und Geschichtswissenschaft*, pp. 92-95, 134. Christhard Hoffmann, *Juden und Judentum in Werk deutscher Althistoriker des 19. und 20. Jahrhunderts* (Leiden: Brill, 1988); Norbert Kampe, *Studenten und 'Judenfrage' im Deutschen Kaiserreich: Die Entstehung einer akademischen Trägerschicht des Antisemitismus* (Göttingen: Vandenhoeck & Ruprecht, 1988); W. Boehlich (ed.), *Der Berliner Antisemitismusstreit* (Frankfurt: Insel, 1965). The distinction occasionally drawn between racism and

such as Schmoller wanted to tolerate Social Democrats because of their radical view of university liberties or because they wished to see a *rapprochement* between State and workers, though this did not require cessation of discrimination against Social Democrats. The often quoted words 'The "freedom of science" exists in Germany within the limits of ecclesiastical and political acceptability.

Outside these limits there is none' come from Max Weber, the occasion being the failure of Robert Michels, Social Democrat and freethinker, to secure professorial qualifications in Marburg or Jena.[63]

Examination of historiography opens our eyes to the contents of historical works, the choice of topics, the methodological tendency and the so called lessons of history. At first approach a reconstruction of the main streams of specialist scholarly discourse on history displays the following characteristics:

1. The state was the central topic, its relationship to other states (foreign policy) and its activity as organizer and initiator in society, industry and culture (domestic policy). The state was objective: Georg von Below knew the problem of value judgements in scholarship and knew that 'facts cannot be viewed in combination without value judgements' but that: 'these judgments rest on a system of values that we present-day historians follow', a system which was provided by the state, which was 'the most comprehensive human association', the 'authoritative organisation of the people', the 'strongest bulwark of culture'. Following Oexle one can perceive in this a 'decisionistic determination of a recognition-forming highest value, that of the

denominational anti-semitism needs further discussion in the case of the late nineteenth century.

63. Max Weber, 'The alleged "academic freedom" of the German universities', p. 17 in E. Shils (ed.), 'M. Weber, The Power of the State and the Dignity of Academic Calling in Imperial Germany. The Writings of Max Weber on University Problems', *Minerva* 11.4 (1973), pp. 1-62. German version in a letter to the Frankfurter Zeitung 1908: 'Tatsache ist doch, dass die angebliche "Lehrfreiheit" offenkundig 1) an den Besitz politisch hof- und salonfähiger Ansichten und überdies 2) daran geknüpft ist, dass man ein bestimmtes Minimum kirchlicher Gesinnung betätigt und, eventuell, heuchelt. In Deutschland besteht die "Freiheit" der Wissenschaft innerhalb der Grenzen der politischen und kirchlichen Hoffähigkeit– ausserhalb derselben nicht' (*Frankfurter Zeitung* 20.9 [1908], Morgenblatt 5th edn, quoted by Ulrich Sieg, in vom Brocke, *Wissenschaftsgeschichte und Wissenschaftspolitik*, p. 299).

state relationship, which gave the historian the 'direct scale' for "consideration of individual portions of culture"'.[64] The state was thus not merely a preferred topic; this preference had a methodological dimension.

2. The history taught was national, consisting of the reconstruction of the genesis of the German nation and the history of other nations in their relationships with Germany, direct or indirect. The state of the past was also seen as a power-political Nation State.

3. It followed from the above that General History was coextensive with nation state history viewed from the national perspective.

This picture requires qualification.

1. We cannot ignore the so-called *Historismus*. However, this term has no generally accepted definition, and it is questionable to what extent the norms implicated in it (principle of individuality, doctrine of *Verstehen*, ideas as prime movers behind events) were really relevant in historiographical practice.[65] The 'Ranke renaissance' at the close of the nineteenth century thus clearly offered an opportunity for finding historical explanations at an idealistic remove from the cruder concepts of the power-state.[66]

64. Quotations from Georg von Below's *Die deutsche Geschichtsschreibung von den Befreiungskriegen bis zu unseren Tagen* (Munich: Oldenbourg, 1924 [repr. Aaten: Scientia, 1973]), as in Otto Gerhard Oexle, 'Ein politischer Historiker—Georg von Below', in Notker Hammerstein (ed.), *Deutsche Geschichtswissenschaft um 1900* (Stuttgart: Steiner, 1988), pp. 283-312, here p. 302 (transl.).

65. Thomas Nipperdey, 'Historismus und Historismuskritik', in E. Jäckel and E. Weymar (eds.), *Die Funktion der Geschichte in unserer Zeit* (Stuttgart: Klett, 1975), pp. 82-95; Otto Gerhard Oexle, '"Historismus". Ueberlegungen zur Geschichte des Phänomens und des Begriffs', in *Braunschweigische Wissenschaftliche Gesellschaft, Jahrbuch 1986*, pp. 199-255. *Historismus* must not be translated by 'historicism', cf. Georg G. Iggers, 'Historicism', in *Dictionary of the History of Ideas* (1973), II, pp. 127ff., and Hans Schleier, 'Epochen der deutschen Geschichtsschreibung seit der Mitte des 18. Jahrhunderts', in Wolfgang Küttler, Jörn Rüsen and Ernst Schulin (eds.), *Geschichtsdiskurs. I. Grundlagen und Methoden der Historiographiegeschichte* (Frankfurt a.M.: Fischer Taschenbuch Verlag, 1993), pp. 133-56 nn. 6-8. [—For more details, cf. G. Scholz above, pp. 149ff.]

66. Elisabeth Fehrenbach, 'Rankerenaissance und Imperialismus in der wilhelminischen Zeit', in Bernd Faulenbach (ed.), *Geschichtswissenschaft in*

2. Other topics and approaches were certainly treated, such as cultural, economic, administrative, social, urban and guild history. In these areas, structural approaches were clearly present. But as far as Berlin was concerned these were not really history, but peripheral specialities. Any attempt to suggest a validity for these disciplines beyond their marginal status produced violent defensive reactions (for example, in the Lamprecht case and the Breysig affair). At least as important as the combatting of 'incorrect' historical methods was the aim of keeping 'unworthy' topics out of university research and teaching and setting the right order of precedence: state and politics before society, individual before masses. In the framework thus set, specialist topics could be treated with methods that were not envisaged by *Historismus*, as the beginning of Otto Hintze's career demonstrates.[67]

After reconstructing the prevailing consensus within historical scholarship, I encountered the question as to how these features of discourse relate to the situation of the historian between society, state and university. Speaking from a considerable distance, I could maintain that it was the form of discourse required by the state for its own

Deutschland (Munich: Beck, 1974), pp. 54-65; Hans-Heinz Krill, *Die Rankerenaissance: Max Lenz und Erich Marcks: Ein Beitrag zum historisch-politischen Denken in Deutschland 1880–1935* (Berlin: de Gruyter, 1962).

67. Cf. vom Bruch's conclusions (*Wissenschaft, Politik und öffentliche Meinung*, pp. 388ff.); on the situation of History, see Simon, *Staat und Geschichtswissenschaft*, pp. 19ff.; on the framework within which social and economic topics were tolerated or considered desirable in History the classical work on the subject is Gerhard Oestreich, 'Die Fachhistorie und die Anfänge der sozialgeschichtlichen Forschung in Deutschland', in *HZ* 208 (1969), pp. 320-63. On the Lamprecht conflict see Lutz Raphael, 'Historikerkontroversen im Spannungsfeld zwischen Berufshabitus, Fächerkonkurrenz und sozialen Bedeutungsmustern: Lamprecht-Streit und französischer Methodenstreit der Jahrhundertwende in vergleichender Perspektive', *HZ* 251 (1990), pp. 325-63; Luise Schorn-Schütte, *Karl Lamprecht: Kulturgeschichts-schreibung zwischen Wissenschaft und Politik* (Göttingen: Vandenhoeck & Ruprecht, 1984); Emil Spiess, 'Die Geschichtsphilosophie von Karl Lamprecht' (Diss. Freiburg (Schweiz), Erlangen, 1921); Matti Viikari, *Die Krise der 'historistischen' Geschichtsschreibung und die Geschichtsmethodologie Karl Lamprechts* (Helsinki: Suomalainen Tiedeakatemia, 1977); Georg G. Iggers, 'The Methodenstreit in International Perspective', *Storia della Storiografia* 6 (1984), pp. 21-32.

justification. History can thus be seen as a legitimating discipline for the constitutional monarchy in the form of the 1870 Empire (but not of the Wilhelmine variety with its claim to monarchic neo-absolutism). This can be substantiated on the one hand, on the grounds of the arguments in favour of monarchy, of the strong state, and of power/unity before liberty; and on the other, on the basis of the rejection of alternative models such as parliamentarianism, democracy, the so called priority of society (and of its forces such as class and economic interests) over the state (as superfactional embodiment of the nation).

Here, too, discrimination is required, since the intentions of speakers and actors should not remain unexamined; they served the state only inasmuch as they considered that the state served and represented the nation (and élite culture). In approach this was a critical attitude, which permitted opposition at all times except those of emergency. Behind this one can recognize secularized religion (*religion civile*) and the posture of the prophet/priest pillorying the behaviour of the mighty. The priest-historian guarded those central standards which society had to follow unconditionally if it were to survive and prosper. On the other hand, in what were considered times of emergency, there was practically no mental limit to the historians' readiness for self-sacrifice; criticism was required to give place to service.[68]

Thus a bridge between intention and effect becomes evident, which gives a more profitable line of argument than a coarse analysis on functionalistic principles. '[Professorial politics] does not render service, rather more it presents itself for service and is accepted', said Hermann Lübbe.[69] Historians served the state because they wanted to serve the nation; they thus sought proximity to the state where they expected to be heard, respected and protected. Their thoughts proceeded from the state's position, as the Left noticed long ago, and thus wrote 'history from above', putting state activity at the centre of their questioning and

68. Klaus Schwabe, *Wissenschaft und Kriegsmoral: Die deutschen Hochschullehrer und die politischen Grundfragen des Ersten Weltkrieges* (Göttingen: Musterschmidt, 1969); Bernhard vom Brocke, 'Wissenschaft und Militarismus: Der Aufruf der 93 "An die Kulturwelt!" und der Zusammenbruch im internationalen Gelehrtenrepublik im Ersten Weltkrieg', in William M. Calder III, H. Flashar and T. Lindken (eds.), *Wilamowitz nach 50 Jahren* (Darmstadt: Wiss. Buchgesellschaft, 1985). Cf. also Hans Peter Bleuel, *Deutschlands Bekenner: Professoren zwischen Kaiserreich und Diktatur* (Munich: Scherz, 1968).

69. Hermann Lübbe, *Politische Philosophie in Deutschland* (Basel: Schwabe, 1963), p. 10 (transl.).

regarding society from the perspective of the administration and politics from the monarch's throne or minister's bench.

It was national and scholarly interest that led to the state-related perspective; *religion civile* cried out for this. The relationship to the state was the consequence of a hierarchy of values which was in itself a consequence of the history of this section of citizens in its relationship to the state. This should not, however, divert attention from the fact that certain other libertarian critical values (liberal in their terms) were accepted and esteemed. When there was no necessity of confirming the pre-existent hierarchy of values in discourse, then other values could determine choices; in such situations the stage was dominated by professorial liberalism. In its historical content, national liberalism continued to exist as a constituent of that discourse which bound the German professors of history together as a community and determined their tradition.

It must often be emphasized that the Empire was not a dictatorship (or at least, not compared with the Third Reich); that within the framework as outlined above, thought was, or could have been, as free as in the preceding period of reaction had never been the case, and as it was not intended to have been in Germany 'for a thousand years' afterwards.

I think that this praise of liberty and the use made of it under the three *Kaiser* can only be qualified by looking at it in comparison with other, democratic-republican conditions; but this is exactly how I do look at it, and I would certainly wish to proceed to such a qualification. Thus, for example, Marc Bloch criticized his German colleague George von Below from just this standpoint. He was extremely disturbed by the 'cult of the state' in the 'collective mentality' of German history from 1871–1918.[70] Oexle assumed from Bloch's text that von Below's concentration on Germany prevented his achieving what Bloch had demanded, that historians should be good Europeans, and on this basis he attempted to explain why the renewal of historical scholarship did not proceed from Germany but from France.[71]

---

70. Marc Bloch, 'Un tempérament—Georg von Below [Review of Minnie von Below, *Georg von Below: Ein Lebensbild für seine Freunde*]', in *Annales ESC* 3 (1931), pp. 553-59.

71. Otto Gerhard Oexle, 'Ein politischer Historiker. Georg von Below (1858–1927)', in Notker Hammerstein (ed.), *Deutsche Geschichtswissenschaft um 1900* (Stuttgart: Steiner, 1988), pp. 283-312. Further arguments in Karl Ferdinand Werner, 'Marc Bloch et la recherche allemande', in *Marc Bloch aujourd'hui: Histoire*

When I adopt this external viewpoint, then I am relating the history of a social group from the intellectual élite that chose a conservative option based on a specific interpretation of their own history and on their proprietary group interest (in the social position of culture and education due to its proximity to the ruling body), which banned other options from their ranks and which retained the conservative option for a very long time; too long to appear sympathetic, too long for them to maintain their leading position in the European *République des lettres* into the twentieth century.

comparée et sciences sociales (Paris: Ed. de l'Ecole des Hautes Etudes en Sciences Sociales, 1990), pp. 125-33: Before 1914 the French wanted to write history like the Germans but better; after 1918 they were in search of a completely different kind of history, as proposed by Febvre and Bloch after being appointed to Strasbourg after 1919.

BARON FRIEDRICH VON HÜGEL AND THE CONVEYANCE OF GERMAN PROTESTANT BIBLICAL CRITICISM IN ROMAN CATHOLIC MODERNISM*

Hans Rollmann

Introduction

Modernism, the ill-defined 'poison of all heresies' of Pius X's encyclical *Pascendi dominici gregis*, was a mixed bag of teachings that engaged Roman Catholic scholars and thinkers of the nineteenth and twentieth centuries, especially those who wanted to see the Church involved in a dialogue with contemporary thought and feeling. Condemned side by side with a person-centred philosophy of religion were methods and results of modern biblical and church-historical scholarship, which had become part of Protestant theology during the eighteenth and nineteenth centuries. The encyclical showed little sensitivity for the employment of this scholarship in the service of Roman Catholicism and rejected it wholesale and without regard for its theological or even apologetic potential. While much of the encyclical was directed against the so called 'new apologetic' and its religio-philosophical underpinnings, the entire current of modern biblical scholarship, which had been developing cautiously in Roman Catholicism since the pontificate of Leo XIII, was indicted as well. Among the efforts to convey this modern historical-critical thinking in the biblical field to receptive Roman Catholic theologians in France, England, Italy, and Germany, one figure in particular looms large, that of the layman Baron Friedrich von Hügel. The Baron—as he was affectionately known among his friends, and whom the French liberal protestant Paul Sabatier once called the 'Pope of the Modernists'—was indeed an intellectual clearinghouse and pivotal for

* The research in the von Hügel papers at St Andrews University Library (SAUL), Scotland, and at the British Library in London was made possible through a grant of the Social Sciences and Humanities Research Council of Canada, which the author wishes to acknowledge gratefully.

the dissemination and stimulation of biblical scholarship among modern-minded Catholics in Europe.

In this paper I shall deal with von Hügel's role as the conveyer of German Protestant biblical scholarship within the Modernist Movement. Scholarly work on von Hügel has been extensive but until now has dealt almost exclusively with his philosophy of religion, spirituality, and with the historical specifics of his involvement in the modernist crisis.[1] With the exception of a series of articles by myself, which explored the personal relationships and intellectual contexts of von Hügel's German correspondents,[2] no study has yet appeared which deals specifically with von Hügel's contribution to and use of biblical criticism. And yet it was modern biblical criticism which—besides a person-centred philosophy of religion—was rejected by the anti-Modernist decrees in the outgoing nineteenth and early twentieth centuries and which von Hügel made a main focus of his scholarly work from the 1880s on. Von Hügel's central role in acquainting *fin de siecle* Catholicism with state of the art biblical criticism is also evident from his scholarly correspondence and publications. There is an obvious need to fill the gap in our understanding of the historical-critical component in von Hügel's thought and influence. The following paper shall address this patent need in a modest

---

1.   Lawrence F. Barmann, *Baron Friedrich von Hügel and the Modernist Crisis in England* (Cambridge, 1972); Peter Neuner, *Religiöse Erfahrung und geschichtliche Offenbarung: Friedrich von Hügels Grundlegung der Theologie* (Munich, 1977); Thomas Michael Loome, *Liberal Catholicism, Reform Catholicism, Modernism: A Contribution to a New Orientation in Modernist Research* (Mainz, 1979).

2.   The following articles of mine deal with von Hügel's relations to German scholarship: 1. 'Troeltsch, von Hügel, and Modernism', *DR* 96 (1978), pp. 35-60; 2. 'Adolf von Harnack's Answer to a Recently Published Letter of Friedrich von Hügel', *JAAR* 44 (Suppl., Dec. 1978), pp. 499-507; 3. 'Holtzmann, von Hügel, and Modernism', *DR* 97 (1979), pp. 128-43 and 221-44; 4. 'Baron Friedrich von Hügel's *Mystical Element of Religion*, Reviewed by Himself', *DR* 97 (1979), pp. 304-307; 5. 'Introduction', *Liberal Catholicism—Reform Catholicism—Modernism: A Critical Discussion of Thomas Michael Loome's Agenda for a New Orientation in Modernist Research* (Hans Rollmann and Ronald Burke [eds.], Modernism issue of *DR*, vol. 100 [1982]), pp. 157-61; also 6. 'Critical Assessment of Loome's German Sources', *ibid.*, pp. 193-200; 7. 'Von Hügel and Scheler', *DR* 101 (1983), pp. 30-42; 8. 'Ernst Troeltsch, Friedrich von Hügel, and the Student Christian Movement', *DR* 101 (1983), pp. 216-26; 9. 'Franz Xaver Kraus and John Henry Newman', *DR* 109 (1991), pp. 44-51; 10. 'Liberal Catholicism, Modernism and the Closing of the Roman Mind: Franz Xaver Kraus and Friedrich von Hügel', *DR* 109 (1991), pp. 202-16.

and preliminary way and is divided into two parts. In the first and larger part, entitled 'Appropriation', the reception and significance of German Protestant biblical scholarship for von Hügel's own thinking is examined. In a shorter and more tentative second part, entitled 'Communication', there is a focus on the public and private conveyance of exegetical expertise by von Hügel to his Modernist friends, especially to George Tyrrell.

Appropriation

Von Hügel's role as a mediator of German biblical scholarship must be understood from his role as a private scholar and layman. He never attended a school or a university, yet became the first Roman Catholic since the Reformation to receive an honorary doctorate from Oxford University for his contributions to theology. As the son of the Austrian ambassador to Florence and later to Brussels, Carl Alexander Freiherr von Hügel, the youth received private tutoring from, among others, a Lutheran pastor, under the supervision of the Prussian diplomat and historian Alfred von Reumont. His private education included thorough training in Latin and Greek. Socially, he achieved fluency in German, English, French, and Italian. His family ties with the Catholic nobility of England and Europe enabled him, like Lord Acton, to lobby in the highest ecclesiastical circles without embarrassment and oblige scholars, academics, and the clergy when initiating a private correspondence on scholarly matters. His later course of studies, after the arrival in England, was self-prescribed and without any regard for confessional barriers. Much of this scholarly and personal independence was a precondition of his role as mediator between Protestant exegetical and philosophical expertise and Roman Catholic theology. A personal circumstance, his near deafness, prevented him from ever attending a university. Thus he never felt the constraints of a contemporary theological education. Unlike other Modernists and Catholic liberals, von Hügel's training was never characterized by a process of intellectual liberation from the confinements of a neo-scholastic seminary training. But he was united with a group of other liberal Catholics and clergy who attempted to bring Catholicism into touch with modern realities without sacrificing its Catholic substance.[3]

---

3. Still useful for the development of von Hügel is the biography of Michael de

It seems that von Hügel's early interest in biblical matters revolved around questions of textual criticism arising from his theological readings. He was particularly concerned with the textual sufficiency of the Vulgate. And here, as he would do so often later, he went to discuss matters with the authorities in the field. On 21 March 1882, for example, von Hügel engaged in a lengthy conversation with one of the most eminent textual critics of the day, Dr Scrivener. Scrivener introduced him to the principles of textual criticism, judged for him the value of the Codex Vaticanus and the Vulgate, and offered his opinion on the Westcott and Hort text and the relevant grammars and linguistic aids.[4] Later, in 1885, to cite another example, John Wordsworth in Oxford made available to him during a visit his unpublished critical text of the Vulgate.[5] The diaries from 1879 to 1885 confirm this preoccupation with textual questions. During this time he acquired and used the major critical editions of the Greek text, notably those of Tischendorf. A decade later he also pursued with as much rigor the study of the Hebrew text. From August to October 1890 in London he received his first private instructions in Hebrew by the Innsbruck orientalist and convert from Lutheranism to Catholicism, Gustav Bickell. This study of Hebrew was continued for five years with the German Jewish scholar Julius Spira and even included, in 1895, Aramaic lessons by Ignazio Guidi of the Urban College in Rome.[6]

Besides these face-to-face encounters, the correspondence preserved at St Andrews, Scotland, and in other European archives reads like a who's who of late nineteenth- and early twentieth-century scholarship and learning. Von Hügel never hesitated to pose questions of fact and interpretation to the leading biblical scholars, historians, theologians, and philosophers of his day. His correspondents include the following non-Catholics: Charles A. Briggs, Gustav Adolf Deissmann, Samuel Rolles Driver, Rudolf Eucken, Adolf von Harnack, Friedrich Heiler, Heinrich Julius Holtzmann, F.J.A. Hort, William James, Claude Montefiore, Rudolf Otto, Salomon Reinach, W. Robertson Smith, Paul Sabatier,

la Bedoyere, *The Life of Baron von Hügel* (London, 1951); but see also Loome, *Liberal Catholicism*.

    4.   'Interview with Prebendary Scrivener', 21 March, 1882 (St Andrews University Library, von Hügel Papers [hereafter: SAUL], MS 2653).

    5.   1885 Diary, 23–24 February (SAUL).

    6.   The diaries at SAUL for those years detail his preoccupation with learning Hebrew. The Hebrew lessons are preserved at SAUL too.

William Sanday, Albert Schweitzer, Nathan Söderblom, Ernst Troeltsch, Hans Vaihinger, James Ward, and Clement Webb. Among his fellow Catholics were liberals from Cardinal Newman and Franz Xaver Kraus to Albert Ehrhardt, Max Scheler, Hermann Schell, and Archbishop Mignot, as well as nearly all the figures involved in the Modernist crisis proper. This network of international scholarship was, as we shall see, crucial in furthering the Modernist cause and conveying the latest critical opinion from Germany. It also served as a significant resource for the Baron's own thinking and for maintaining and reinforcing a consciousness of the universality of scholarly methods and results among Modernists amid an increasingly restrictive ecclesiastical policy towards scholarly endeavours in the historical and theological disciplines.

Among the intellectual resources of the Baron, his private library, preserved at St Andrew's University in Scotland, is an impressive witness to the scope of his scholarly study of the Bible. During a research stay at St Andrew's, I examined this library closely. Von Hügel personally owned all major reference tools of the day, from editions, commentaries, lexica, dictionaries and monographs to the appropriate journals in the field. He subscribed, among others, to the *Zeitschrift für die Alttestamentliche Wissenschaft, Zeitschrift für Neutestamentliche Wissenschaft, Zeitschrift für Teologie und Kirche*, and the *Archiv für Religionswissenschaft*. A careful examination of the books in this library permitted me to trace the intellectual development of von Hügel. This was made possible especially because of the copious annotations in his books. Von Hügel not only underlined significant passages, he also developed a system of marginal outlines and annotations and furnished on the inside covers four types of comments: *Annotanda*, *Criticanda*, *Admiranda*, and *Corrigenda*. Frequently he also supplied the reasons for his purchase and exact dates of his reading, and, occasionally, even the degree of closeness of this reading. In addition to the library, there is also a wealth of pamphlets, offprints and brochures, which von Hügel read with differing degrees of closeness.

It is impossible to convey even an overview of this intellectual exposure. I shall thus provide here two examples by focusing on the two German scholars who were very important for the Baron's own work and who represented the height of German critical achievements of the day: Julius Wellhausen and Heinrich Julius Holtzmann. Of Wellhausen, von Hügel owned *Die Composition des Hexateuchs und die historischen Bücher des Alten Testaments; Israelitische und jüdische*

Geschichte; *Prolegomena zur Geschichte Israels*, both in German and English; volumes 1, 3, and 5 of *Skizzen und Vorarbeiten*, that is, *Geschichte Israels und Judas, Reste arabischen Heidentums*, and *Die kleineren Propheten*; also, in the area of New Testament studies, Wellhausen's *Das Evangelium Marci*; *Das Evangelium Matthei*; *Das Evangelium Lucae*; *Das Evangelium Johannis*; and his *Einleitung in die drei ersten Evangelien*. Besides these primary works, von Hügel owned and carefully read Johannes Meinhold's 1897 appreciation of Wellhausen, which appeared in the fascicles of the *Christliche Welt*. It was Bickell who first enthused von Hügel for Wellhausen, while W. Robertson Smith and Heinrich Julius Holtzmann reinforced the high esteem of the German Old Testament scholar.[7] It seems the appropriation of Wellhausen and Kuenen in Alfred Loisy's 1890 work on the canon of the Old Testament was also the reason for their first personal encounter. To his friend Wilfred Ward, the Roman Catholic historian and publicist, von Hügel recommended Loisy's study as 'the very thing we [Catholics] want'. And as to what this 'very thing' consisted of, von Hügel left no doubt. Loisy's book contained 'every date and composite authorship demanded by Wellhausen and Kuenen: you don't get that every day!'[8]

While the *Composition des Hexateuchs* is only moderately lined, the *Prolegomena* was, as von Hügel tells us on the inside, read twice and completed on 2 September, 1890. To judge from his linings, the book was absorbed quite selectively. His special interests were the source question and the history of the cult, notably the contrast between priest and prophet in Judaism, a theme of special religio-historical relevance for the Baron. The *Geschichte Israels und Judas im Umriss*, which was purchased upon the suggestion of Bickell, von Hügel worked through thoroughly in September of 1894. The *Israelitische und jüdische Geschichte*, which he read first in Rome in the fall of 1895, is thoroughly lined, outlined, and paralleled with, for example, references to Kuenen's work. It seems to have served, as did the *Umriss*, as a major reference work for von Hügel. The Baron's preoccupation with the Mosaic authorship questions, then sweeping Roman Catholic scholarship, may have been the personal motivation for his initial interest. In the process, however, he acquired a methodology, which he sought to

---

7.   See von Hügel's own estimate of his exposure to Wellhausen in the obituary, 'Julius Wellhausen', *TLS*, 7 March, 1918, p. 117.
8.   Von Hügel to Wilfred Ward, 31 October, 1890 (SAUL).

impart to his fellow Roman Catholics as well. Thus he contributed in 1897 a knowledgable survey of existing scholarship on hexateuchal studies to the Fourth International Catholic Scientific Congress in Freiburg, Switzerland.[9] The essay appeared one year later in an English version in America in the Modernist *The Catholic University Bulletin*, for which von Hügel also translated Lagrange's contribution on the Pentateuch given at the same congress.[10] In the essay von Hügel attempts to convince his Roman Catholic readers that the methodology of Reuss, Kuenen and Wellhausen is by no means anti-Catholic. He links the exegetical concerns of such Roman Catholic pioneers as Richard Simon and Jean Astruc with these modern endeavours and argues in a comparison between the source analysis in Kautzsch's German Bible and that of Jean Astruc in 1753, that of 137 verses attributed to Astruc's source 'A', 110 were still attributed to its modern equivalent 'P'.

The appropriation of such scholarly work into Roman Catholic theology was a prime concern for von Hügel, who stressed again and again the consensus emerging on major issues in international and inter-confessional biblical scholarship. This insistence on a consensus was no attempt to become non-Catholic as it was interpreted by the anti-Modernists. It rather represented an attempt to catch up and compensate by moving into the mainstream of the universal scholarly enterprise. At their core, the Modernists were apologists for Roman Catholicism, albeit with modern methods in philosophy and history. When the Pontifical Biblical Commission in 1906 rejected this scholarship altogether and declared as a matter of faith the Mosaic authorship of the entire Pentateuch, von Hügel engaged with the American scholar Charles Briggs in a published correspondence, which reaffirmed the critical inquiry he had learned initially from Wellhausen.[11] Upon Wellhausen's

9. Von Hügel, 'La methode historique en son application à l'étude des documents de l'hexateuque', *Compte rendu du quatrième congres scientifique international des catholiques, tenu à Fribourg 16–20.8, 1897*, Part 2: *Sciences exégétiques* (Freiburg, 1898), pp. 231-58.

10. Von Hügel, 'The Historical Method and the Documents of the Hexateuch', *CUB* 4 (April, 1898), pp. 198-226.

11. Charles A. Briggs and Friedrich von Hügel, *The Papal Commission and the Pentateuch* (London, 1906). On the exchange, see William J. Hynes, 'A Hidden Nexus between Catholic and Protestant Modernism: C.A. Briggs in Correspondence with Loisy, von Hügel and Genocchi', *DR* 105 (1987), pp. 193-223; Gerald P. Fogarty, *American Catholic Biblical Scholarship: A History from the Early*

death, von Hügel published a personal appreciation of the German scholar in the *Times Literary Supplement*. The only critical stance of von Hügel toward Wellhausen concerned his New Testament studies, which he considered, 'for the most part, distinctly less solid and sober than...his OT labours'. The radical conclusions about the non-historicity of Jesus' messianic predications in the *Einleitung in die drei ersten Evangelien* were especially objectionable to the Baron, who followed here not Wellhausen but his New Testament mentor Heinrich Julius Holtzmann, when arguing against Wellhausen that Jesus identified himself with a spiritually understood Messiah.[12]

The appropriation of Holtzmann by von Hügel was not purely confined to his New Testament expertise but was based upon a wider historical and speculative interest, which the two men had in common.[13] Since his first major work in 1859 on *Kanon und Tradition*, Holtzmann was interested in everything Catholic. This was reinforced by repeated visits to Rome and numerous reviews of Roman Catholic scholarship in the major Protestant journals. The personal friendship with von Hügel intensified and sustained this concern. Also Holtzmann's speculative work, notably his study of Richard Rothe, became an important source for the Baron's own religio-philosophical studies on time and duration. But the decisive influence was indeed in the biblical area. Nearly all of Holtzmann's books and articles are preserved in the Baron's library. Most important among them were his *Lehrbuch der historisch-kritischen Einleitung in das Neue Testament*, the *Lehrbuch der neutestamentlichen Theologie*, and three editions of the *Handkommentar zum Neuen Testament*, all of which became indispensable reference works for his own scholarship and which he used even when preparing religious instructions for his children.

At first, Holtzmann represented to von Hügel merely a reliable Protestant exegete who could be used when clarifying issues inherent in the debate about the dogmatic position of scripture.[14] Von Hügel had

Republic to Vatican II (San Francisco, 1989), pp. 140-70.

12. See above n. 7. The judgment as to Wellhausen's New Testament studies relies on an examination of von Hügel's annotations of Wellhausen's books in SAUL.

13. The following draws on my previous articles on von Hügel and Holtzmann, titled 'Holtzmann, von Hügel, and Modernism', *DR* 97 (1979), pp. 128-43 and 221-44.

14. See James Tunstead Burtchaell, *Catholic Theories of Biblical Inspiration since 1810: A Review and Critique* (Cambridge, 1969), pp. 164-229; Oswald Loretz,

engaged in discussing these matters with Cardinal Newman and his successor at the Birmingham Oratory, H.I.D. Ryder.[15] They became acute, however, with the publication in 1893 of Leo XIII's encyclical *Providentissimus*. Von Hügel entered the interpretative debate with three articles in the *Dublin Review*, entitled *The Church and the Bible*.[16] The articles represent an uneven study, which aims at accomplishing too much at once: the legitimacy of the historical-critical method for biblical studies; a limited doctrinally protective role for the Church's *magisterium* as far as historical-critical questions were concerned; a demonstration of how modern biblical scholarship was able to help Catholic apologetics; and a survey sketching the results of Old and New Testament criticism for Roman Catholics. Thus the original intention of the articles, to clarify the issues raised by *Providentissimus* regarding divine authorship, plenary inspiration, and inerrancy of the Bible became obscured. But they help us to gauge the scope and nature of von Hügel's reliance on German Protestant scholarship for his theological work. Here von Hügel revealed a thorough knowledge of Holtzmann's *Handkommentar*, from which he quoted on numerous occasions in support of exegetical points, especially those that supported a traditional Catholic position, for example, a traditional chronology; the positive appreciation of the life of Jesus as found in the gospels; Petrine priority; the reliability of Jesus' messianic self-proclamation and the historicity of his predictions about the destruction of Jerusalem. In the trilogy, the Baron, who at the time considered himself as a 'member of the Catholic Left or Protestant Centre', judged Holtzmann as a 'radical and representative Rationalist'. The ideological pigeon-holing, however, is not fully consistent and changed considerably over time. On other occasions he described Holtzmann's world view and scholarship as 'rationalist' with 'moderate' views on chronology to 'the ablest living representative of

Das Ende der Inspirations-Theologie. I. *Untersuchungen zur Entwicklung der traditionellen theologischen Lehre über die Inspiration der Heiligen Schrift* (Stuttgart, 1974), pp. 95-98.

15. See von Hügel's privately printed *Notes Addressed to the Very Reverend H.I.D.R.* [Henry Ignatius Dudley Ryder] *upon the Subject of Biblical Inspiration and Inerrancy* (July 1891); see also J.D. Holmes, 'Von Hügel's Letter to Ryder on Biblical Inspiration and Inerrancy', *Historical Magazine of the Protestant Episcopal Church* 38 (1969), pp. 153-65.

16. Von Hügel, 'The Church and the Bible: The Two Stages of their Inter-Relation', *DubR* 115 (October, 1894), pp. 313-41; 116 (April, 1895), pp. 306-37; 117 (October, 1895), pp. 275-304.

the Rationalist Left' or simply 'the ablest of the Radical Exegetes'.[17]
In a lengthy correspondence in 1893 with Madame Rhoda von
Schubert about the Petrine claims, which was published posthumously
as *Some Notes on the Petrine Claims*, von Hügel availed himself of a
similar argumentation and classification. In order to establish that the
gospels favoured Petrine priority he found support in Holtzmann,
Bernhard Weiss and the exegete Meyer for the traditional Roman
Catholic interpretation of Mt. 16.18 and related passages. Holtzmann was
especially important to the Baron because of his alleged radical criticism
and historical objectivity beyond any confessional considerations. The
Baron described him as 'the ablest of the living advanced-left critics,
who sniffs forgery and late ecclesiasticism wherever he can: he is so
entirely "natural" in all his views that he cares not two straws as to
what he says benefiting Rome or Wittenberg'. In due time, however,
Holtzmann would become, in the Baron's estimate, rather moderate,
while his friend Loisy and the representatives of the *Religionsgeschichtliche Schule* were viewed as the radicals. Incidentally, Harnack's work
was employed in a similar fashion by von Hügel. His *Dogmengeschichte*
furnished the necessary *dicta probantia* for a support of the Petrine
claims while his personal reputation as church historian enhanced the
argument. For von Hügel, Harnack was 'the first-rate, though intensely
sceptical and deeply anti-dogmatic and anti-hierarchical Berlin authority'.
Ironically, reputation and radical objectivity among the Protestant
scholars became here moral qualifications in support of traditional
judgments, although the tenor of the articles espoused scholarly
objectivity for its own sake. The Bible, von Hügel argued, was to be
investigated by 'ordinary critical and historical standards'. I shall come
back to this shared ethos of historical objectivity later.[18]
   The strictly historical inquiry in the area of biblical studies, which von
Hügel and his liberal Catholic friends had hoped for in the outgoing
nineteenth and early twentieth century, became less and less a reality
under the new pope, Pius X, and his secretary of state Merry del Val. A
severe setback was the decision of 27 June, 1906, by the Pontifical
Biblical Commission affirming the Mosaic authorship of the Pentateuch.
Von Hügel's published response represents a passionate plea for the
historical-critical method in biblical studies. The method, which to him
was Catholic in nature, represented ultimately no opposition to theology,

17. For details see Rollmann, 'Holtzmann, von Hügel and Modernism', pp. 132-33.
18. Rollmann, 'Holtzmann, von Hügel and Modernism'.

despite its temporary and necessary frictions. In 1907 he discussed these views in person with Holtzmann in Baden-Baden and in a generous appreciation of Wellhausen in the *Times Literary Supplement*. By now von Hügel's ideological scale of scholarship had shifted considerably. Holtzmann, the 'radical' representative of the 'Rationalist Left' in 'The Church and the Bible' articles of 1894–1895, had mellowed into a 'highly competent, assuredly not over-conservative critic'. This ideological readjustment took place during von Hügel's continual defence of Loisy and amidst an avid reading of biblical scholarship, including the monographs issued by the Göttingen *Religionsgeschichtliche Schule*. In his review of Loisy's *Les Evangiles synoptiques*, von Hügel compared method and results of Loisy's researches with those of Holtzmann and noted the greater elimination of Markan texts by Loisy. While he shared Loisy's methodology and his reliance on Holtzmann's source theories, he considered his interpretation of the alleged Markan expansions 'excessive' and trusted instead Holtzmann's more positive view of the 'historical' character of Mark.[19]

In dealing with the reception of German biblical scholarship within Roman Catholic Modernism, intellectual historians have made so far no distinction as to its types. Wellhausen is mentioned in one breath with Gunkel, and Holtzmann with Wrede and Weiss. And yet, the differing reception is crucial for understanding the degree of distance between traditional Roman Catholic theology and its liberal re-interpretation. Whereas the literary-critical analyses of Holtzmann and Wellhausen could still be accommodated in liberal Catholicism and remained extrinsic to the Roman Catholic self-definition, the ideological gulf opened up by the *Religionsgeschichtler* between the first century and the nineteenth and twentieth had potentially more serious consequences. Loisy confirms such a qualitative difference in scholarship between his own biblical studies and von Hügel's appropriation of Holtzmann. Von Hügel advised George Tyrrell in 1905:

> The careful detailed study of his [Holtzmann's] H[and] C[ommentar] Commentaries, the NT Theologie, and, I should say, his 'Einleitung in das Neue Testament' would be the best equipment for New Testament judgments that I know.[20]

19. Rollmann, 'Holtzmann, von Hügel and Modernism', p. 226-27.

20. Von Hügel to George Tyrrell, 18 September, 1905 (British Library: ADD MSS 44,929), 40rv.

Contrast with this the judgment of Loisy about Wellhausen and Holtzmann in his *Memoires*:

> There is a method of literary criticism, accurate and meticulous, which in the times of Reuss, Wellhausen and Holtzmann rendered the most eminent services to the exegesis of the Old and New Testament. But this method, always pushed in one and the same direction by the meticulous analysis of texts, has driven biblical criticism to a sort of impasse. One is too accustomed in considering the principal books of the Old and New Testament as patients that old idle men would have the humour to cut up, without any other concern but to put into good place all the pieces prepared and cut to size; the whole point would be now to dissect the system, to see of how many pieces it is composed, and which the pieces are that could have been cut into the same scroll; the most ancient scroll was supposed to be the best. There would remain only the task of sewing the pieces together in order to obtain an old legend or an old story, beyond which there would be nothing more to search for.[21]

This method, however, as the German *Religionsgeschichtler* saw correctly, was inimical to experienced religion and rendered the biblical texts lifeless and meaningless.[22] For von Hügel, however, the sources of the Pentateuch and those of the synoptic gospels as analyzed by Wellhausen and Holtzmann guaranteed a historically reliable picture of Israel's history and Jesus' life. No so Loisy. His critical remarks on von Hügel's confidence and the insecurity of *positiva* in his own work are telling and deserve quoting:

> My critical work...has had as its subject inexhaustible scholarly topics which expand with each day. Thus von Hügel thought to have the last word on the criticism of the Gospels with Holtzmann's conclusions: what an error! He believed himself to be equally on unshakeable ground with Wellhausen concerning the OT: what an illusion! With what new obscurity are not the origins of Israel covered even as certain aspects of the

21. Alfred Loisy, *Memoires pour servir à l'histoire religieuse de notre temps* (3 vols.; Paris, 1930–31), III, p. 410.

22. On the *Religionsgeschichtliche Schule* and their vitalistic conception of religion see my articles 'Duhm, Lagarde, Ritschl und der irrationale Religionsbegriff der Religionsgeschichtlichen Schule: Die *Vita hospitis* Heinrich Hackmanns als geistes- und theologiegeschichtliches Dokument', *ZRGG* 34 (1982), pp. 276-79; 'Theologie und Religionsgeschichte: Zeitgenössische Stimmen zur Diskussion um die religionsgeschichtliche Methode und die Einführung religionsgeschichtlicher Lehrstühle in den theologischen Fakultäten um die Jahrhundertwende', *ZTK* 80 (1983), pp. 69-84; 'Religionsgeschichtliche Schule', in *Evangelisches Kirchenlexikon* (Göttingen, 1992), IV, pp. 60-61.

history of the Mediterranean peoples are revealed! And what does one know even of this history...[Even] in terms of Christian origins, nothing is more obscure for us than the historical role of Jesus—however certain the historicity of his person may be—and that of the conditions in which Christianity developed between the beginnings of the gospel sermons and the establishment of the church...in the last quarter of the second century.[23]

Loisy became increasingly sceptical about furnishing either a reliable course of the history of Israel or a life of Jesus, whereas the Baron retained with tenacity Wellhausen's and Holtzmann's scholarly reconstructions. The later Holtzmann, too, knew the difference between Loisy's and his own work and did not fight it but received it with as much generosity as he had welcomed in Protestant exegesis the devastating critique of his life of Jesus and his New Testament theology by William Wrede. To von Hügel he wrote in 1909 about Loisy:

> No one can esteem more highly than I do the merit which this thorough and equally unprejudiced scholar has earned for gospel criticism and the Life-of-Jesus question...Myself, I am, as you know, somewhat more conservative than Loisy, at least regarding the historical reconstruction of the Life of Jesus, but I can take it rather well if one labours more resolutely than I dare to do. Loisy has now completely joined the *religionsgeschichtlich* camp—as his inaugural lecture [at the College de France] demonstrates...[24]

Von Hügel never gave up faith in the basic historical outline of Jesus' life that Holtzmann had reconstructed in *Synoptische Evangelien*, whereas Loisy followed more and more the *religionsgeschichtlich* approach, which explained even considerable Markan materials as having their origin not in the life of Jesus but in the life and faith of the early Christian community. Von Hügel's unquestioned trust in a basic historically reliable outline of the life of Jesus—and the alleged development in Jesus' life and mission—is reflected in his article *Du Christ éternel*. Here he ventured radical views on the Gospel of John. The different character of the synoptic and the Johannine witness, the one being historical and earthly, the other suprahistorical and divine, was— according to the Baron—analogous to the God-human doctrine of classical Christianity. I am almost tempted to state that von Hügel's development as a biblical scholar resembles the second great revolution

23. Loisy, *Memoires*, III, p. 460.
24. Rollmann, 'Holtzmann, von Hügel, and Modernism', pp. 239-40.

in Protestant Life of Jesus research according to Albert Schweitzer: the victory of the synoptic Christ over the Johannine one. The radical questions put to the synoptics by the *Religionsgeschichtliche Schule*, especially Wrede, never seriously affected von Hügel's theology. The appropriation of the *Religionsgeschichtliche Schule* was very selective. Gunkel's *Wirkungen des heiligen Geistes* and even Duhm's *Das Geheimnis in der Religion* were important to both von Hügel and Tyrrell for what they yield in religio-psychological and philosophical data and insights. They were appropriated by the Baron for an understanding of religion in general and made fruitful for an understanding of mysticism and devotion, but did not create a gulf in horizons between the first century and the nineteenth and twentieth.[25]

Likewise, von Hügel only reservedly followed the eschatological researches and conclusions of Johannes Weiss's *Die Predigt Jesu vom Reiche Gottes*, which he had read closely in its first and second editions. The book was of great significance for Modernism, in that it served as a powerful apologetic tool both for Loisy and Tyrrell to criticize Harnack's timeless ethic of the Kingdom and alleged Christian essence. Von Hügel, even where he recognized the eschatological dimension in Jesus' proclamation, neutralized radical eschatology by demonstrating a dual conception in the teachings of Jesus. In his essay on the 'Apocalyptic Element in the Teaching of Jesus', he refused radical eschatology by pointing out a second, 'slow and peaceful' character in the proclamation of Jesus. The psychological and historical division of Jesus' life into a pre- and post-Caesarea Philippi period (Mk 8.27) largely followed Holtzmann's psychological developmental view. The penetrating critique by Wrede of this view did not influence the Baron. In fact, to judge from the lack of lining and the occasional comments in von Hügel's copy, he read Wrede's *Messiasgeheimnis* in an almost angry manner.

Von Hügel was much less reserved as far as the theologies of Paul and John were concerned. Here he could even borrow from representatives of the radical *Religionsgeschichtliche Schule*. In *The Mystical Element of Religion*, von Hügel discussed Pauline and Johannine theology as literary sources of Catherine's conceptions. Von Hügel reconstructed the theology of the two principal New Testament witnesses on the basis of Holtzmann's *Lehrbuch der Neutestamentlichen Theologie*. His

25. Rollmann, 'Holtzmann, von Hügel, and Modernism', pp. 227-28.

indebtedness to Holtzmann is acknowledged in the Preface to the first edition with the words:

And already in Part First, but especially in Part Third I have utilized as largely, although here with still more of personal knowledge and of careful re-examination, considerable sections of Professor H.J. Holtzmann's *Lehrbuch der Neutestamentlichen Theologie*, 1897—sections which happen to be, upon the whole, the deepest and most solid in that great but often daring work.[26]

The 'personal knowledge' and 'careful re-examination' on the part of the Baron consisted primarily in the adaptation and selection of relevant materials from Holtzmann's vast and complex *Lehrbuch der Neutestamentlichen Theologie* to suit von Hügel's purposes. Fundamentally, the Paul and John of von Hügel are those of Heinrich Julius Holtzmann. Paul has as complex an anthropology, his theology is characterized by the same antinomies, the eschatology is equally minimized, the strands of his objective-juridical (Judaic) and those of his subjective-ethical (Hellenistic) soteriology remain unreconciled, and the conversion experience of Paul holds the significance it has for Holtzmann, while Paul's idea of sanctification witnesses the 'contrasting couples' which Holtzmann's *Lehrbuch der Neutestamentlichen Theologie* also exhibited. The treatment of Paul from Holtzmann's standard work was repeated four years later in the same selective and adaptive manner in von Hügel's *Eternal Life*.[27]

His Johannine theology, with its dual Pauline and Philonian orientation, also owed much to Holtzmann. Immediacy of eternity, allegory in method, and ontology are Johannine features which the Baron clarified under Holtzmann's guidance. And the relative devaluation of Johannine theology in *The Mystical Element of Religion, Eternal Life* and his *Encyclopaedia Britannica* article of St John's Gospel took place against the background of his faith in Holtzmann's ability to reconstruct the wellspring of the *ipsissima verba Jesu* by literary criticism. Besides, the current difficulties with Rome may have had a considerable effect upon his negative assessment of John's explicit authoritarian ecclesiology in contrast with the synoptics.[28]

It is in his 1911 article on the Gospel of John in the famous eleventh

---

26. Von Hügel, *The Mystical Element of Religion as Studied in Saint Catherine of Genova and her Friends* (2 vols.; London, 1908), I, p. xxx.

27. See Rollmann, 'Holtzmann, von Hügel and Modernism', pp. 230-31.

28. Rollmann, 'Holtzmann, von Hügel and Modernism', p. 231.

edition of the *Encyclopaedia Britannica*, that we find von Hügel's most serious exegetical contribution. Von Hügel acknowledged his chief indebtedness to Holtzmann and Loisy. In the article, the Baron, like Holtzmann, left the clashes with the synoptics unreconciled. He admitted, with Cardinal Newman, the 'symbolic' character of the Johannine 'signs', pointed out the 'pervadingly allegorical' method and 'profoundly mystical' aims of John, while locating its intellectual and religious horizon in St Paul's universalism and Alexandrian Judaism. The advanced scholarly character of von Hügel's judgment of John's Gospel becomes comprehensible when contrasted with the decision of 29 May, 1907, of the Pontifical Biblical Commission *De auctore et veritate historica quarti Evangelii*, which rejected any serious symbolic interpretation of the gospel and required Roman Catholic scholars to view the gospel as a 'strictly historical document'.[29]

Loisy felt that the Baron's views on scholarly autonomy were more restrictive, despite a shared ethos of historical objectivity. The factors limiting it lay in his tenacious allegiance to institutional Catholicism and mystical religiosity. This oversimplifies von Hügel's fundamental conceptions of the significance of the historical-critical method for theology. I have shown already that the 1894 articles in response to the encyclical *Providentissimus* espoused the study of the Bible by 'ordinary critical and historical standards'. Von Hügel never tired of insisting on objectivity in the service of the historical disciplines, even when he placed them into a constructive and practical context. There emerged in Modernist circles a consensus regarding the morality of historical knowledge and the legitimacy of systematic doubt in academic matters. Like most of the Protestant scholars of the day, this morality was largely expressed in an objectivist hermeneutic, which did not clarify the problem of subjectivity in interpretation. In the case of von Hügel, it did include, however, an anchoring of these scholarly requirements within a larger understanding of religion and even devotion. In his 1906 defence of Pentateuch scholarship, von Hügel wrote:

> If they [science and scholarship] are, in the long run, simply irresistible
> within these limits of their own, they as demonstrably presuppose and
> require a fuller, deeper world of reality and life than is theirs; and religion
> will be able to find room for these other levels of life on the day when it
> has fully learnt, on its side, that it cannot henceforth attain again to its
> deepest fruitfulness, unless it can and will frankly accept and encourage

29. Rollmann, 'Holtzmann, von Hügel and Modernism', pp. 232-33.

such autonomies within its ampler life. Theology will only slowly and approximately be able to resolve the antinomies thus occasioned, but the religious soul will again be conscious of how much fuller are the religious life and reality than are even their best analyses; and the sciences themselves will then be pointing to, without themselves directly reaching, religion as thus practised and understood.[30]

For him, the scientific element in religion was only one besides the institutional and the mystical elements. Thus dogmatic faith and historical-critical scholarship, according to von Hügel, stood in conflict. But this conflict and friction was far from being ultimately destructive, because it resulted in fruitfulness. The process was one in which out of conflict, friction and tension there arose a new synthesis. Biblical and historical criticism were not simply subservient to tradition, as they were in Blondel, but opportunities for personal purification and the formation of a deep personal faith. In fact, they seem to play a purificatory role in faith and theology once held by eschatology and asceticism. It is at once cross and purification, quest and striving for unity amid great clashes and diversity. Individual results of biblical criticism were in the Baron's judgment not capable of shaking his personal faith. Rather, he saw in them opportunities to purify and unify the individual. He also felt that Roman Catholicism as the 'most historical' of all religions was selling itself short and denied its Catholic character if it pursued biblical studies and church history by any other methods than the historical-critical ones.[31]

And yet what had appeared hopeful during the Pontificate of Leo XIII became less and less a reality. The Pontifical Biblical Commission, envisioned as an ecclesiastical forum for biblical questions by competent theologians, was emptied of its scholars who were replaced with neo-scholastic theologians and church officials. These reduced the differentiating probability judgments of history to the final propositional statements 'negative' or 'positive'. Its decisions about the authorship of the Pentateuch, the *Comma Johanneum*, and the historical character of the Gospel of John destroyed any faith von Hügel and the Modernists may have had in the commission, as did the condemnation of Loisy's works and his eventual excommunication. The degree *Lamentabili*, the

---

30. Charles Briggs and Friedrich von Hügel, *The Papal Commission and the Pentateuch*, pp. 56-57.
31. On von Hügel's grounding of biblical criticism in his philosophy of religion, see the splendid treatment of Peter Neuner: *Religiöse Erfahrung*, pp. 151-68, 185-94.

encyclical *Pascendi* and the eventual *Oath against Modernism* sealed the fate of Roman Catholic scholarship for decades to come. Von Hügel increasingly devoted himself to the philosophy of religion, in which he produced his major works. And yet—as the articles on the Johannine literature for the eleventh edition of the *Encyclopaedia Britannica* show—he never compromised on the basic approach in biblical studies that he had learned from Holtzmann and that he shared, with modification, with Loisy.[32]

The sweeping and quick demise of critical biblical scholarship from Roman Catholic seminaries and university faculties shows how limited the reception of critical Bible studies had been and how poorly its results and methods had been communicated to the clergy and integrated into the theological curriculum. The scope and nature of this communication or conveyance of exegetical expertise I shall examine next in a very brief overview and with special reference to von Hügel.

Communication

On the whole, the Modernist movement remained elitist in character, being supported largely by intellectuals and private individuals from among the Roman Catholic clergy and upper class laity. It is thus not surprising that the foremost channels of communication would be literary. They include books, journals, and newspapers. The journals played a very important role both for the reception of exegetical opinion and for its articulation. The *Revue biblique*, the *Revista bibliografica italiana*, and *Studi religiosi* or specific Modernist publications: the French *La Quinzaine* and the Italian *Il Rinnovamento* or the American *Catholic University Bulletin* provided such forums, as did non-Roman Catholic journals such as the *Hibbert Journal* or even newspapers.[33]

As far as the spread of and international dialogue with Modernist contributions were concerned, von Hügel carefully arranged reviews and articles through his network of scholars. Once again, Heinrich Julius Holtzmann became invaluable as far as German Protestant exposure was concerned. Not only did he review individual contributions on biblical studies and theology in the major review organs such as the *Theologische*

---

32. Von Hügel, 'John, Gospel of', *EncBr* (11th edn, 1911), XV, pp. 452-58.
33. The transmission of ideas within the movement called Modernism has been explored by Lester R. Kurtz, *The Politics of Heresy: The Modernist Crisis in Roman Catholicism* (Berkeley, 1986).

Literaturzeitung, Deutsche Literaturzeitung, Historische Zeitschrift and *Theologischer Jahresbericht*, he also kept a German audience abreast with lengthy review articles in the *Protestantische Monatshefte* and furnished state of the art summaries on select New Testament and Early Christian topics in the *Archiv für Religionswissenschaft*. His command of Italian, French, and English and his reputation as the pre-eminent theological reviewer in Germany saw to it that the Modernist case was laid before a wide cultured public. I shall mention here especially the meticulous and comprehensive contributions of Holtzmann's *Das Urchristentum und der Reformkatholizismus* of 1903, *Der Fall Loisy* in 1905, and *Reformkatholisches aus Italien, Frankreich und England* in 1908. More than anything else, these literary links with international scholarship in major German theological publications gave credibility to the Modernist cause and reinforced a cognitive consensus of a universality in approach and scholarship, even where liberal Roman Catholics aimed at defending Roman Catholicism with these modern approaches.[34]

Other forums which aimed at nurturing critical Bible studies were the scholarly conferences and study groups, often of an ecumenical nature or international scope. I have alluded already to von Hügel's role in acquainting Roman Catholic scholars with German Old Testament criticism at the fourth International Catholic Scientific Congress in Freiburg in 1897. Another example of a grassroots attempt to discuss biblical matters in a critical fashion was the *Società degli Studi Biblici* in Rome in 1896–97, which had the patronage of the learned cardinal Lucido Parocchi, and before which von Hügel delivered a redaction-critical study of Lucan transpositions. To judge from the summary in the *Revue biblique*, von Hügel showed in his paper that the arrangement of pericopes in Luke not only follows a chronological scheme but is motivated very much by theological considerations.[35] The discussions were contagious among some young theologians as shown by the case of the young Eugenio Pacelli, the future Pope Pius XII whom von Hügel took under his wings in 1896. Von Hügel's diary from January to March 1896 shows an intense exchange with Pacelli, who met in von Hügel's presence other major figures of international Catholic liberalism, including the German Reform Catholic Franz Xaver Kraus.[36]

---

34. For Holtzmann's role in the academic dissemination of Modernist literature, see Rollmann, 'Holtzmann, von Hügel, and Modernism', pp. 221-39.

35. 'Bulletin', *RB* 5 (1896), pp. 470-72.

36. 1896 Diary, 26 January–4 April (SAUL).

Thoughout his life von Hügel also stimulated an ecumenical study group in London, the 'London Society for the Study of Religion', where he discussed, among other topics, synoptic studies and which repeatedly entertained distinguished visitors from the continent, such as Albert Schweitzer and Gustav Deissmann.[37] This public spread of 'Modernism' by education, publication and exchange became an object of special concern among institutional anti-Modernists. The encyclical *Pascendi* addressed this issue and sought to devise definite means that might help check the spread of the heresy.

More important, however, for the reception and dissemination of exegetical opinion within Roman Catholicism was the private network among scholars and theologians, which was largely sustained by correspondence. Von Hügel's fluency in German, Italian, French, and English as well as his financial and professional independence enabled him to maintain this network on a large scale. To this must be added his visits and conversations in England and on the continent. The Baron spent his winters in Italy and visited annually his liberal Catholic friends in France and, occasionally, also in Germany. The correspondence was accompanied by a private distribution system of significant scholarly literature, exchanged largely at the Baron's expense. Von Hügel's correspondence with the major figures of international scholarship served both to clarify theological and exegetical issues and at the same time arranged publicity for Modernist publications. The Baron's personal efforts in acquainting his friends with German biblical scholarship can be well illustrated with reference to the chief Modernist in England, George Tyrrell. Almost all letters of the exchange are preserved in five large folio volumes in the British Library in London.

Until he met von Hügel, Tyrrell's Modernism drew much upon the liberal tradition of Cardinal Newman.[38] But this quickly changed. After initiating their life-long correspondence in 1898, von Hügel wrote in connection with the religio-philosophical work of Rudolf Eucken, 'how I

---

37. On the LSSR, see Lawrence F. Barmann, 'The Origins and Early History of the London Society for the Study of Religion (1904–1918) as an Expression of Modernism', in Francis S. Fiorenz and James C. Livingston (eds.), *Culture Protestantism and Catholic Modernism* (Papers of the Nineteenth-Century Theology Working Group; Berkeley, 1977).

38. On the theological development of George Tyrrell, see David G. Schultenover, *George Tyrrell: In Search of Catholicism* (Shepherdstown, WV, 1981).

wish you had German, so as to read him'.[39] This wish was expressed repeatedly and with increasing insistence, finally with reference to his own late study of Hebrew at the age of forty and the self-taught German of Loisy and Duchesne.[40] Tyrrell eventually complied and studied German. His reading of German theological scholarship began with Wernle's *Anfänge unserer Religion*. Von Hügel quickly introduced him to the scholarly journal literature in New Testament and other areas. He sent to Tyrrell copies of the *Theologische Literaturzeitung*, which he recommended to him since

> its scriptural and Early Christian reviews are simply first-rate, and generally real contributions, often first communications of important results or discoveries; and its religious-philosophy notices are always intelligent and sometimes admirable.[41]

Much of Tyrrell's German reading concerns the philosophy of religion, where Eucken, Troeltsch and Fichte became especially important. But his von Hügel-inspired exposure to the *Religionsgeschichtliche Schule*, notably Johannes Weiss, Hermann Gunkel, and Bernhard Duhm, but also to Sohm's *Kirchenrecht*, led to a re-orientation of his theology, the mature product of which can be found in his book, *Christianity at the Crossroads*.[42] Throughout their correspondence, von Hügel sought to inspire Tyrrell with Holtzmann, whose *Hand-Commentar* and *Neutestamentliche Theologie* he read dutifully and used with benefit in his understanding of the Gospel of John.[43] Once he had mastered German, Tyrrell also followed with delight Holtzmann's critical review essays on himself and the Modernists. In fact von Hügel distributed widely among his European friends the assessments of Modernist literature reviewed by Holtzmann, and even quoted repeatedly from their private correspondence, as he did also with Troeltsch and Eucken. The most decisive theological impulse Tyrrell received came, however—as with

39. Von Hügel to George Tyrrell, 26 January, 1898 (British Library: ADD MS 44,927), fol. 16v.

40. Von Hügel to George Tyrrell, 6 August, 1901 (British Library: ADD MSS 44,927), 168v–169r.

41. Von Hügel to George Tyrrell, 8 January, 1902 (British Library: ADD MSS 44,928), 5v–8v.

42. George Tyrrell, *Christianity at the Cross-Roads* (London, 1909).

43. George Tyrrell to Friedrich von Hügel, 12 October, 1903 (British Library: ADD MSS 44,928), 121r; von Hügel to George Tyrrell, 18 September, 1905 (British Library: ADD MSS 44,929), 40rv.

Loisy—from Johannes Weiss's *Predigt Jesu vom Reiche Gottes*. The book served a two-fold task: to criticize Harnack's and the liberal Protestant essence of Christianity; but also to understand the apocalyptic nature of early Christianity in its own right. Both Weiss and Schweitzer convinced Tyrrell that the liberal Protestant conception of Christ was 'as mystical as the miraculous Christ [of Roman Catholicism]'. He also came to recognise that his own previous work was greatly dominated by such a 'liberal-theological Christ'. Tyrrell took this insight not without considerable personal strain and subsequently alternated between states of utter disillusionment over his own 'theological bankruptcy' and a heroic affirmation of otherworldliness with categories furnished by Weiss's eschatological and christological researches.[44]

Although I have chosen Tyrrell's case to illustrate the influence of German biblical scholarship mediated by von Hügel, similar cases could be made for many of the Baron's Modernist friends, although among professional exegetes, independence of judgment was much more pronounced. Loisy, as we have seen already found Holtzmann's and Wellhausen's literary-critical studies much less satisfactory and moved increasingly into the religio-historical camp. While the Modernist exegetes and theologians appropriated much of the German Protestant scholarship, they did not succeed in communicating these insights to the ecclesiastical authorities and the educational institutions. Here a remarkably unhistorical and non-scientific consensus prevailed and ultimately doomed the efforts of von Hügel and his liberal Catholics.

Franz Xaver Kraus, the Freiburg Church historian and publicist, the mentor of German Reform Catholics, had observed the danger in separating Roman Catholic theological education from the general university education.[45] He warned repeatedly of the isolation of theology from the cultural and scientific developments of the western world. That this danger was real became obvious even in the German theological faculties within the university, which preserved a curricular independence and were increasingly affected by an ahistorical neo-scholasticism. Von Hügel felt this isolation of biblical scholarship painfully. In 1897 he wrote to Kraus that he lacked co-workers in biblical studies, especially in Germany and England.

44. See especially George Tyrrell to Friedrich von Hügel, 9 April, 1909 (British Museum: ADD MSS 44,931), 92rv.

45. On von Hügel's association with Franz Xaver Kraus, see Rollmann, 'Liberal Catholicism', pp. 202-16.

And yet biblical criticism and the philosophy of religion will demand also in the future my best energies. Especially the first subject has among Catholics obviously few open-minded supporters. Happily, I have thus in France and (less so) in England rather than in Germany some close co-workers and like-minded [individuals]. And even a few must suffice.[46]

Later, in 1899, in a letter to Albert Ehrhard, he lamented the fact that the biblical roots of Catholicism, for the Baron the 'most "historic" of all religions', were neglected by Catholic scholars. He writes that the good Roman Catholic historians and exegetes Bardenhewer, Hummelhauer, van Hoonacker and Poel were too hesitant and conservative in the application of the historical-critical method in biblical studies. Von Hügel was struck, as he expressed it once to Tyrrell, that almost all German Catholic scholars

> admit and some practice sound whole-hearted *historical* criticism in Church history—and Patristic literature—matters: they are still practically unanimous in carefully and laboriously thinking out excuses for not really thinking about *Biblical* problems at all…[Otherwise] excellent scholars… design and carry out whole series of 'Biblical Studies' carefully contrived for all the thinking and working away from the living problems, on to archaeological trifles or harmless accumulations of mere materials.[47]

It seems that besides a lack of training among many seminary professors, the dogmatic status of scripture in theology prevented the thoroughly historical consideration of the Bible as contrasted with patristics or church history. The latter became at times places of refuge for censured or weak-kneed biblical scholars.

The situation worsened when the Pontifical Biblical Commission, designed to examine biblical issues of a theological nature, was turned into a neo-scholastic tribunal issuing ideological judgments on historical questions. Only a thorough re-orientation of the seminaries and theological faculties could have achieved a change in these disciplines. But the case of Loisy's expulsion from the *Institute Catholique* and the growing alienation of the liberal-minded and reforming Archbishop of Albi, Monsignor Mignot, a friend and correspondent of von Hügel, show that the Modernist's cause was a scholarly movement only and could not hope for popular support. As Troeltsch observed in response to the encyclical *Pascendi*, 'without a great revolution, there is in my judgment

---

46. Rollmann, 'Liberal Catholicism', p. 212.

47. Von Hügel to George Tyrrell, Addendum to Letter of 18 and 20 December, 1901 (British Library: ADD MSS 44,927), 178rv.

no return possible from the ways of the curia'. He felt that the future for a changed Catholicism was bleak, since the few aristocrats and scholars were incomparably outnumbered by the obliging masses in the Church who had never been affected by the theological reformers.[48] The quick pace of change among those attracted to modern biblical studies such as Eugenio Pacelli illustrates the lack of popular support. This suppression and lack of academic support seems to prove Thomas Kuhn right, in that a sufficient number of converts to a new paradigm is a precondition of its academic success.[49]

Conclusion

The case study of von Hügel shows that his position as private scholar of means and social standing provided him with opportunities for the dissemination of exegetical expertise not commonly available to his clerical friends. His classical training and linguistic ease facilitated the encounter between European scholars. The historical-critical method became entrenched in his theological work because of its universality and emerging cognitive consensus about its moral propriety. Further, it recommended itself because of its relevance to Roman Catholicism, to the Baron 'the most historical' of all religions. Moreover, the tensions, frictions, and antinomies posed by this method furnished opportunities for constructive spiritual growth, in which the scientific element became a substitute for earlier friction-producing elements of theology such as eschatology and asceticism. The process of his development as a private scholar was characterized by a competent private training and exchange with leading European scholars. The Protestant biblical scholarship of Wellhausen and Holtzmann became for von Hügel firm points of reference in a fast-growing and ever-changing discipline. But Wellhausen's efforts were understood within a wider context which, according to the Baron, reached far back in history and included Roman Catholics such as Richard Simon and Jean Astruc. Their modern exponents, Kuenen and Wellhausen, provided answers for the ongoing Roman Catholic debate about the authorship of the Pentateuch. Wellhausen's reconstructions of the history of Israel confirmed to the Baron the fruitfulness of the whole approach. Likewise Holtzmann became a firm exegetical

---

48. On Troeltsch's views of Modernism see Rollmann, 'Troeltsch, von Hügel, and Modernism', pp. 35-60.
49. Thomas S. Kuhn, *The Structure of Scientific Revolutions* (Chicago, 1970).

anchor for von Hügel's theology. The literary-critical work enabled him to reconstruct with confidence a historically reliable outline of the life of Jesus. The radical questions posed to this approach and reconstruction by the *Religionsgeschichtliche Schule* were never experienced as deeply by von Hügel as they were by Loisy and Tyrrell. The Baron's religio-philosophical constructivism appropriated the *religionsgeschichtlich* scholarship largely for religion in general, for spirituality, or the safer areas of Johannine or Pauline theology. In appropriating Protestant scholarship for Roman Catholic theological purposes, we can observe in von Hügel the development from a pragmatic use of *realia* for specific theological positions to a much more factually oriented appropriation of exegetical results in their own right. Correlated with this is a shift in the ideological classification of scholars and their *ad hominem* or ideological employment for confessional purposes. In the case of Holtzmann, the growing personal relationship with von Hügel, his help in the Modernist crisis, an intellectual kinship in religio-philosophical questions, and the more radical turn of Loisy to *religionsgeschichtlich* questions may have contributed to this change.

The intensive reception of Protestant scholarship within liberal Catholicism was ultimately an elite endeavour which never penetrated the educational institutions of the day or reached the ecclesiastical authorities. The conveyance of German Protestant scholarship took place largely in books, journals, professional meetings and study groups as well as in correspondence and private conversations. Von Hügel was the centre of a network of liberal Catholics and communicated religio-philosophical and historical-critical expertise of German Protestants to his Roman Catholic friends in England, France, Italy, and Germany. In the case of Tyrrell, this led to a significant exposure to German philo-sophical and exegetical thought and had theological consequences. The link with non-Catholics established opportunities for the dissemination of Modernist work in international scholarly and theological journals, as the case of Holtzmann shows. The feedback of the Baron to his Modernist friends about their reception in Germany contributed to a sense of universality of the scholarly task but may also have rendered the Modernists vulnerable within their own Church, which was unable to appreciate the apologetic potential of the Modernist work. The deficiency in communicating modern philosophy and critical history to the Church at large and to the seminaries seriously weakened the Modernist movement and contributed to its temporary demise. All the more surprising has been the thoroughgoing overcoming of anti-Modernist attitudes within Roman Catholic scholarship since the publication of 1943 of Pius XII's *Divino afflante spiritu*, a process that calls for an examination in its own right. The clash between the Modernists and their Church was one in intellectual horizons. Or—to speak with Thomas Kuhn—it was the drama of a shift in paradigms: from a qualitatively different way of approaching sacred scripture from a faith perspective, to a treatment of the Bible and of church history by an autonomous historical-critical method, with all of its probability judgments, anthroprocentrisms, and frightening relativities. The Baron of the *The Church and the Bible* articles joined hands with Ranke, Wellhausen, and Holtzmann in treating the subject matter of the Bible with ordinary critical and historical standards. Kuhn speaks of crises in explanation and understanding which precede such paradigm shifts. The nineteenth and early twentieth century were full of them. The anti-Modernist decrees, which celebrated once again neo-scholasticism and an absolute view of religious history were stop-gap measures and apologetic acts of desperation. Confronted with the ongoing research in ancient history, archaeology, and comparative religion, the traditional explanations became more qualified and complicated than their explanatory sufficiency. Thus the institutional defeat of the Modernists, who sought to normalize Roman Catholic biblical scholarship with that of their Protestant and secular colleagues, was only temporary. The ecclesiastical decrees of the first decade of this century were overcome, with a delay in the fourth, the fifth and the sixth decades. The delayed blossoming of the historical-critical method in Roman Catholic scholarship has since been remedied by an accelerated growth process and has brought about in our generation the normalization that the Baron and his few friends had hoped for but were never allowed to see themselves.

THE OLD FAITH AND THE NEW:
THE LATE THEOLOGY OF D.F. STRAUSS

Friedrich Wilhelm Graf

'The name of David Friedrich Strauss is unknown, since quite a long time, to only but a few of the educated in Germany, nay one can almost say in Europe, and even among the broad mass of people he has reached a fame which an educated person rarely attains.' This quotation appeared in 1848 in a popular encyclopaedia entitled *Die Gegenwart* (The Present), which was published by the most influential German printers in the nineteenth century, F.A. Brockhaus in Leipzig. The author of the article was Eduard Zeller, a son-in-law of Ferdinand Christian Baur and a significant philosophical representative of the critical Tübingen School.[1] The hint at wide popularity of his friend Strauss was doubtlessly correct: among the German Protestant theologians of the nineteenth century Strauss surely was, theologically, not the most important one. But no other theologian—not even Friedrich D.E. Schleiermacher— had such an effect on the educated bourgeois public as Strauss had. His literary success is nearly without parallel in the German intellectual history of the nineteenth century. Strauss's contemporaries traced this high popularity back to his proximity to the bourgeoisie. 'I am a Bourgeois and I am proud to be one' Strauss confessed in 1872.[2] This confession illustrates the noteworthy continuity of his theologico-philosophical works. The theological programme of David Friedrich

---

1. Eduard Zeller, 'David Friedrich Strauss', in *Die Gegenwart: Eine encyclopädische Darstellung der neuesten Zeitgeschichte* (The Present. An Encyclopaedic Presentation of the History of the Newest Times for All Classes), I (Leipzig: H. Kurtzel, 1848), p. 342.
2. *Der alte und der neue Glaube: Ein Bekenntnis von David Friedrich Strauss* (= *The Old Faith and the New: A Confession by D.F. Strauss* [trans. from the 6th edn by M. Blind; 2 vols.; Berlin: Asher, 1873]) (Leipzig: Hirzel, 1872), p. 268—This first print of Strauss's final book which appeared between the 10 and 15 of October.

Strauss[3] can be interpreted as an attempt to legitimize the bourgeois claim to socio-political emancipation in the medium of classical theological subjects.

The Life of Jesus Critically Examined

Strauss already had become the object of intense public debate by the time of his first theological book, *The Life of Jesus Critically Examined* which was published in 1835–36. Many contemporaries celebrated this book as a 'theological revolution', as the epoch-making breakthrough of genuinely modern theology. The preceding history of this work, important beyond the narrow boundaries of theology, is swiftly told. Strauss, born in Ludwigsburg in 1808, in the same year as Charles Darwin, passed through the different educational institutions of Old Württemberg with brilliant success. After leaving the Tübingen *Stift* in 1830, getting a curacy in the country and a philosophical doctorate in Tübingen, he travelled to Berlin, the mecca of his intellectual passions. Finally fled from the provincial narrowness of the *Stift* and that of the village pulpit, he intended to complete a thorough understanding of Hegel's main works through the direct study of the representative of the most progressed philosophical consciousness. But the absolute spirit, who rules the course of history, does not even in historical self-explanation necessarily coincide with the particular interests of the finite subject. Only a few days after Strauss's arrival in the Prussian capital, Hegel died. Thus the grasp of Hegel of the young Württemberg theologian had to remain a second-hand Hegelianism, not only from a biographical but also from the systematic point of view.

Back in the *Stift* as a tutor in 1832, Strauss gave philosophical lectures

3.   As the most recent German analysis of Strauss's theological program, see my *Kritik und Pseudo-Spekulation: David Friedrich Strauss als Dogmatiker im Kontext der positionellen Theologie seiner Zeit* (Criticism and Pseudo-Speculation: D.F. Strauss as a Dogmatic in the Context of Positional Theology of his Time) (Munich: Kaiser, 1982). Here you will also find a comprehensive bibliography of the contemporary debates about Strauss as well as new literature. At the same time a French monograph on the whole work of Strauss appeared: Jean-Marie Paul, *D.F. Strauss (1808) et son époque* (Paris: Les belles lettres, 1982). Among the newer English books a special mention may be made of Marilyn Chapin Massey, *Christ Unmasked: The Meaning of the Life of Jesus in German Politics* (Chapel Hill: University of North Carolina Press, 1983).

at the university in which he succeeded in 'opening with great skill the understanding even of such a difficult matter as Hegel's Logic is'.[4] His overwhelming success as a teacher provoked the resistance of the chair-holders and is, in this respect, inscribed in the history of the faculty. At the same time he began preparations for the *Life of Jesus* with which he founded the fulminating programme of a new, critical theology. Since Kant, criticism had meant first and foremost to trace back seemingly objective conceptions to the human being as their subject of production. With the help of a painstaking exegetic analysis and detailed recollections of the biblical critique of the deists and the Enlightenment of the seventeenth and eighteenth centuries, Strauss tried to prove that the gospels' reports of Jesus' life, death and resurrection are for the most part just unhistoric myths. Myths he understood as narrative texts, in which a pre-modern collective subject—the primeval community (*Urgemeinde*)—for the sake of the expression and strengthening of their identity elevates a great historical individual, that is Jesus of Nazareth, into an acting subject *sui generis*. So, by the application of this theory of myth, the God-like Christ of faith is re-transfigured to a normal human among humans. This human being, however, was gifted, as Strauss underlined, with outstanding ethical qualities.

Hegelians do not resign themselves to radicalizing rationalist criticism of the intellect. They want to apply this criticism, by the negation of the negation, to criticism itself thus re-establishing the negated in a speculative way. In the medium of concepts, in the sphere of a higher reason, Christ who was killed by a cold intellect shall be resurrected as a supra-historically universal, purely notional truth. After Strauss was sacked from the *Stift* as a consequence of the publication of the first volume— tutors in the *Stift* should train future parsons!—he then, in the *Last Dilemma* of the second volume, aimed at refining the truth inherent in traditional doctrine as an only inadequately unconscious truth in christology, to a rational notion of it. This fascinating theoretical program amounts to dissolving historical particularity for an actual partici-pation of autonomous reason:

> This is indeed not the mode in which Idea realizes itself; it is not wont to lavish all its fulness on one exemplar, and be niggardly towards all others—to express itself perfectly in that one individual, and imperfectly in

4. *David Friedrich Strauss in seinem Leben und seinen Schriften geschildert von Eduard Zeller* (D.F. Strauss: His Life and his Works described by E. Zeller) (Bonn: E. Strauss, 1874), p. 30.

all the rest: it rather loves to distribute its riches among a multiplicity of exemplars which reciprocally complete each other—in the alternate appearance and suppression of a series of individuals...

This is the key to the whole of Christology, that, as subject of the predicate which the church assigns to Christ, we place, instead of an individual, an idea; but an idea which has an existence in reality, not in the mind only, like that of Kant. In an individual, a God-man, the properties and functions which the church ascribes to Christ contradict themselves; in the idea of the race, they perfectly agree. Humanity is the union of the two natures—God become man, the infinite manifesting itself in the finite, and the finite spirit remembering its infinitude; it is the child of the visible Mother and the invisible Father, Nature and Spirit; it is the worker of miracles, in so far as in the course of human history the spirit more and more completely subjugates nature, both within and around man, until it lies before him as the inert matter on which he exercises his active power; it is the sinless existence, for the course of its development is a blameless one, pollution cleaves to the individual only, and does not touch the race or its history. It is Humanity that dies, rises, and ascends to heaven, for from the negation of its phenomenal life there ever proceeds a higher spiritual life; from the suppression of its mortality as a personal, national, and terrestrial spirit, arises its union with the infinite spirit of the heavens. By faith in this Christ, especially in his death and resurrection, man is justified before God; that is, by the kindling within him of the idea of Humanity, the individual man participates in the divinely human life of the species. Now the main element of that idea is, that the negation of the merely natural and sensual life, which is itself the negation of the spirit (the negation of negation, therefore), is the sole way to true spiritual life.

This alone is the absolute sense of Christology.[5]

For his speculative *christology of ideas* Strauss thus recruited a biological notion, namely that of the *human species*. The prominent position of that notion, species, is a consequence of the desire to make the basic notions of traditional metaphysics empirical. To speak of species now instead of God and Christ and to transfer these traditional predicates of the absolute to it, should result in a gain of precision, because now the relation between the finite subject and the universal one can be thought of as being (more) immediate. So every human individual in itself is directly a part of the universal species. So, Strauss's demand to open the christology traditionally oriented at *one* privileged individual and

5.   David Friedrich Strauss, *The Life of Jesus Critically Examined* (trans. George Eliot; The Lives of Jesus' Series; Edited and with an introduction by Peter Hodgson; London: S. Sonnenschein; New York: Macmillan, 1898; Philadelphia: Fortress Press, 1972[3]; repr. London: SCM Press, 1973[5]), pp. 779-80.

perceived as being abstract, to the general conception of species, can also be explained politically: as the demand to democratize ecclesiastical christology by the means of the socialization of Jesus Christ's private property.[6] What once was valid for only *one* human being and exclusively for him, is now valid for humanity as a whole and thus for every single human being. Strauss applies the notion of species to advance individual liberty. The constitution of autonomy which he intends is accomplished through a transfer of divine predicates: when the predicates of the absolute are related to the species, they can be used in a mediated way of the individual, too. So, by Strauss's description of cultural progress (*Kulturfortschritt*) and the growing dominance of nature it can be discerned that he, in the medium of christology, raised emancipatory progress in the realization of liberty in his program. Thus, he understood a growing intensity in the dominance over nature as an enhancing of liberty.

Following the *Life of Jesus* and the fervent political discussions about the book, Strauss could never start an academic career at a German university. He could not even enter a chair of dogmatics in Zürich, to which he was called by the liberal government of the Canton; because of heavy protests from the conservative, ecclesiastical and political authorities, and because of the fall of the government. Nevertheless, the Zürich affair had an important impact on Strauss's further theological biography. For facing the chance so much hoped for, to hold lectures in dogmatics in a theological faculty, Strauss since 1838 had begun again to follow his old plan, to supplement the *Life of Jesus* with a critical-speculative dogmatic. Even after the deep disappointment over the result of the Zürich call, Strauss continued with these plans. But certainly the definite deference from academic theology contributed towards a growing inner distance from ecclesiastical Christendom. And so the critical ring was sharpened yet again compared with the *Life of Jesus*.

---

6. Marilyn Chapin Massey and I, independently of each other, presented political interpretations of Strauss's christology: see Massey, *Christ Unmasked*, especially pp. 30ff. and 142ff.; and my *Kritik und Pseudo-Spekulation*, pp. 574ff. Strauss's own political opinion is, however, only rudimentarily taken into consideration; compare my review, 'D.F. Strauss' radikal-demokratische Christologie' (D.F. Strauss's radical-democratic Christology), *TRu* 54 (1989), pp. 190-95.

Christian Dogmatic Presented in its Historical Development and in the Struggle with Modern Science

In 1840–41 Strauss published his systematic principal work *Christian Dogmatic Presented in its Historical Development and in the Struggle with Modern Science*. The two volumes of a critical-speculative dogmatic is, in all dogmatic sections, given to a certain understanding of historical criticism: there is nothing which is not historical; this is why all the contents of dogmatic conceptions stand under the stipulation of development, the essence of historical exactitude. The old dogmatic corpus which is set with normative objectivity for the orthodox understanding of theology, is consequently historically interpreted by Strauss, that means liquified for the human being as a productive subject. Strauss wrote his dogmatic as the 'history of the development of Christendom, especially the history of dogma'.[7] He offered a 'genetic demonstration' of its genesis, ecclesiastical formation, heretic dubitation and finally its critical destruction in the paradigm-shift of the Enlightenment for every single 'locus'. 'The real criticism of dogma is its history.'[8]

Strauss presented the intended destruction of traditional theist metaphysics as a process which, with historical necessity, results in the autonomy of the subject. He reflected categories from Hegel's *Phenomenology of Spirit* in the totality of history such that they become steps in a one-directional process which is uniform and at the same time one-dimensional. Thus, the history of dogmatic becomes influenced by the evolutionary logic of reason, and so reason, through the successive presentation of conceptions of the world (*Weltbild*) or stages of consciousness relieving one another, comes to itself. So the history of dogma and theology, too, followed 'the basic law of all historical development',[9] progress. Strauss described the inner principle of this

---

7.   Strauss, *Die christliche Glaubenslehre in ihrer geschichtlichen Entwicklung und im Kampfe mit der modernen Wissenschaft* (Christian Dogmatic in its Historical Development and in the Struggle with Modern Science), I (Tübingen: Osiander'sche Buchhandlung, 1840), p. 71.

8.   Strauss, *Dogmatic*, I, p. 71.

9.   In Strauss's view, Schelling, concerning 'the historical development of mankind', had maintained that 'its first state must have been one of high culture'. For Schelling, not progress but decline marked the path of history. But this opposed 'all historical science' and ran 'strictly against the basic law of every historical development' (*Dogmatic*, I, p. 714). In another argument Strauss speaks of the 'law

progress as an enhancing of liberty through cognitive and practical acts of the suspension of a given dependence. The full realization of the history of the development of theological consciousness should, for the sake of contemporary self-determination, lead to a new interpretation of the reality as theology comprehends it.

All theology is determined by a specific understanding of reality. Theology talks of a reality which determines or oversteps all finite being. Theology tries to understand everything finite in its relation to the absolute. Thus the set of its themes presents the most radical case of the determination of the subject: namely humanity's utter dependence on God. Should human liberty exist, this religious dependency either has to be conveyed critically into liberty or religious dependency itself has to be thought of as a determined figure of conscious liberty. Strauss writes the history of dogmatics for the sake of transferring dependence into liberty. Modern consciousness is genetically referred to in the medium of the history of dogmatics, to free it from the burden of the past (which has now expressly become its own).

The epitome of human dependence for Strauss was to be found in the leading concept of Christian metaphysics, aristotelian since long ago, the idea of God's transcendency as one absolutely self-dominating sovereign subject. Where human beings imagine the absolute to be a personal Creator, they have not yet an adequate consciousness of their own personal liberty. The more transcendent God is imagined, the more the human being is alienated from his or her true destination. It was in the interest of human liberty that Strauss, therefore, wanted to enforce a new notion of the absolute. The traditionally transcendent relation between humans and God shall be exchanged for an immanent relation. For the sake of human liberty Strauss dismissed the traditional idea of the difference between God and human beings.

This critical process would be misunderstood, if one saw it as a principal destruction of metaphysics in general. Strauss stuck to the necessity of a metaphysic even in modern conditions. Liberty would be fictive or the mere illusion of a void transcendental subject circling around itself in a blind delusion of autonomy, if people, who claim the ability of sovereignty, were not sure of being in accord with the world which is in reality different from them. Where practical realization of liberty is required, autonomy cannot sufficiently be based on the pure self-reflection of the subject. This rather needs the presentation of an

of the relative imperfection of all beginnings' (I, p. 180).

adequacy between the subject and worldly reality, which allows the accomplishment of liberty. In other words: it needs a theory which over-steps mere theories of the subject, looking at the seizing of more general coherences of reality—a metaphysic, consequently. Strauss introduced this metaphysic of liberty in his *Dogmatic* of 1840–41 as the 'new or modern conception of the world' (*Weltanschauung*).[10]

The expression 'conception of the world' (*Weltanschauung*) served Strauss to define the specific force of religion. Individuals, like collective subjects, need a unitary conception of the world for the sake of their identity. Only if the knowledge of the status of the world and individual self-perception can be integrated into a closed conception of the world (*Weltanschauung*), can the world successfully be shaped and dominated. Strauss understood religion as being an exemplary case of such a con-ception of the world (*Weltanschauung*). With a consequence that is without parallel in the theology of his time, but later rapidly became the obligatory standard of sincerity in and outside academic theology,[11] Strauss interpreted Christendom as such a conception of the world. It is the foundation for Christian religion, he said, to see God as the creative ground of all reality. It generated a totality of knowledge, unitary in itself, of the worldly reality, which comprised all single facts about the world, the human being and the relations between the two. Strauss applied this concept (*Weltanschauung*) first of all to describe the problem forming

10. Strauss sees that his present time is determined by conflict about whether the 'autonomy or the heteronomy of the mind' is the principle of self-understanding of the world formation of the human being. So it was 'a wasted toil to quarrel about single definitions in the doctrines of original sin, vindication, sacrament, etc'. Autonomous reason, thus, not only had single elements but 'the whole of those doctrines, including the conception of the world, which is its base, to call in question' (*Dogmatic*, I, pp. vi-vii). So, 'the old faith' (I, p. viii) and the 'new conception of the world' (I, p. 66) or the 'modern conception of the world' (I, p. 671; II, p. 98) stand as the 'main contrast' (I, p. vii) of present time against each other. Because 'our contemporary conception of the world' is dominated by 'the principle of immanence' (II, p. 17 cf. II, p. 97), cf. also the characterization of dogma as 'the conception of an idiotic consciousness' (II, p. 625).

11. For the contemporary use of the term 'conception of the world' compare Helmut G. Meier, '"Weltanschauung". Studien zu einer Geschichte und Theorie des Begriffs' ('"Conception of the World". Studies in the History and the Theory of a Notion') (Diss. Phil., Münster, 1967), and Eilert Herms, 'Weltanschauung bei Friedrich Schleiermacher und Albert Ritschl' ('Conception of the World in F. Schleiermacher und A. Ritschl'), in Herms, *Theorie für die Praxis—Beiträge zur Theologie* (Munich: Kaiser, 1982), pp. 121-43.

the starting-point of his theology: can Christian tradition standing under the conditions of the change of paradigm in enlightenment and idealism and leading to modern subjectivity, justify its conceptual (*weltanschaulich*) function to establish a unity constituting identity? Was it not just this change of paradigm that led to the far-reaching implausibility of traditional Christian metaphysics, *because* that was opposed to elementary findings of modern science? In addition, Strauss, with the help of *Weltanschauung*, intended to make clear what the constructive design of his theoretical work was like. Thus, howsoever one might answer the question of the actual capacity of the concepts of Christian tradition, in the interest of an increase in dominance over the world, individual and society need a unitary conception of the world (*Weltanschauung*). Therefore, Strauss presented a conception in which the findings of modern science were included. He tried in his *Dogmatic* to develop this 'new or modern conception of the world' (*Weltanschauung*) from the genetic description of old European theist metaphysics, via criticism and criticism of criticism. The leading question of his dogmatic is, consequently, whether there is also a genuinely positive relation above the merely negative one which can be thought between old and new metaphysics. Is this modern conception of the world still genuinely Christian?

Strauss's answer can be clearly exemplified by one of the dogmatic instructions: the dogma of creation. How did Strauss describe the genetic criticism of this dogma? Could he make any constructive sense of it?

Johann Gottlieb Fichte had already named the notion of creation as the basic error of all false metaphysics, because the notion implies a difference between the subject and the object of creation. This, however, calls the absolute into question. If the world was defined as creation, no adequate notion of the independence of the created world and, moreover, no sufficient notion of human liberty could be thought. Friedrich Wilhelm Joseph Schelling then tried to undermine Fichte's criticism of the theist doctrine of creation by identifying *natura naturans* and *natura naturata*. Strauss followed this endeavour to surpass Fichte's criticism. Accepting the meaning of Schelling's identification of *natura naturans* and *natura naturata*, he chose the expression 'absolute life'. This 'absolute life' stands in the place of the old theist notion of God. Where there was transcendental creation there is now the eternal process of the creative self-preservation of nature. The traditional dogmatic doctrine of the divine *creatio continua*, the doctrine of the preservation and reigning of the created world through God, is transformed by Strauss into the idea of a self-regulation of nature. He thus interpreted nature, in the way of idealist speculation, as a renunciation of the absolute reason. The government of the world was not to be seen as the determination of the course of the world by an extra-worldly reason but as the reason immanent in the cosmic powers themselves and in their relations. Under the influence of the romantic-idealistic notion of the unity of everything natural, Strauss named this self-preservation of nature as the *natural development* of all 'organic beings...from the unorganic'.[12] With the help of the notion of development he, at the same time, tried to state the inner unity of nature and mind:

> First there is matter as the primary alienation or more precise the imme-
> diate existence of the idea, where it is completely in its order that it, in
> ascending steps, first as life in nature then as mind in the human being, and
> by this in the course of his historical development comes more and more
> to itself.[13]

According to this unity of nature and history Strauss replaceed the traditional doctrine of the 'genesis of the human being from immediate divine creation'[14] by an explanation of 'the first formation of the human being as a natural process, as the result of a coincidence of certain physical conditions'.[15]

How far can this critical-speculative reformation of the old doctrine of creation fulfil the demands of being adequate to the basic conceptions of modern times? An important contemporary scientist like Alexander von Humboldt, who explicitly agreed to the critical tendency of the *Dogmatic*, attributed 'natural-historical thoughtlessness' to Strauss in 1842.[16] Strauss had demanded, in 1840, to integrate the actual positions

---

12. Strauss, *Dogmatic*, I, p. 681.

13. Strauss, *Dogmatic*, I, pp. 716-17.

14. Strauss, *Dogmatic*, I, p. 686.

15. Strauss, *Dogmatic*, I, p. 685.

16. Alexander von Humboldt had borrowed Varnhagen von Ense's copy of Strauss's *Dogmatic* and then read it with acclaim (at the beginning of 1842). At the beginning of April 1842 Humboldt wrote: 'What I didn't like in Strauss's book at all was this natural historical levity, where he doesn't find any problem with the genesis of the organic from the unorganic, even in the formation of the human being from the chaldaic original sludge' (Ludmilla Assing [ed.], *Briefe von Alexander von Humboldt an Varnhagen van Ense aus den Jahren 1872* [sic]*–1858:* [1782 or 1842 intended?] *Nebst Auszügen aus Varnhagens Tagebüchern, und Briefen von Varnhagen und*

of science or 'our widened knowledge of nature' into speculative dogmatics. So, in the forties, after the appearance of the *Dogmatic* he intensified the study of new natural historical publications. Much more strongly than before, he recognized the difficulties of formulating a fully speculative interpretation of natural history facing an open situation in science. Nevertheless he loyally adhered to the central thesis, which he received through idealist natural philosophy, to define nature as a process of life, which reproduces itself eternally in ever higher forms. This Theo-Logy of absolute life is oriented decisively at the ideas of progress and evolution in nature. This then especially facilitated Strauss's reception of Darwin's publications. Intensive study of Darwin's theory of evolution reinforced the inherent distance from traditional Christian metaphysics.

The Old Faith and the New

In 1869 Strauss reported to his old fellow-student Christian Käferle, that theological books did not interest him for the time being:

> More scientific ones; especially Darwin's theory and what is related to it, is important and attractive to me. Darwin is the first to liberate us from (the notion of) creation; we philosophers, though, always wanted to escape but only Darwin showed us the door.[17]

Strauss consequently used Darwin's reconstruction of natural evolution for the program of his own theory. Darwin had worked out a material definition of how evolution functioned which excellently fit in the frame of the Theo-Logy of absolute life. Further than being mere assertion it was now clear for the 'history of the development of nature', how evolution is accomplished without the theist presumption of a transcendental navigating subject. Strauss now could, with reference to Darwin, explain his criticism of the anti-liberal negative transcendency of a Creator as at once more radical and more plausible. New constructive

anderen an Humboldt (Letters from Alexander von Humboldt to Varnhagen van Ense) (Leipzig, 1860), p. 117.

17. Strauss to Christian Käferle, a friend since his school days, 17 January, 1869, in Eduard Zeller (ed.), *Ausgewählte Briefe von David Friedrich Strauss* (D.F. Strauss, Selected Letters) (Bonn: E. Strauss, 1895), pp. 505-506. Strauss was a friend to the famous liberal historian Georg Gottfried Gervinus. For Gervinus see Gangolf Hübinger, *Georg Gottfried Gervinus: Historisches Urteil und politische Kritik* (G.G. Gervinus: Historical Judgment and Political Criticism) (Göttingen: Vandenhoeck & Ruprecht, 1984).

potentialities were now opened up, to present the absolute in the modern conception of the world as much more definite in its inner coherence. The monist integration of nature and mind into absolute life could now be developed much more consistently than before, from the side of nature. Earlier interpreters of Strauss saw this as a radical change of position, the transgression of a late idealist into materialism.[18] This is wrong at least insofar as the basic categorical scheme of Strauss's argumentation stayed the same. Despite the quarrel of materialism which he studied closely, Strauss maintained that the antithesis of idealism and materialism is, philosophically seen, a mere 'quarrel of words'.[19] Both positions coincide in the intention to universalize the principle of a general interpretation of reality such that it may include every possible counternotion. Whether the totality of the real was developed from absolute spirit or from absolute matter, would make no difference concerning the inner logic of the claim of the universal deduction of reality:

> They have a common foe in the dualism which pervaded the conception of the world throughout the Christian era, dividing man into body and soul, his existence into time and eternity, and opposing an eternal Creator to a created and perishable universe. Materialism, as well as idealism, may, in comparison with the dualistic conception, be regarded as Monism, i.e., the endeavour to derive the totality of phenomena from a single principle—to construct the universe and life from the same block. In this endeavour one theory starts from above, the other from below; the latter constructs the universe from atoms and atomic forces, the former from ideas and idealistic forces. But if they would fulfil their tasks, the one must lead from its heights down to the very lowest circles of Nature, and to this end place itself under the control of careful observation; while the other must take into account the higher intellectual and ethical problems.[20]

This description of the structural equivalence of idealism and materialism lets us discern why Strauss put a privilege on the 'departure from below' when exercising his monist program: the materialist

---

18. E.g. Konstantin Schlottmann, *David Friedrich Strauss als Romantiker des Heidenthums* (Strauss as a Romanticist of Paganism) (Halle a.S.: Buchhandlung des Waisenhauses, 1878), pp. 49ff.; August Wandt, *David Friedrich Strauss's philosophischer Entwicklungsgang und Stellung zum Materialismus* (Strauss's Philosophical Development and his Position Related to Materialism) (Münster, 1902), pp. 37ff.; Adolph Kohut, *David Friedrich Strauss als Denker und Erzieher* (Strauss as a Thinker and a Teacher) (Leipzig: Kröner, 1908), pp. 88ff.

19. *The Old Faith and the New*, I, p. 207.

20. *The Old Faith and the New*, II, pp. 19-20.

practice of the monist program should again result in a gain concerning the empirical realization of the reasons for human liberty. Experience-oriented exact science fascinates by enhancing liberty in the sense of dominance over nature further than the contemporary state of historico-social development:

> ...those [,too], who taught the steam-engine to shoot along the iron road, thought and speech to flash along the electric wire-works of the devil, according to the consistent view of the pious—are from our standpoint fellow-labourers in the kingdom of God.[21]

But even under the conditions of modernity one has to walk quite a long way, to reach its heavenly salvation.

In *The Old Faith and the New* of 1872, the basic text of Strauss's later theology, one can recognize his clearly more radical criticism of Christendom. This was now expressed primarily as cultural criticism on a historical basis. Strauss underlined the wide historical gap between the beginnings of Christianity and the contemporary bourgeois spheres of life, looking especially at christology. Contrary to his statements about Jesus of Nazareth in the thirties and in the widely known *Life of Jesus treated for the German people*[22] he now drew a rough and realistic picture of Jesus. In many *Life of Jesus* presentations of liberal theologians, Jesus, as is well known, was declared an exclusive or outstanding subject of moral perfection. In opposition to this, Strauss pulled Jesus into the dirt of his Palestinian homeland with calculated directness. For the later Strauss, Jesus is an enthusiast, and a modern bourgeois who is conscious of the progress in culture and civilization can only worship in a cult at the price of schizophrenia. And whoever, as a bourgeois, worships Jesus, discloses a bourgeois striving for success and an economic-rational mentality of efficiency. But 'We cannot imagine life in the villages and

---

21. *The Old Faith and the New*, II, p. 58: 'Man not only can and should know Nature, but rule both external Nature, as far as his powers admit, and the natural within himself. Here again a most important and productive field of human activity finds the recognition and the sanction denied it by Christianity.' However, it is also valid: 'Man ought to rule the Nature around him—not like a fierce tyrant however, but like a man. Part of the Nature whose forces he constrains to his service consists of sentient beings' (*ibid.*). For the required 'warm sympathy with sentient Nature', 'Buddhism has done more (...) than Christianity' (p. 60).

22. David Friedrich Strauss, *The Life of Jesus Treated for the German People* (Leipzig, 1864).

small towns of Galilee to be dirty and wretched enough'.[23] Surely a bourgeois does not easily accept a Palestinian itinerant preacher with village dirt on his naked feet in his well-tidied living room, in which there is a piano beside a bookcase, containing 'our great classics', the reading of which gives him the superior feeling of cultural progress. This religious connection to a world-denying, eschatological fanatic, who, being wrong in this case, as we all know, tried to convince people that the coming of God's kingdom was near, is not useful for worldly business. The religious 'cult of poverty and begging', which, concerning the ascetic attitude, Christianity had in common with Buddhism, had to be confronted with the instinct of business, which in the doctrine of Jesus was 'unacceptable to start with'.[24] 'If theologians were able to extirpate it (the love of money) we would relatively fall back onto barbarian standards,' Strauss quoted Buckle's *History of the English Civilization* with consent.[25]

Strauss's criticism of Christian theism now had won a sociological realization, in which there are clearly traces of the history of economic emancipation of the bourgeoisie. Because Christianity taught a difference between this world and the world to come and so, via its institutions, also established a dualism of transcendency concerning cultural practice, it had to be dismissed, as a 'principle hostile to culture'.[26]

> If we open our eyes, and are honest enough to avow what they show us, we must acknowledge that the entire activity and aspiration of the civilized nations of our time is based on views of life which run directly counter those entertained by Christ. The ratio of value between the here and hereafter is exactly reversed. And this is by no means merely true of the luxurious, the so-called materialistic tendencies of our age, nor even of its marvellous progress as regards technical and industrial improvements; but even of its discoveries in science, its astronomy, chemistry, and physiology, as well as its political aims and national combinations, nay, even its

23. *The Old Faith and the New*, I, p. 75.

24. *The Old Faith and the New*, I, p. 72: 'Could theology succeed in extirpating it (i.e. the love of money), all these influences would cease, and we should in a measure relapse into barbarism'.

25. *The Old Faith and the New*, I, p. 72. You can compare the characteristic of the book in a letter to his friend Ernst Rap, the 6 February, 1869: 'The author tries to present his story as a history of reformatory ideas, of the spiritual forces in general, instead of writing war- dynastical- or literary-history like before, but he plans his work most strangely' (Zeller, *Briefe* , p. 506).

26. *The Old Faith and the New*, I, p. 73.

productions in poetry and the sister arts. Everything, therefore, of best and happiest which has been achieved by it has only been attainable on the basis of a conception which regarded this present world as by no means despicable, rather as man's proper field of labour, as the sum total of the aims to which efforts should be directed.[27]

In a society which becomes increasingly industrialized, 'in this age of material interests, unchained egotism'[28] the conscious contemporaries could not answer the central question of post-Enlightenment consciousness, 'Are we Christians yet?' other than with a clear no, insofar 'as they speak as honest and upright men'.[29] 'Today's life and action prone humanity' could not accept the word from Good Friday's cross, the symbol of the 'absolute idolatry of passion at all' any more as the valid 'expression of its religious consciousness'.[30]

In contrast to this, the answer to the leading question of the second main part—'Don't we have any religion?'—is clearly more positive. So Strauss now defined religion as a productive effect of reason by which the human being tries, based on 'an intensive drive for well-being', to put the predominance implied in his bio-physical structure in relation.[31] Historical progress in the cultural dominance over nature leads, as Strauss says, necessarily to a decline in the need to compensate for the dependence on nature with the help of religion. At the same time—though admittedly not very successfully—Strauss combined Schleiermacher's famous definition of religion as the feeling of utter dependence with Feuerbach's thesis 'the real essence of religion is the wish'.[32] Religion should have a function even under the condition of modernity: the *single* human being, therefore, despite all *social* domination of nature, stayed dependent on it by constitution. Even if the God of the Church became substituted by the idea of the living universe, humans could experience 'our power (only) as nothing compared to the

27. *The Old Faith and the New*, I, p. 86.
28. *The Old Faith and the New*, I, p. 98.
29. *The Old Faith and the New*, I, p. 107.
30. David Friedrich Strauss, *Gesammelte Schriften* (ed. E. Zeller; Bonn: E. Strauss, 1877), VI, p. 61. This sixth volume of the collected works contains the ninth printing of the extremely successful *The Old Faith and the New*. This passage which begins at p. 60 about 'the image of Jesus on the cross, the so called crucifix', 'the most one-sided and bluntest incorporation of Christian flight from the world and passivity', is not yet to be found in the first edition of *The Old Faith and the New*.
31. *The Old Faith and the New*, I, pp. 108-109.
32. *The Old Faith and the New*, I, p. 155

omnipotence of nature'. In the eternal change of becoming and passing away of life, people are able, nevertheless, to perceive 'something lasting, an order and a law' and 'a step, a formation of the higher from the lower'. To imagine 'the cosmos or universe, not in the sense of being the sum of all phenomena', but as the 'one epitome of all acting forces and fulfilling laws', so, to look at all life in the perspective of 'order and law, reason', and to give oneself up to this order of the world 'in loving confidence'[33]—this was the new religion.

The new religion primarily reflected the dependence of the human being upon the transcendent, eternal cycle of nature. Beyond such a dependence of the individual on the whole, it should vindicate human liberty. As in his *Dogmatic* Strauss conveyed the definition of the transcendent totality of nature over to the explication of an immanent relation between nature and the human being as a fixed particular natural living-being. Endowed with consciousness, human beings experience that they are not *only* dependent on life, the original force of all living forms. They can experience their dependency as liberty at the same time through religion because they know themselves to be congenial to this original force in the inner self. This definition of human liberty does not in fact contain any real independence of the human being compared to natural worldly reality. On the contrary, Strauss only repeated the subject's fixation to nature or inclusion in the whole of nature. Of course, the new religion might result in a practical increase of liberty, but Strauss could not concoct a plausible argument that human beings are conscious of their dependence on nature and even in spite of that, may discover themselves to be free. However much trouble he may have taken to legitimate bourgeois emancipation in the medium of the topics concerning religion and Christianity, in his late theology he stayed under the standard he had claimed for his criticism of old Christian dualist metaphysics. This he overthrew, because it only defines liberty in a deficient way. But he could not fulfil in a constructive way, what his quite justified criticism of the old-fashioned ontology of substance had provoked: an interest in the promotion of individual autonomy. Nowhere was he able to illustrate the transition he claimed from religious dependency into a religiously mediated experience of liberty of the individual. So here one could argue with Strauss against Strauss: to explain religious dependence as liberty would merely be to play with the expression 'liberty'.

33. *The Old Faith and the New*, I, p. 161

A look back to the historical as well as systematic starting-point of Strauss's theology is, so to speak, fatal. From the *Life of Jesus* onwards, Strauss staged an increasingly radical criticism of ecclesiastical traditions. Again and again he tried to transform the old dogma into a specifically modern, reasonable shape, to liberate the individual from false dependencies. Strauss tried to perform such a transition of a religiously founded dependency to a cognitive-practical liberty of the individual, continuously from his first book onwards, by certain argumentative strategies, which can be described as follows. The difference between God and humankind becomes neglected, in order to to transfer certain qualities of the absolute to the finite subject. Just because of the argument and the guarantee for the intended individual liberty, Strauss developed a new theory of the absolute or a metaphysic. He was looking for a new notion of the absolute, which he could present more decisively as a post-Christian one. But the categories with which he tried to develop a new notion of the absolute did not allow an adequate realization of the emancipatory interest, which the effort of such a formation had, first and foremost, provoked. So, in the context of these new basic notions, individual liberty could only be thought of as being more deficient than in the parameters of the old European metaphysic. To transfigure the God of ecclesiastical dogma into the idea of a universal totality of life, to convey transcendence into immanence, dualism into monism, these notional operations did not result in a gain, but brought about a loss of the consistent liberty of the individual. Under the conditions of aloneness and monism it was impossible to think of a real difference or an individuality of the finite subject against the all embracing, contingent reality. The only definition of humanity which could now be won with strict argumentation was this: to be part of a part of a whole, which continues itself in the disappearance of its infinite number of elements, and the consistency of which does not depend on any of its fixed parts.

But even the idea of this wholeness which might be imagined by human consciousness, should not represent an ideal outside of the totality. The *monism* which Strauss proclaimed for the progress of liberty in consciousness and reality, exactly implied the liquidation of the liberty of the subject. This now could not claim a reasonable tran-scendency against worldly reality. A monist reduction of the factual complexity of reality always means the fall of the individual. Facing the depressing omnipotence of a totally closed, 'natural' reality, there remains only one chance for the single subject: in a (new) piety, a primarily aesthetic observation of the world, it could accept the fate of its biological nullity and contemplate the 'eternal harmony of the universe' in the eternally valid works of art.[34] In fact, this whole harmony only consists of every birth being death at the same time, in that by the fading of the individual the generality of species triumphs and that in the infinite change of genesis and decline there is only one thing for sure, change itself.

From Darmstadt, Strauss reported to a friend, the art historian Julius Meyer, on 22 March 1871:

> The day before yesterday I was in Heidelberg to see the corpse of Gervinus…The town was dressed with flags for the homecoming troups, so the corpse went besides, ignored. How the single individual, even the most famous one, is nothing, compared to the whole, one had a disheartening feeling of.[35]

The new faith tried to meet such depressions with the help of an artistic treat: 'in the ether to which our great poets transport us, in the ocean of harmony in which we are enisled by our great composers, all earthly woe vanishes and dissolves, and as if by magic we see all those stains removed which otherwise, with all our labour, we cannot wipe away'.[36] Such aesthetic disclosure of reality could, as Strauss himself underlined, help individuals 'only for an instant' and 'only in the realm of fantasy' to a transcendental compensation of their factual frailty. After this the individual is swiftly back 'in a rough reality and a narrow life':[37]

> In the enormous machine of the universe, amid the incessant whirl and hiss of its jagged iron wheels, amid the deafening crash of its ponderous stamps and hammers, in the midst of this whole terrific commotion, man, a helpless and defenceless creature, finds himself placed, not secure for a moment that on an imprudent motion a wheel may not seize and rend him, or a hammer crush him to powder. This sense of abandonment is at first

---

34. *The Old Faith and the New*, I, p. 122: 'The function of art in all its branches is, no doubt, to reveal, or at least display to us in miniature, the harmony of the universe, which, ever maintaining itself amid the apparent confusion of phenomena, exceeds our comprehension as an infinite whole. This is the reason of the intimate connection which, with all nations, has always existed between art and religion. The great creations of the plastic arts have also in this sense a religious influence. Poetry and music, however, exert the most direct influence of this kind on our inner life'.

35. Zeller, *Letters*, p. 527.

36. *The Old Faith and the New*, II, p. 211.

37. *The Old Faith and the New*, II, p. 211.

something awful. But then what avails it to have recourse to an illusion? Our wish is impotent to refashion the world; the understanding clearly shows that it indeed is such a machine.[38]

The radicalism of this mechanist view of the world is enhanced, because 'from our point of view' of decisive modernism 'all the consolations' of Christianity—especially the christologic doctrine of satisfaction, the belief in providence and the idea of an eschatological counter-world are seen to be mere illusions. Nevertheless, the subject of the new faith should not stay without pious consolation. The world, in fact, is a 'machine' threatening the individual. 'But not this alone: there are not only uncompassionate wheels moving, but soothing oil is flowing, too', which is produced first and foremost by our great poets and composers.[39] Strauss so used the aesthetic 'surrogate of religion'[40] to become a diffuse stabilizing requirement of the individual.

This seems to be justifying the rigor of the polemic against *The Old Faith and the New* which the then quite unknown Basel professor, Friedrich Nietzsche, published in August 1873 as the *First Piece* of his *Untimely Observations*, under pressure from Richard Wagner who was held up in his career by Strauss in 1868. The idea that in the medium of art a universal harmony is inferred, which transcends the individual negative experiences with the 'world-machine', Nietzsche tried to unmask as being a class-specific narrow-mindedness of the ideology of the 'intellectual middle class'.[41]

> The universe won't be grateful to the frenzied master that he couldn't invent a better allegory to praise it, even if it should allow itself to be praised by Strauss. How then is the oil called that trickles down the

---

38. *The Old Faith and the New*, II, p. 213.
39. *The Old Faith and the New*, II, p. 213, cf. pp. 119ff.
40. So Strauss's New Faith was qualified by Albrecht Ritschl, *Die christliche Lehre von der Rechtfertigung und Versöhnung* (The Christian Doctrines of Justification and Reconciliation), III (Bonn: A. Marcus, 1874[1] = Bonn, 1985[4]), p. 218.
41. Friedrich Nietzsche, 'Unzeitgemässe Betrachtungen. Erstes Stück: David Strauss der Bekenner und Schriftsteller' ('Untimely Observations, First Part: David Strauss, the Professor and Writer') (1873), in *idem, Sämtliche Werke: Kritische Studienausgabe* (15 vols.; ed. Giorgio Colli and Mazzino Montinari; Munich: Deutscher Taschenbuchverlag, 1980), I, pp. 157-242, 168.

hammers and stamps of a machine? And how would it console the worker
to know that this oil is poured forth on him while the machine is seizing
his limbs?[42]

Nietzsche's criticism of Strauss is based on a strategy of argumentation equally simple and effective that can be described as an application
of the criticism to itself. Nietzsche made the claim of critical rational
enlightenment completely his own, which Strauss used against the
ecclesiastical figures of interpretation of Christian religious consciousness. But then he imputes the ideas and construction of Strauss's post-
Christian art-religion themselves to the conditions of this criticism. To
radicalize this criticism leads to a principal neglect of any religious consciousness at all. Religion, for Nietzsche, is untrue because, for the sake
of universal harmony, it wants to integrate every difference and with this
robs the never-to-be-abrogated antagonism between the individual and
the world of its specific negativity. In the 'terribly sincere impetus of
negation in the first centuries of Christianity', that is, in the first
Christians' distance from the world, which was motivated by eschatology,
there were, by all means, certain moments of truth which showed in the
history of religion. But facing the bourgeois elevation of culture,
according to Nietzsche, these moments of truth can be kept present only
through a criticism of religion which destroys all finalizing reasonings
and all constructions of a universal sense. The gist of Nietzsche's criticism concerning the 'doctrine of comfort' of the 'chief of the
philistines', Strauss,[43] lies in this redefinition of exactly those elements of
Christianity which Strauss had made responsible for the cultural practical
deficits of old fashioned dualism; the eschatologic-ascetic contents of
Christian consciousness. By criticizing the *predominant* religion,
especially the religious elevation of given cultural institutions into objec-
tivised trans-historically prevailing values, Nietzsche realized the
momentum of transcendence belonging to the old religion in the direction of a principal autonomy of the individual against the coherence of
the world. But if the individual is exclusively thought of as a counter-
instance of the 'world machine', his or her independence will remain
threatened by abstract negation. Insofar as Nietzsche explained the
individual as a strong subject of activities, he tried to realize individual
liberty in its historical practice in an empirical way, which is essentially
coined in its contents by a difference to the world or by a criticism of

42. Nietzsche, 'Untimely Observations', p. 189.
43. Nietzsche, 'Untimely Observations', p. 191.

cultural stocks. But looking at this activity of liberty itself, no further liberty can be vindicated. The strong individuals lose to the constraints of practical pressure, without having the contents of their activities at their disposition.

Based on these (religious) critical implications of Nietzsche's criticism of the 'new faith' it seemed more attractive to theologians to opt for Strauss's than for Nietzsche's party. With Strauss the piety of a good nature, in spite of all negative experiences of the individual, could be testified. But could his aesthetic ointments successfully heal the deep wounds which Nietzsche's ideological criticism inflicted on the religious consciousness? A theology understanding itself as a reflexion of the special claims to truth of the Christian faith would have to deny this question. Theologically it may be much more plausible, to follow Nietzsche's criticism of Strauss and to protest against a religious glorification of the extinction (or elevation) of the individual, as it is implied as a natural fact in finite life.

Strauss's *The Old Faith and the New* aroused a widespread literary debate in Germany. In a short span of time hundreds of refutations and critical reviews appeared. None among the countless theologians who then criticized *The Old Faith and the New*, was tempted to apply Strauss's gracious and rational universe to a theological meta-criticism of Nietzsche's criticism of religion. Many theological critics of the late Strauss rather worded their protests against the 'New Faith' in a surprising proximity to Nietzsche. Prominent representatives of the learned liberal protestantism like Willibald Beyschlag,[44] Richard A. Lipsius,[45] Heinrich Lang,[46] Alexander Schweizer,[47] Adolf Hilgenfeld,[48] Alois

---

44. Willibald Beyschlag, 'Ein antiker Spiegel für den "neuen Glauben" von D. Fr. Strauss. Vortrag gehalten zu Erfurt und Halle im März 1873' ('An antique mirror for the "new faith". Lecture presented in Erfurt and Halle') (Berlin: Rank, 1873).

45. See R.A. Lipsius, Review of *Der Alte und Der Neue Glaube*, by D.F. Strauss, in *Literarisches Centralblatt für Deutschland*, Nr. 4 v. 25, January, 1873, pp. 97-102. Friedrich Nippold, 'Die literarischen Ergebnisse der neuen Straussischen Controverse. Kritische Studie' (The Literary Results of the New Strauss Controversy...) in *Strauss's Alter und neuer Glaube und seine literarischen Ergebnisse: Zwei kritische Abhandlungen von L.W.E. Rauwenhoff und F. Nippold* (Leipzig: Harrasowitz, 1873), pp. 129-246, 228, asserts that the theologian Lipsius wrote this critique.

46. For Heinrich Lang's numerous critiques of *The Old and the New*,

Emanuel Biedermann[49] claimed traditional Christian concepts proclaim a principal singularity of the individual against a more and more overpowering objective world. By this concentration on a principal liberty or a world-transcendency of the individual, which should be disclosed through Christian religion, Strauss's liberal theological critics tried to justify theologically certain bourgeois claims of emancipation.

Strauss's program of criticism can only be interpreted in the context of the politico-cultural endeavours of bourgeois emancipation. If this proposal for an interpretation is striking, then the theological reactions to Strauss can be explained from the perspective of 'intellectual history' or a 'sociology of knowledge' (K. Mannheim) or even a 'social history of ideas'. Without exception, Strauss's liberal theological critics objected to 'The New Faith' that the practical autonomy of the individual was only defined in a deficient way, and that, in this respect, Strauss missed the central content of the doctrines of Protestant tradition. Therefore they claimed to overcharge Strauss. Their decisive argument here was that one could symbolize a principal world-transcendency of the individual much more successfully by the old faith than using Strauss's religion of art. The determination with which the theological critics of *The Old Faith and the New* pushed the autonomy of the individual into the centre of their interpretations of Christianity, is not only a *critical* reaction to Strauss. The reaction also shows how deeply Strauss was able to influence the transformation of Protestant theology in the

cf. Alois Emanuel Biedermann, *Heinrich Lang* (Zürich: Schmidt, 1876), pp. 96ff.

47.   Alexander Schweizer, '"Der alte und der neue Glaube. Ein Bekenntnis", von David Friedrich Strauss 1872', in *idem, Nach Rechts und Links: Besprechungen über Zeichen der Zeit aus den letzten drei Decennien* (To the Left and to the Right. Discussions of the Signs of the Time from the Last Three Decades) (Leipzig: Hirzel, 1876); Schweizer, 'Die Zukunft der Religion' ('The Future of Religion'), *ZWT* 20 (1877), pp. 433-86; enlarged separate printing: *Die Zukunft der Religion* (Zürich: Füssi & Co., 1878), IV, p. 10, pp. 19-23, pp. 32-39.

48.   Adolf Hilgenfeld, 'Der alte und der neue Glaube, nach den neuesten Schriften von D.F. Strauss und Lagarde geprüft' (The Old Faith and the New in the New Writings of Strauss and Lagarde), *ZWT* 16 (1873), pp. 305-54.

49.   Alois Emanuel Biedermann, 'Strauss und seine Bedeutung für die Theologie: Rektoratsrede, gehalten an der Stiftungsfeier der Züricher Hochschule, den 29. April 1875', in *Ausgewählte Vorträge und Aufsätze mit einer biographischen Einleitung von J. Kradolfer* ('Strauss and his Importance for Theology...', also in: Selected Lectures and Essays, with a Biographical Introduction) (Berlin: G. Reimer, 1885), pp. 211-30.

process of the modernization of German society in the nineteenth century. His programme to legitimize bourgeois emancipation by critical theology or a criticism of theology shaped Protestant theology at the universities even where they kept a distance from Strauss. So, David Friedrich Strauss reached a central position in the process of modernizing theological reflection. He succeeded in forcing his subject on his opponents: the subject of bourgeois autonomy and its theological justification. His liberal theological critics have only tried to find a way to legitimize the bourgeois claims of emancipation in their theology.

THE INTELLECTUAL BACKGROUND OF H.H. MILMAN'S
THE HISTORY OF THE JEWS (1829) AND ITS IMPACT
ON ENGLISH BIBLICAL SCHOLARSHIP

R.E. Clements

To the modern reader, familiar with the subject of the history of Israel as a major component in the modern scientific study of the Old Testament, H.H. Milman's three volumes on *The History of the Jews* which date from 1829, do not appear to offer much of lasting interest. In spite of the *History*'s considerable popularity in the latter half of the nineteenth century as a textbook, Milman is now better remembered for his Palm Sunday hymn 'Ride on, ride on, in majesty, in lowly pomp ride on to die'. Yet, when the first volume of the *History* appeared as a rather dull looking volume in a popular series called 'The Family Library', it caused an immense stir. Milman was preached against from pulpits all over England; pamphlets and tracts were hastily published to oppose his view of the Old Testament history, and leading figures of the English Church felt called upon to dissociate themselves from his attempt to popularize and interpret the Bible in this novel fashion.

Yet Milman had proclaimed no heresy, rejected no creed and denied no essential part of the biblical tradition. On the contrary, in his own estimation he had striven hard to confirm it and its historical veracity. His offence was simply to have written an account of the Old Testament story as a secular history. Because he believed it to have been a real history he presented it in the dress of the age and setting to which he knew that it belonged and made it conform to principles of historical causation and development which any serious historian would look for. It is true that he rationalized the biblical emphasis upon the miraculous reports of divine intervention in Israel's history by speculating about what may have actually happened to have left the contemporary partici- pants with the belief that God had directly intervened in their affairs. However, it is not simply such rationalizing explanations which caused offence, but rather the whole tone of Milman's presentation which made his work appear to be a rebuttal of the accepted norms of Christian biblical interpretation. He was rebuked for having described Abraham as an oriental vizier, or nomad sheik, and for having cast the biblical history as part of a larger ancient oriental movement of events.

Henry Hart Milman—Poet and Scholar

Henry Hart Milman was born in Westminster, London, in 1791, where his father Francis Milman was physician to the monarch, George III. He was educated at Eton College and at Brasenose College, Oxford, where he matriculated in 1810 and took his BA in 1813, his MA in 1816. He was ordained into the Church of England in 1816 and, after a curacy in Ealing, London, he took the living of St Mary's Reading in 1817. He was elected to be Professor of Poetry at Oxford in 1821, a position to which he took his BD and DD and was re-elected in 1826, subsequently being succeeded by John Keble. In 1849 he was appointed to be Dean of St Paul's Cathedral, London. Among his close friends from these early years he numbered J.T. Coleridge, a nephew of the distinguished poet, and John Murray the publisher. His acquaintances also included J.G. Lockhart, the biographer of Sir Walter Scott, and this distinguished literary circle provides evidence of Milman's strong literary ambitions and interests in his early years. This series of connections was to have a bearing upon the circumstances surrounding the writing and publication of *The History of the Jews*.

Lockhart served as editor from 1826 of *The Quarterly Review*, a literary journal to which Milman contributed, and acted as agent and friend to John Murray.[1] It was on behalf of the publisher John Murray that Lockhart was instrumental in proposing the subject of Milman's controversial work. All told, for a literary-minded clergyman of the 1820s, he appears to have had a talented and ambitious circle of friends whose company often brought Milman from Reading to London.

Apart from brief memoirs written shortly after the time of his death, no full length biography appeared until his son Arthur Milman, a physician, published one in 1900.[2] Milman himself had given instructions

---

1. Lockhart's connection with Milman and 'The Family Library' is recounted in Marion Lockhead, *John Gibson Lockhart* (London: John Murray, 1954), pp. 179ff.

2. Arthur Milman, *Dean Milman: A Biographical Sketch* (London, 1900); cf. the earlier essay, written at the time of Milman's death in 1868 by A.P. Stanley, 'Dean

for all his correspondence to be destroyed after his death. Unfortunately, the biography is undistinguished and sheds only a little light on the controversy of 1829. Few copies of the first edition of *The History of the Jews* appear to have survived the ravages of time and decay very well. However, the storm which it provoked gave rise to many critical reviews and published sermons which highlight the issues which it brought to the surface. It remains an often cited title, intimating the early appearance of a new critical approach to biblical scholarship entering English life. It remains almost alone as an Anglican contribution from the first half of the nineteenth century to the subject of serious criticism of the historicity of the Old Testament. A.P. Stanley was later to describe it as 'the first decisive inroad of German theology into England'.[3] Yet this is certainly to over-rate its importance, and contemporary readers may have wondered where the evidence of 'German rationalism', with which it was labelled, is to be seen.

It was not until more than twenty years later, when the work of Heinrich Ewald received wide popularity and following in England, that other comparable studies began to make their appearance. Even then, apart from a few liberal Anglicans like Milman and Stanley, the middle years of the nineteenth century largely witnessed critical Old Testament scholarship advancing in England almost entirely through Unitarians, such as Francis W. Newman, and independents, such as Samuel Davidson. At the very least Milman's *The History of the Jews* was a work born out of due time, and Milman's son and biographer reports the Oxford bookseller, Parker, saying that the three-volume work was published 'thirty years too soon'.[4] Yet the work is totally innocent of the source criticism which later dominated the critical approach to Old Testament studies, and seems, in the first instance, not to have been intended as a critical essay in biblical research at all. Certainly Milman had had no prior experience of this and makes no allusion to contemporary critical work by such scholars as Eichhorn and de Wette. Moreover

Milman', *MM* 19 (1869), pp. 177-87; repr. in *Essays Chiefly on Questions of Church and State from 1850–1870* (London: John Murray, 1870), pp. 572-91; W.E.H. Lecky, 'Henry Hart Milman', *EdR* 191 (1900), pp. 510-27; repr. in *Historical and Political Essays* (1908), pp. 249-74.

   3.   Stanley, 'Dean Milman', *Essays on Church and State*, p. 576.
   4.   Milman, *Dean Milman*, p. 93. In the preface to the third edn (1863) of the *History*, Milman himself reflects illuminatingly on the great changes that had taken place in English research into Old Testament history in the intervening years.

it clearly was intended to be a history of the Jews, reaching from biblical times to the age of Napoleon.

Milman began his literary career while still a student at Oxford, where he wrote and produced, in 1813, a drawing-room drama entitled *Fazio* (published at Oxford in 1816). This enjoyed a brief popularity, being produced subsequently in both London and Bath. As a result of the lax copyright system prevailing at the time, Milman was surprised to discover that a play being produced at the Surrey Theatre with the title *The Italian Wife* was, in reality, his play *Fazio*.

Milman's first ambition was to become a poet in the Romantic tradition and it is this fact, combined with his close association with central figures of the Romantic Movement, which makes his conversion to become a historian significant. What he drew into the tradition of serious historical research of antiquity, in which Edward Gibbon served as his model and mentor, was something of the natural-supernaturalism of the Romantic School linked with the names of Coleridge and Wordsworth.[5]

The first publications from the energetic young Milman, incumbent of the Parish of St Mary's Church in Reading, were epic poems conceived in the Romantic tradition.[6] First came *Samor: Lord of the Bright City* in 1818, recounting the adventures of a British tribal chieftain fighting against Saxon invaders. Then in 1820 came a poem entitled *The Fall of Jerusalem: A Dramatic Poem*, to be followed in 1822 by two more, *The Martyr of Antioch* and *Belshazzar*. The martyr theme focused on an incident reported in Gibbon's *Decline and Fall*. His poem *Anne Boleyn* (1826) continued, and was the final offering, in the same style. From the point of view of what was to come later, the poem *Belshazzar* illustrates well the mixture of Romantic and mythological themes which characterised much early nineteenth century interest in the Bible as literature. It anticipates the appeal of the subject to contemporary English minds, as illustrated by the major paintings on the same theme from John Martin and Edward Poynter.

D.H. Reiman points out that Milman very much belonged spiritually to the English ecclesiastical and cultural establishment. He describes him

---

5. Cf. M.H. Abrams, *Natural Supernaturalism: Tradition and Revolution in Romantic Literature* (New York: W.W. Norton, 1971), *passim*.

6. The modern reader is indebted to Garland Publishing of New York for reprints of Milman's poetry. So *The Poetical Works of H.H. Milman* (3 vols.; selected and arranged by D.H. Reiman; in the series 'Romantic Context: Poetry. Significant Minor Poetry 1789–1830'; New York: Garland Publishing, 1976–77).

as 'a fossil-poet', and ventures the comment: 'Milman's writings are instructive as to how a firm allegiance to the political, religious and academic establishment can vitiate a genuine, if limited, talent.' Nevertheless Milman was, in his early days, regarded as something of a rival to both Byron and Shelley.[7] J.G. Lockhart clearly had serious misgivings about Milman's abilities as a poet, describing his dramatic poem on *The Fall of Jerusalem* as 'feeble and poor in the extreme'.[8]

Milman's election to become Professor of Poetry at Oxford confirms the impression that, for the first decade of his ecclesiastical career, he saw himself as essentially a poet in the Romantic tradition. However, he clearly became increasingly aware that his talent in this field was undoubtedly limited, in spite of encouragement from friends and some success in publishing. It is significant therefore that when he was invited to give the Bampton Lectures in the University of Oxford in 1827, he chose a historical subject, *The Character and Conduct of the Apostles Considered as Evidence of Christianity*. From this point on, Milman clearly saw his future academic career pointing in this direction.

After publication of *The History of the Jews* in 1829, Milman wrote little more on the Old Testament, apart from substantially revising the *History* for a third edition in 1863. By this time, the country was more ready for it. He preached, in 1865, the annual sermon at Oxford University on Hebrew prophecy in which he reiterated his concern with the national dimensions of the faith of the Old Testament. W.E.H. Lecky comments that his mind was essentially secular in its outlook[9] and his theological position strongly coloured by his desire to see a truly 'national' Church in which the spiritual and intellectual life of England would find its natural centre. His interests were those of the historian, constantly looking up to Edward Gibbon, of whom he wrote a biography (1839). His other major writings were histories of the spread of the Christian Church in the West. He died in 1868.

Overall, the publication of *The History of the Jews* in 1829, appears as a rather abberant departure in the life of a scholar who wished primarily to be a Church historian. It is even more distinctive and out of place in the context of the state of Old Testament studies in England at the time. Perhaps most striking of all is the point that it clearly did not originally set out to be a major venture into critical biblical studies, for which

---

7.   Reiman, *Poetical Works of H.H. Milman*, I, p. ix.
8.   Lockhead, *John Gibson Lockhart*, p. 181.
9.   Lecky, *Historical and Political Essays*, p. 267.

Milman had little real taste. It aimed to be, as its title states, a history of the Jewish people, whose condition in Europe had been profoundly changed as a result of the upheavals following on from the French Revolution.

Biblical Scholarship in England in the Early Nineteenth Century

In order to understand the nature and causes of the storm of controversy aroused by Milman's book,[10] it is important to consider briefly the state of biblical scholarship in England at the time. The figure whose influence appears most prominently here is S.T. Coleridge (1772–1834),[11] the philosopher poet, whose visit to Germany in 1798–99 enabled him to bring back to England an intellectual stimulus greatly affected by Romanticism, coupled with a new critical approach to the Bible which had found inspiration in the work of J.G. Eichhorn. Alongside Coleridge, whose influence on Milman was undoubtedly strong in encouraging his early desire to become a Romantic poet, we should also mention Connop Thirlwall (1791–1875), whose English translation of F.D.E. Schleiermacher's commentary on Luke, with a lengthy introduction, was published in 1825.[12] Thirlwall was primarily an ancient historian, proceeding to publish the first of an eight-volume

---

10. For H.H. Milman cf. J. Estlin Carpenter, *The Bible in the Nineteenth Century* (London: Longmans, Green & Co., 1903), p. 19; V.F. Storr, *The Development of English Theology in the Nineteenth Century, 1800–1860* (London: Longmans, Green & Co., 1913), pp. 112-14; John Hunt, *Religious Thought in the Nineteenth Century* (London: Gibbings & Co., 1896), pp. 113-14; J.W. Rogerson, *Old Testament Criticism in the Nineteenth Century: England and Germany* (London: SPCK, 1984), pp. 184-88.

11. The literature on Coleridge and the rise of biblical criticism in England is now immense. Cf. now especially E.S. Shaffer, *'Kubla Khan' and the Fall of Jerusalem: The Mythological School in Biblical Criticism and Secular Literature 1770–1880* (Cambridge: Cambridge University Press, 1975); A.J. Harding, *Coleridge and the Inspired Word* (Kingson, Montreal: McGill–Queen's University Press, 1985); R. Ashton, *The German Idea: Four English Writers and the Reception of German Thought 1800–1860* (Cambridge: Cambridge University Press, 1980); R. Holmes, *Coleridge: Early Visions* (New York: Viking–Penguin, 1990); Stephen Prickett, *Words and The Word* (Cambridge: Cambridge University Press, 1986), *passim*.

12. F.D.E. Schleiermacher, *A Critical Essay on the Gospel of Luke* (ET Connop Thirlwall; London: John Taylor, 1825).

History of Greece in 1835.[13] Herbert Marsh (1757–1839) had probably done as much as anyone to interest British scholars in the newer methods of criticism developed in Germany. He had studied in Germany under J.D. Michaelis and was elected Lady Margaret Professor in Cambridge University in 1807. The lectures he delivered there between 1809 and 1816 were among the first attempts to popularise a new critical approach to the Gospels, such as had become established in Germany. They aroused fierce criticism from the Calvinists and Evangelicals within the Church.

More directly related to the study of the Old Testament was the work of E.B. Pusey (1800–1882), who had travelled in Germany during the years 1825–27, hearing lectures in Göttingen and Berlin from such diverse scholars as J.G. Eichhorn and E.W. von Hengstenberg. His publication of the researches that he conducted there under the title *An Historical Enquiry into the Probable Causes of the Rationalist Character lately predominant in the Theology of Germany* (Part I, 1828; Part II, 1830), was widely interpreted as a strongly negative evaluation of the German developments.[14]

Not all English attention to German biblical scholarship was as critical, however, and mention should be made of Thomas Arnold (1795–1842), who had learnt German in 1825 in order to read B.G. Niebuhr's *History of Rome* and Julius Hare (1795–1855). Together Julius Hare, Connop Thirlwall, Thomas Arnold and Henry Hart Milman were leading and representative figures of what can best be described as liberal Anglicanism.[15] They each displayed a strong interest in German scholarly developments, particularly as they affected the study of the ancient world.

Later they came to be supported by A.P. Stanley (1815–1881), who became a close friend and London colleague of Milman's (as Dean of Westminster) effectively continuing and developing the critical interest in the Old Testament which Milman himself did not follow up to any

---

13. C. Thirlwall, *A History of Greece* (8 vols.; London: Green & Longman, 1835–44).

14. Cf. David Forrester, *Young Doctor Pusey* (London: A.R. Mowbray, 1989), pp. 32-50.

15. Cf. Duncan Forbes, *The Liberal Anglican Idea of History* (Cambridge: Cambridge University Press, 1952). Milman is particularly dealt with by Forbes for his concern with the concept of 'Providence'; cf. *Liberal Anglican Idea of History*, pp. 73ff.

significant extent. Stanley's special contribution was to have travelled in the Holy Land in the years 1852–53, and to have drawn a close link between geography and sacred history.[16] He also did much to popularize the work of the German orientalist and historian Heinrich Ewald.[17] The intellectual tools of these scholars were primarily those of the historian, yet they saw little separation between ecclesiastical and secular history.[18] Each of them saw the study of ancient history as a primary educational and cultural discipline for maintaining a sense of continuity with the past and for the promotion of its values. Within this history they saw a divine providential order at work. Stanley, in particular, came to see in the new critical developments in Old Testament scholarship a prime factor in demonstrating the necessity for a radical revision of traditional Anglican theology, and for claiming that the values of the past could be retained, even though the forms of society, and the norms of intellectual life, must undergo change.[19] They saw historical research as demanding a new kind of theological insight, revealing the divine governance of the world and its providential significance. Together they each shared a concern with national educational reform both in the schools and universities, finding in the ancient classical histories of Greece and Rome a model of intellectual enlightenment.

In a general assessment, it must be noted that the English Church felt increasingly divided over the critical study of the Bible during the first half of the nineteenth century. In spite of the fact that, during the eighteenth century, England had contributed much to biblical learning, there were deep fears abroad after the French revolution, of a social, political and theological kind. The most radical theological ideas were readily combined with radical social perspectives, as by the Presbyterian philosopher scientist, Joseph Priestley (1733–1804). His move into

---

16. Cf. A.P. Stanley, *Sinai and Palestine in Connection with their History* (London: John Murray, 1856, 2nd edn, 1883).

17. Cf. his *Lectures on the Jewish Church* (3 vols.; London: John Murray, 1863; rev. edn, 1889) Stanley points out the extent of the influence that Ewald's work had, both on his own work, and on the later editions of Wm. Smith's *Dictionary of the Bible*; cf. vol. I, p. 24.

18. Cf. Forbes, *Liberal Anglican Ideas of History*, p. 42: 'there could be no real division between "ecclesiastical" and "secular"'.

19. Cf. especially his essay on 'Theology of the Nineteenth Century', *Essays on Church and State*, pp. 352-76. He could venture the claim that the critical study of the Bible 'enables us to understand in a Christian, and at the same time philosophic spirit, the whole history of mankind' (p. 361).

Unitarianism in 1791, and his defence of the French Revolution, came to be seen as dangerous signs that critical scholarship could be linked to dangerously radical political and theological views. It is not surprising, therefore, that in 1829 the English Church was preoccupied with other issues, and by no means ready to offer a calm and welcoming response to volumes from a young scholar that appeared to embrace wholeheartedly views that had become, largely mistakenly, associated with German Rationalism. They were far more dependent upon a newly developing English historicism. The popular misguided assumption concerning its German rationalistic origin, however, was the unhappy fate that befell Henry Hart Milman's hastily prepared attempt to reach a wide public with his three-volume account of Jewish history from biblical times to the age of Napoleon.

The assumption of an origin in German critical biblical scholarship was especially applied to the first volume, which was the one that caused the greatest consternation. Nonetheless, once alerted to feel suspicion, an ungenerous critic could find evidence of dangerous tendencies in the absence of any treatment of the ministry of Jesus in the second volume. There are, however, additional features that make Milman's popular presentation of the biblical history interesting. Not least among these is the fact that a great deal of public attention had been drawn to the ancient Bible lands as a result of the Napoleonic campaigns in Egypt and the subsequent beginning of serious Egyptology. The first major treasures from that land had become a popular subject for exhibition.

A new wave of interest in the ancient East, most especially Egypt but certainly also including Palestine, was sweeping Great Britain. In large measure cultured English society was rediscovering the art, architecture and distinctiveness of the biblical world. Within a half-century the first surprise discoveries from the Bible Lands had become a major ongoing source of new treasures and new knowledge. The result was that a whole range of ancient languages had been rediscovered and a new depth of understanding of the world from which the Bible had emerged had been attained. It is a striking feature of Milman's volumes that they reflect very effectively much of the romantic and cultural appeal of this oriental world.[20] The mix of Romanticism and Orientalism, which by 1830 had acquired a strong popular appeal in England, is markedly

---

20. Cf. E.W. Said, *Orientalism* (London: Penguin Books, 1978); cf. especially his comment, p. 18: 'There has been some important recent work on the background in Biblical scholarship to the rise of what I have called modern Orientalism'.

evident in Milman's writing. Without them it is doubtful whether the first volume of *The History of the Jews* would have enjoyed the popular reception that it gained, or stirred up the opposition that it did. Perhaps even more to the point, it seems improbable that Milman would ever have ventured to write such a work, had it not been that he felt the time was ripe for an orientalized and historicised account of the Bible story. Nor was he reluctant to believe that he, as a poet turned historian, possessed the necessary literary talent to pursue such a subject.

Great Britain and The History of the Jews

There is a further reason for reconsidering the significance of Milman's three-volume work which, from the intellectual historian's viewpoint, has been almost totally neglected. This lies in the choice of its subject: the history of the Jews from biblical times to the end of the eighteenth century. It is dealt with by him in three periods, covered respectively in the three volumes. Roughly outlined, volume one covers the Old Testament period down to the Babylonian Exile and the activity of the prophet Jeremiah; volume two covers the Post-exilic, Intertestamental and New Testament periods, although without treatment of the rise of the Christian Church; volume three continues the story after the separation of Christianity from Judaism and extends down to the Napoleonic era. Since the readership of 'The Family Library' was intended to be popular, and predominantly Christian, such a drawing of attention to the complex, and often tragic, character of Jewish experience, seems a strange choice for a young and ambitious writer.

However the choice of subject, especially for a young Christian scholar with a strong English national interest and loyalty, becomes immediately clear when we consider the immense revival of attention to the subject of Jewish history at this period. Ever since the seventeenth-century English Puritanism had maintained a strong interest in the fate of the Jewish people, not wholly out of a theological altruism, but out of belief that they held the key to the divine plan for all human history.[21] The twin themes of the return of the Jews to their ancient homeland in

21. Cf. Ian H. Murray, *The Puritan Hope* (London: Banner of Truth, 1971), pp. 59ff.; earlier valuable information is to be found in Christopher Hill, 'Till The Conversion of the Jews', *Millenarianism and Messianism in English Literature and Thought 1650–1800* (ed. R.H. Popkin; Clark Library Lectures; Leiden: E.J. Brill, 1988), pp. 12-36.

Palestine, and their conversion to accept Jesus as the Messiah, had been ideas closely intertwined with Christian millennialism.

The French Revolution, and the subsequent Napoleonic conflicts, had given rise in England to a strong revival of this millennial expectation.[22] The time appeared to be ripe for the conversion of the Jews to begin, encouraging Christian missionary endeavours in this direction. Yet along with this, and arguably inseparably linked to it, was the belief that flourished in some Evangelical circles that the Jewish people must first return to their ancient homeland, not in isolated numbers, but as a veritable host returning to their rightful domain. The Napoleonic campaign in Egypt and its aftermath had suggested to some that such a move was shortly to happen. Moreover, even though tinged with not a little national triumphalism, the belief was being openly discussed that it was a unique commission from the Most High, no less, that Great Britain should have the leading role to play in making possible such a return.

This revival of millennial expectation has been widely noted, but the relevant fact so far as Milman's work is concerned, is that by 1825 this re-awakened interest in the conversion of the Jews had come to enjoy a quite remarkable degree of popular attention. Seen against such a backdrop, the contemporary interest in Milman's choice of subject becomes a great deal clearer.

This is certainly not to suggest that Milman personally embraced either strong millennial expectations or deep convictions that the work of assisting the return of Jews to Palestine was a uniquely British assignment in a divine plan. Rather it is simply to point out that, when he published the first volume of his *History* in 1829, the British reading public had stronger reasons for wanting to know a great deal more about Jewish history after the biblical period than were usually to be found. Yet it was, for the most part, almost completely ignorant of it.

The rekindled eagerness for Christian missionary work among Jews was exemplified in the formation in 1809 of the London Society for the Promoting of Christianity among the Jews. Originally this was an interdenominational venture, but after 1815 it became a predominantly Anglican one. This quickly led to exploratory moves to set up a mission station in Jerusalem, a venture which, by 1819, was closely matched

---

22. Cf. W.H. Oliver, *Prophets and Millenialists: The Uses of Biblical Prophecy in England from the 1790s to the 1840s* (Auckland, NZ: Auckland University Press, 1978), pp. 69ff.

from the USA.[23] The combination of interests in resettling Jews, led subsequently to the joint establishment in 1840 by the Anglican Church and Frederick William IV of Prussia of a Protestant Anglican Episcopate in Jerusalem.[24] Certainly this venture had some hopes of revitalising what were seen at the time as degenerate oriental churches. Nevertheless the primary objective was to facilitate Christian missionary work among Jews.

In 1826 the English gentleman Henry Drummond invited approximately forty clergy and interested lay persons to his residence at Albury House, near Guildford, in Surrey for the first of three conferences on the subject of biblical prophecy.[25] Others were held in 1827 and 1829. The first of these has drawn particular attention from historians because of its considerable impact on the eccentric Scottish preacher Edward Irving, and the subsequent rise of the so-called 'Irvingite' movement in British Church life.[26] Central to the discussions was the question of the divine purpose for the Jewish people and their return to their ancient homeland. This marked a revitalising of what had been a prominent motif of English Puritan theology, with attention to the link between this Return to the Holy Land and Jewish conversion to recognize Jesus as Messiah. All these interests were tied to a more imminent hope of the dawning of the millennial era.

These developments had been greatly advanced by the way in which English interests had been drawn into the Near East in the wake of the Napoleonic wars. Accordingly they were linked in speculative minds to a concern with the role that God intended that Great Britain should play in the further unfolding of events, which many believed would shortly lead to the dawning of the millennium. For any English Christian writing a book about the history of the Jews in the late 1820s, this level of intense contemporary expectation relating to that history could not be

23. A.L. Tibawi, *British Interests in Palestine 1800–1901* (Oxford: Oxford University Press, 1961); cf. also Tibawi, *American Interests in Syria 1800–1901* (Oxford: Clarendon Press, 1966), esp. pp. 23ff.

24. Cf. Julius Richter, *A History of Protestant Missions in the Near East* (New York: F.H. Revell, 1910), pp. 181ff. Richter describes this development (p. 237) as 'one of the most interesting episodes of mission history in the Near East'.

25. Oliver, *Prophets and Millenialists*, pp. 90ff.

26. Cf. Edward Miller, *The History and Doctrines of Irvingism, or of the So-called Catholic and Apostolic Church* (2 vols.; London: Kegan, Paul, 1878), I, pp. 30-47. Prominent among the five major conclusions reached at the Albury House Conferences was that 'the Jews will be restored to their own land' (*Irvingism*, p. 44).

missed. It must undoubtedly have played a major role in the choice of subject, even for an author who viewed its associated millennial leanings with considerable reserve.

In 1827 George Croly had published a strongly national-millennialist interpretation of *The Apocalypse of St John*.[27] The Scottish Church also participated in these developments by sending four leading ministers on a fact-finding tour in 1839.[28] Although not at all their primary purpose, these exploratory developments were to lead to a major awakening of interest in a knowledge of the geography and archaeology of the Holy Land as a primary subject for biblical research. It is this feature of the high degree of contemporary interest in Christian work among Jews which adds a unique dimension of interest to the publication of Milman's work in 1829. The timing of its publication and the intended popular readership clearly indicate that it was the level of popular discussion and ecclesiastical debate regarding Christian attitudes to the Jewish people, that suggested the subject. Seen in this light, it also becomes evident that the particular critical assessments of the biblical history which caused so much consternation, were never intended to be more than an incidental feature of the work. Milman really did have a reason for wanting to carry the story of the 'Jews' of the Bible down to his own time.

The Writing of The History of the Jews

The circumstances surrounding the origin and intentions of the writing of Milman's *The History of the Jews* are of interest. The publisher John Murray had begun to plan a series of popular works under the title 'The Family Library' and enlisted Milman's interest as a potential contributor. So it came about that, in a letter dated July 17 1828, J.G. Lockhart, acting at the request of the publisher John Murray, put the following proposition to Milman: 'What do you say to a volume about the history of the Jewish people? Surely it might be made more entertaining than any romance, and really useful besides.'[29] Milman responded affirmatively to this suggestion and began work immediately. The first volume took him only a few months and was ready by December of the same year. All three volumes of the *History* then duly appeared in 1829 as numbers 5, 6, and 9 in the series. Curiously Milman's name did not

27. Oliver, *Prophets and Millenialists*, p. 67.

28. Murray, *The Puritan Hope*, p. 175.

29. Milman, *History*, pp. 84.

appear on the title page, although it was readily known who the author was and his name was included on all the later editions. Perhaps this reticence was an indication that Milman felt some qualms about the controversial style of the book. He himself apparently commented 'I expect wise heads will be shaken at my views' [30] but more probably it merely reflects the point that all Milman was setting out to do in the first volume was to retell the familiar Bible history.

In the event, there was a storm of controversy as soon as the volume appeared, and the book quickly sold, calling for a reprint. In this, according to one critic, 'some of the more objectionable passages have been corrected or qualified'. Soon afterwards the series 'The Family Library' was discontinued, and it was widely believed that it was the controversy over Milman's book which had occasioned this.

More than three decades later, in 1863, a third edition was published thoroughly revised and extended. By this time it was presented in a well bound form, on high quality paper, as befitted a publication by an author who was now the Dean of St Paul's and a highly respected historian. A fourth edition appeared in 1866, and was republished in 1878 in Routledge's Standard Library. In 1880, it was published yet again in 'The World Library of Standard Works'. All of these later editions include references to some of the wide range of books dealing with Old Testament historical themes from the middle of the century. In particular, illustration and support are drawn from works dealing with the rapidly developing fields of Palestinian (as it was described) geography and antiquities.

Such new information was becoming widely known in Great Britain through the popularity of W. Smith's *Dictionary of the Bible*, as well as through the work of H. Ewald, which was well received in England by such liberal Anglicans as Milman and A.P. Stanley. This publishing history is relevant and of significance because, after the original edition of 1829, Milman's *The History of the Jews* scarcely remained the same book. Indeed, by the last quarter of the nineteenth century it had come to appear as a rather old-fashioned and conservative approach to the biblical history.

In spite of the initial hostile reaction to the book, Milman's subsequent ecclesiastical career was a distinguished one. Having been appointed Dean of St Paul's Cathedral in London, his work as a historian of the western spread of the Christian Church was highly regarded. Perhaps

30. Milman, *History*, pp. 84-85.

more surprisingly, the first volume of *The History of the Jews* came to be regarded as something of a standard work upon its subject until its lack of any stringent source criticism of the biblical material eventually rendered it totally obsolete.

Milman's Historical Presentation of the Biblical Story

It is, essentially, the first of Milman's three volumes that drew the most criticism and which came to be regarded as the most significantly pioneering of his contributions. The interest in the history of the Jews from biblical times to the present, which had grown out of a distinctive period of Christian missionary zeal, came largely to be seen in a different context altogether and Milman's original attempt at contributing to this was forgotten. His book was read and criticised as though it were primarily an essay in biblical criticism—a goal which was almost entirely peripheral to its original purpose.

The first edition of Milman's *The History of the Jews* bears every sign of its hasty preparation and contains very few footnotes. It mentions (p. 58), in regard to the contemporary popularity of interest in the rediscovery of ancient Egypt, the work of J.F. Champollion (1790–1832) and the hope is expressed that future discoveries from the hieroglyphic writings of that land might serve to shed confirmatory light on the event of the Hebrew exodus. There are some maps of the biblical lands and a few illustrative sketches of the biblical setting, including the high-priestly dress, the Ark and the Tabernacle.

What Milman assumes throughout to be the case, that the biblical history from Abraham onwards represents a real history, has allowed him to make his account conform to the principles of historical writing, such as one versed in Gibbon's ideas of historical connectedness and causation felt bound to adhere to. An anonymous critic published an open letter to him, urging that he should not allow the work to be reprinted on the grounds that 'It stands altogether on the footing of an ordinary history, having no other pretensions to notice than a history of Egypt, Greece, or Rome'. This critic then continued: 'Its aim is, not to improve the heart, but to inform the understanding'.[31]

It is precisely this feature that makes Milman's work interesting, and

---

31. *A Letter to the Rev. Henry Hart Milman, M.A., reputed author of A History of the Jews*, by 'One Who is Also an Elder' (Oxford: J. Parker/London: Rivingtons, 1830), p. 7.

which provoked such a sharp and stormy response to it. It recognizes that the biblical narratives write about events and record their occurrence from their own ancient oriental perspective. This is taken to be substantially different from the point of view which a modern, scientifically aware and critically minded, observer would be bound to adopt. What Milman wanted to do therefore was to recast the manner of reporting the biblical material so as to relate it more closely to the style and assumptions of a critical modern observer. It is interesting to note that one of the more moderately critical suggestions proposed, as a result of the controversy which the book aroused, that the publisher, John Murray, should publish a new edition setting out Milman's text alongside that from the Bible. The idea was not taken up.

This highlights the feature of the work that is uppermost. Written as it was very hastily, in just a few months, it aims to blend together literary skill with sound, if largely speculative, historical judgment. Apart from the broad aim of writing Israel's history 'like any other history', it was on the grounds of its treatment, and apparent rejection, of biblical miracles that it was most heavily criticised.

The treatment of the overthrow of the cities of Sodom and Gomorrah is a case in point (Gen. 19.23-29). Milman takes it for granted that an actual event occasioned the biblical story and feels free therefore to suggest what may really have happened:

> The cities stood on soil broken and undermined with veins of bitumen and sulphur. The flammable substances, set on fire by lightning, caused a tremendous convulsion; the water courses, both the river and the canals by which the land was extensively irrigated, burst their banks; the cities, the walls of which were perhaps built from combustible materials of the soil, were entirely swallowed up by the fiery inundation; and the whole valley, which had been compared to Paradise, and to the well-watered corn fields of the Nile, became a dead and fetid lake. (*History*, I, p. 15)

From this speculation Milman could proceed to suggest how Lot's wife came to meet her tragic end:

> Lot, warned of the impending ruin, fled with his daughters; his wife lingering behind was suffocated by the sulphurous vapours, and her body encrusted with the saline particles which filled the atmosphere. Later tradition, founded on a literal interpretation of the Mosaic account, pointed to a heap or column of salt, which bore perhaps some resemblance to a human form, and was believed, even by the historian Josephus, who has seen it, to be the pillar into which she was transformed. (*History*, I, p. 16)

Since the supposed denial of the Old Testament miracles was the foremost of the offensive and irreligious features in the book which Milman's critics objected to, it is important to observe that this denial did not consist in any argument that they never really happened, but simply that they could not have happened as a result of direct supernatural intervention in the way that the biblical narrative describes. From the perspective of gaining some understanding of the wider intellectual background to Milman's approach it is interesting to note that he shows little awareness of either the complexity of myth and its origins, or the complex literary character of biblical narrative. A simple historical realist type of interpretation is regarded as sufficient to enable modern readers to find their way back to an understanding of ancient stories. The influence of the natural-supernaturalism which Abrams notes as characteristic of the Romantic movement is obvious. It is this, as much as the critical historicism of Gibbon, that has shaped Milman's interpretation.

As a second illustration of Milman's interpretation and the hostility which it aroused we can look at the account of the reversed movement of the sun on Hezekiah's steps:

> On this sign, and on the dial, volumes have been written. It is not necessary to suppose that the sun actually receded, but that the shadow on the dial did; a phenomenon which might be caused by a cloud refracting the light. Whether the Jews possessed sufficient astronomical science to frame an accurate dial, can neither be proved or disproved; still less the more rude or artificial construction of the instrument itself; for as the dial was probably set up by Ahaz, who was tributary to the Assyrians, it might have come originally from Chaldea. (*History*, I, p. 308)

There are two features here which are worth pausing over. The first is the speculation which is made that Hezekiah's sun-clock, or steps, could have been an Israelite copy of a similar artefact designed and fashioned in Mesopotamia. The second is as significant. This is the supposition that is openly expressed that a sun-clock of this nature would certainly have been 'rude' in its design, and might be thought by many to have lain beyond the technical competence of ancient Israelites, a point which Milman almost dares the reader not to accept! Clearly anthropological assumptions concerning technological primitivism and of the spread of cultural skills from a common centre are already being taken for granted.[32] Such aspects of Milman's work might appear to be no more

32. Cf. Glyn Daniel and Colin Renfrew, *The Idea of Prehistory* (Edinburgh:

than superficial and pointless guesswork, were they not interesting reflections of the changing intellectual climate in England in 1829.

This consistent reinterpretation of the miraculous and supernatural element in the Old Testament proved to be the central, and most highly publicised, aspect of the work which drew forth such sharp criticism. John Rogerson describes the book as 'a very traditional account of the history of ancient Israel, with occasional mild instances of rationalization'.[33] This is no doubt true, but such a description calls for a good deal of fuller evaluation. The *History* is traditional in the sense that it accepts the fundamental historical reliability of the biblical tradition as a record of actual events from the time of Abraham onwards, even as to its relatively minor details. Yet it must be said that no one had previously put together an Old Testament history of this kind. It marks a major step forward in its whole understanding of the historical dimension of the biblical revelation.

The Reaction to The History of the Jews

The ferment of opposition to Milman's presentation of biblical history concentrated on the first volume and was widespread throughout England. It appears to have been voiced from pulpits across the breadth of the land. To this extent the inclusion of the book in a series called 'The Family Library' had achieved its intended goal of reaching a lay readership of interested and literate persons. Opposition was most vociferously led by Godfrey Faussett, the Lady Margaret's Professor of Divinity in Oxford. His sermon delivered before the university on February 28, 1830 was reprinted several times. By this time a reprint (nominally a second edition) of the original first volume by Milman had appeared with some relatively minor alterations. Its overall character, however, remained unchanged, as is true of the later editions also, so far as its critical stance was concerned. The aim of these later revisions was to make the work conform to a more exacting scholarly format, which rather contrasts with the hasty manner of its original preparation.

Milman himself disliked public controversy and refused to be drawn into open debate, although he had little respect for the views expressed by Faussett. He commented: 'The sermon is feeble—for a man in his

Edinburgh University Press, 2nd edn, 1988), pp. 25ff.; George W. Stocking Jr, *Victorian Anthropology* (New York: The Free Press, 1987), pp. 30ff.

33. Rogerson, *Nineteenth Century Criticism*, p. 187.

situation miserably so!' Faussett's view of the Old Testament, and of Israel's history reflected in it, can be demonstrated from a single quotation. It was probably not at all untypical of much of the popular attitude to the Old Testament in England in 1830:

> Israel was rescued by stupendous miracles not only from Egyptian bondage, but from the arrows and abominations of their heathen neighbours, and securely established in their land, as the sole depositories of the true religion, the sole witnesses of God's name, in the midst of an idolatry otherwise hopeless and universal.[34]

It is noteworthy that neither Milman's three volumes, nor Faussett's sermon show any particular anti-Jewish feeling. Faussett himself reflected much of the contemporary popular interest in the significance of Judaism, which had become associated in the English Church with a strong millennial expectation. He noted that the Jews 'still subsist, for purposes yet unfulfilled in the scheme of Providence...'[35] Not all Milman's critics were as generous, but it is noteworthy that the three-volume work as a whole was evaluated for what it implied about biblical criticism, and most of all about the nature of the biblical history, rather than for what light it shed upon the Christian understanding of, or significance of, post-biblical Jewish history.

In one respect Faussett's sermon serves to pick out the central aim of Milman's work which he describes very pertinently in the following fashion: it was 'to obliterate, as far as may be, the prominent features of distinction between God's peculiar people and the general mass of mankind; to humanize, if I may so express it, a history'.[36] This was undoubtedly a concern which Milman felt very strongly: to show that the biblical history was a real history and must therefore have conformed to the normal canons of historical interpretation and causation.[37]

Something of the deep mood of suspicion felt in Oxford concerning the contemporary trend in German biblical scholarship is appropriately voiced by Faussett. He claims that Milman's history was 'too closely analogous to the unhallowed speculations of German rationalism'[38] and

---

34. Faussett, *Sermon on 2 Sam. 7.23* (Oxford, 1830), p. 5.

35. Faussett, *Sermon on 2 Sam. 7.23*, p. 6.

36. Faussett, *Sermon on 2 Sam. 7.23*, pp. 8-9.

37. Lecky's comment is entirely apposite that Milman was happiest 'when he could treat his subject like secular history' (Lecky, *Historical and Political Essays*, p. 267).

38. Faussett, *Sermon on 2 Sam. 7.23*, p. 9.

goes on to point out that J.J. Semler was guilty of 'the most revolting impieties'.[39]

We have already noted that the hostile reaction to Milman's book, with its enduringly interesting subject, did not affect his own ecclesiastical career, nor did the adverse responses to its initial appearance preclude its revision and use as a textbook, once a couple of decades had passed. In many respects all that Milman had done was to draw attention to the need for a serious reconsideration of the nature of the biblical history and the way in which the new critical approaches to ancient history, which were strongly felt in the early nineteenth century in regard to the histories of ancient Greece and Rome, affected biblical interpretation.

The Significance of Milman's Achievement

A look back to this first volume of Milman's *The History of the Jews* as though it represented a credible and well researched account of the history of ancient Israel in the Old Testament period is likely to be very disappointing. It was hastily written by an intending historian who clearly had had neither the time nor the exposure to critical reflection which the subject demanded. On the other hand, if we regard it for what it actually is, a draft sketch, hurriedly written for popular consumption, of the issues and perspectives with which a serious history of ancient Israel would have to deal, it is full of interest.[40] It sets an agenda which, during the next century, occupied the central place in European Old Testament research. It lays out a number of historiographic principles which any serious future historian would have to take into account. What it chiefly lacks, and what shortly afterwards became central to further forays into the subject, is any awareness of the importance of careful analysis of the age and historical worth of the biblical sources.[41]

---

39. Faussett, *Sermon on 2 Sam. 7.23*, p. 10.

40. Not since the writing of Humphrey Prideaux (1648–1724), the Bishop of Norwich in the previous century had an Anglican clergyman formulated a sketch of the biblical history in this fashion. In 1716–18 he published *The Old and New Testaments Connected in the History of the Jews* (2 vols.; repr. New York: Harper Bros., 1836, from the twentieth London edn).

41. Lecky, *Historical and Political Essays*, pp. 260-61, claims that Milman was familiar with the contemporary German source criticism, and was firmly opposed to it. If this is true, then it nonetheless displays a major weakness in Milman's judgment. It

Milman clearly had no inkling at this stage of the vital importance of this issue. Nor does he show any awareness that this question was already being seriously addressed in Germany and Switzerland by W.M.L. de Wette. Yet to be fair, we must acknowledge that it was clearly never his intention to discuss major literary problems relating to the Bible for the benefit of the kind of readers he envisaged.

There are some further issues which the appearance of Milman's *The History of the Jews* in 1829 raises for the theological historian. I have noted that the volume which caused the greatest consternation was the first of three which carried the story of Jewish history from Bible times down to the Napoleonic era. I have urged that the early nineteenth century witnessed in Great Britain and America a greatly increased Christian interest in the significance of Jewish existence and that its relationship to Christian millennial expectations undoubtedly formed part of the contemporary background explaining the choice of subject for Milman's book. Almost unwittingly, therefore, the three-volume work could not but raise in a new way the question of the Jewishness of the Old Testament. This was an issue which the prevalent typologogical conventions of Christian Old Testament interpretation had largely left out of most British approaches to the biblical text.[42] In reacting against Schleiermacher, E.W. von Hengstenberg had reconstructed a new, and extensive, form of crypto-messianic typological exegesis of the Old Testament which enjoyed a striking, and little deserved, popularity in Great Britain, especially among the Evangelicals.[43] Even the conservative Pusey had recognized that such encoded messianic prophecies could not provide a clear and convincing understanding of the Christian worth of the Old Testament.[44] At the time of publication of Milman's volumes,

seems more likely that Milman had not, in 1829, seriously engaged with such questions.

42. Cf. George P. Landow, *Victorian Types, Victorian Shadows: Biblical Typology in Victorian Literature, Art and Thought* (London: Routledge & Kegan Paul, 1980).

43. E.W. von Hengstenberg, *The Christology of the Old Testament and a Commentary on the Messianic Predictions of the Prophets* (ET J. Martin; Edinburgh: T. & T. Clark; 2nd edn, 1854–58). An earlier English translation by R. Keith was published in Alexandria 1836–39. The original German edition was first published in Berlin in three volumes 1829–35; cf. my studies, 'Messianic Prophecy or Messianic History', *Horizons in Biblical Theology* 1 (1979), pp. 87-104; 'The Messianic Hope in the Old Testament', *JSOT* 43 (1989), pp. 3-19.

44. Cf. Forrester, *The Young Doctor Pusey*, p. 44.

the question of Christian–Jewish dialogue over the meaning of the Hebrew Scriptures was only just beginning to reappear as a major theme in the light of the new Science of Antiquity. It does not appear to have been an issue which aroused much comment from Milman's critics, although at least one of them averred that Milman had failed to display an adequate exposure of the errors of Judaism.

Certainly from the point of view of Christian missionary interest in Jews and Jewish life, Milman's volumes stood at the starting point of a greatly renewed attention to the subject. That he had recognized a deep continuity between the Old Testament and contemporary Jewish existence was an important departure for renewed Jewish–Christian debate.[45] Nor can I set aside as insignificant the immense importance that this re-awakened attention to a recognition among Christians that Jews were also 'a People of the Book' was to have. Its link with Christian millennial hopes through a doctrine of Dispensationalism became one of the major characteristics of evangelical thinking later in the nineteenth century, both in Great Britain and the USA.[46]

There is a larger theological feature regarding Milman's approach to his subject which has considerable importance in the recognition of a major shift in the understanding of the nature of divine revelation. The history of the Jews is the disclosure of the working of Providence. It is understood as that ordering of life and the development of all nations which emanates from the spiritual nature of the created order. God uses the biblical history of the Jews as a paradigm of a process of self-disclosure. In this direction we can see how the historicist legacy of the Enlightenment was expressed in the foundation of a new path of biblical

---

45. A similar awareness from the Jewish side, although with a very different perspective, was adopted by the major historian Heinrich Graetz; cf. my essay 'Heinrich Graetz as Biblical Historian and Religious Apologist', in *Interpreting the Hebrew Bible: Essays in Honor of E.I.J. Rosenthal* (ed. J.A. Emerton and Stefan C. Reif; Cambridge: Cambridge University Press, 1982), pp. 35-55.

46. The leading figure in the rise of British Dispensationalism, which accorded a certain measure of independence to the revelation of the Old Testament as a revelation to the Jews, was J.N. Darby (1800–1882). Cf. Stanley J. Grenz, *The Millenial Maze* (Downers Grove, IL: IVP, 1992), pp. 91ff. This was to have widespread repercussions for American evangelical biblical interpretation later in the nineteenth century; cf. Timothy P. Weber, *Living in the Shadow of the Second Coming* (Chicago: University of Chicago Press, 1983; rev. edn, 1987), pp. 87ff.; Clarence B. Bass, *Backgrounds to Dispensationalism: Its Historical Genesis and Ecclesiastical Implications* (Grand Rapids: Wm. B. Eerdmans, 1960).

interpretation. History, rather than theological propositions, brought to light the divine ordering of reality.

From the biblical point of view God is presented as an essential participant in Israel's history, and Milman found it helpful to give room to this feature of the biblical God-language by writing extensively of Providence. It is vital to Milman's whole presentation, and is essentially simply a surrogate term for God. Duncan Forbes draws attention to this as a central feature of what he calls the 'Liberal Anglican' idea of history: 'Their absolute presupposition was God's Providence; it is this which they took for granted and which they never questioned or doubted.'[47] 'Providence' becomes a convenient multi-purpose term by which historical and theological ideas can be merged into one another.

Forbes proceeds to show how this notion of Providence was later developed by Thomas Arnold and A.P. Stanley along lines similar to those which Milman had adopted. It becomes a very convenient bridge concept between history and theology, all the more useful because of its undefined character. Although Milman may unwittingly have left himself a hostage to his critics by giving so much attention to the narrative incidents in which miracles appeared to have taken place, and by offering natural explanations for them, this attention was incidental to a larger purpose. The idea of Providence, conceived as the overarching sense of a divine hand shaping all human history, had become embedded in the biblical tradition in the form of particular providences in which specific events had been ascribed directly to the hand of God. In reality, as Milman's much-criticised rationalisations illustrated, these specific occurrences, with their seemingly miraculous nature, were no more than natural events seen from a particular religious perspective.

History as Revelation in Liberal Anglical Theology

This leads on to a wider consideration as to how far Milman conceived of all history as, *in some sense*, revelatory. It is arguable that his treatment of the continuation of Jewish history into the post-biblical era implicitly declared that this too was subject to a special overarching divine care and purpose, although Milman does not explicitly declare that to be the case. Nevertheless the popular discussions concerning the future of the Jews at the time when Milman's *History* was first published strongly point in the direction of recognizing this to be so. It must

---

47. Forbes, *The Liberal Anglican Idea of History*, p. 7.

be regarded as slightly ironic that Milman's three-volume work; which clearly set out to present a true history of the Jews, should, in the outcome, have been almost exclusively remembered as an essay in biblical criticism. It was so, more as a consequence of unplanned necessity than by genuine design and forethought. Only the major revisions introduced into the later editions could properly be said to have aimed seriously in this direction.

Ultimately, however, it appears that, at the early stage in his development represented by the publication of the history, Milman had not deeply thought through the issues of a historical revelation. How a specific and unique biblical history, with saving and revelatory significance, related to a much larger and comprehensive history of the Jewish community and how, in turn, this related to a universal history are not worked out. There is only a general movement in the direction of arguing that the particular nature of the biblical story finds its theological relevance as a disclosure of the universal principles of the providential governance of the world.

Another important aspect of the assumptions that shaped Milman's work, and which aroused the ire of his critics, is his consistent orientalizing of the biblical story. I have pointed out that Abraham and Jacob are portrayed as oriental viziers, of the kind that the increasing numbers of European travellers in the biblical lands were encountering. The scenery and geography of the Old Testament, as the dress of its people, are all shown to be typically oriental as this term was being understood. The particularism of the biblical world is being unconsciously emphasised, and even exaggerated. There is something here of the Romantic ideal which, at the period of the book's appearance, was exercising a strong fascination for English readers. To a considerable degree Milman was attempting to present the biblical history as the kind of history that was still occurring in the Near East of the early nineteenth century. The oriental nature of the biblical world was being stressed, even more than its antiquity, out of a recognition that 'ancient' and 'modern' were not qualitatively distinct kinds of historical happening. On this issue Milman was at the very opposite pole to the Dispensationalist patterns of biblical interpretation which subsequently achieved such popularity among the Evangelical party. No doubt Milman had merely touched upon a sensitive theme which, by the middle of the nineteenth century, had become a major one, so far as biblical studies were concerned. When William Smith's *Dictionary of the Bible* first appeared in three volumes in 1863, this oriental aspect of the culture of the biblical history had become dramatically prominent. Illustrations abounded concerning every aspect of dress and daily life which reflected a particular Palestinian setting.

On the one hand this orientalizing of the biblical world created an appetite for travel in the region which rapidly become a flood, with the subsequent publication concerning the character of life in Bible lands. At another level it generated an awareness that the new science of archaeology offered the possibility of bringing a whole new wealth of knowledge about the Bible which could transform the modern interpretation of it. Overall Milman's presentation of the history of ancient Israel in the Old Testament period very decisively can be characterized as a particular history. Its ancient and oriental context is something which is to be accepted, even though it poses difficulties for its interpretation as a universal revelation. It is also something to be emphasized and made the subject of particular exposition.

The first volume of Milman's *A History of the Jews*, viewed as essentially a work in its own right and as constituting a draft attempt at writing a history of ancient Israel, reveals much that is interesting. Its very innocence of anything resembling a serious source criticism of the historical narratives of the Hebrew Bible enables us to see that there are principles of historiography which are very bit as important as the source criticism which subsequently drew the lion's share of attention in the nineteenth century. Even when, as with Milman, the major part of the narrative tradition of the Old Testament is assumed to be reliable and historically true, this still raises the question of what would 'true' mean in such an assessment. Milman's critics argued as though miracles were commonplace in biblical times and that, in those days, God exercised a providential governance of events, very different from that which is experienced in the modern world. To this extent Milman's critics supposed the world of the Bible to be very different from the painful realities experienced in the modern world. They regarded direct divine intervention as wholly to be expected by, and on half of, those whom God had uniquely chosen. Clearly Milman realised that he could not subscribe to any such position as this, for then the whole question of the natural-supernatural character of the world, such as the Romantics had perceived it,[48] would have had to be abandoned.

It is worthwhile noticing that, in spite of the sharp outburst of criticism

---

48. Cf. Abrams, *Natural Supernaturalism*, pp. 65-70; Prickett, *Words and the Word*, pp. 123ff.

directed against it, Milman's *History* proved to be a remarkably popular and widely read work. Once the first volume had been revised in the third edition to give it more the appearance of a work of critical biblical scholarship for serious students, rather than for a popular readership, then it came to be widely read and used as something approximating to a textbook. That it dealt with a serious subject, *viz.* the historicity of the tradition which underlies the biblical story, was quickly recognized, and the subject seen to be a relevant and inescapable one. It is not surprising therefore that, as a sketch of the Old Testament history, it remained a widely read book, preparing the way for the much larger, and more substantial, translations of the histories of Heinrich Ewald and Julius Wellhausen which eventually supplanted it among English readers. Even then, because of its brevity and literary style, it continued to be enjoyed as a popular introduction to the historical background of the Old Testament. To a degree, its lack of any discursive introduction on the problems of the dates and reliability of the historical sources of the Old Testament enabled it to escape some of the censorious critique of later generations of Churchmen. To their sensitive theological minds the radical revisions of the dates of the biblical source documents, as recognized by J. Wellhausen and S.R. Driver, betokened a lack of trust in the inspiration and authority of the Bible.

At a best estimate, Milman's *History* was a challenging work, born out of its proper time, which prepared the way for the fuller investigation of a major subject of biblical research. On a lower level, it was no more than a hastily conceived draft of its subject, designed and written to pander to a current mood of curiosity concerning the connection of nineteenth-century Jews with their biblical past and their ancient homeland.

APPENDIX

CONDITIONS AND PRESUPPOSITIONS OF BIBLICAL CRITICISM IN GERMANY IN THE PERIOD OF THE SECOND EMPIRE AND BEFORE: THE CASE OF HEINRICH JULIUS HOLTZMANN

Henning Graf Reventlow

Biblical criticism is a very specialized endeavour. It involves observing meticulously every detail of a text, looking upon the finest nuance of an expression, comparing and dissecting, using seemingly objective methods. But one has to stress: *seemingly*, as we know that the guiding motives for posing specific questions, for giving answers which fit into an overarching picture of a biblical book, of Scripture as a whole, are preconditioned by the leading interests of scholars, by the training they have gone through, by their education and ideals, by the time in which they live.[1] In the frame of this conference dealing with the conditions of the second half of the nineteenth century, the aim of this paper will be to show by the example of one famous scholar, Heinrich Julius Holtzmann (1832–1910),[2] in what way biblical research in Germany in that period is to be understood in the context of the ideological heritage and the political conditions of this country, which was rightly regarded as the Mecca of biblical research. But what I want to show is that one has to differentiate,

1. Cf. H. Holborn, 'Der deutsche Idealismus in sozialgeschichtlicher Bedeutung', *HZ* 174 (1952), pp. 359-84 = H.U. Wehler, *Moderne deutsche Sozialgeschichte* (Cologne: Kiepenheuer & Witsch, 1973⁴), pp. 85-108: 'Ideas are never simple projections of a concrete outer situation, but creative attempts of often highly sublime sort, to put the real conditions of life in harmony with the inner needs of man' (p. 94).

2. For a detailed review of his scientific work from the pen of a well known pupil, cf. W. Bauer, *Heinrich Julius Holtzmann: Ein Lebensbild* (Giessen: Töpelmann, 1932); cf. Bauer, *Aufsätze und kleine Schriften* (ed. G. Strecker; Tübingen: Mohr–Siebeck, 1967), pp. 285-341. The description, however, does not take into consideration the aspects we are interested in. For a comprehensive summary of work and life, O. Merk, 'Holtzmann, Heinrich Julius (1832–1910)', *TRE* 15 (1986), pp. 510-22 (with lit.).

that one has to look upon more detailed conditions than usual, that one has to avoid one-sided conclusions before having considered the very special circumstances which decided the position of this scholar and the role he played in the larger development of scientific theories which are typical of the period and gained a large following.

The hypothesis which indirectly caused my research by the initiative of William Farmer and David Dungan, is the theory of the primacy of the gospel of Mark. I shall not say a word about the correctness or otherwise of this hypothesis itself, as I am not a specialist in the field of New Testament exegesis. What can be spoken about are the conditions which furthered the rise of this theory and its popularity and the whole ideological and political environment in which a liberal biblical scholarship flourished in the second half of the century.

Methodologically—that seems important to me—one has to differentiate between two major aspects which are in no way identical. They are not without connection, but they are independent and must not be mingled or even identified, as sometimes a one-sided approach is in danger of doing. One aspect is the history of ideas. Former generations of scholars took this history as a completely self-sustained development living in the hearts of people in the freedom of the spirit uninfluenced by outer conditions. This opinion had to be corrected and was followed by the sociological approach which is still in high favour, regarding thoughts basically as the products of social and political conditions. Even if those theories are not developed in the wake of dialectical materialism, which takes human thought as the mere expression of material conditions, and originated as a counter-stroke to German idealism, their exponents are not infrequently prone to isolating their point of view and forgetting that similar external conditions can produce very different ideologies. The way to be taken will, therefore, be on the one hand to reflect the mutual impacts that streams of thought have wrought upon people acting in the realms of scholarship and of political practice; on the other hand, to become acquainted with the specific social and political conditions which formed the background to such a seemingly purely theoretical question as the problem of the relative age of the Synoptic Gospels.

After these methodological considerations I enter the specific problem of the origins and conditions of the growth and wide acceptance of an exegetical theory, using the example of the Markan Hypothesis and its most influential promoter Heinrich Julius Holtzmann.

The first thing to be observed is the remarkable fact that Holtzmann's *Die synoptischen Evangelien*[3] in which he substantiated Markan primacy in detail, is obviously free of any ideological reasoning. Holtzmann gives no reason why he develops his theory; apparently he regards what he says as the objective results of observations in the biblical text itself, and the whole argumentation moves on the level of textual comparisons etc. It should not be forgotten that the theory was not invented by Holtzmann but (after indications of Schleiermacher and Lachmann) had already had its best known promoters in C.G. Wilke[4] and C. Weisse[5] a quarter of a century before. Whereas Wilke's book is also a collection of exegetical details, Christian Hermann Weisse (1801–1866), a gifted philosopher,[6] added to his two-volume work a closing chapter— 'Philosophical closing consideration on the religious relevance of the personality of Christ and the evangelical tradition'[7]—in which he communicated his leading motives for writing his book. If not planned, it was completed, as he declares in his foreword,[8] as a sort of answer to D.F. Strauss's *Life of Jesus*.[9] This work, which explained the largest part of the evangelical tradition as mythical inventions, fell like a bomb[10] among contemporaries and shook the ideological foundations of both orthodox believers and rationalists. It was not completely rejected by Weisse, who as a philosopher felt free from ecclesiastical restrictions, although he did not follow the rationalists in explaining away miracle

---

3.   *Die synoptischen Evangelien: Ihr Ursprung und geschichtlicher Charakter* (Leipzig: W. Engelmann, 1863).

4.   C.G. Wilke, *Der Urevangelist oder Exegetisch kritische Untersuchung über das Verwandtschaftsverhältnis der drei ersten Evangelien* (Dresden: G. Fleischer, 1838).

5.   C.H. Weisse, *Die evangelische Geschichte kritisch und philosophisch bearbeitet* (2 vols.; Leipzig: Breitkopf & Härtel, 1838); cf. Weisse, *Die Evangelienfrage in ihrem gegenwärtigen Stadium* (Leipzig: Breitkopf & Härtel, 1856). On Weisse's first book, C.M. Tuckett, 'The Griesbach Hypothesis in the 19th Century', *JSNT* 3 (1979), pp. 29-60, 37-40.

6.   On Weissee, cf. A. Schweitzer, *Geschichte der Leben–Jesu–Forschung* (Tübingen: Mohr–Siebeck, 1923[2]), pp. 124-27; E. Günther, *Die Entwicklung der Lehre von der Person Christi im 19. Jahrhundert* (Tübingen: Mohr–Siebeck, 1912), pp. 201, 214.

7.   Weisse, *Die evangelische Geschichte*, II, pp. 441-543.

8.   Weisse, *Die evangelische Geschichte*, I, pp. iii-iv.

9.   *Das Leben Jesu, kritisch bearbeitet* (2 vols.; Tübingen: Osiander, 1835–36).

10.   Cf. E. Zeller, *Erinnerungen eines Neunzigjährigen* (Stuttgart: Uhland, 1908), p. 100.

stories and similar passages in the gospels by natural explanations. Strauss was right in uncovering the mythical character of most of the gospel traditions. But if that proof did in fact destroy the fundament on which the orthodox belief in the letter of the Scripture was built, and the basis of rationalist explanations likewise, there does still exist a third way which has been opened by Schleiermacher,[11] who taught Christians to find salvation for their personal souls in the person of Jesus Christ. One goes the wrong way, however, to find this person, if one sees with Schleiermacher and 'almost all the more recent theology' in the idealized Christ of the Gospel of John the historical Jesus Christ.[12] Instead, one needs a historical basis for a truly historical picture of the personality of Christ.[13] This picture, according to Weisse, is to be found in the oldest gospel, the closest to Jesus' lifetime, the gospel of Mark. Weisse also distinguishes between two conceptions of the personality of Christ: an 'inaesthetical-historical' (a picture which can be gained by religious experience in the way of Schleiermacher and his followers) and a 'moral-religious' one which takes this personality as 'the divine proto-type of humankind'.[14] To reach that personality one needs the individual, historical figure of the personal Christ',[15] which is important in the smallest details and has been preserved in the tradition in its originality, though this tradition is not free from later accretions. But as the approach to the personal Christ is not through the letter, these admixtures should not disturb the reader.

These considerations of Weisse seem to be important as they show the impetus which guided generations of scholars who belonged to the liberal school of exegetes in their search for a picture of the historical Jesus. The problem of the most genuine Gospel is closely connected with this intention. That can be seen also with Holtzmann, who closed his book on the Synoptic Gospels with a chapter on 'The Synoptic Gospels as Sources of History'[16], which includes a paragraph entitled 'Picture of the Life of Jesus according to Source A' (which means the original

11. Weisse speaks of 'a recently deceased famous theologian', *Die evangelische Geschichte*, II, p. 448.
12. Weisse, *Die evangelische Geschichte*, II, p. 459.
13. Weisse, *Die evangelische Geschichte*, II, p. 500.
14. Weisse, *Die evangelische Geschichte*, II, p. 500.
15. Weisse, *Die evangelische Geschichte*, II, p. 501.
16. Holtzmann, *Die synoptischen Evangelien*, pp. 359-514.

Mark),[17] taken as the closest to historical truth. This picture was instantly overtaken by D. Schenkel in embellished form for his sensational and much debated *Charakterbild Jesu*[18] and is a summary of the classical liberal ideal.

The 'moral-religious' picture of Jesus has two ideological components: the moralism of Kant (in the wake of the Enlightenment) and the idea of personality, which originated in the period of neo-classicism. Both together form the typical *Weltanschauung* (world-view) of German (and also British) *Bildungsbürgertum*. Goethe and Thomas Carlyle (1795–1881) put the figure of the historical personality as hero (including the religious genius), in the centre of their works, and gained wide popularity in Germany in the nineteenth century.[19] But the largest influence was the humanist education in the classical *Gymnasium* which remained the predominant higher school of *Bildungsbürgertum* throughout the century.[20] The impact of this predominant world-view on the history of

17. Holtzmann, *Die synoptischen Evangelien*, pp. 468-96. On the criticism by Holtzmann's famous pupil A. Schweitzer of this picture cf. E. Grässer, *Albert Schweitzer als Theologe* (Tübingen: Mohr, 1979), esp. pp. 73, 75-76 and *passim*.

18. D. Schenkel, *Charakterbild Jesu für die Gemeinde* (Wiesbaden: C.W. Kreidel, 1864); A. Hausrath, *Richard Rothe und seine Freunde* (2 vols.; Berlin: Grote, 1902–1906), I, p. 490: 'In the new book he followed in the question of the sources simply the results of his younger colleague Holtzmann…The summary of Holtzmann he clothed with the wide, puffy garment of his rhetorics and polemics…'

19. Cf. H. Kahlert, 'Der Held und seine Gemeinde: Untersuchungen zum Verhältnis von Stifterpersönlichkeit und Verehrergemeinschaft in der Theologie des freien Protestantismus', *EH XXIII/238* (Frankfurt a.M.: Lang, 1984); J. Kedenburg, *Theologisches Geschichtsbild und theokratische Geschichtsauffassung im Werke Thomas Carlyles* (Frankfurter Arbeiten aus dem Gebiete der Anglistik und der Amerika-Studien, 6; Heidelberg, Winter, 1960).

20. Cf., for instance, the description of the ideological foundations of the National Liberal Party in the Reichstag by the known Badenian liberal politician J. Jolly, *Der Reichstag und die Partien* (Berlin: Reimer, 1880), p. 93: 'On the liberal conception of the state…the common national education [had] a very strong impact…Our modern national education is in its foundations and its highest flourishments specifically humanist and ideal…It poses the highest task in the development of the fine, free personality.' Jolly also stresses the popularity of 'our poet-heroes' and their impact on the thinking and feeling of the whole nation. Goethe, Schiller and W. von Humboldt are the best known names. Cf. also K. Vondung, 'Zur Lage der Gebildeten in der wilhelminischen Zeit', in Vondung (ed.), *Das wilhelminische Bildungsbürgertum* (Göttingen: Vandenhoeck & Ruprecht, 1976), pp. 20-33, 251; C.E. McClelland, *State, Society and University in Germany* (Cambridge: Cambridge University Press, 1980), pp. 111-22.

biblical exegesis has not yet sufficiently been observed.[21] But in its critical form it is a part of the broad stream of liberal thinking. The idealistic thinking also formed the theories of history which became the ground of the historical sciences. For W. von Humboldt[22] the notion of individuality is constitutive of the understanding of history, which is nevertheless a totality, being on the way to a certain end. The historical school also stressed the endeavor for historical objectivity,[23] to be approached by the use of sources and a scrutiny employing every available philological mean.[24] This philological heritage of humanism and the Enlightenment is an important factor in the practice of biblical research and not to be undervalued. Holtzmann, for example, in his work on the gospels was sure to offer objective facts built upon methodologically gained observations in the text.[25]

But now I come to the other factors that have to be taken into consideration in order to avoid the one-sidedness of a purely intellectual history. What were the external conditions in which a certain theory of biblical criticism could be developed and brought to acceptance in a public willing to hear? Who were the bearers of such a critical tradition and who formed the audience? Who were the adversaries? Of course it

21. The work of Kahlert, *Der Held und seine Germeinde*, is a beginning. However, he is biased in his examples.

22. On Humboldt, see G.A. Benrath, 'Humboldt, Wilhelm von (1767–1835)', *TRE* 15 (Berlin: de Gruyter, 1986), pp. 685-87 (Lit.).

23. Cf. the famous sentence of L. von Ranke that the historian just wants to show 'what actually happened' (*Sämtliche Werke, Bd. 33/4* (Leipzig: Duncker & Humblot, 1877³), p. vii; H. White, *The Historical Imagination in Nineteenth Century Europe* (Baltimore, London; Johns Hopkins University Press, 1973), pp. 163ff.; R. Vierhaus, 'Rankes Begriff der historischen Objektivität', in R. Koselleck, *et al.* (eds.), *Objektivität und Parteilichkeit in der Geschichtswissenschaft* (Munich: Dtv, 1977), pp. 63-76; J. Wach, *Das Verstehen*, III (Tübingen: Mohr, 1933), pp. 121ff.

24. Cf. J. Mehlhausen, Art. 'Geschichte. Geschichtsschreibung. Geschichts-philosophie', §VI/2: '19–20 Jahrhundert', *TRE*, XII, pp. 643-58, 649-50. Cf. also above, pp. 149ff.

25. In fact, he was dependent upon the wish to win a picture that would be fitting for a 'modern view' of Jesus. Cf. J. Héring, 'De H.J. Holtzmann à Albert Schweitzer', in *Ehrfurcht vor dem Leben: Festschrift A. Schweitzer* (Bern: P. Haupt, 1955), pp. 21-29; E. Grässer, *Albert Schweitzer als Theologe*, p. 75. For the problem of the 'historical Jesus' and its ideological background, R. Slenczka, *Geschichtlichkeit und Personsein Jesu Christi: Studien zur christologischen Problematik der historischen Jesusfrage* (Göttingen: Vandenhoeck & Ruprecht, 1967), esp. pp. 128ff. Real 'objectivity' was never reached.

would be too simple to presume that the theologians and the members of the Church, that the general educated public would unanimously accept the results of Bible criticism or, especially, a certain theory. So it must be remarked first, that the promoters of such theories belonged to the general liberal movement which played a certain role in the society, in the Church and in political life. Liberalism as a movement can be observed in several aspects of social life, but all of them belong together because a common ideology is the moving force behind the respective engagements on different fields. Religious liberalism[26] and the political liberal movement[27] are not far from one another, and that they belong together can be seen by the partial identity of the persons engaged in both.

It is not easy to define the beginnings of the liberal movement, but it is clear that it originated about the close of the eighteenth century in the educated class of *Bürgertum* and among state officials who had been trained in the universities.[28] The ideas of progress and the freedom of the individual which were developed theoretically in the philosophy of German idealism stood at the forefront of the movement and formed the moving force through the different stages of its development. As education was a condition for belonging to the relevant class, the universities were a prominent place for its preferment. The newly founded ones in particular (above all Berlin, founded 1810, which gathered the elite of intellectual protagonists, such as Fichte, Hegel, Schleiermacher among others) promoted the liberal ideas. In Prussia, the political reforms of the minister vom Stein and the educational ones of W. von Humboldt, to which belonged the principles of freedom and independence of scientific teaching and research, set rather early into practice central postulates of the liberal program. To say it at once: at least this part of inner autonomy of the universities was preserved throughout the century even under changing conditions. Only later totalitarianism (nazism and communism) was able to destroy it. To understand the special situation in

---

26. Cf. W. Nigg, *Geschichte des religiösen Liberalismus: Entstehung–Blütezeit–Ausklang* (Zürich: Max Niehans, 1937).

27. E.g. L. Gall, 'Liberalismus und "bürgerliche Gesellschaft"', *HZ* 220 (1975), pp. 324-56 = Gall (ed.), *Liberalismus* (Cologne: Kiepenhauer & Witsch, 1976), pp. 182-86, and the other essays collected in this work.

28. Cf. J.J. Sheehan, 'Liberalism and Society in Germany 1815–1848', *JMA* 45 (1973), pp. 583-604 = 'Liberalismus und Gesellschaft in Deutschland 1815–1848', in Gall (ed.), *Liberalismus*, pp. 208-31.

Germany one has also to note that the national idea of a united German people and state originated early, namely in the years of oppression by the emperor Napoleon and the victorious wars of national liberation. The wave of national enthusiasm flooded the whole country and found expression in patriotic poetry that was to become a standard reading in the schools to be learnt by heart throughout the century and later. Though a reaction followed for both German nationalism and the liberal political ideas (in the Vienna congress 1815 and the period of restoration, which was shortly interrupted by the revolutionary events in the famous March 1848, leading to the St Paul's Church Parliament and a short-lived hope for a constitutional German empire ruled according to liberal principles), both ideals were not abandoned but kept alive, although they had for some time lost a direct influence on the government in the numerous German, mostly monarchically ruled, states. But it is wrong to say that national pathos is a late form of depravity in German liberalism; in a way it belongs to its earliest sources.

Not only in secular politics, but also in the Church the period after 1830 (roughly the time of the death of Schleiermacher and Hegel) brought a change to more conservative and orthodox movements. Lutheran confessionalism reared its head in several places in connection with a religious awakening (Tholuck, K. Harms, W. Löhe *et al.*). In 1840 in Prussia, King Frederic-William IV came to the throne. He favoured a romantic idea of his office in the Church and the use of liturgical forms. For the Roman-Catholic Church the pontificate of Pius IX (1846–1878) was decisive. Pope Pius IX started as a liberal but ended up strengthening Roman centralism and steering an orthodox dogmatic course.[29] So the influence of liberals in both churches was minimized and they nowhere became a majority—with one exception we have to speak about. After the disappointments of 1848–49 most liberals, who did not emigrate to the United States or elsewhere, were prepared to compromise and adapted their aims to the possibilities of a centralized government under a monarchical head, so far as possible mitigated by the parliamentary rights of the estates. In several cases the universities were repositories of liberal thinking, though mostly restricted to the inner circles of their members.

There is a remarkable exception which has to be regarded in more detail, because it leads us back to our specific topic, the Markan

29. *Syllabus Errorum*, 1864; Vatican I with the dogma of the infallibility of the Pope, 1870.

Hypothesis and its famous promoter Holtzmann. Holtzmann was the son of a Badenian pastor and was from 1847 a parishioner in Heidelberg and simultaneously a teacher at the Evangelical Protestant Seminary. He later became a prelate for long periods also and was a member of the General Synod and influential in Church politics.[30] Born in Karlsruhe, Holtzmann was a Badenian indigene and for many years a citizen of Heidelberg, where he spent his *Gymnasium* years and most of his study. Whereas the Heidelberg Theological Faculty in those years has been characterized as stamped by the climate of restoration,[31] Holtzmann was very much impressed during a stay of one year in Berlin by Wilhelm Vatke and his class on 'Introduction to the New Testament'.[32] Vatke was one of the last Hegelians: a critical mind, an outsider in his faculty (never more than *extraordinarius*), and ingenious in his way, impressing his students by his eloquence and overarching perspectives. After his study and some practical years, Holtzmann became lecturer in his home faculty in 1858 by passing the examinations for the degree of licentiate. Whoever is accustomed to contemporary rules of academic profession will be astonished when hearing the topic of Holtzmann's dissertation: its title was *De corpore et sanguine Christi quae statfuerint in ecclesia examinantur* and it contains a description of the differences between the Lutheran and the Reformed positions regarding the eucharist. His following work on 'Canon and Tradition'[33] is also dogmatical and historical in content. In the nineteeth century and beyond, a professor in a German university was not obliged to restrict himself to teaching a narrowly described subject as, for example, the New Testament. It was usual to cover more than one field according to the needs of instruction. Most faculties had no more than five full professors;[34] in Heidelberg at the time of Holtzmann's lectureship there were just four.[35] Even later,

---

30. On Holtzmann, cf. W. Hönig, in F. von Weech (ed.), *Badische Biographien III* (Karlsruhe: Braun'sche Hofbuchhandlung, 1881), pp. 59-62.

31. Cf. Bauer, *Holtzmann*, p. 288.

32. Cf. Bauer, *Holtzmann*, p. 289 and Holtzmann, *Lehrbuch der historisch-kritischen Einleitung in das Neue Testament* (Freiburg i. Br.: Mohr, 1892), p. viii.

33. *Kanon und Tradition: Ein Beitrag zur neueren Dogmengeschichte und Symbolik* (Ludwigsburg: Ferd. Riehm, 1859).

34. Cf. the statistics in W. Lexis, *Die Universitäten im Deutschen Reich* (Berlin: A. Asher, 1904), *passim*.

35. Cf. R. Riese, *Die Hochschule auf dem Wege zum wissenschaftlichen Grossbetrieb: Die Universität Heidelberg und das badische Hochschulwesen 1860–*

when he got a call to Strasbourg university in 1874, he was commissioned to teach New Testament, dogmatic and early Church history.[36] During the whole time of his activity in Heidelberg and Strasbourg he taught also catachetics and practical theology.[37] But the New Testament was the main field in which he was engaged.

Shortly after Holtzmann's entrance into the Theological Faculty in Heidelberg the political situation in Baden changed remarkably.[38] The immediate occasion was the conclusion of a treaty with the Vatican by the government after long protracted negotiations concerning the rights of the Roman-Catholic Church. It followed an energetic struggle of the Church to gain more control over its own matters, especially the right of free instalment of priests without formal sanction by the governmental *Oberkirchenrat* (High Church Council) and the independent administration of Church finances and of religious education. These demands look moderate and in their substance to be taken for granted to a modern spectator. It was not so much the material regulations of the treaty, but the fact that it had been concluded with the Vatican, that roused a storm of protest throughout the country. To understand this one has to grasp the special national feeling that dominated the leading classes in the German states. The Roman Church was not out of favour as a religious community (there was even a liberal movement among catholics; a prominent member was the later minister F. von Roggenbach),[39] but ultramontanism was unpopular. Ultramontanism was a term for loyalty to an outward political power (as the Pope and the Vatican were characterized, as trying to erect a state in the state, ruled by the emissaries of

---

1914 (Stuttgart: Klett, 1977), p. 97-98 (the date on Holtzmann has to be corrected to 1861).

36. Cf. Bauer, *Holtzmann*, p. 309.

37. Cf. H. Bassermann, 'Heinrich Holtzmann als praktischer Theologe', *PM* 6 (1902), pp. 172-84.

38. For the following details cf. e.g. F. von Weech, *Baden in den Jahren 1852–1877* (FS Grandduke Frederic I; Karlsruhe, 1877), pp. 8ff.; R.G. Haebler, *Badische Geschichte* (Karlsruhe: Braun, 1951; repr. Baden: Battert; Bad Liebenzell: B. Gegenbach, 1987), pp. 109ff.; L. Gall, *Der Liberalismus als regierende Partei: Das Grossherzogtum Baden zwischen Restauration und Reichsgründung* (Wiesbaden: Steiner, 1968); H. Färber, 'Der Liberalismus und die kulturpolitischen Fragen in Baden von 1850–1870' (Diss. phil., Freiburg i. Br., 1959).

39. About him, K. Samwer, *Zur Erinnerung an Franz von Roggenbach* (Wiesbaden: J.F. Bergmann, 1909); Gall, in Gall (ed.), *Liberalismus*, esp. pp. 71-73 (with lit.).

the Pope and an obedient hierarchy), which competed with the loyalty citizens owed to their own prince and government and their duties as German patriots.[40] When Bismarck opened the *Kulturkampf* in Prussia in the seventies he acted according to a widespread popular feeling. His proceeding was in no way isolated but has parallels in other places, for instance in Baden.

The treaty with the Vatican needed a formal ratification in the two houses of parliament, which was refused, as the Liberal party had gained the majority in the lower house. The result was the demise of the government and the installation of a new one, led by the Liberals. After the failure of the constitutional movement in 1848–49 this was the only German state where the Liberals came to power. It was possible only because the young Grandduke himself[41] was won over to Liberal intentions. He had studied with the liberal historians F.C. Dahlmann in Bonn and L. Häusser in Heidelberg and was now inclined to clear the way to internal reforms in his territory. The Catholic Church was awarded the internal freedom it needed, by state legislation. In its political relations the Church remained subject to the state. A reform of the school-system followed which ended the supervision of the schools by the clergy of both churches.

The centre of liberal resistance against the restoration was the university of Heidelberg, where the historians Gervinus and Häusser were leaders of the liberal movement, which had most adherents among

---

40. This tendency can still be detected in the utterances of the leaders of the liberal movement. E.g. D. Schenkel, *Der deutsche Protestantenverein und seine Bedeutung für die Gegenwart* (Wiesbaden: Kreidel, 1868), p. 4: 'We are to Catholicism, as far as it does not aspire to anti-cultural aims and does not try to renovate the horrors of Jesuit intolerance and priestly persecution mania, of a friendly mind; it may continue its religious and cultural-historical mission without hindrance...' Similarly Jolly, 'Der Reichstag und die Partien', p. 75: 'For the Catholic Church as church the battle could be very well avoided...The state has in its own interests much more reason to support the pure churchdom in its development and activity...' But the conflict rages against the hierarchy, the popish theocracy. 'The sharp weapon of ultramontanism is the mixture of the pure theology of the church with the theocratic rule of the pope' (p. 81).

41. Frederic I (1852[56]–1907). Cf. e.g. H. Oncken (ed.), *Grossherzog Friedrich I von Baden und die deutsche Politik von 1854–1871* (2 vols.; Stuttgart: Deutsche Verlagsanstalt, 1927; repr Osnabrück: Biblio, 1966), Oncken, *Grossherzog Friedrich I von Baden, ein fürstlicher Nationalpolitiker im Zeitalter der Reichsgründung* (Stuttgart: Deutsche Verlagsanstalt, 1926).

the natural scientists. In the Faculty of Theology the mild confessionalists were reigning,[42] but also there the situation changed in the new political climate. Influential above all was R. Rothe (1799–1867), member of the faculty 1837–49 and again from 1854 on,[43] who advocated his own peculiar speculative system, expecting that the Church would be merged into the state, in a common christianized society. Holtzmann was closely befriended by Rothe and co-operated with him in his church politics; he shared 'his basic theological conviction about the relation of religion and moral',[44] but did not fully subscribe to his particular system,[45] although he later edited Rothe's *Ethics*.[46]

The change in the political situation brought about a re-organisation of the protestant Church government, for which the professor in the Theological Faculty and director of the Preacher's Seminary, D. Schenkel, was a leading figure. In a session of the newly elected General Synod (1861) with a liberal majority, a new constitution of the Church was accepted which introduced the congregational principle as basis. Holtzmann's father became prelate in the *Oberkirchenrat*.

The most spectacular undertaking was the founding of the Protestant Union which happened in 1863.[47] The promoters were Rothe, Schenkel and Holtzmann. The aims were formulated by Rothe in an inaugatory speech at the first assembly in Eisenach near the Wartburg: the most prominent was the gaining back of the protestant masses which had emigrated out of the visible church, but were still members of a people

42. The introduction of a more ornate liturgy which met a strong opposition lapsed in the fifties, shortly before the period interesting us.

43. About Rothe, see A. Hausrath, *Richard Rothe und seine Freunde* (2 vols.; Berlin: Grote, 1902–1906). On his theological thinking, cf. H.-J. Birkner, *Spekulation und Heilsgeschichte: Die Geschichtsauffassung Richard Rothes* (Munich: Kaiser, 1959); C. Walter, *Typen des Reichs-Gottes-Verständnisses* (Munich: Kaiser, 1961), pp. 117-36; P. Kessler, *Glaube und Gesellschaftsgestaltung: Die Bedeutung Richard Rothes für das Verhältnis von Kirche und Welt* (Essen: R. Hobbing, 1969); F. Wagner, 'Theologische Universalintegration: Richard Rothe (1799–1867)', in F.W. Graf (ed.), *Profile des neuzeitlichen Protestantismus. I. Aufklärung, Idealismus, Vormärz* (Gütersloh: Mohn, 1990), pp. 265-86.

44. Bauer, *Holtzmann*, p. 291.

45. Bauer, *Holtzmann*, pp. 291-92.

46. Rothe, *Theologische Ethik* (Wittenberg: Koelling, 1871²).

47. Cf., e.g., Schenkel, 'Protestantenverein', in *Charakterbild Jesu*; W. Hönig, *Der Deutsche Protestantenverein* (Bremen, 1904); Hausrath, *Rothe*, pp. 465ff.; J.E. Groh, *Nineteenth Century German Protestantism* (Washington, DC: University Press of America, 1982), pp. 342ff.

formed by Christian traditions and customs. We know now that this aim was not reached, and the crisis of the first world war ended the optimism standing behind the whole enterprise, but at its beginning it was carried by a high enthusiasm. The will to form the society according to these ideals motivated the members of the Protestant Union to engage themselves in practical politics. So Holtzmann became deputy in the lower house of the Badenian Parliament 1867–71,[48] engaging himself in cultural politics, especially the schools debate, as a prominent expert.[49] Another important question which affected the Badenian external politics was the German problem. There were two possible solutions for a prospective united Germany: the Great German project including Austria and the Small German politics, in which Prussia, as the predominant protestant power, would be leading. In 1866, the Prussian–Austrian war over dominance in Germany broke out and ended with a swift victory of Prussia. Public opinion in Baden was divided; at last Baden went into the war on the side of Austria. After the defeat, the government had to be exchanged, but the territory remained untouched. In the university of Heidelberg there were two parties among the liberals: one favouring Austria, the other Prussia. Whereas Gervinus was the head of the pro-Austria group, the protagonists of the friends of Prussia were, among others, Wilhelm Oncken and Heinrich Holtzmann.[50]

Holtzmann, after having refused a call to Vienna—the imperial university had already rewarded him an honorary doctorate—in 1865 became a full professor and now belonged to the inner circle of the faculty. After the appearance of his book on the Synoptic Gospels he had gained an international reputation. His future would not be to stay in Heidelberg. There, the situation became worse after the establishment of the second empire under Prussian leadership. To adorn the imperial university in Berlin, the Prussian minister of cultural affairs called the best professors from the smaller universities. From Heidelberg, Helmholtz, Zeller and Treitschke went to Berlin.[51] The struggle between

48. Cf. W. Hönig, 'Heinrich Holtzmann und sein Heimatland', *PM* 6 (1902), pp. 184-87, 186; Bauer, *Holtzmann*, p. 307.
49. Cf. Hönig, *Deutsche Protestantenverein*, p. 186: 'He was one of the best experts of the basic educational system at all, especially the Badenian'.
50. Cf. Hausrath, *Zur Erinnerung an Julius Jolly* (Leipzig: Herzel, 1899), p. 155. According to J.C. Bluntschli, *Denkwürdiges aus meinem Leben*, III (Nördlingen: C.H. Beck, 1884), p. 158, 'Just Holtzmann and Nippold were on the side of the national movement' in the theological faculty.
51. Cf. Hausrath, *Rothe*, pp. 279-81.

Great and Small Germans had caused dissension even among the leaders of the university. Liberal politics had reached a crisis, as the politics of Bismarck had strengthened the monarchical, bureaucratic, military state. Even the Badenian army had been incorporated into the Prussian troops. Von Roggenbach left the cabinet in 1865 as a man whose plans had failed. In the Theological Faculty the number of students had noticeably decreased after the conservatives in the Church had decried Schenkel for his *Charakterbild Jesu*.[52] Between the Badenian liberals themselves, from 1868, dissension broke out under the antagonism of the two liberals A. Lamey and J. Jolly.[53] So there were many reasons for Holtzmann to become discontent with his present position, as the documents concerning his appointment to Strasbourg in 1874 show he was. Those documents, which are preserved in the archives of the High Rhine Department in Strasbourg,[54] are an interesting source regarding university and Church politics in the first years of the Second Empire. I may be allowed to premise that the documents do not confirm the theses of W. Farmer (which the courtesy of the highly esteemed author has brought to my knowledge in manuscript form) according to which the appointment of Holtzmann to a chair in the Theological Faculty of the university of Strasbourg was an act of imperial politics belonging to Bismarck's anti-Roman measures during the *Kulturkampf*. On the contrary, they show that the Emperor and his Chancellor in Berlin only very reluctantly, and after having imposed important restrictions on Holtzmann, accepted his nomination, the initiative to which did not come from Berlin but from the faculty in Strasbourg itself. The archives contain the correspondence of the university Curator Ledderhose with the office of the Chancellor in Berlin. The Alsace had been gained from France during the war 1870–71 and put under the direct administration of Berlin as an imperial territory.[55] It did not belong to Prussia. The

---

52. Cf. A. Hausrath, *Geschichte der theologischen Facultät zu Heidelberg im neunzehnten Jahrhundert* (Heidelberg: J. Hörning, 1901) = *PM* 6 (1902), pp. 1-13, 17/12. This notice is confirmed by the statistics in Lexis, *Die Universitäten*, p. 550: 1860: 105; 1870: 52; 1880: 24. In 1890 the number had recovered to 91.

53. Cf. Bluntschli, *Denkwürdiges aus meinem Leben*, III, pp. 239ff. ('struggle of Offenburg'); von Weech, *Baden* (n. 38), pp. 43ff.

54. Archives du Bas-Rhin, Strasbourg, versement AL 103, paquet 74, no. 255-58.

55. For the political and administrative situation, see H.-U. Wehler, 'Unfähig zur Verfassungsreform: Das "Reichsland" Elsass-Lothringen von 1870–1918', *Krisenherde des Kaiserreichs 1871–1918* (Göttingen: Vandenhoeck & Ruprecht, 1970), pp. 17-63.

university of Strasbourg had been founded anew as a German institution, though some professors of the French period were kept in office. The right of appointment of full professors in the monarchical states belonged to the sovereign, in this case the Emperor himself, William I.[56] The Chancellor was obliged to report about each candidate to win the Emperor's consent for signing the decree of appointment. Procuring the necessary information belonged to the duties of the Curator as the state commissioner responsible for the administration of the university.

The official initiative for the nomination, too, came from the Curator. Among the documents a secret account of the Curator to the Chancellor dated June 2, 1874, is of high interest. The Curator reported that the function of the Theological Faculty had been impaired for a long time by the old age and illness of several members; so much so, that a completion of the staff appeared to be urgent. Besides, the younger members of the faculty, A. Krauss[57] and Hermann Schultz[58] had more than once confidentially complained 'that the majority, consisting of the elder Alsatian members, clings to the old-fashioned', so that they *'are not able to get through with motions for very desirable improvements'*. 'After careful investigations I have come to the conviction that the existing need could be redressed most efficiently by the appointment of Professor Holtzmann in Heidelberg. The local faculty has acknowledged his importance as author and teacher long ago by proposing him already in January of the last year (1873).'

The Curator subsequently explains why he had for a long time hesitated to follow the wishes of the younger faculty members and similar suggestions from the Church of Alsace. The reason was—and now we come to the main objection playing a role in all the documents—that Holtzmann was a prominent member of the Protestant Union, 'which seemed to be offensive to the party of the positively believing Lutherans, who are represented in a not insignificant number in this country'. In fact in most parts of the protestant territories, the clergy and the more active laiety were deeply divided into opposing parties which fought

56. Cf. C. Bornhak, *Die Rechtsverhältnisse der Hochschullehrer in Preussen* (Berlin: Reimer, 1901), §7, pp. 34-36. For appointing extraordinary professors the right was delegated to the ministry.

57. 1836–92. A practical theologian and author of a well-known compendium of homiletics.

58. 1836–1903. Known as author of a famous Old Testament Theology (1895[6]).

bitter battles against one another. The positive Lutherans (and Reformed) were mostly followers of the confessional awakening in the first half of the century. The liberals in most territories were a minority (Baden was an exception) confined to the *Bürgertum* and academic intellectuals. We can follow these battles in the periodicals of both parties. The organ of the Protestant Union was the *Protestantische Kirchenzeitung*;[59] the 'positive' Lutherans fought in the *Evangelische Kirchenzeitung*, led by Hengstenberg, and in the *Allgemeine Evangelisch-Lutherische Kirchenzeitung*. On June 3 a group of fifty nine pastors of the Alsace had sent a petition to the Chancellor demanding the appointment of a professor 'in a positive-believing sense'.[60] The Curator ended his report by informing the Chancellor that according to reliable authorities 'Mr Holtzmann is prepared to dissociate himself from confessional activity and that he wishes to leave Heidelberg for exactly that reason'. As the matter is urgent, he begs for permission to contact Holtzmann regarding an appointment. 'As Professor Schultz of the faculty here informs me, Mr Holtzmann is assigned to the University of Berlin and has received...a letter of the Royal Prussian High Consistory in this matter. He would, however, prefer a professorship in the university here, if offered in time.'[61] After getting permission, the Curator met Holtzmann in Baden-Baden and urged him to sign a contract, in which Holtzmann expressly declared his resignation from his position in the Protestant Union and his full time dedication 'to his studies and the education of the theological youth'. This document was sent to the Chancellor together with an accompanying letter, out of which I cite just the following passage:

> I have gained the full conviction that Professor Holtzmann is earnestly interested, in his position here, to keep a distance from any public engagement, which could further a sharpening of the differences in the protestant church of the Alsace, and that his appointment here is especially welcome to him because it would make possible or at least easier his disengagement from his present party position in Heidelberg.

---

59. 1854ff.; later *PM*.

60. Text in *Allgemeine Evangelisch-Lutherische Kirchenzeitung* 7 (1874), p. 676 (August 28, 1874).

61. In the following year (1875) a hoped-for call by the communal government of Berlin to become provost of St Petri failed, because the Prussian High Church Council intervened. Cf. Merk, 'Holtzmann', p. 519.

While the Curator was away on his journey to Baden, a decree from Berlin arrived (dated June 13) in which the Curator was charged in similar words to urge Holtzmann to a declaration expressing his readiness to abstain from confessional party movements. The Curator answered after his return that he regarded this demand as already fulfilled in the Baden agreement. Later he received a further letter from the Chancellor in answer to his report of June 16,[62] instructing him not to keep Holtzmann in the dark about the conditions of his appointment and to keep his eye on his future behaviour.[63] In early July on the occasion of a visit of Holtzmann preparing for his move to Strasbourg the Curator asked for and received from him a second, more detailed declaration about his future behaviour, which, however, is not preserved in the documents.[64]

The whole dimension of the problem becomes visible in a letter of Bismarck to the President of his Chancellor Office, minister Delbrueck,[65] a copy of which has been kept among the documents. Bismarck writes at the express request of the Emperor,

> that the execution of this appointment document had cost His Majesty a great effort. His Majesty felt troubled in his conscience, that the declaration of Professor Holtzmann on the future state of his relation to the Protestant Union…is formulated in a very general way and extensible in the matter. If His Majesty nevertheless agreed to the application…, so with the expressed wish, that the sorrows…may not be confirmed by future experiences.

This is a moving testimony to the conscientiousness of the monarch who was a believing Lutheran but respected academic freedom in the universities which were formally under his supervision. Also Holtzmann in his Baden declaration had expressed that he reserved his complete freedom in research and teaching.

Though some exceptions are known, generally one cannot maintain that the German governments intervened arbitrarily in the universities.[66]

---

62. Undated sketch in the collection, no addressee given, but obviously the curator Ledderhose.

63. 'I request you…to turn your special attention to the behaviour of Professor Holtzmann and, in case he should against any expectation not stay true to this condition, to remind him of it in a fitting manner, eventually to report to me.'

64. The accompanying letter to the Chancellor bears the date of July 7.

65. Dated June 27, from (Bad) Ems, Document no. 4082.

66. Cf. Lehmann's judgment regarding the influence of the famous F. Althoff,

Academic freedom was preserved in an impressive way. The Prussian minister of cultic affairs after World War I, C.H. Becker, formulated in 1925: 'I believe that there does not exist a land in the world, however free and liberally ruled, in which the freedom of teaching for university teachers is so unconditionally and universally postulated and preserved as in Germany.'[67] His conviction that this would endure in the future[68] was wrong, but he knew what he wrote about the past. There is no doubt that the government reserved the final decision about appointing professors for itself, and the appointments were made often without or against the expressed wishes of a faculty.[69] But in the case of the theological faculties the trend did not favour the liberals. When in Strasbourg, shortly after Holtzmann was appointed, the chair of H. Schultz became vacant, the positive Lutheran group of the clergy sent petitions to the Chancellor claiming their right to the nomination of a successor of their own tendency. Bismarck asked the advice of the minister of religious and educational affairs and received a letter in response (which has been preserved in the Strasbourg documents), in which the minister recommended the appointment of the Old Testament positive scholar Kleinert[70] in preference to calling back H. Schultz from Heidelberg.[71] This move was intended to satisfy the confessionalists,

who was responsible for the appointment of professors in Prussia 1882–1902: 'Also here his pretension did not go so far that he would have endeavoured to make appointnments by the faculties of their own staff a mere formality, and to replace it by the appointment by the state…In fact he heard the faculties not just formally, but considered their votes carefully…' ('Der gelehrte Unterricht bis zum Weltkrieg 1892–1914', an Appendix in F. Paulsen, *Geschichte des gelehrten Unterrichts*, II [Berlin and Leipzig: Veit, 1921³; repr. Berlin: de Gruyter, 1965], pp. 693-797 [705]).

67. C.H. Becker, *Vom Wesen der deutschen Universität* (Leipzig: Quelle & Meyer, 1925), p. 24.

68. 'In front of this demand of the intellectual Germany even the most violent rulers stop' (Becker, *Vom Wesen der deutschen Universität*, p. 24).

69. Cf. Becker, *Vom Wesen der deutschen Universität*, p. 23: 'Whereas in England and America the universities…have a free hand in filling posts…the universities in Prussia–Germany are institutions of the state. Everywhere the government appoints the professors. It fills the posts and it theoretically has the authority—which it exercises frequently—to engage lecturers over the head of universities and faculties.'

70. P. Kleinert (1837–1920), cf. *RGG* III³, p. 1653. Actually Kleinert remained in Berlin and the chair was left vacant.

71. 'Both (Holtzmann and Schultz) are able and serious scholars, but they will not satisfy those circles of the clergy from which your Serene Highness received

following the appointment of the liberal Holtzmann.

In any case: the Markan Hypothesis played no role whatever in Holtzmann's appointment so far as the government was concerned. In the scientific world, Holtzmann was a scholar of fame. Whatever one might think about liberal theology in general, about the Markan Hypothesis in particular, the testimonies we have about the personality of Holtzmann[72] and the breadth of his universal knowledge are impressive. If we are critical of ancestors and object to the results of their research, the first step must be to evaluate them in the circumstances in which they lived, and that will prevent us from condemning them.

petitions, because with them one misses faithfulness to the confession.'

72. Curator Ledderhose writes (letter of June 16, 1874 to Bismarck): 'The impression which I received from the personality of the p. Holtzmann I can only describe as a very favourable one.' In the popular retrospective view on the history of the church of Elsass, O. Michaelis, *Grenzlandkirche: Eine evangelische Kirchengeschichte Elsass-Lothringens* (Essen: Lichtweg, 1934) (which also contains a photograph of Holtzmann, opposite p. 12), one reads: 'At any case the university of Strasburg possessed a teacher who had internalized nearly the whole education and culture of his time in an admirable way...How little was his subject able to limit the view of this great theologian, how much was this universal spirit at home even in subjects which were far from theology!' (etc.), p. 54. The jubilee volume of *Protestantische Monatshefte* for Holtzmann's 70th birthday (6.5. [1902]) contains articles on different subjects in which Holtzmann's contributions were important. W. Hönig, 'Heinrich Holtzmann und sein Heimatland', pp. 184-87 (184), praises him not as a pioneer, but as 'the embodiment of the scientific consciousness of the time'.

INDEXES

INDEX OF BIBLICAL REFERENCES

JOURNAL FOR THE STUDY OF THE OLD TESTAMENT

Supplement Series